Neural Networks and Nebbiolo

Artificial Intelligence for Wine

Shengli Hu

shenglihu@ai-for-wine.com

Find more interactive visualizations, demos, other topics, technical details, and more at http://ai-for-wine.com.

Table of Contents

SECTION 1

Introduction

Everything about wine appears intricate and complex, and mastering wine appears an ever daunting endeavor with the fast changing landscape of the worldwide wine industry, that encompasses a wide range of subjects such as geology, geography, viticulture, viniculture, chemistry, law, marketing, operations.

From the meticulous handling by experienced sommeliers of delicate aged bottles that have been perhaps scrutinized for provenance at the dinner table, to the selection of distribution and marketing channels possibly subject to the arguably unnecessarily complex three-tier system, from different regimes at bottling that might cause or prevent wine faults in years to come, to numerous experiments done at different stages of *élevage* in the winery to finetune the final product, from intimate decisions on soil treatment, irrigation, vine training and trellising based on vintners' experience, ideals, and terrior, to the processes and experiments revolving around scions and rootstocks in the nursery, it might strike as without doubt that there is perhaps little space for artificial intelligence (AI) at its current state to take hold in the wine industry in the near future.

After all, the thought of ordering a bottle of wine with personal recommendations through a robot at a dinner table, or conversing with Alexa or Siri about the intricacies that make Musigny more different from Bonnes Mares than Les Amoureuses, devoid of any human touch of hospitality, would easily make one squirm.

On the other hand, artificial intelligence has made breathtaking breakthroughs in multiple fields in the past decade, not only solving some of the world's most pressing and challenging puzzles, but also penetrating various aspects of our daily lives. AI is making it easier for people to do things every day, whether it's searching for photos of loved ones with a simple query, breaking down language barriers with smart online translators, typing emails with automatic completion, or getting things done with the Google Assistant. AI also provides new ways of looking at existing problems, from rethinking healthcare to advancing scientific discovery. One particularly relevant research theme that is quickly emerging is AI for Social Good, which uses and advances artificial intelligence to address societal issues and improve the well-being of the world. In an excellent review article by the AI and Social Good Lab at Carnegie Mellon University, over one thousand relevant academic articles published in top computer science conferences were summarized and steady growths were seen in various application areas heralded by AI for Healthcare, AI for Transportation, AI for Environmental Sustainability, AI for Education, AI for Agriculture, and so forth.

With the steady (or even exponential) growth of AI technology in various public domains, there is no reason why the wine industry overlapping with so many other industries wouldn't benefit from AI technology. It is my strong conviction that various AI technologies can already resolve many issues of the wine industry in a surprisingly efficient manner, and I am going to show you how in this book in a relatively less technical way that starts with wine storytelling and segues into proposed AI solutions.

1.1 Objectives of This Book

How could AI assist wine professionals in various aspects of the wine world, perhaps change the wine industry for the better, and ultimately enrich consumers' experience? I try to illustrate by

- examining the essential qualities and responsibilities of wine professionals or sommeliers through the lens of AI, and detailing how to use AI to help with relevant tasks;
- identifying components of the wine industry where AI could potentially improve upon wine professionals, or make their job easier and more efficient at the very least;
- solving challenging problems that have shaken the sommelier circles in recent years;
- laying out plans to building an ultimate sommelier-in-the-loop AI system for the wine industry.

1.2 The Structure of This Book

Chapter by chapter, I will discuss wine-related topics and the associated challenges, followed by to what extent could AI be of help, and in what ways, with introductions to the relevant topics in AI. I try to include visualizations and demos when possible to make it less dry. More *interactive* visualizations, technical versions of the AI parts in the form of literature review in scientific papers from a previous version of this book, and other topics are and will be available online at http://ai-for-wine.com.

This book can be read in three distinctive ways. First, each chapter provides visualizations (can be accessed online) that aggregate certain wine knowledge in a (hopefully) creative way. Second, every chapter addresses one or more of the wine-related challenges faced by wine professionals and/or enthusiasts with a set of AI solutions, introduced in a relatively nontechnical way alongside visualizations, sample results, and demos when possible and applicable. Third, every chapter furthers the discussion, in subsections, of relevant AI methods with a self-contained review of method development and evolution over the past decade in the AI community where citations are included for scientific accuracy. Therefore, each chapter assumes in parallel two themes, one relevant to the wine industry, the other the AI industry. Yet both parts would be self-contained thus no previous knowledge is required to grasp the texts, except a curious mind and a playful heart. In addition, each chapter is in itself self-contained and can be read separately with pointers to other sections throughout the book when necessary, therefore readers are welcome to read in whatever order.

Hopefully, this book makes a unique and novel addition to the wine literature and the AI literature, while being broad enough in scope to be of use across the wine profession, and perhaps inspire AI applications in other fields as well. Because of the fast-evolving nature of the AI technology (and the wine industry too), I hope to continuously update the chapters with the newest methods and introduce new topics.

1.3 A Preview of Chapters

Chapter 2 discusses in-depth about what wine professionals and enthusiasts love (and hate): blind tasting. It has been an essential part of training for wine professionals. However, it does appear that everyone has his or her own unique marker or method, on top of the generally accepted "deductive tasting" approach. I detail some of the many schools of thought about how to conduct deductive tasting, highlighting their major flaws and inconsistencies, while illustrating how this exact problem corresponds to some of the most classic machine learning methods, which in turn could be used to prevent pitfalls and identify the optimal strategy of deduction for each individual.

Chapter 3 gets into the weeds of the vast body of wine knowledge touching on various distinct yet intertwined subjects such as geology, geography, chemistry, viticulture, vinification, economics, etc. A solid grasp of a large body of wine knowledge is fundamental to being a qualified wine professional, just as how knowledge graphs are fundamental to various AI models and their generalizability[1] and flexibility. We recount the important roles knowledge graphs have been playing in modern AI ecosystems, and illustrate with examples how knowledge graphs could be integrated to build question-answering systems like chatbox applications tailored to the wine industry.

Chapter 4 broaches the classic topic of wine pairing, whether it be with food, or music and art. Given the textual description of a dish and the identity of a bottle of wine, how could AI methods be used to help determine their compatibility? Given an image of a dish, how would AI models recommend a wine to pair with, with rationales? Furthermore, given a bottle wine, how could we generate a recipe for a dish that goes well with it, with personal preference customization? We will break down each of the scenarios, and explain AI solutions module by module.

Chapter 5 explores the colorful landscape of wine maps, by compar-

[1]The extent to which these models can be applied to and perform well in other domains.

ing various wine map collections and cartography projects. Mapmaking, or cartography, has long been a labor intensive and time-consuming process that requires extensive and in-depth knowledge of visual design, geography, perception, aesthetics, etc., on the part of cartographers or designers, despite the powerful modern softwares like Adobe Illustrator and ArcGIS that have partially eased the process. When it comes artisanal wine maps that are artistically stylized, however, manual hand-drawing appears inevitable. Could AI help automatically generate artistic maps with style and precision in no time? The answer is yes, yet not without challenges.

Chapter 6 describes the phenomena of flying winemakers, and globe-trotting wine professionals and enthusiasts, and introduces the wine equivalents of the fun game Geo Guessr: Vineyard Guessr — given an image of a vineyard, guess where it is located in the world, and Cellar Guessr — given an image of a cellar, guess which winery it is! Can you score more correct guesses than our AI Guesser? You might be surprised. We will discuss the ins and outs of image geolocalization and how it applies to vineyards and cellars.

Chapter 7 details the fascinating world of grape varieties. Which grape varieties in the world are similar in terms of fruit profile, or structure, or growing patterns? What are the varieties that share something in common with both Riesling and Viognier? To answer such questions and many more, with the help of some of the widely used methods in AI, we produce a comprehensive map of the world's thousands *vitis vinifera*, from which links and associations among grape varieties could be easily identified. Could AI help with grape variety identification in the vineyard with a single photo of the grape vine on the ground? The answers are indeed positive, with the help of fine-grained visual classification applications in computer vision.

Chapter 8 maps out the kaleidoscopic space of (craft) cocktails as a semantic network[2]. What makes a cocktail creative? There is a pop-

[2] A network of interconnected concepts.

ular misconception that a great idea strikes from out of the blue, much like the apple that supposedly fell on Newton's head. In fact, almost every idea, no matter how groundbreaking or innovative, depends closely on those that came before. We analyze the creativity of craft cocktails through the lens of semantic networks and network theory, and provide creative tools and insights for aspiring mixologists. Furthermore, with the help of recent advancement in text generation technologies, we demonstrate how to automatically generate creative cocktail recipes, given minimal inputs.

Chapter 9 examines some of the world's best curated wine lists and explores what makes a great wine list in a data-driven manner. We introduce AI methods particularly adapted to parse a wine list, provide a comprehensive evaluation of any given wine list, and ultimately, generate a wine list given certain constraints such as budget, restaurant theme, perceived creativity, target consumer segments, etc., envisioning the future of AI assistants to wine directors at Michelin-starred restaurants and rustic bistros alike.

Chapter 10 seeks to tease out the causal effects of *Terrior* vs. *Vignerons* on wine quality, as opposed to spurious correlation, by introducing the most classic methods in Econometrics[3] and Statistical Learning[4] of causal inference, as well as their modern renditions in AI research.

Chapter 11 touches on the good old problem of trust-building among supply chain partners in the wine industry. Unsurprisingly, this is by no means a problem unique to the wine industry, therefore we review research efforts and practical insights over the past decade or so on the topics of automatic deception detection, and information concealment detection in text and speech with practical demos as potential solutions to some issues in the wine industry.

---

[3]The subject of the application of statistical methods to economic data for meaningful interpretation of economic behaviors and activities.

[4]The sub-field of machine learning drawing from the fields of statistics and functional analysis.

Chapter 12 elaborates on the worldwide wine auction scene. What are the optimal strategies for the auctioneer and the customers, respectively? What are some pitfalls corresponding to different mechanism designs from the perspective of customers? How could we induce truth-telling and perhaps greater market efficiency with mechanism design of auctions? In this chapter, we delve deep into the classic game theory and mechanism design that prove wildly relevant in the modern world.

Chapter 13 summarizes the entire life cycle of wine from vine to glass, with various interactive visualizations of viticulture and viniculture processes and strategies. More importantly, I detail existing and potential applications of AI techniques to every step of the production production and distribution processes by conducting a comprehensive review of the landscape of AI for Agriculture or Viticulture, AI for Disaster and Crisis Response, AI for Logistics, and AI for Marketing.

Chapter 14 details the ever-increasing popularity of wine as an alternative asset of investment, which is no longer exclusive to the most wealthy bunch. How does wine compare to traditional assets in terms of volatility, return on investment, etc., regardless of how wine funds keep painting you rosy pictures? What are the optimal portfolio management strategies when it comes to wine investment? What are some behavioral pitfalls to avoid when investing alternative assets like wine? And how and which AI techniques could best assist you in making the best-informed investment decisions?

1.4 Background Information

Before we start, let us clarify the meaning of artificial intelligence with some background information, as well as several closely related terms you will frequent in this book, and the AI community in general.

With the ever increasing amounts of data in digital form, the need for automated methods for data analysis continues to grow. The goal of **machine learning (ML)** is to develop methods that can automatically detect patterns in data, and then to use the uncovered patterns to predict future data or other outcomes of interest. Machine learning is thus closely related to the fields of statistics and data mining, but differs slightly in terms of its emphasis and terminology.

Data mining deals with challenges particularly in the areas of data storage, organization and searching.

The learning problems that we consider can be roughly categorized as either supervised or unsupervised, with those in-between termed semi-supervised. In supervised learning, the goal is to predict the value of an outcome measure based on a number of input measures; in unsupervised learning, there is no outcome measure, and the goal is to describe the associations and patterns among a set of input measures. **Statistical learning** brings together many of the important new ideas in learning from data, and explain them in a statistical framework.

The desire of creating machines that think dates back to at least ancient times when the tales of giant bronze robot Talos, artificial woman Pandora and their creator god, Hephaestus, filled the imaginations of people in ancient Greece. When computers first came into being, people had wondered whether they might become intelligent. Today, **Artificial intelligence (AI)** as a field has come a long way with numerous practical applications and active research topics, from intelligent software for automating routine labor, to speed and language understanding, from image and video perception, to scientific diagnoses in medicine, and many more. In the early stages of AI, problems that are intellectually difficult for human beings but relatively straightforward for computers were quickly solved. These are the ones that can be described by a list of mathematical rules. The real challenge to AI remains those easy for humans to perform that are difficult to articulate — those we solve effortlessly and intuitively, such as recognizing faces in images, or recognizing spoken words in a speech. The solution to such tasks — natural for human but challenging for machines, is to allow computers to learn from experience, mostly in the form of data, and understand the world in terms of a web of concepts, the hierarchy of which allows the computers to learn complicated concepts by building them upon simpler ones, just like how humans learn. If we draw graphs of these learned concepts built on top of one another, these graphs are deep with many layers. Therefore, this approach to AI is termed **Deep learning.** Deep learning allows us to handle unstructured data inputs (pixels, texts, audio signals, etc.) without hand-engineering features as in machine learning paradigms before deep learning, and with less domain knowledge. And they work exceedingly well in a variety of situations across various domains, with broad generalization enabled by large and diverse datasets.

Natural language processing (NLP) is the use of human languages, such as English or Japanese, by a computer. Different than computer languages that were designed to allow efficient and unambiguous parsing, natural language processing commonly revolves around resolving ambiguous and informal descriptions, and includes applications such as question answering (covered in Section 3.2), text generation (covered in Section 9.2, and Section 8.1), machine translation (touched on in Section 3.1), named entity recognition (touched on in Section 3) and many more.

Speech recognition aims to map an acoustic signal containing a spoken natural language utterance into the corresponding sequence of words intended by the speaker. The **automatic speech recognition (ASR)** task aims to identify an automatic function for that mapping, nowadays mostly based on *deep learning* methods. We will touch on some parts of it in Section 11.1.

Traditionally one of the most active research area for deep learning applications since vision is a task effortless for humans and animals but challenging for computers, **computer vision (CV)** is a very broad field consisting of a wide variety of methods of processing images resulting in an amazing diversity of applications, ranging from reproducing human visual abilities, for instance, recognizing faces, to creating new categories of visual abilities, such as recognizing sound waves from silent videos based on vibrations induced in objects visible therein. Many of the most popular standard benchmark tasks for *deep learning* methods are forms of *object recognition*, covered in Section 4, Section 7 and Section 6, as well as *optical character recognition*, covered in Section 5.5. Computer vision also overlaps with *computer graphics*, surfacing creative and efficient solutions to problems such as repairing defects in images, coloring black and white images, artistically stylize photos, and many more. We will discuss some of these in Section 5.

1.5 About the Author

Shengli Hu is an AI research scientist in New York City. Her research experience and interests lie in intersdisciplinary research bridging social sciences, computational linguistics, computer vision, and speech. She has published in top conferences and journals in natural language processing, computer vision, speech, and applied statistics including Association of Computational Linguistics (ACL), Empirical Methods in Natural Language Processing (EMNLP), Computer Vision and Pattern Recognition (CVPR), European Conference on Computer Vision (ECCV), International Conference on Computer Vision (ICCV), InterSpeech, and Annals of Applied Statistics (AoAS). Her research works have been featured in spotlight talks, and nominated for Best Paper Award. She received her PhD from Cornell University in 2019. She is also a wine professional with credentials including Diploma in Wine with Merit (Wine & Spirits Education Trust), Certified Sommelier (Court of Master Sommelier), Certified Specialist of Wine and Spirits (Society of Wine Educators). She is studying for the Master of Wine diploma (Institute of Master of Wine).

SECTION 2

Deductive Tasting

Blind tasting is one of the favorite games among wine enthusiasts. A mysterious bottle of wine wrapped in opaque papers or pouches, poured into a delicate hand-blown crystal glass, revealing its clear deep crimson color. Rich and opulent, pure and high-toned bouquet jumped out of the glass. Beautiful wild red cherries, vigor, fresh, and reverberant. A hint of roses and violets crackling with a touch of white pepper. Stony satiny tannins perfectly balanced with its tension and energy. What is it, you wonder in ecstasy, swirling the elixir gently to take in all its intricate aromatics. Familiar memories conjured up in your mind. *You were wondering within a deep forest, thick with pristine primeval growths. As the humid scent of life wafts from the moss-covered trees. You walked towards the heart of forest in search of solace. Suddenly you noticed a ray of light. You smelt flowers and red fruits that seem out of place in these woods. Unexpectedly the forest opened to a small clear spring, pouring forth like a miracle, like an oasis in the desert. The restoring water appears out of nowhere, and the surface glitters like so many jewels lit by the heavens. Drawn by the beauty, you quietly approached the spring. In that moment, the breeze rippling across the water, delivers to your nostrils the smell of sweet flowers and wild red fruit, so sweet and exalted. Up in the air, a pair of violet butterflies tangling in flight!*[5] There is no

Figure 1: An illustration of the imagery that possibly captures G. Roumier Les Amoureuses 2001.

other *lieu-dit* in the world that could lead you to a virgin forest like this than Les Amoureuses, the premier cru in Chambolle Musigny, in Cote de Nuits of Cote d'Or, Burgundy. This is George Roumier Les Amoureuses. Vintage... let's say, 1999? You announce to your

[5]Drops of God, Volume 4. The First Apostle, a.k.a. George Roumier Les Amoureuses. 2001. In the words of Yukata Kanzaki, the fictional world-known wine critic.

wine lover friend with whom the bottle is shared, with a somewhat confident smile.

Blind tasting is perhaps one of the essential skills of many wine professionals. For an importer or retailer, to be able to pick out the best quality wine (or the wine most likely to sell) at the most reasonable price contributes directly to the profitability or survival rate of the business. For a wine writer or critic, the capability of correctly judging wine's quality and ageability is likely what his or her own reputation depends on. For a sommelier, correctly identifying wines blindly not only creates the wow factor for the restaurant[6], but also helps tremendously with building a best wine program given a limited budget.

Therefore, it is no wonder that most well-known wine study programs include a section on blind tasting in examinations. In The Court of Master Sommelier's tasting exams required to earn the title Master Sommelier, for instance, candidates have to pass an oral example of 25 minutes to identify six wines — three white, three red — correctly in terms of grape variety, region of production, and vintage, by first describing them, one by one, from colors in sight, to aromas on the nose, to flavors or other elements on the palate, and then concluding with deduced identities. In The Institute of Master of Wine's tasting exams required to obtain the diploma of Master of Wine, as another example, candidates have to sit a written exam of three hours while tasting 12 wines, answering in the form of essays different winemaking techniques or climatic characteristics exemplified in the color, aromas, and tastes of wines, with attempts to identify either the vintage, region, or grape variety, possibly funneling[7] when uncertainty arises.

---

[6]Like the tales around well-known sommeliers Raj Parr, Fred Dame (exposed in New York Times articles on scandals though), Larry Stone, and the likes.

[7]For instance, if at one point you think the closest you could get with a wine is that it is an Italian red wine due to perhaps its volatile acidity, drying tannins, prominent herbal characters, and an acidic spine. But no clue if it is a Brunello

There have been quite a few different schools of thought regarding how to blind taste, what makes an excellent blind taster, and what to look for to improve blind tasting skills. One of the most widely known is *deductive tasting,* possibly popularized by The Court of Master Sommelier and Wine and Spirits Education Trust, which essentially separates the process of blind tasting into two steps: first, describe the wine in terms of color, aroma, and flavor, and structure, as precisely and objectively as possible; second, given the resulting descriptors, logically deduce the identity of the wine without referring back to the liquid in the glass. The first step requires a palate tuned to accurately identify a wide range of aromas and flavors in different forms and levels of doses, from exotic fruits like lychee or tamarind to esoteric flowers like marigold or azalea, from Asian five spices to Comte cheese and Herbes de Provence, from potting soil after an early summer rain, to pencil shavings and graphite, let alone cat urine, dirty socks, wet dogs, barnyard funk, and leather belts. And that is why "licking rocks and eating dirt" are not uncommon perhaps not only among geologists, but also sommeliers — at least those serious about improving palate sensitivity, I guess. It is only when one can objectively identify all the elements in a wine precisely in a consistent manner, can the second step — logical deduction — really shine.

In this chapter, I will focus on this second step, the logical deduction. Various advice and toolkits for tuning your palate for the first step have been passed down: constant training with wine aroma kits, the sniff and scratch book series by Richard Betts, roasting plain popcorns with different spices — a tip by Jill Zimorski, cooking with a wide range of ingredients and condiments, paying attention to not

di Montalcino, a Barolo, or an Etna Rosso, you could potentially *funnel* by putting down that you think it could be all three with a slight inclination towards Etna Rosso due to its volanic characteristics.

only the flavors but also the structural elements, the textures, and types and shapes of acidity, popularized by Nick Jackson's book *Beyond Flavor*, to name just a few. Let's assume for now — don't worry, we have solutions to be discussed later for when this assumption is hardly met — that we have reached the point when we have the perfect palates capable to accurately and comprehensively identify the entire spectrum of aromas, flavors, and sensations in a glass of wine.

To logically deduce the identity of any given wine, is to compare the wine in question to stereotypes of wines with known identities in our memory, and find the identity of the most similar stereotype. Therefore, the second step of deductive tasting — logical deduction — can be further divided into two parts.

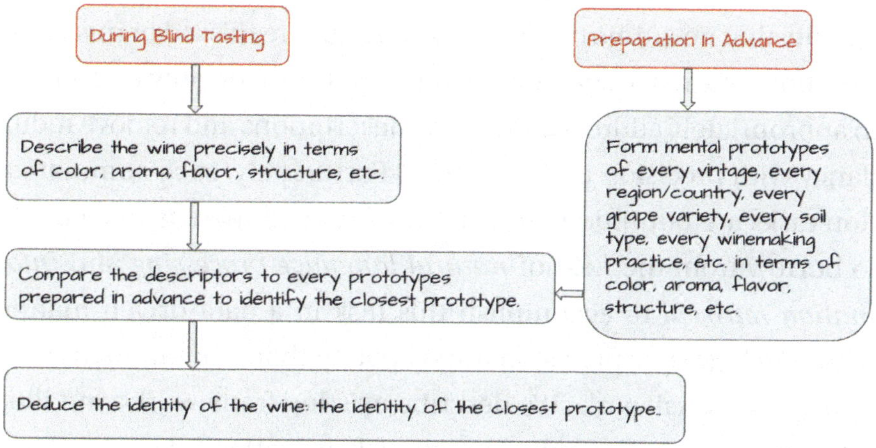

Figure 2: A flowchart of the deductive tasting process.

A first and major part of training for logical deduction, is to build up a robust and comprehensive database of archetypes of wines of different origins, varieties, vintages, and producers, etc. with objective and consistent descriptors. How would you describe an archetypal

10-year-old Condrieu from the 2010 vintage? What are the signature characteristics of a 2013 Aglianico del Vulture in 2020? A common and manual approach among wine students is to first obtain wines from well-recognized classic producers of each region, style, appellation, etc., then taste them comparatively and take notes of descriptors for each of them as precisely, accurately, consistently, and objectively as possible, and finally summarize the common themes among these descriptors for that particular region, style, appellation, etc., oftentimes referencing authoratative sources such as Jancis Robinson's purple website, Vinous, etc. Such a manual process is apparently prone to various biases and human errors. How could one be certain the set of wines obtained and tasted are indeed representative of the particular region or style one tries to understand? How could one be confident of one's own tasting sensibility and capability that no aroma or flavor compounds are missed or misjudged? How does one make sure that in the final step of forming an archetype to appropriately address conflicting descriptions and remove redundancy with precision and accuracy? Fortunately, such summarization tasks are not unique to wine tastings and there is indeed a lot to borrow from the field of *natural language processing* and *information retrieval* to accomplish this task in a data-driven manner with much greater precision and capacity than human memorization and manual work. We describe existing frameworks and illustrate how it could be applied to our task in Section 2.1.

Secondly, comparing the descriptors of the given wine to those of stereotypes in our collected database in the first step. Humans are notoriously bad in such tasks. For example, in the case of blind tasting, one taster decided to narrow down to only Savennieres, the most "cerebral" wine producing region, after detecting both Botrytis — honey, marmalade, saffron — and oxidative — almond paste, bruised apple, cheese rind — aromas. However, wouldn't an aged

Montrachet from certain vintages and producers also best exemplify both Botrytis and oxidative notes? One might further confirm or refute the choice of Savennieres with the level, shape, and structure of acidity, as well as unique aromatics since Chenin supposedly is of searingly high and crescendo acidity according to Nick Jackson's blind tasting book *Beyond Flavors*, and radiant of fragrances like chamomile, jasmine, honeysuckle, wasabi, and dried stone and tree fruits sometime a touch of tropical too.

However, more often than not, one starts to hallucinate certain aromas signature of Savennieres with such an objective in mind, falling victim to the confirmation bias. Blame it on the subjectivity of wine tasting! In another example, one taster might have quickly eliminated varieties like Nebbiolo, Grenache, Pinot Noir, Gamay(, and more indigenous varieties such as Freisa, Ruche, Prie Rouge, Nerello Mascalese, Baga, etc.) simply based on the deep purple color in the glass. However a Hubert Lignier Charmes-Chambertin, a Château de Beaucastel Châteauneuf-du-Pape, or a Yvon Metras Moulin-a-Vent would easily defeat that assumption, in which case the taster would have simply bypassed the correct identities at the initial judgment. The advice of funneling, or enlisting all the possible "grape laterals" — easily confused or similar grape varieties — has been circulated among some wine study circles. But a Pinot Noir might be similar to Gamay, which might be similar to Nebbiolo in some capacity, which then is similar to Sangiovese (ever mistook a Brunello for Barolo?) or Nerello Mascalese or Xinomavro, and the chain never stops. . . .

Such begs the question, is there an optimal or systematic way to move the deduction process consistently towards the correct answer as much as possible? In what steps and based on what characteristics should one eliminate or funnel? For example, Abigail might start with color, then aromatics on the nose, then flavors and finally structural components on the palate, therefore deduce by eliminating most varieties by color, draw initial conclusions based aromatics on the nose and palate, and narrow down to or confirm the final conclusion with the structural components. But Bob perhaps might argue one should use the structural components to come up with a list of initial conclusions and drill down to a few based on aromatics and flavors, and finally confirm with color or quality indicators. Yet another pro Claire might instead use fruit categories and conditions (crunchy tree fruit or jammy stone fruit?) on the nose versus on the palate (if fruit went tart on the palate compared to the nose it might be indicative of certain regions) for initial conclusions, and structural components for final conclusions. Or if Claire is not good at judging the level or type of acidity, she might choose to not rely on structural components as much and use them sparingly.

Whose strategies might most consistently lead to the most correct answers in blind tasting sessions? What is the optimal strategy based on one's strengths and weaknesses? For instance, if Claire is confident in her ability to detect spices but lacking in acidity calls, whereas Bob can never detect Rotundone (the chemical compound supposedly responsible for smells of black pepper) but is excellent in accessing fruit aromas and flavors. How should their blind tasting strategies differ to accommodate these strengths and weaknesses? Let us dive into personalized optimal deductive tasting strategies in Section 2.2.

What if we were blind tasting for vintage alone, or variety alone, or country? How would the optimal deduction strategy change according to the target? Intuitively, there might be a much smaller set of characteristics we watch out for if we are trying to decide on the country alone, compared to vintage or variety. Such questions and beyond are exactly what we seek answers to in Section 2.3.

2.1 Summarization

The focal task we are trying to accomplish, as the first step towards becoming an accurate deductive taster, is to generate precise and comprehensive archetypal descriptions for each wine, with aggregate archetypal descriptions for every wine region, grape variety, vintage, style, and sometimes even every vineyard and every producer, by leveraging the universe of tasting notes and reviews written by either others or ourselves. The purpose of such descriptions is to provide tasters with details about the differentiating characteristics of wines based on which tasters could tell one apart from another. Therefore, a good resulting description should be accurate, informative, readable, objective, and relevant to the focal wines based on defined granularity of the summarization task. For instance, if we were to summarize for Sancerre Blanc based on all the tasting notes and wine reviews we could find, the resulting description should be relevant only to white wines in the Central Loire Valley of France labelled as Sancerre, as opposed to a specific producer (e.g., Domaine François Cotat), or lieu-dix (e.g., Monts Damnés in Chavignol), or wines from Central Loire, or Sauvignon Blanc in general.

Let us call our task *wine summarization* for the sake of referencing convenience as we familiarize with similar tasks to be introduced in this section.

Fortunately, solutions to similar tasks have been researched upon for decades in the machine learning and natural language processing communities, the experiences, insights, and techniques from which could be adapted to our *wine summarization* task in question.

Text summarization is one of the most important tasks of *natural language processing* that automatically converts a piece of text or a collection of texts on the same topic into a concise summary that contains key semantic information of the topic. Text summarization techniques have enabled a wide range of downstream applications of practical relevance in our daily lives , ranging from automatic creation of news digests from a collection of news articles, to automatic generation of captions and subject titles from an article or a paragraph, from automatic summary of research highlights from a series of research articles, to automatic abstract generation based a single research paper, from generating retail product descriptions from user reviews for fashion and motor industries, to review summarization aimed at extracting opinions about a product from various reviews, to mention just a few.

Let us define the task of text summarization more explicitly by specifying its inputs and outputs. The input(s) to a text summarization algorithm could be one sentence, one passage or paragraph, one article, one document, or multiples of them centering around the same theme or topic or event. And the output(s) of a text summarization module would largely be a concise piece of information that summarizes the input(s), either in the form of a caption, a title, a sentence, or a paragraph, depending on the nature and length of the input(s). According to the number of input documents, text summarization can be cast into two categories: **single document summarization** and **multi-document summarization**. Single document summarization tasks refer to those that summarize from one document whereas multi-document summarization accommodates a set of related documents for a single concise summary, which aligns with our task of *wine summarization* since we take as inputs many documents of reviews or articles about a particular wine to form a wine description that captures the essence and distinctive characteristics of the focal wine.

Technically speaking, multi-document summarization is perhaps indeed more complicated and difficult to tackle than single document summarization, due to the increasing volume of and the more intricate relations between a non-trivial number of documents that are be complementary to, overlapping with, and contradicting one another. Additionally, most mainstream natural language processing techniques are notorious for handling long documents as inputs that lead to noticeable performance drop. Therefore, it has been a real challenge for AI models to retain critical contents from complex input documents, while generating coherent, non-redundant, factually consistent and grammatically correct summaries. It demands efficient and effective summarization techniques capable of analyzing a large corpora of long and complex documents, identifying and merging consistent information while removing subjective noises and conflicting or unreliable information. Moreover, multi-document summarization tasks could end up more computationally expensive, due to the increasing sizes of documents and model parameters.

The size of input documents is but one criterion based on which text summarization techniques could be categorized. To provide a bigger picture of the topic, let me illustrate the landscape of text summarization with Figure 3 where automatic text summarization systems are classified according to different criteria: the input size, nature and type of the output, technical approaches, etc. And we further illustrate the process of multi-document text summarization with breakdowns of different techniques for each processing module in Figure 4.

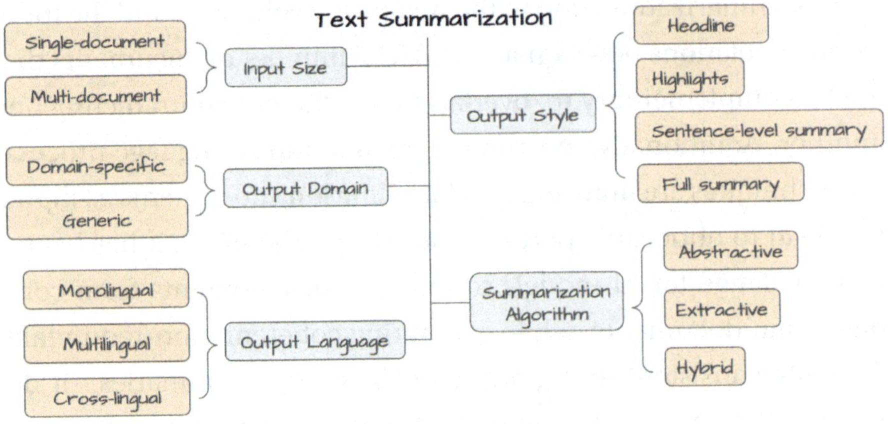

Figure 3: Classification of automatic text summarization systems.

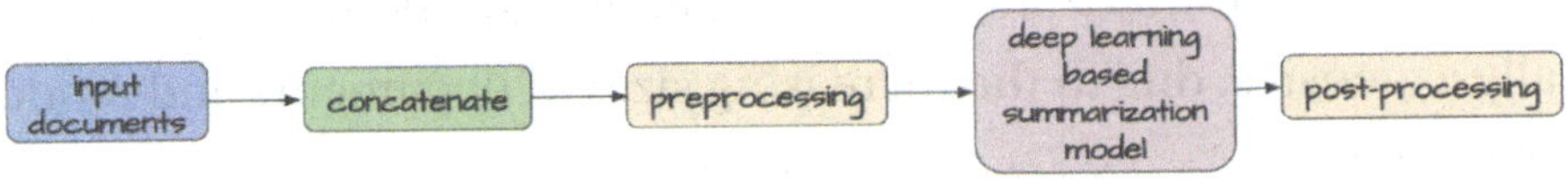

Figure 4: A framework of multi-document summarization.

Starting with multiple input documents, we concatenate them, either by spanning and treating them as a flat sequence of words and sentences, or by exploiting hierarchical structures within documents to accommodate complementary, redundant, and conflicting information in the input documents such that richer semantic information is preserved with hierarchical concatenation. After concatenation and preprocessing such as tokenization or removing punctuations, a deep-learning-based model then learns semantically rich representations from the concatenated and preprocessed documents for summarization: either extractive or abstractive, with some recent approaches combining both. In an **extractive summarization** task, snippets from input documents are selected to form the final summary, whereas in the case of **abstractive summarization**, the output summary is generated by the deep-learning-based text generation model given preprocessed input documents.

Different than the standard multi-document text summarization task in literature, where the goal is to generate a concise summary for multiple documents. Our task of *wine summarization* is perhaps more similar to the task of review summarization that focuses on summarizing multiple reviews about a product. Most studies on review summarization first identify the key attributes (usually termed *aspects*) of the focal product and then extract keywords or phrases that describe or express sentiments about them respectively. There exists a key difference between our *wine summarization* and review summarization in that the ideal output summary about a particular wine (or region, style, vintage, etc.) should be not only concise and informative, but also objective and factually consistent, whereas most review summarization systems focus on extracting opinions and sentiments rather than objective descriptions at the appropriate granularity. In summary, in *wine summarization*, we seek a distinctively informative set of content that is uniquely descriptive of the focal wine, out of a large number of wine reviews.
Figure 5 plots the processing framework of our multi-document wine summarization, built upon Figure 4 with modifications tailored to our application.

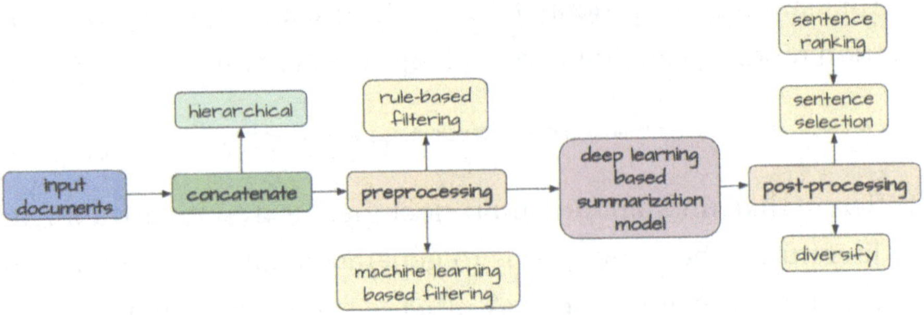

Figure 5: Multi-document wine summarization.

We start with our **input documents**, which are wine articles and reviews related to our focal wine (or region, style, vintage, etc.) of diverse types and lengths across various platforms and media outlets possibly written in diverse communication styles. They could be many short documents such as wine reviews either by wine professionals and critics or consumers, few long documents such as in-depth articles with a plethora of background information and inside scoop, or a mix of both.

Because of the contrasting features of the inputs (subjective wine reviews and articles) and outputs (objective archetypal descriptions of particular wines) of wine summarization, **candidate sentence extraction** becomes a critical component in the process, where the goal is to automatically identify a set of sentences among input documents that could potentially be used for objectively describing the wines. This is essentially a filtering step that removes contents from input documents that are subjective or uninformative with respect to the wines to be described. Let us detail both rule-based methods and machine or deep learning model based methods that could be used in tandem to achieve the best result:

- Rule-based filtering. Given our clear goal of generating informative and objective descriptions, there are at least several straightforward linguistic features for filtering out sentences that will not make the cut: *short, personal,* or *irrelevant.* For instance, we remove sentences of three or fewer words, with first-person or second-person pronouns, and are of irrelevant topics, based on the observation that such sentences rarely contain useful information for the output summary.

- Machine- or deep-learning-based filtering. More nuances and reasoning-based filtering could be implemented with a tailored machine- or deep-learning-based model trained for classifying sentences into relevant or irrelevant for the final summary.

After all the pre-processing steps, the central component of the multi-document text summarization pipeline lies in the machine learning model that converts multiple documents into a concise summary, which usually takes the form of a sequence-to-sequence deep learning network.

As was briefly touched on earlier in this section, multi-document summarization methods could be grouped into three types according to the nature of summary construction: abstractive, extractive, and hybrid that combines the former two:

- Extractive summarization: extractive summarization methods focus on selecting the most suitable snippets, whether it be sentences, phrases, or words, from input documents to form final summaries. Sentence ranking and sentence selection are important components of an extractive summarization pipeline, which preserves semantic and linguistic structure of the input documents, with major challenges revolving coherence, flexibility, redundancy, etc.

- Abstractive summarization: abstractive summarization methods generate final summaries to be as succinct and coherent as possible given input documents, typically allowing greater flexibility and less redundancy than extractive methods, with higher levels of natural language understanding skills required.

- Hybrid summarization: combining both extractive and abstractive summarization methods could prove particularly effective for multi-document summarization tasks with more involved relational structure between input documents. Canonical hybrid structures involve a two-stage process where in the first stage a module of either extractive or abstractive summarization is implemented to greatly consolidate information, followed by an abstractive summarization module in the second stage.

Deep learning methods dominate the landscape of automatic text summarization methods today as they have been shown to consistently achieve better performance than traditional methods, especially for multi-document summarization due to the expressiveness of non-linearity and capacity afforded by deep and wide neural networks. Figure 6 summarizes some state-of-the-art deep-learning-based multi-document summarization frameworks according to neural network architectures.
Without getting lost in the weeds of deep neural networks architecture, let us briefly familiarize with each of the illustrated architectural design in Figure 6:

- Simple networks: deep neural networks are used to extract features as multiple documents are concatenated and passed through the deep neural network for word-level, sentence-level, or document-level representation, which is used for summary generation or sentence selection later on. Such a simple pipeline acts as a starting point for the following more involved architectures;

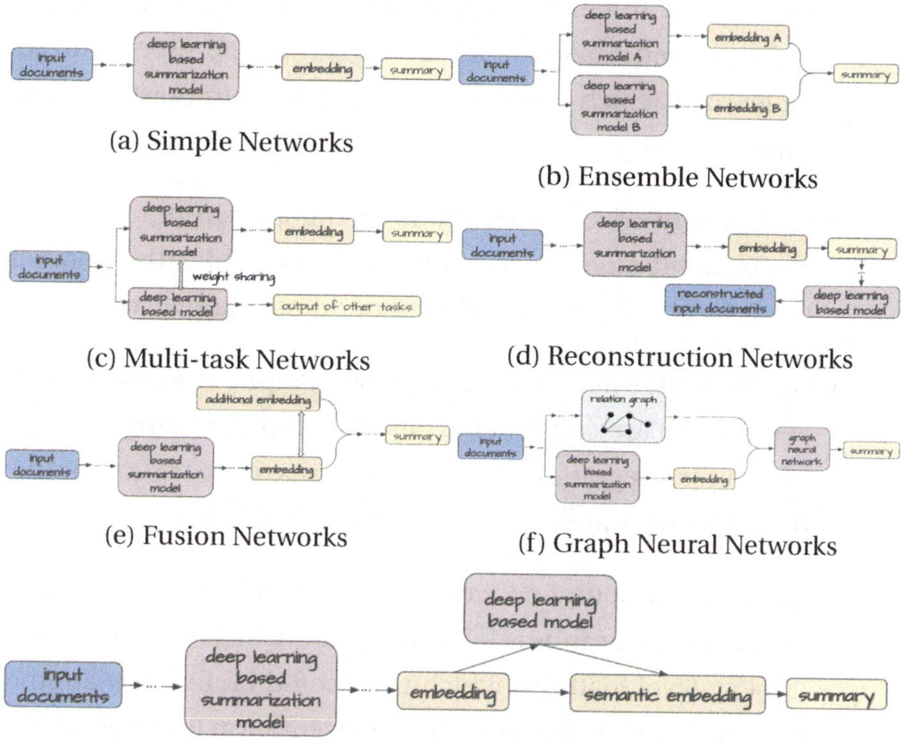

(g) Hierarchical Networks

Figure 6: Deep learning networks for text summarization.

- Ensemble networks: multiple machine learning or deep learning models are combined for potential improvement over individual models. Input documents are passed through different machine learning models in terms of network architectures and operations, and the outputs are aggregated by the majority vote or average mechanisms;

- Multi-task networks: relevant tasks other than summarization are introduced as auxiliary tasks to be learned concurrently to potentially improve feature extraction in terms of generalization ability as a regularization mechanism;

- Reconstruction networks: by leveraging unsupervised learning with document reconstruction tasks as main tasks and summary generation as auxiliary, better feature representation could be learned which could in turn improve summarization results;

- Fusion networks: representation generated from neural networks, hand-engineered features, and possibly other modalities is fused to incorporate prior or domain knowledge;
- Graph neural networks: knowledge graphs (more details in Section 3.1) are constructed based on input documents to allow better integration of how documents relate to one another, thus possibly improving summarization results;
- Hierarchical neural networks: multiple documents could be concatenated as inputs into a deep neural network for extracting low-level features, which then could be fed into another network for high-level feature representation learning. In this way, information of different granularities would be more likely separated and aggregated efficiently for summarization.

Within each of the aforementioned neural architectural design, the deep learning based (summarization) backbone model pictured in the dark pink boxes could take on any of the following forms:

- Convolutional neural networks (CNN) based models: the convolution operation could scan through word-, sentence-, and document-level embeddings. Convolutional neural networks have been proved to be effective for various natural language processing as well as computer vision tasks. In general, CNN-based multi-document summarization models use convolutional networks for extracting semantic and syntactic feature representation, replacing the generic fully-connected neural network architecture;

- Recurrent neural networks (RNN) based models: recurrent neural networks are well-suited for capturing sequential information such as relations and syntactic or semantic information from word sequences. To avoid potential optimization problems of exploding or vanishing gradients during stochastic gradient updating processes, Long Short-Term Memory (LSTM), Gated Recurrent Unit (GRU), and Bi-directional Long Short-Term Memory (Bi-LSTM) are frequently used in practice, which then are superseded by Transformer-based models as well as large-scale language models that we will dive into in Section 7.4;

- Transformer based models: Transformer architecture [Vaswani et al., 2017] known for its design of multi-headed self-attention enjoys advantages over convolutional neural networks with sequential input data, and over recurrent neural networks with long-range sequences and parallelization, and thus has been proved effective in multi-document summarization tasks;

- Graph neural networks (GNN) based models: to better capture relations between words, phrases, sentences, documents, as well as other information, graph neural networks are better suited than CNNs or RNNs to capture the semantic and syntactic relations that could lead to better summarization results (more details will be introduced in Section 4.3);

- Pointer-generator networks based models: based on earlier works such as pointer networks [Vinyals et al., 2015] that allow strategic selection from either input documents or algorithm-generated content, pointer-generator networks [See et al., 2017] excel at avoiding factual inconsistencies or redundancies in summarization;

- Auto-encoder based models: by minimizing the distance between inputs and reconstructed outputs, the auto-encoder architecture reduces the dimensions of feature representation, which could be leveraged for abstractive summarization tasks with less supervision overall;

- Hybrid models: multiple neural networks enlisted above could be integrated for more powerful and expressive architectures. For instance, Transformer and pointer-generator networks have been combined in a two-stage summarization method [Lebanoff et al., 2019] jointly scores single sentences and sentence pairs to identify representative single sentences and most compatible sentence pairs from the input documents, based on the observation that the majority of human-written summary sentences are generated by fusing one or two input sentences .

Diversification is an indispensable step to remove any potential redundancy in the final summary. This is usually done by calculating sentence similarity measures among candidate sentences based on learned representations of sentences, either sparse (e.g., tf-idf) or dense (contextualized embeddings, detailed in Section 7.4), average or weighted. Similarities measures range from the lossy Euclidean, to cosine distance, from the Kullback–Leibler (KL) to the Jensen–Shannon (JS) divergence, from machine-learning to deep-learning-based metric learning (detailed in Section 4.1).
If we were to opt for extractive summarization techniques, sentence ranking and sentence selection are two indispensable post-processing steps for quality assurance.
A **sentence ranking** step could be included to maximize the quality of our final outputs in terms of informativeness and readability. Deep learning based models such as those described above as candidate networks for text summarization could be readily repurposed for sentence ranking tasks with modifications to the training objectives.

Sentence selection is the final step of the summary generation pipeline. From the previous steps, we have obtained a list of candidate sentences ranked by their informativeness, readability, and relevance, and pairwise similarity scores of each possible pair of sentences within our candidate pool. Given a desired number of sentences in the final summarized description, let us detail several common and straightforward approaches to coalesce selected sentences into the final output:

- Greedy: traverse the list of candidate snippets based on their respective scores of informativeness, readability, relevant, etc., ranked from the highest to the lowest, and add a candidate to the final descriptive summary if and only if it is not similar to any candidates already chosen until a pre-specified length of output summary is reached.

- LexRank: a graph-based extractive summarization method that relies on the concept of sentence salience to identify the most important sentences in a document or set of documents. Salience is typically defined in terms of the presence of particular important words or in terms of similarity to a centroid pseudo-sentence. It computes sentence importance based on stochastic random walks and the concept of eigenvector centrality in a graph representation of sentences. When applied on top of the list of snippet candidates for the output summary, the importance scores could be used to re-rank the candidate sentences as the scores indicate how well the candidate covers the information included in other candidates. After the importance-based re-ranking, the candidate list is traversed in a decreasing order of the assigned scores and a sentence or snippet is added to the final output if and only if it's not similar to any already added.

- Clustering: after partitioning candidate sentences into a pre-specified number of clusters using clustering algorithms such as K-means, the resulting clusters could be traversed based the size of the cluster in a decreasing order where the most representative (for instance, closest to the cluster centroid), relevant, informative, and readable snippet from each cluster is added to the descriptive summary.

Finally through these steps, multiple documents are converted and transformed into concise, informative, objective, and readable descriptive summaries of the particular wine (or region, style, vintage, etc.) at the specified granularity. Table 1-Table 2 showcase some examples of automatically generated summaries given specific regions, vintages, or styles.

Variety	Vintage	Region, Country	Summary
Cabernet Sauvignon	1984	Napa Valley, US	Sweet mushroom. Spiced red plum. Rich dark chocolate. A lot of American oak. Blackcurrant, cedar, plum. High acidity. Very long.
Riesling	1990	Mosel, Germany	Gold with green. Clean and rich. Mineral and dense. Botrytis. Tart finish. Racy honey dust. Nervy and lively. Long finish.
Pinot Noir	1996	Nuits-Saint-George, France	Savory with quite some depth. Lovely red fruit with a touch of darker fruit. Fig and raisin. Mushroom and licorice. Hints of spices. Sweet finishes. A bit tart and austere,
Merlot	2001	Pomerol, France	Rich and velvety. Opulent on the palate. Sweet and mineraly. Poise. Floral. Lifted. Thick sweet tannins. Very heady.

Table 1: Examples of generated summaries of specific regions, vintages, and varieties.

Variety	Vintage	Region, Country	Summary
Syrah	2003	Hermitage, France	Some sweet liquorice. Sweet and powerful. Big and rich. Savory and long. Slightly herbal note. Cooked.
Chardonnay	2006	Puligny-Montrachet, France	Honey and butter. Lemon oil. Mineral complexity. Creamy oak on the palate. Intense. Spicy oak. Lively with a refreshing finish.
Chenin Blanc	2007	Vouvray, France	Searing acidity. Fennel. Tingly structured acidity. Focused and nervy. Honeysuckle and lime. Lime and flowers. Richly toasty.
Semillon	2010	Hunter Valley, Australia	Smoke and toast. Creamy. Grassy. Green fruits. Low alcohol.
Agiorgitiko	2010	Nemea, Greece	Round tannins. A lot of smoky spice. Red cherry fruit. Deep ruby. Garnet. Dark fruited. Sweet dusty tannins. Real freshness. Lovely perfume. Serious,
Grüner Veltliner	2011	Wachau, Austria	Oily on the palate. Mineral nose. Rich and broad. Big and broad. Power. Oily mineral textured. Peppery, citrus, creamy texture.
Nebbiolo	2014	Barbaresco, Italy	Brick color. Savory fruit. Tension. Powerful and intense. Dusty fruit on the nose. Grippy tannins. Orange tinges. Tart acidity. Drying tannins. Soft red fruit. Stalky and reductive.
Mencia	2016	Bierzo, Spaon	Freshness. Floral and acidic. Light. Mineral character. Heady sweet berries with freshness. Fine tannins.

Table 2: Examples of generated summaries of specific regions, vintages, and varieties. (Continued)

2.2 Decision Tree

Decision trees are classification (predicting samples' category or categories) or regression (predicting samples' value or values of some sort) models formulated in a tree-like architecture. With decision trees, data samples are progressively organized in smaller and more uniform subsets, while an associated tree graph is generated. Each internal node of the tree structure represents a different pairwise comparison on a selected feature, whether it be red-fruit markers or dusty tannins, whereas each branch represents the outcome of this comparison. Leaf nodes represent the final decision or prediction taken after following the path from root to leaf, which is referred to as a classification rule. The most common learning algorithms in this category are the classification and regression trees (CART) for categorical and numerical prediction targets, respectively.

We classify grape varieties to reveal how we can select the blind tasting strategy with the lowest out-of-sample[8] error by only using in-sample[9] characteristics of color, aroma, and flavor. This enables us to answer the central question: given a set of descriptors based on an unknown glass of wine, which blind tasting strategy best identifies the wine.

The winning strategy — the decision rule, given wines we sample from and practice with, is determined by the identifying the model with the minimum error among all possible alternatives.

The classification tree provides cutoff values of characteristics, whether it be of color, aroma, flavor, or structure, to place samples of wines into "buckets." This classifies wine samples in an easy-to-interpret manner. Each bucket of wine samples has a similar profile in terms of characteristics.

---

[8]Any new wines we have never tasted.

[9]Wines we have tasted and know what they taste like.

When a new flight of wines is encountered, it can be classified using this decision rule to identify which kinds of wines each will most likely be. This allows us to uncover relationships between observed feature patterns in the data and model fit[10] that are easy to interpret while avoiding the need to make any additional assumptions.

The classification trees in this section can be easily read by starting at the top and following a series of "if-then" decisions down to a terminal node (leaf) at the bottom of each branch. These terminal nodes represent data sets with the same observed characteristics.

Let us experiment with three different sets of available characteristics reflective of different tasting and sensory abilities and compare the resulting optimal blind tasting decision rules as strategies, for both white and red wines:

1. characteristics of colors, aromas, and flavors without structural descriptors;
2. characteristics of colors, aromas, flavors, and structures (structural descriptors indicating low, medium, or high levels of acidity, tannin or phenolic bitterness, intensity, body, alcohol);
3. characteristics of colors, aromas, flavors, and fine-grained structures (structural descriptors indicating low, medium, or high levels of acidity, tannin or phenolic bitterness, intensity, body, alcohol, as well as shapes and types such as dusty, coarse, clayey, zesty, etc.).

Figure 7 illustrates the resulting decision tree when blind tasting white wines without structural information, suitable for tasters not confident about gauging the acidity or alcohol levels of wines.

[10] How the particular decision rule compares to truth in data.

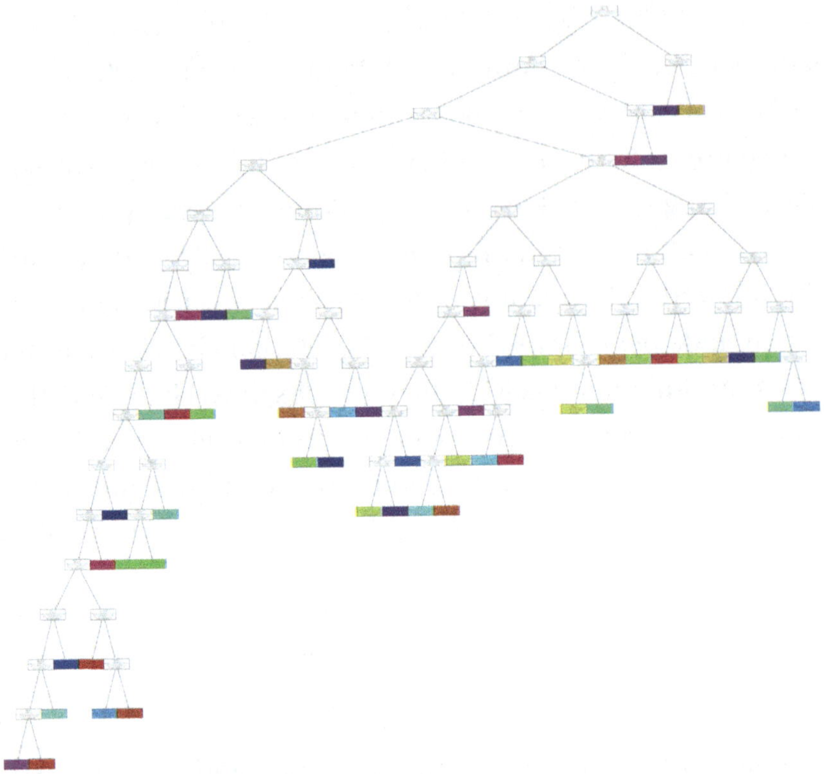

Figure 7: The decision tree for white wine deduction without structural information. This is only showing the skeleton due to page limit. Visit http://ai-for-wine.com/tasting for full-sized visualizations and details.

Over a dozen characteristics out of a total of over two dozen were selected by the classification tree's sequential variable selection algorithm as being diagnostic, ordered by decreasing importance: TDN (petrol), pyrazine (green bell pepper), color, minerality, guava, phenolic bitterness, orchard fruit, passion fruit, foxiness, herbal notes, malolactic notes, tropical fruit, dried fruit, Botrytis, oily texture, smokiness, salinity, florality, etc. To illustrate how to use the decision tree for deduction while tasting, given a glass of white wine, one may start by asking if petroleum character is present. If the answer is no, one would proceed by gauging the presence of green bell pepper or grassy notes. If the answer is still no, minerality would be next trait to be vetted. If minerality is indeed detected on the nose or the palate, we could further narrow it down by paying attention to phenolic bitterness on the finish, if any. If there is indeed a phenolic grip, we would keep investigating if there's any herbal characteristics. If the answer is yes, we are fairly confident that the final answer in terms of grape variety is one of a small subset of varieties we started with: Chenin Blanc, Grüner Veltliner, Malvasia Istriana, Gros Manseng. We could further distinguish Malvasia Istriana or Gros Manseng from Albariño or Grüner Veltliner based on the presence of orchard fruits. Once we narrow it down to either Albariño or Grüner Veltliner, notes of Botrytis such as honey, saffron, and ginger are among the markers that set Grüner Veltliner apart from Albariño, whereas smokiness is among the distinguishing characteristics between Malvasia Istriana and Gros Manseng, indicative of the type of soils they show affinity to, respectively. Such a tree is but one demonstration of how to leverage decision trees for deductive tasting given a particular set of markers, personalized to reflect individual strengths and weaknesses, and customized for different objectives (grape variety, vintage, region, country, soil type), based on whatever input provided to decision tree algorithms based on *wine summarization* (Section 2.1).

Such a deduction process deviates from the conventional approaches such as the grid popularized by The Court of Master Sommelier, and SAT popularized by The Wine and Spirit Education Trust, but could be easily tailored for anyone to accommodate strengths and weaknesses and improving the efficiency of the deduction process by eliminating factors that wouldn't contribute the deduction results and prioritizing more distinguishing characteristics one should focus on. In the language of the Master of Wine program, decision trees also conveniently facilitate identifying grape laterals —

easily confused grape varieties in a blind tasting — as neighboring tree leaves, personalized with individual strengths and weaknesses, and customized with specific objectives and contexts. Better yet, with each pair of identified grape laterals, decision trees identify the most distinguishing characteristics to tell them apart. The same applies to identifying laterals of vintages, regions, countries, styles, etc. For instance, in the same example of a decision tree of white wines without structural information for grape variety calls. Semillon and Hárslevelű are identified as grape laterals and notes of tropical fruit help set one apart from the other. Verdejo and Irsay Oliver are identified as laterals with underripe fruit being one of the important traits to look for telling them apart. Chenin Blanc and Vermentino are also laterals with aromatic intensity being one of telltale signs of distinction. These laterals are identified based on flavors and aromas exclusively without any structural information such as acid and body, and we shall compare the laterals identified with structural information later on in this section.

For those confident in accurately identifying the structural information and comfortable with replying on such for deduction, Figure 8 illustrates the resulting decision tree when blind tasting white wines with such structural information of acidity, body, and alcohol. Overall, the resulting tree is wider and shallower than the one without structural information, indicative of the distinguishing power of structural information.

Again, over a dozen — though fewer than the decision tree without structural information — characteristics out of a total of over two dozen were selected by the classification tree's sequential variable selection algorithm as being diagnostic, ordered by decreasing importance: florality, grapefruit/guava, nuttiness (oxidative), aromatic intensity, herbal character, acidity, salinity, leesy character, Botrytis,

stone fruit, etc. To illustrate how to use the decision tree for deduction while tasting with structural calls, given a glass of white wine, one may start by asking if the wine is particularly floral. If the answer is no (yes), one would proceed by gauging the presence of guava (grapefruit) notes. If the answer is still no, any herbal characteristics would be next trait to be vetted. If herbal characteristics are indeed detected on the nose or the palate, we could further narrow it down by paying attention to the level of acidity on the palate. If the acidity level turns out medium to high, we could further determine if pyrazine (grass or green bell pepper) is indeed present. If the answer is no, together with hints of orchard fruit and phenolic bitterness, we are fairly confident that the final answer in terms of grape variety is among the following: Pinot Gris, Furmint, Macabeo, and Friulano. Among them, the most distinguishing factor to single out Friulano could be less prominent orchard fruit compared to the other three. Macabeo appears to be slightly lighter in color compared to Pinot Gris and Friulano and the presence of minerality might help in distinguishing Friulano from Pinot Gris in general.
The decision based on both structural information and flavor or aroma information identifies a different set of grape laterals than the one without structural information. Equipped with additional structural information, for instance, Verdicchio, rather than Irsay Oliver (identified as a lateral by the decision tree without structural information), is the lateral of Verdejo, even though leesy characters are more commonly present in Verdejo but not in Verdicchio, making it a distinguishing factor. Roussanne, rather than Chenin Blanc (identified as a lateral by the decision tree without structural information), is the grape lateral of Vermentino. Interestingly, Falanghina and Petit Manseng are identified as laterals too with Petit Manseng being spicier than Falanghina, whereas Fiano and Greco appear to be somewhat similar too, with Greco generally exhibiting riper fruit profiles.

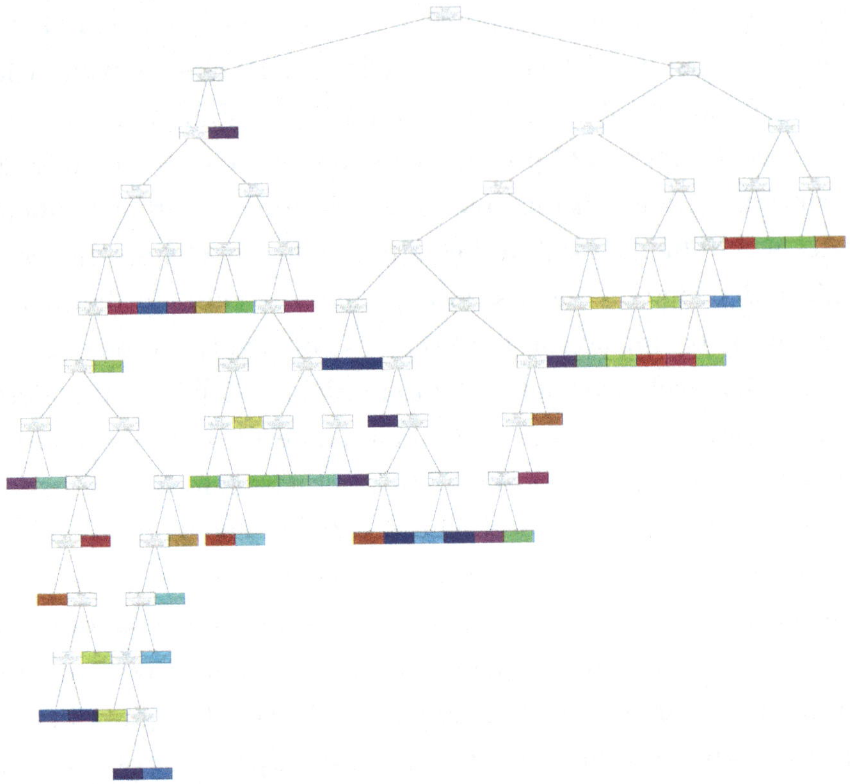

Figure 8: The decision tree for white wine deduction. This is only showing the skeleton due to page limit. Visit http://ai-for-wine.com/tasting for full-sized visualizations and details.

For those with more defined palates that can confidently judge the finer details of structural information, one example being Nick Jackson's theory detailed in his book *Beyond Flavor* where the shape and type of acidity could be articulated as crescendo, zigzag, linear, vertical pole-shaped, waveform, watershed, etc. With such additional fine-grained structural information as input and possibly proper decision tree pruning, the resulting tree could learn to better select information features to rely on for greater overall deduction accuracy.

Figure 9 illustrates the resulting decision tree when blind tasting red wines without structural information, mimicking situations for tasters less confident in gauging the acidity or tannin levels of wines. Characteristics selected by the classification tree's sequential variable selection algorithm as being diagnostic, ordered by decreasing importance are: florality, meaty or gamey characters, notes of olives, color concentration, minty characters, tobacco, cherry, underripe fruit characters and red fruit characters, volatile acidity, minerality, new oak characters, herbal notes, and flavors and aromas associated with carbonic maceration, etc. To illustrate how to use the decision tree for deduction while tasting with structural calls, given a glass of red wine, one may start by asking if the wine is particularly floral. If the answer is yes, one would proceed by gauging the color and concentration. If the wine appears medium to dark in color concentration, any minty notes could be the next informative piece of information to consider. If minty characteristics are indeed detected on the nose or the palate, we could further narrow it down by the presence of cherry notes or any suggestions of carbonic maceration. If no obvious carbonic maceration could be detected but there exists positive evidence of the use of new French oak barrels in the vinification process, we perhaps could have some confidence in the variety of the wine being Cinsault, or Tempranillo, with Tempranillo being perhaps more red-fruited, tart and dried and more traditionally aged in at least a proportion of new French oak barrels.

Once again, a diverse set of grape laterals based on flavor and aroma information alone is identified in this process. For instance, Saint Laurent and Gamay are identified as laterals distinguished by spiciness, so are Baga and Portugieser with Portugieser being more red-fruited, Sciacarello and Brachetto with Brachetto perhaps more herbal, Lagrein and Lacrima with Lacrima slightly more red-fruited, Cinsault and Barbera with Cinsault more likely associated with carbonic maceration, etc.

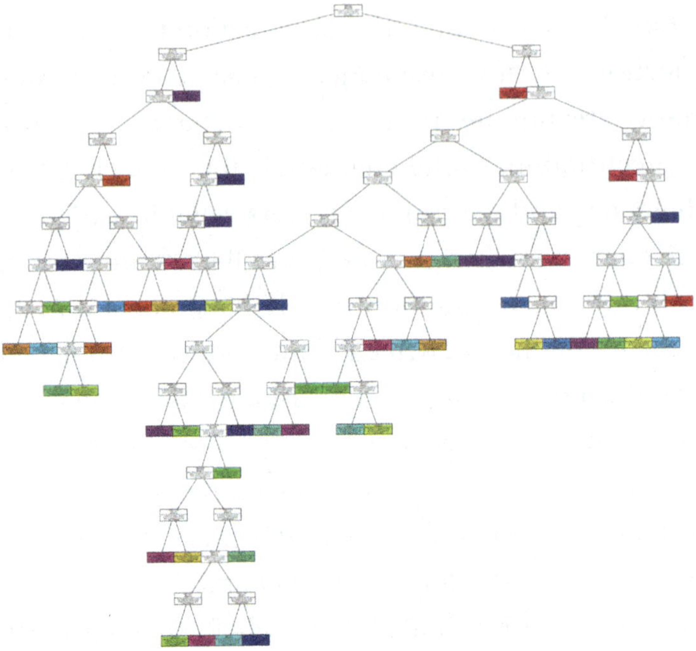

Figure 9: The decision tree for red wine deduction without structural information. This is only showing the skeleton due to page limit. Visit http://ai-for-wine.com/tasting for full-sized visualizations and details.

For those confident in accurately identifying the structural information and comfortable with replying on such for deduction, Figure 10 illustrates the resulting decision tree when blind tasting red wines with such structural information of acidity, tannin, body, and alcohol. Overall, the resulting tree is wider and averages shorter branches than the one without structural information, indicative of the distinguishing power of structural information.

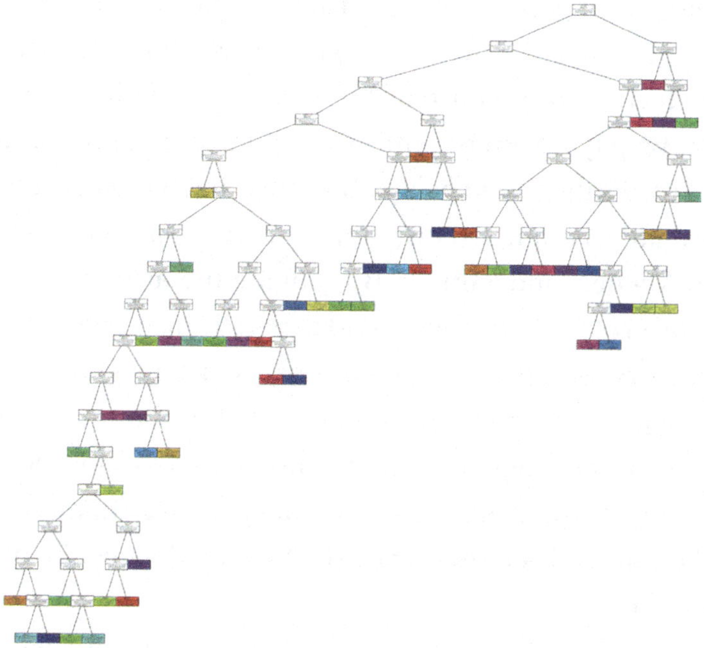

Figure 10: The decision tree for red wine deduction. This is only showing the skeleton due to page limit. Visit http://ai-for-wine.com/tasting for full-sized visualizations and details.

With structural information, characteristics selected by the classification tree's sequential variable selection algorithm as being diagnostic turn out rather different than without structural information, especially when it comes to their relative importance: olive, mint, game and meat, tar and leather, powder sugar, new French oak, purple fruit like pomegranate, tart cherry, herbal character, black pepper, minerality, acidity, alcohol level, etc. To illustrate how to use the decision tree for deduction while tasting with structural calls, given a glass of red wine, one may start by asking if the wine reminds one of olives. If the answer is no, one would proceed by gauging the presence of gamey characteristics. If the answer is still no, any purple fruit would be next trait to be vetted. If purple fruits are indeed detected on the nose or the palate, we could further narrow it down by paying attention to the ripeness of fruit and the presence of blue fruit on the palate. If there is indeed blue fruit, and the fruit is relatively ripe and lush, then our varietal candidates include Merlot, Malbec, and Tannat. By gauging the alcohol level and the tannin level of the wine, one could generally distinguish Tannat and Malbec from Merlot as Merlot tannins are usually more velvety and supple at a lower level than Tannat or Malbec tannins and the alcohol levels usually higher. Tannat, compared to Malbec and Merlot, supposedly features even riper and deeper fruit characters. Therefore, the final call is rather straightforward following the path of the decision tree.

The decision based on both structural information and flavor or aroma information identifies a different set of grape laterals than the one without structural information. Equipped with additional structural information, for instance, Dornfelder, rather than Barbera (identified as a lateral by the decision tree without structural information), is the lateral of Cinsault, with the level of acidity of Cinsault perhaps a touch higher than that of Dornfelder. Zweigelt, rather than Lacrima (identified as a lateral by the decision tree without structural information), is the grape lateral of Lagrein, with perhaps slightly differentiating levels of tannins. Rightfully, Aglianico and Sagrantino are identified as laterals too with Aglianico perhaps less brooding than Sagrantino, whereas Dolcetto and Nero d'Avola appear to be laterals as well, with Nero d'Avola generally showcasing

a higher level of tannins. Moreover, laterals such as Graciano and Schioppetino, Mencia and Saint Laurent, Merlot and Malbec, Ciliegiolo and Teroldego, Touriga Nacional and Negroamaro, etc. returned by the decision tree with structural information are indeed reasonably plausible as I for one, constantly mix up new world Merlot with Malbec in blind tastings.
And yet, those with exquisite palates that can confidently discern the finer details of tannin structures and characteristics, one example being Nick Jackson's theory detailed in Beyond Flavor where the shape and type of tannins could be articulated as felt-at-the-gum, coarse-grained or grainy, sandpaperly, clayey, felt-at-the-cheek, dusty, etc. With additional fine-grained structural information as input and possibly proper decision tree pruning, the resulting tree could learn to better select informative features to rely on for even higher deduction accuracy overall.

2.3 Multi-task Learning

Multi-task learning comes into play where standard supervised deep learning methods generally struggle. It is when we would like a general-purpose AI system that could rapidly ramp up for new tasks, with a limited amount of data that follows a long-tail distribution[11], that multi-task learning really shines. Multi-task learning refers to the machine learning training regime where multiple tasks are learned at the same time by a shared model, by way of shared architecture or optimization designs that enable learning of common patterns across tasks that improve outcomes on the entire collection of tasks, as opposed to training one model for every task in isolation. For instance, in the case of blind tasting, given the wine sample and all the observable features associated with it, our collection of tasks

[11]Most datasets we could easily collect in real life follow long-tailed distributions where data samples concentrate on a few common classes and for a vast majority of classes available data samples are lacking.

could include: deducing its vintage, identifying its grape variety or varieties, pinpointing its growing region, guessing the producer, and rating its quality. In a multi-task learning setting, one would complete all the tasks all at once for the same wine sample, perhaps allowing answers to be influenced by one another in the process, as opposed to accomplishing each and every task one by one in isolation independently. Indeed, multi-task learning perhaps mirrors human learning process more precisely as humans could be remarkably good at solving multiple tasks simultaneously.

There are at least three advantages when it comes to multi-task learning:

1. Due to the shared structure or optimization designs, it could result in tremendous memory-efficiency especially when the number of tasks grows;

2. Since all the tasks are accomplished all at once (with sequential exceptions for good reasons), multi-task learning could be especially advantageous when it comes to speed;

3. In many cases, multi-task learning could lead to improved performance especially when associated tasks share relevant and complementary information that flows freely in-between or act as regularizer for one another that improves generalization ability.

On the other hand, one of the major challenges of efficient multi-task learning lies in circumventing *negative transfer*, which happens when independently trained networks work better than the jointly trained one, and that the data and training of one task is adversely hurting the training of other tasks. Such is a rather prevalent phenomenon and potential causes include:

1. *Optimization challenges* due to cross-task interference in training[12], diverging learning rates of different tasks[13], etc.
2. *Limited representational capacity* of the multi-task network which often is required to be much larger than their single-task counterparts. And if not met, network underfitting could result where the model struggles to learn meaningful patterns from the training data.

Multi-task learning techniques had been commonly classified into soft and hard parameter sharing paradigms. Hard parameter sharing refers to the practice of sharing model weights between multiple tasks such that each weight is trained to jointly minimize loss functions, whereas soft parameter sharing means individual task-specific models are trained for different tasks with separate weights with additional terms in the objective function that constrain these weights to be similar. With the rapid growth of multi-task learning community, such a delineation is perhaps a bit limiting to encompass the landscape of multi-task learning strategies. The class of hard parameter sharing methods could be loosely extended to methods that focus on *multi-task architectures*, while soft parameter sharing in the form of regularization could be perhaps loosely mapped to *multi-task optimization* methods with some works focusing more on architectural design as well. Let me summarize the kaleidoscope of these two classes of multi-task learning methods in tables Table 3 and Table 4 respectively, which provide an outline of the following discussions of multi-task learning methods. Some

[12]For instance, when updating gradients during one iteration, the gradient of one task hurts the weights of another task, and the optimization process gets challenging.

[13]In which case, the optimization process could get stuck in a local optimum as the slower-learning task struggles to catch up.

works enlisted, in fact, straddle between multiple categories as they are not necessarily mutually exclusive.

Besides multi-task architectures and optimization methods, the other class of methods that we loosely refer to as *task relationship learning* is where a recent body of active research efforts center around, thus is perhaps worth highlighting to complete the picture. Task relationship learning methods focus on learning an explicit representation of the relationships between tasks, which helps inform the optimal architecture of optimization designs of the multi-task learning paradigm.

In the soft parameter sharing paradigm, each task initiates its own tailored neural network with feature sharing mechanisms in place to provide the crosswalk between different tasks. It could involve searching an enormous space of possible parameter sharing architectures to find the optimal solution, raising concerns about scalability of such a sharing regime. Such feature sharing mechanisms could take on different forms. Cross-stitch network [Misra et al., 2016] consists of individual networks for different tasks but uses "cross-stitch" units to linearly combine the activations from multiple task-specific networks and learn an optimal combination of shared and task-specific representations for each task. Sluice networks [Ruder et al., 2019] generalize cross-stitch networks to allow greater flexibility and granularity in that each layer is divided into shared and task-specific representations, and the input to each layer is a linear combination of the task-specific and shared outputs of the previous layer for each task network. Neural discriminative dimensionality reduction convolutional neural networks (NDDR-CNNs)[14] [Gao et al., 2019] further reduces dimensions discriminatively which enables automatic feature fusing at every layer from different tasks, while multi-task attention networks (MTAN) [Liu et al., 2019a] in-

[14]What a mouthful...

troduces a single shared network containing a global feature pool, together with a soft-attention[15] module for each task to allow for learning of task-specific features from the global features, while simultaneously allowing for features to be shared across different tasks. In the hard parameter sharing paradigm, model weights are shared between multiple tasks, and each weight is learnt jointly across tasks, as opposed to in soft parameter sharing, different tasks have individual task-specific models with separate weights, with feature sharing mechanism in-between to incentivize similar parameters across the task-specific models. A common structure of hard parameter sharing architecture consists of a shared feature encoding network that branches into feature decoding heads tailored for each task. In such structures, when to branch out and where to branch out are sometimes arbitrary, which could lead to less than optimal results. Followup works proposed tree-like structures [Lu et al., 2017b, Vandenhende et al., 2019] that start from a minimal trunk, and branch out dynamically and strategically based on task characteristics to grow into the full structure.

Among architecture-based methods, we could perhaps further categorize into encoder-based and decoder-based approaches. In encoder-based methods, task features are shared in the encoding stage with a backbone network to learn a generic representation for task-specific heads. Along this line, the focus appears to be on *where* and *how* feature sharing should be carried out in the encoder. Decoder-based architectures, on the other hand, instead of directly predicting task outputs from the same input all at once, allow for sequential feature sharing that include an initial stage of task prediction, the results

[15] Soft attention is a global attention mechanism where all image patches are given some weight, whereas with the hard attention mechanism, only one image patch is considered at a time. More details in Section 7.4 and the Transformer [Vaswani et al., 2017] literature.

of which could be leveraged to improve feature learning recursively, facilitating information sharing during the decoding stage.

Orthogonal to encoder- and decoder-based architectures, *conditioned architecture* based on conditional or adaptive computation refers to where specific parts of a neural network architecture are executed depending on characteristics of network inputs, enabling greater generalization across various tasks and inputs.

Lastly and unsurprisingly, neural architecture search (NAS) has been applied to multi-task architectures as well. In particular, it serves as one of the solutions to mitigate negative transfer between tasks, as there could exist parts of the network where positive transfer still happens, in which case searching for the specific configuration for partial positive transfer could get unwieldy with hand-designed architectures with a large number of tasks and scale of networks.

Among optimization-based multi-task learning methods, interesting methodological equivalences could perhaps be identified between various loss weighting and task scheduling methods. They were largely originated from their respective fields with loss weighting perhaps more prevalent in computer vision, whereas task scheduling in natural language processing. Loss weighting could perhaps been viewed as a relaxed form of task scheduling and various task scheduling methods could be adapted to loss weighting techniques, despite the fact that most studies follow the convention of their field in terms of naming and intuition.

Despite advances in architectural and optimization design for multi-task learning, joint learning of multiple tasks is prone to *negative transfer*, when the joint learning outcomes degrade compared to individual learning outcomes for at least some tasks within a set. It could be due to the fact that some tasks are unrelated. Such a

	Method	Summary	Drawback	Reference
Encoder-based	Cross-stitch networks	Cross-stitch units combine activations from multiple networks to learn optimal combination of shared and task-specific representations	Scales linearly with task count; restrictive feature fusion, etc.	[Misra et al., 2016]
	Sluice networks	Extends cross-stitch networks with elective sharing of feature representations and skip connections.	Scales linearly; restrictive feature fusion, etc.	[Ruder et al., 2017]
	Neural discriminative dimensionality reduction CNNs (NDDR-CNNs)	Extends cross-stitch networks with dimensionality reduction by channel-wise concatenation and reduction.	Scales linearly; limited local info sharing.	[Gao et al., 2019]
	Multi-task attention networks (MTAN)	Extracts generic features with a shared backbone, with task-specific attention modules selecting features from generic features through a soft attention mask.	Limited local info sharing for the attention mask.	[Liu et al., 2019b]
Decoder-based	Prediction-and-distillation networks (PAD-Net)	Predicts intermediate auxiliary tasks as multi-modal input to distillation modules with spatial attention for final tasks.	Limited local info sharing for spatial attention mask.	[Xu et al., 2018]
	Pattern-affinitive propagation networks (PAP-Net)	Cross-task and task-specific propagation to adaptively diffuse similar patterns across & within tasks as regularization.	[NA]	[Zhang et al., 2019]
	Joint task-recursive learning (JTRL)	Recursively predicts two tasks at increasingly higher scales to gradually refine results based on past states.	Not directly applicable to more than two tasks.	[Zhang et al., 2018b]
	Multi-scale task interaction networks (MTI-Net)	Accounts for multi-scale interaction while distilling task information.	[NA]	[Vandenhende et al., 2020]
Conditioning	Neural module networks	Stanford parser determines composition of neural modules & relationships.	Module composition not learned.	[Andreas et al., 2017]
	Routing networks	A principled approach to gauge connectivity of network modules via routing.	Lack of architectural diversity.	[Rosenbaum et al., 2018]
	Compositional recursive learner (CRL)	Iteratively chooses a task-agnostic module through which to route inputs.	Potential module collapse.	[Chang et al., 2019]
	Soft modularization	Routing networks relaxed: a linear combination of (not discrete) modules.	Lack of architectural diversity.	[Yang et al., 2020]
Neural architecture search (NAS)	Multi-task neural model search (MNMS)	MNMS controller trained on all tasks to generate one architecture for each task.	Incremental at best, expensive.	[Wong and Gesmundo, 2017]
	MTL-NAS	NAS in a set of fixed-architecture single-task backbone networks over feature fusion operations between network layers.	Computationally expensive.	[Gao et al., 2020b]
	Fully-adaptive feature sharing (FAFS)	Dynamically grow the model from a simple network where tasks share all layers into a tree structure based on sample difficulty.	Sample difficulty as a task affinity metric suffers from dataset bias.	[Lu et al., 2017b]
	Soft layer ordering	A flexible layer ordering approach that learns how shared layers are applied in different ways for different tasks.	Computationally expensive.	[Meyerson and Miikkulainen, 2018]
	Piggyback	Learns binary masks that "piggyback" on an existing network (or applied to unmodified weights of that network) for good performance on a new task.	Restrictive application; unclear generalization beyond classification.	[Mallya et al., 2018]

Table 3: Architecture-based Multi-task Learning Techniques.

problem motivates this other class of multi-task learning methods — task relationship learning. Task relationship learning methods learn an explicit representation of tasks or their relationships with techniques such as clustering, the results of which could in turn be leveraged to improve learning outcomes. As a solution to negative transfer, many task relationship learning methods are designed to

	Method	Summary	Drawback	Reference
Loss weighting	Uncertainty weighting	Task-dependent uncertainty for balancing losses.	Restrictive.	[Kendall and Gal, 2017]
	Dynamic weight averaging	Downweights fast tasks, upweights straggling ones.	Suffers if validation results fluctuate.	[Liu et al., 2019b]
	Dynamic task prioritization	Prioritizes learning difficult tasks by assigning them a high task-specific weight.	Clean groundtruth annotations needed; manual tuning.	[Guo et al., 2018]
	Gradient normalization	Aligns task gradients at a similar magnitude.	May not align with testing performance.	[Chen et al., 2018]
Regularization	Trace-norm regularized	Encourages learning parameters of similar tasks.	Weak results.	[Yang and Hospedales, 2017]
	Multilinear relationship nets	Regularizes with priors over parameters by task relations.	[NA]	[Long et al., 2017]
	Deep asymmetric multi-task feature learning	Regularizes with an auto-encoder term to allow asymmetric information flow.	Computationally expensive.	[Lee et al., 2018]
	AdaShare	Regularizes shared parameters, not module parameters.	Potential module collapse.	[Sun et al., 2019b]
	Maximum roaming	Randomly partitions parameters during training.	Lack of theoretical understanding.	[Pascal et al., 2021]
Gradient modulation	Gradient episodic memory	Constrains new task gradients to be non-conflicting.	Computational burden.	[Lopez-Paz and Ranzato, 2017]
	Projecting conflicting gradients (PCGrad)	Resolves conflicting task-specific gradients by gradient projection.	Strong assumption, unclear efficiency if it is used alone.	[Yu et al., 2020a]
Task scheduling	Adaptive task scheduling	Prioritizes difficult tasks by assigning higher weights.	Clean groundtruth annotations needed.	[Jean et al., 2019]
	Proportional sampling	Samples tasks with probability proportional to size of datasets.	Prone to dataset biases.	[Sanh et al.,]
Multi-objective optimization	Multi-objective optimization	Finds one Pareto optimal solution with good trade-off among different tasks.	One Pareto solution might not satisfy as many exist.	[Sener and Koltun, 2018]
	Pareto optimization	Finds a set of Pareto solutions representing trade-offs among different tasks.	Rank among well-distributed Pareto solutions unclear.	[Lin et al., 2019]

Table 4: Optimization-based Multi-task Learning Techniques.

control information flow strategically — share information between related tasks and block if it could jeopardize the performance of one another.

There are several classes of task relationship learning methods that have emerged over the past few years, among which *task grouping* and *learning transfer relationships* are the major ones, as detailed below:

Task grouping methods operate on the rule of thumb that if two tasks exhibit positive transfer, keep them grouped with parameter sharing or tying regimes in multi-task training, whereas if two tasks exhibit negative transfer, separate their learning from start. Such methods usually require a great deal of computing resources in preparation for the large-scale trail and error especially when the number of tasks scales up.

The first few large-scale studies in natural language processing that empirically tested the effectiveness of multi-tasking learning across 1440 task combinations and 90 task pairs, each with a main task and one or two auxiliary tasks, found that the performance on the main task improves the most with auxiliary tasks whose label distributions exhibit informative properties such as high entropy and low kurtosis, as well as, if not even more, the rate at which learning happens (gradient) if the main task is trained on its own. Multitask learning is perhaps particularly beneficial when individual task learning rate begins to plateau at the beginning, since adding auxiliary tasks might help prevent it from being stuck in a local solution that would be sub-optimal. Furthermore, additional simple linear models were trained to predict whether an auxiliary task would improve or compromise the performance of the main task based on dataset features and learning characteristics.

In computer vision, there exists similar studies, perhaps less comprehensive than the aforementioned natural language processing studies, in the context of self-supervision, that have documented findings that multi-task learning appears to always improve performance compared to single-task learning.

More recently a milestone dataset Taskonomy was introduced by Stanford computer vision researchers, who conducted an in-depth investigation on tasking grouping. They vetted potentials answers and rationales to the question: which tasks should and should not be learned together in one network when employing multi-task learning? By examining task cooperation and competition in different learning settings, a framework for assigning tasks to a few neural networks was proposed such that cooperating tasks are computed by the same neural network, while competing tasks are computed by different networks. This framework offers a time-accuracy trade-off and promises to produce better accuracy using less inference time than not only a single large multi-task neural network but also many single-task networks. Some of their empirical findings are perhaps surprising and thought-provoking:

1. there were mixed evidence regarding whether or not multi-task training improves over single-task training baselines;
2. performance gains from single-task training to multi-task training varies wildly with training setups, which calls into questions the common assumption that the effectiveness of multi-task learning strategies depends on the nature of the tasks or the relationships in-between;
3. there appears no clear correlation between multi-task affinity (tasks when grouped together in multi-task learning perform better) and transfer affinity (tasks from or to which transfer learning achieves better performance) between tasks, which invites more unsolved questions about what affects joint task learning such as multi-task and transfer learning.

Learning transfer relationships as a class of methods is related to tasking grouping, even though they do not necessarily correlate, as was indicated by insights from analyses done on the dataset Taskonomy, which was perhaps one of the first few studies that attempted to learn transfer affinities between tasks. It consists of 4 millions images with respect to 26 tasks, from which a computational method to automatically construct a taxonomy of visual tasks based on transfer relationships between tasks was proposed. It was the first large-scale empirical study to analyze task transfer relationships and compute an explicit hierarchy of tasks based on their transfer relationships, and by doing so they are able to compute optimal transfer policies for learning a group of related tasks with little supervision, despite being computationally expensive.

A few similarly spirited but more computationally efficient method proposed to compute a measure of similarity between tasks, using either Representation Similarity Analysis borrowed from computational neuro-science, or attribution maps common in computer vision, among others. Both methods boosted a tremendous speedup compared to Taskonomy without compromising performance.

This line of research is still nascent, and there remains plenty of opportunities ahead. In summary, these existing models leverage neural networks to better train neural networks, by drawing on information learned by the single-task networks to inform training strategies downstream.

SECTION 3

Theory Knowledge

The title for this section "Theory Knowledge" might come off as a misnomer for anyone outside the wine trade, especially those with a science or engineering background. Let me preface by defining what is meant by Theory Knowledge to be a most comprehensive set of factual knowledge that covers each and every aspect of the wine trade, an aggregate of all the knowledge of every wine professionals and enthusiasts in the world combined, if you will. Before we dive into the scope of this body of "theory knowledge", let us take a shortcut first by reviewing what is required to obtain some of the most highly regarded certifications in the wine world, which might provide some clues about whatever wine knowledge is required for a qualified wine professional.

In fact, this particular nomenclature of Theory Knowledge largely follows the term used in Master of Wine (by The Institute of Master of Wine, IMW, hereafter) and Master Sommelier (by The Court of Master Sommelier, CMS, hereafter) programs. In order to achieve the title Master of Wine, besides the final thesis that culminates the program as well as the practical exam of 12-wine blind tastings in which wines must be assessed for variety, origin, commercial appeal, winemaking, quality and style, one has to pass a Theory exam at the second stage, which consists of writing essays for five papers on viticulture, vinification and pre-bottling procedures, the handling of wine, the business of wine, and contemporary issues. These topics are designed to test the breadth and depth of a candidate's theoretical knowledge in the art, science and business of wine. Example questions are publicly available on the official website of the Institute of Master of Wine, but here are some samples for each of the five papers from the past few years:

- Paper 1: Mildews continue to afflict vineyards. What strategies might a vineyard manager employ to reduce the risk?
- Paper 2: With new French oak barrels becoming increasingly expensive, what alternative options and techniques are available to the winemaker wishing to make high-end wines?
- Paper 3: Many winemakers are reducing the levels of free and total sulphites in wine. Consider the role of sulphites at bottling and until the wine reaches the end consumer. What are the implications of reduced levels of free sulphites?
- Paper 4: How do wine consumers in mainland China decide what wine to buy and what are the implications of their choices for producers and distributors?
- Paper 5: Does a changing climate place greater emphasis on terroir or on choice of grape variety?

On the other hand, a Master Sommelier candidate is faced with a three-part exam that includes a theory portion, a tasting portion, and a service portion. The theory and tasting portions overlap with Master of Wine exams' theory and tasting portions but they are of different formats and with different focuses. Master of Wine (MW, hereafter) exams are all written exams in the form of essays, whereas Master Sommelier (MS, hereafter) exams are all oral exams that require candidates all dressed up in formal attire conversing directly with the examiners.

Some have argued that both exams are somewhat opaque, with MS exams to a much greater extent in that the wines in the blind tasting exams were never revealed, nor were any of the exam questions, correct answers, or records of candidates' performance — it seems whatever happened in the room stayed in the room, wheras IWM releases the exam questions and wines used in the tasting exams immediately after the exam every year. The implications and consequences of such practices have engendered a series of misconducts and problematic culture that took the center stage when exposed in the past few years, which is a whole another story to tell. Fortunately, or perhaps unfortunately at the same time, such problems are not exclusive to the wine industry but have permeated our society as a whole, and therefore AI research scientists have long been dedicating their ingenuity towards a better society by orchestrating AI solutions for social impact. We will devote the entire Section 11 to AI solutions to some of the most glaring issues exposed in a series of scandals unfolded in the past few years in the wine trade.

Other than the different formats associated with the MS and MW exams, more distinguishing features of the two exams and certification bodies are perhaps their respective focuses. Master of Wine program focuses a lot more on the production side than the MS program which perhaps leans more on the hospitality side in that all the theoretical and practical knowledge are in service of better serving consumers from all walks of life. Take the tasting exams for example, MW programs places more emphasis on **why** a wine tastes like what it tastes like, drawing on knowledge from viticulture, vinification, distribution, and consumer psychology, etc., and there could be some non-classic exams thrown in the mix, whereas for MS tasting exams, there are unofficial *fair game* grape varieties and regions that are considered classic examples and the odds of something unusual or non-classic in the tasting exams are rather slim, thus perhaps putting more emphasis on **how** or **what** should a particular style, region, variety, or quality level taste like.

Another major distinction between MS and MW programs is perhaps the level of breath and depth of knowledge expected from candidates. Even though both require both depth and breath, there are perhaps abundant signals that the MS program leans towards breath whereas the MW leans towards depth, relatively. This is implied by the title of Master Sommelier versus Master of Wine, in that sommelier covers all sorts of beverage with wine being a major part but a strong grasp on cocktail, spirits, beer, sake, cider, tea, coffee, and even cigar, among others, are all essential parts of the sommelier's knowledge for a successful beverage program at a fine dining restaurant or a beverage establishment, whereas for Master of Wine, only in-depth know knowledge is necessary but with a greater level of original and critical thinking best exemplified in a thesis on a novel topic of practical relevance. Some recent Master of Wine thesis titles include: What factors impacted the presence of American wines on US wine lists during the period 1900-1950? (Kryss Speegle MW); Arrived with COVID-19, here to stay? Experiences of German wineries with online wine tastings (Moritz Nikolaus Lueke MW); Depictions of grapes, vines and wine in the work of four seventeenth century English poets (Nicholas Jackson MW); Stock Movement for 2005 Red Bordeaux purchased En Primeur through a UK Wine Merchant 2006-2016: Have Buyers' Intentions Changed?

(Thomas Parker MW).

Now after a long digression of the required knowledge of MW and MS title holders, let us resume and refine our definition of the universe of wine knowledge to the a superset of the Theory Knowledge required for both MW and MS programs, that is, both combined, and much more. In fact, many would argue MW and MS programs are simply the beginning of a life-long learning journey in the ocean of wine knowledge, from vine growing in the eyes of geneticists like Carole Meredith (whose stories we will touch on in Section 7), viticulturists like Pedro Parra , geologists like Francois Vannier and Brenna Quigley; to wine production from the perspective of *chefs de cave* or cellar masters like Jean-Baptiste Lecaillon and Pierre Morey; from global distribution in the shoes of flying merchants like wine distributors Kermit Lynch and Neal Rosenthal, to consumer education through wine specialists at retailers and auction houses like Astors Wine (one of the largest retailers in NYC) and Sotheby's.

Let me try to summarize this all-encompassing body of wine knowledge by its scope, nature, and practical applications, and in doing so, identify AI solutions as well as what these AI solutions could make wine professionals lives better and perhaps ultimately consumers, and the society as a whole a better more efficient place.

First, the wine knowledge is fragmented, decentralized, and unstructured.

Fragmented in the sense that pieces of knowledge are scattered everywhere in different geographical regions, in different people's minds, and in different periods of time. How and why certain wines go through periods of closing down and opening up, for which certain wines are particularly known for, for instance, including white

Rhones like , Chateauneuf-du-Pape Blanc, Condrieu, Hermitage Blanc, and white Burgundys like Meursault Perrieres as well as various long lasting red wines such as Vosne-Romanée Conti or La Tache[16]. Such intimate knowledge of how certain wines age, how different vintages would fare differently a decade from now, what changed in the flavor and texture of wines throughout the last few decades of vintages, and when to best enjoy them and on what occasions, etc. is scattered with different vignerons, wine merchants, sommeliers, collectors, and consumers, scattered around the globe. Even though social media and digital marketing have greatly reduced the information fragmentation, for instance, Guillaume d'Angerville[17] suggested using the estate's social media account to provide real-time advice to consumers around the globe on when would certain vintages of Clos des Ducs reach the peak within the drinking window, we are still far from achieving any centralized information base or repository of the world's wine knowledge, ideally open-sourced for everyone to access.

In addition, despite the vast amount of available information online and off-line, the majority is unstructured in the sense that it is noisy — the factual consistency of which not easily verifiable, in free form texts in various languages or high-dimensional data such as images and video clips that are not easily parsed into clean machine readable format for large-scale information extraction and processing compared to clean tables and spreadsheets of numbers and statistics.

[16]With mixed evidence, as while some say La Tache is more approachable in youth and Vosne-Romanée Conti takes at least 15 years to come around, others say the exact opposite.

[17]The former executive at JP Morgan, who took over the iconic Marquis d'Angerville in Volnay following the sudden passing of his father Jacques due to leukemia in 2003.

Second, the wine knowledge is multilingual, and semantically integrated across languages. It does not come as a surprise statement that to master wine, one would surely be at an advantage if one could master multiple languages including English, French, Italian, German, Spanish, Portuguese, etc.

Take French for example, there is an enormous amount of historical accounts of wine knowledge only written and distributed in French, especially on fine wine regions in France. It was Dr Jules Lavalle, whose opus magnum *Histoire et Statistique de la Vignes des Grands Vins de la Côte d'Or*, published in 1855, that later proved to have cemented the importance of the Burgundy *climats*. It was an expansion of an 1831 dissertation by Dr. Denis Morelot. In it, Dr Lavalle formed a classification of the terroirs of Burgundy in the same year that Bordeaux's own 1855 classification was being presented to the *Exposition Universelle* in Paris, where Bordeaux's ranking went on to gain world renown, leaving the importance of Lavalle's work far less celebrated back then beyond the winemakers of Burgundy and a small circle of experts. A few years after his book, Dr Lavalle went on to head a group in Beaune that pieced together the first comprehensive classification of vineyards in Burgundy. However neither Dr Lavallel's *Histoire et Statistique de la Vignes des Grands Vins de la Côte d'Or* nor Dr Denis Morelot's *Statistique de la Vigne dans le Département de la Côte d'Or* was ever translated into any other languages than French, together with many other significant French literature on vine-growing and wine-making in the 18th, 19th, or 20th centuries such as Dr Claude Arnoux's *Dissertation sur la situation de la Bourgogne, sur les vins qu'elle produit* published in 1728, Claude Courtépée and Edme Béguillet on *Description historique et topographique du Duché de Bourgogne* published in 1778, André Jullien on *Topographie de Tous les Vignobles Connus* released in 1816... until the 21st century, Charles Curtis, Master of Wine, took on the onus to translate into English and aggregate into his book *The Orig-*

inal Grands Crus of Burgundy published in 2014.

To illustrate more concretely, there are many wine concepts or terms common to almost all the wine producing regions but expressed in various different terms and languages locally. Grape variety is one example, in that Grenache is called Garnacha or Garnacha Tinta in Spain, and Cannonau in Sicily, whereas Mourvèdre in France is termed Monastrell in Spain, and Mataro in Catalonia, Australia, and sometimes US. Table 5 aggregates some of the most common grape synonyms in the world.

Besides the different variants of the same clonal mutation, when it comes to grape varieties prone to genetic mutations such as Pinot Noir and Gewürztraminer, as opposed genetically stable varieties such as Riesling, associations in-between all the different grapes and clones in different names of different languages get even more sophisticated and cumbersome. Pinot Gris, Pinot Meunier, Pinot Blanc, Frühburgunder (Pinot Noir Précoce), and Pinot Noir are all clones of Pinot, for instance. The same applies to Chardonnay with two distinct variants: Chardonnay Musqué and Chardonnay Rosé. The former features a higher presence of terpenes and a pungent Muscat-like floral aroma, and the latter is pink-skinned, one notable bottling of which is by Sylvain Pataille in Marsannay. Table 6 documents some of the most popular Pinot Noir and Chardonnay clones in the new world.

Similarly, vessels for *élevage* varies across regions according to local traditions, Burgundian 228-liter large Pièce, Bordelais 225-liter Barrique, Piedmontese large Botte or 550-liter sized Tonneau are but a few among the wide set of similar containers of slightly different sizes and shapes around the globe. Table 7 listed many of these barrel terms according to different regions and languages.

Third, the wine knowledge is multi-domain with a great extent of overlap. Besides across different languages and cultures, studying wine involves, as we have alluded to when we compared and contrasted MW and MS programs, almost every subject on earth one could possibly associate it with. Viticulture, viniculture, biology, geology, geography, accounting, economics, finance, marketing, operations, organizational behavior, psychology, sociology, and even music, literature, cuisine, and art. In today's highly specialized wine world, it is simply not impossible for one individual to be an expert in every sub-area of the wine trade. Jasper Morris MW dedicated his second career (after being a wine merchant for decades) to writing and educating about Burgundy by living on the ground in Hautes-Côtes de Beaune; Jane Anson set out to study Bordeaux inside and out while living and breathing Bordeaux for over a decade; Peter Liem, once the only few Asians living in Champagne, created one of the best English resources of wines from Champagne; Ian d'Agata, one of the most prominent Italian wine scholars, spent at least a third of his time in Italy during the past several decades; Michael Karam lives between UK and Lebanon, while producing film (Wine and War, an amazing wine documentary about the Lebanese wine industry) and writing about Lebanese wine and food culture dating back to the Roman times, and the list goes on... During a WSET alumni seminar with Jancis Robinson and Hugh Johnson at the Rizzoli Bookstore in New York City, Jancis answered the question about her tips to aspiring young wine writers by advising one to pick one topic (whether it be one domain, one region, or one skill set) to focus on and thus put oneself on the map.

Country	Variety					
France	Chardonnay Beaunois (Chablis) Gamay Blanc (Jura)	Chenin Blanc Pineau d'Anjou Pineau de la Loire		Gewürztraminer Heida (Savagnin)	Grenache	
Italy				Traminer (Alto Adige)	Vernaccia Nera (Mache) Cannonau (Sardinia)	
Spain					Garnacha Garnacha Tinta Lledoner (Catalunya)	Albariño
US	Chardonnay	Chenin Blanc		Gewürztraminer	Grenache	Albariño
Portugal						Alvarinho
South Africa		Steen				
Australia				Savagnin Rosé Aromatique		
Germany	Feinburgunder			Gewürztraminer		
Austria	Feinburgunder Morillon		Mosler			
Hungary			Furmint			
Croatia			Moslavac			
Slovenia			Šipon			
France	Ugni Blanc		Pinot Noir Auvernat		Muscat Blanc À Petits Grains Muscat d'Alsace	Muscat of Alexandria
Italy	Trebbiano Toscano			Primitivo	Moscato d'Asti Moscato Bianco	Zibibbo
Spain						
US		Lemberger	Pinot Noir	Zinfandel	Muscat Canelli	
Portugal	Alfrocheiro Branco					Muscatel de Setúbal
South Africa						Hanepoot
Chile						Moscatel
Germany		Lemberger	Spätburgunder Auvernat (Baden) Blauburgunder Blauer Spätburgunder		Gelber Muskateller	
Austria		Blaufränkisch	Spätburgunder Blauburgunder Blauer Spätburgunder		Muskateller	
Switzerland			Blauburgunder Blauer Spätburgunder Cortaillod Clevner			
Hungary		Kékfrankos				
Croatia	Ugni Blanc			Tribidrag Pribidrag Crljenak Kaštelanski		

Table 5: Grape synonyms in various countries and languages.

Clone	Pinot Noir	Clone	Chardonnay
Dijon	Originally from Domaine Ponsot. Widely adopted in Burgundy; 113, 114, 115, 667, 777, and 828 are the most widely planted in the USA. Isolated by Raymond Bernard at Dijon in Burgundy in the 1970s. Known for early ripening. Same as Bernard Clones in Australia.	Dijon 77 & 809	Originally from Domaine Ponsot, isolated by Raymond Bernard at Dijon in Burgundy in the 1970s. Known for elegance and hefty perfume.
Roederer	Brought in to US by Louis Roederer for Roederer in Anderson Valley; widely used for sparkling wine in US.	Dijon 75, 78, 121, 124, 125	Known for high productivity.
Pommard	Originally from Château de Pommard in the 1940s. Known for its weight, dark color, spice, and depth of fruit; widely adopted in Oregon alongside Wädenswil.	Dijon 76, 95, 96	Known for quality potential with complexity. Widely adopted in Oregon (esp. 76), and New Zealand.
Wädenswil	Brought in by David Lett in 1965 from cuttings at UC Davis. Clone 2A excels the most. Known for finesse, perfume, lift; widely adopted in Oregon.	Prosser	Isolated at the Washington State University Prosser Experiment Station in 1960s. Known for small, loose clusters, and low-yielding, with many shot berries.
Jackson	Selected from vines planted in 1889 at Foothill Experiment Station near Jackson in Amador County; low-yielding.	Old Wente	Selected from the Wente Vineyard in Livermore. The original source for most California Chardonnay planted in 1950s and 1960s. Shot Wente is known for small clusters, small berries, with shot berries. Isolated into new clones such as McRae, Martini, Hyde.
Martini	Selected from wines Inglenook and replanted in Carneros in the 1950s; widely adopted in Carneros, Russian River Valley.	Martini	Selected from the Stony Hill (McCrea family) vineyard by Michael Martini, Jr., the clones of which came from the Wente Vineyard. Clones 4 & 5 known for high-yielding, heavy clusters, large berries yet high acidity. 4 & 5 combined into a new clone 108 in the late 1960s widely adopted in California and Washington State vineyards.
Swan	Taken from vines planted in 1969 in Joseph Swan's Russian River Valley estate; originally from Domaine de la Romanée Conti or the Martin Ray Vineyard. Known for elegance and fresh red fruit.	Davis 108	Isolated from Wente clones in 1970s. Known for high-yielding, lower quality potential. Clone 108 is late ripening, suitable for warm regions.
Mt Eden	Selected by Meredith Edwards at the Mt Eden estate in 1975; originally from Burgundy by Paul Masson in the 1890s.	Mt Eden	Selected from Chardonnay vines in the Martin Ray Vineyard in Santa Cruz, originally from Burgundy by Paul Masson in the 1890s. Known for low yielding and virus-prone.
MV6	Mother Vine Six, first few cuttings in Australia by James Busby; originally from Clos Vougeot, widely adopted in Yarra Valley.	Mendoza	Of uncertain origin. Widely adopted in California in early 1950s and 1960s, Western Australia as the Gingin clone, and New Zealand.

Table 6: Common clones of Pinot Noir and Chardonnay in the new world wine producing regions.

Fourth, the wine knowledge is multi-modal. Our knowledge of the wine world not only includes numerical and textual information but also information in other modalities or forms. Numerical knowledge could manifest in information such as, for instance, the number of bottles of Champagne exported to the United States in the year of 2019 (25 million). Textual knowledge refers to entities, events, concepts, or narratives such as, for instance, the name of the English gentleman who staged the famed Judgment of Paris tasting in 1976 (Steven Spurrier). Multimodal knowledge includes but is not exclusive to the following categories:

- visual images: label designs of Le Pergole Torte by Montevertine; images of the proprietor of Hermann J Wiemer winery in Finger Lakes region; images of Jackson Family Wine's warehouses and vineyards; images of aged Musigny and Montrachet bottles;

Region	Barrel	Size
Burgundy	Pièce	228L
Burgundy - Chablis	Feuillette	132L
Burgundy - Côte d'Or	Feuillette	114L
Bordeaux	Barrique	225L
Champagne	Barrel	205L
Alsace	Demi-muid Foudre	600L
Mosel	Fuder	1000L
Rheingau	Stück	1200L
Jerez	Butt	650L
Douro	Pipe	550-630L 534.24L
Italy	Botte	Varies
Italy	Tonneau	550L
Australia	Puncheon	450-500L
Australia	Hogshead	300L

Table 7: Barrels traditionally used in various countries and languages.

- audio signals: pronunciations of wine-producing region Xinjiang or Chateauneuf-du-Pape; the sounds of a biodynamic vineyard with living soils in winter and summer;
- sensory experiences: the smell of TCA or cork taint reminiscent of a musty basement; the fragrance of fresh rose petals, rose water, dried rose petals, lavender, acacia, jasmine, chamomile, orange and peach blossom, marzipan; the earthy mushroomy aroma of forest floors with spring fountains and moss on white

rocks; the leather, the tar, the pencil shaving, Asian five spices, durian, petrol, and truffle;

- video clips: Thibault Liger-Belair video sharing a morning walk through his Richebourg vineyard; Dr Jamie Goode's daily streaming of his wine tasting and sake learning experiences, with colorful and extremely funny T-shirts; a conversation between Jasmine Hirsch and Jeremy Seysses, as Jeremy walks through Nuits-Saint-Georges, on topics such as vineyard work and winemaking adaptations to climate change.

Fifth, the wine knowledge is personalizable or customizable since each distinct individual with distinct background learns and adapts differently. This could be perhaps best explained by how different individuals feel so differently about the concept of *natural wine*, or authentic wine, or wine with minimal-intervention. Some are adamant proponents of the natural wine movements, David Lillie, Pascaline Lepeltier, and sometimes to the extremes like Alice Feiring. Some frequently ridicule such efforts with tirades from the likes of Robert Parker and some snobbish popular podcasters educating normal people. Such drastic reactions might be partially explainable by their educational background, lifetime experiences, cultural believes, and social networks.

In addition, scents and smells are highly personal sensory experiences that transcend time and space. The bottle of Anne Gros Vosne Romanée Les Barreaux might remind a wine lover of his dearly late grandma's rose garden where he used to kill ants and chase after butterflies, and instead conjures up images for another wine lover of her parents' kitchen in the winter permeated with the inviting aromas of Asian five spices and marinated mushrooms.

Sixth, every fragment of the wine knowledge is connected with one another, weaving into an inter-connected knowledge graph as is shown in Figure **??**. In this large knowledge graph each node represents a concept or entity (person, winery, appellation, region, country, grape variety, clone, rootstock, nursery, university, distributor, retailer, style, method, etc.) whereas each edge represents a relationship in-between (is a friend of, did apprenticeship with, interned at, merged with, is located at, is known for, in collaborate with, get allocation from, etc.), and we will define the types of nodes and edges to cover all the concepts, entities, and relationships that one would encounter in the wine trade. Sometimes the type of friendship links encourage multi-way information flows that drive a region's innovation and market success.

The old tale of then new generations of Burgundy vignerons in the 80s and 90s who revolutionized vineyard management and winemaking in and out has never failed to inspire Burgundy lovers. It was a group of (then) young aspiring vignerons who had seen the world outside Burgundy, formed a regular tasting group that met up regularly where individual experimentation trials with different techniques were discussed and analyzed together in-depth such that the experience and lessons learnt magnified beyond each individual's capability. Christophe Roumier, Dominique Lafon, Etienne Grivot, Pascal Marchand, Patrick Bize, Jacques Seysses, Emmanuel Giboulot, Jean-Claude Rateau, Jean-Pierre de Smet, Claude de Nicolay, to name but a few... It was during the group tasting sessions that they made clear strategies to identify and control malolactic fermentation that was commonly overlooked or mistaken for alcoholic fermentation before. It was at these group tasting meetings that they compared traditional, organic, and biodynamic farming practices and what different regimes could bring to the final wine. Many have attributed the explosive growth of Burgundian wines to this generation who changed the landscape for the better with information and knowledge sharing. The same story has been mirrored and relived everywhere else in the world major wine producing regions now, whether it be Barolo or Napa Valley.

Some friendships evolve into apprenticeship and business partnership across the Atlantic Ocean. Jean-Pierre de Smet, a former accountant who had never dreamt of being a vigneron until he became friends with Jacques Seysses through his wife because of shared passion in skiing and racing. His wife and he frequently visited and helped with Domaine Dujac's harvests and eventually apprenticed there for almost a decade during their professional break while sailing around the globe. By the time they returned back to work, they had found a new calling — making wine. Domaine de l'Arlot came next, and the rest is history. Interestingly, Jean-Pierre, being a close friend of Patrick Bize, was also one of the first few witnesses of how Patrick met Chisa on a business trip to Japan, who later travelled to Savigny-les-Beanue for the 1996 harvest, and married him three months later. It is Chisa who took over the Domaine Simon Bize in 2014, together with Marielle, Patrick's sister who married Etienne Grivot, and kept experimenting and innovating with even more exciting releases ever since. Domaine Nicolas-Jay in Willamette Valley of Oregon was the passion project resulting from a thirty-year-old friendship between Jean-Nicolas Meo of Domaine Meo-Camuzet in Vosne Romanée and Jay Boberg, a former musician whose passion for wine connected the two during Jean-Nicolas's college years at University of Pennsylvania.

Seventh, the wine knowledge is context dependent. A bottle opened today enjoyed over dinner with friends and family would evoke much different emotions and memories than if opened ten years later alone. Besides the kaleidoscopic space of wine pairings with cheeses, chocolates, desserts, and various types of cuisines that translates to drastically different memories and sensations, many wine professionals have ventured into wine pairing with books, with music, with fine art, with meditation, and with yoga, to name just a few.

Krug, one of the most celebrated Champagne house in Montagne de Reims launched Krug Echoes in 2014, a project designed to translate specific Champagnes into pieces of music, which has also created 3D music pairing experiences for visitors. They have invited artists to create soundtracks for Grande Cuvée and vintage Champagnes from around the world of distinct genres and instruments. New communication lines were open and beautiful artifacts as ineffable as Krug Champagnes and the world's best music pieces somehow could find ways to connect with one another in a breeze.

On the other hand, the priming effects of music on wine and food perception have been widely studied but food scientists and researchers, and recent studies have shown that people can associate certain music pieces with certain wine styles intuitively when prompted to choose.

Susan Lin, a musian and Master of Wine, devoted her dissertation to studying the influences of classical music on Champagne. She conducted a series of experimental tastings to test the effect of classical music pieces with specific parameter and character attribute combinations, on the tasting experience and sensory perception of a Brut non-vintage champagne. Among all the interesting results she gleaned, there was a significant effect on matching and enjoyment when tasting with the classical music compared to silence. Furthermore, there was evidence that particular musical parameter and character attribute combinations had some influence on the perception of certain sensory characteristics and of the champagne itself, highlighting the potential impact of music on consumers' enjoyment and experience of wine.

Lastly, the wine knowledge is ever dynamic. Just like the fate of way too many wine books (including this one!), information gets obsolete at a lightening speed in today's fast evolving world. Kelli White, the author of Napa Valley Then and Now, lamented the fact that by the time she finally managed to published her 1000-page tome on Napa Valley, five wineries had already been bought out and the information in her book was already outdated even before publishing. The same goes with any static knowledge graph. Therefore regular maintenance of the knowledge graph is just as important as constructing it in the first place to ensure valid and long-lasing adoption thus fueling the AI engine that adapts to the evolving world we are facing now.

Fortunately, Knowledge Graph (KG), an essential building block of modern AI systems, could be designed to accommodate all of the necessary features to ensure wine-centric AI systems. We will detail the history, construction methods, and applications of Knowledge Graphs of wine in Section 3.1, with more detailed introduction and demonstration of how to build a wine-centric Question Answering system (as one potential application) in Section 3.2.

3.1 Knowledge Graph

A Knowledge Graph (KG) is an information structure or representation containing "justified true beliefs" of the universe curated by experts with or without the help of a machine learning algorithm. Knowledge Graphs (KGs) have emerged as a compelling abstraction for organizing the world's structured knowledge, including our wine knowledge, as a way to integrate information extracted from numerous data sources, and have been playing a rather central role in representing the vast amount of knowledge extracted with natural language processing and computer vision techniques, among others. Expansive domain knowledge such as wine knowledge expressed in KGs can be and is being put into AI models to produce more accurate, flexible, generalizable, and ultimately more intelligent systems. Even though the phrase "knowledge graph" dates back to at least

1972, the modern incarnation of the phrase stems from the 2012 announcement of the Google Knowledge Graph, followed by further announcements of the development of knowledge graphs by Airbnb, Amazon, eBay, Facebook, IBM, LinkedIn, Microsoft, Uber, and more. The ever growing industrial uptake of the concept further fueled scientific advances in academia, and a healthy body of literature is being published on knowledge graphs outlining definitions, novel techniques, and surveys of specific aspects of knowledge graphs.

Underlying all such developments is the core idea of using graphs to represent data. A knowledge graph describes objects of interest and connections between them. For example, a knowledge graph may have nodes for a winery, the winemaker and vineyard manager in this estate, the proprietor, the partner, the consultant, the assistant, and so on. Each node may have properties such as a winemaker's name and age. There may be nodes for multiple wineries involving a particular winemaker or consultant. The user can then traverse the knowledge graph to collect information on all the wineries in which the winemaker apprenticed at, or worked for, or, if applicable, consulted with, and so forth.

Many implementations impose constraints on the links in knowledge graphs by defining a *schema* or *ontology*. For example, a link from a winery to its winemaker must connect an object of type Winery to an object of type Person. In some cases the links themselves might have their own properties: a link connecting a particular single-vineyard bottling and a winery might have the name of the specific lieu-dit or climat from which the grapes were harvested. Similarly, a link connecting a winemaker with a winery might have the time period during which the winemaker held that role.

Knowledge graphs usually provide a shared substrate of knowledge within an organization or an aggregate concept like country or region, allowing us to use similar vocabulary and to reuse definitions and descriptions that others create. Furthermore, they usually provide a compact formal representation that Knowledge Graph curators or users could use to infer new facts and build up the knowledge. For instance, by merging the graph connecting wineries and winemakers, with the graph connecting wineries with grape varieties and wine regions, or the graph connecting winemakers with their preferred winemaking styles and techniques, one could easily find out which winemakers make wines in most continents, with a greatest variety of grapes, or prefer cold soak and whole cluster in the southern hemisphere, or are most consistent in winemaking techniques across different wineries — whichever trivia tidbits you are curious about.

Table 8 details some of the largest-scale Knowledge Graphs in use in the industry today.

All of these graph systems have three key determinants of quality and usefulness, as would be the case with most large graph systems in practice:

- Completeness. Is the graph comprehensive? Does it cover all the necessary information? The answer is almost always no, even though over time various techniques have been developed to identify missing nodes and links to alleviate the problem of missing information.

- Factuality. Is all the information in this graph objectively correct and factually consistent in that no outstanding factual conflicts remain? This is what makes the knowledge credible and useful for any downstream applications such as search engines and question answering systems (see Section 3.2).

- Up-to-date. Is the information therein up-to-date? It could have been correct at one point but gone stale. This requirement varies for something that changes almost constantly (auction price) compared with something that rarely changes (official AOCs in Burgundy), with many different kinds of information in-between.

Company	Content	Size of the Knowledge Graph
Microsoft	Bing KG includes descriptions and connections of people, places, things, and organizations, including general knowledge about the world.	2 billion entities 55 billion relationships
Google	Google KG includes descriptions and connections of people, places, things, organizations, etc., including general knowledge about the world.	1 billion entities 70 billion relationships
Facebook	The world's largest social graph: includes information about music, movies, celebrities, and places that users care about.	50 million entities 500 million relationships
eBay	Product KG encoding knowledge about products, entities, and the relationships in-between and the external world.	100 million products 1 billion triples
IBM	IBM's Watson Discovery offers two KGs: one focusing on the use case of discovering nonobvious information, the other on offering a "Build your own knowledge graph" framework.	5 billion relationships 100 million entities
Linkedin	Linkedin Graph includes entities and relations center around people, jobs, skills, companies, locations, etc.	620 million entities

Table 8: Notable Knowledge Graphs (KGs) in industry.

To generate knowledge about the (wine) world, data would be ingested from various sources, which may be very noisy and contradictory, and to collate them into a single, consistent, and accurate graph requires a great deal of scientific and engineering ingenuity. What a user sees at last is the tip of an iceberg — a huge amount of work and complexity is hidden below. For instance, there are at least 9 charmes in Burgundy in different villages, over a dozen Trebbiano grape varieties in Italy, the relationships between many still remain unclear. Figure 11 provides an illustration of what a knowledge graph for wine would look like. Let us define for now different types of nodes and links necessary for a wine knowledge graph with examples:

- Nodes: any entity or concept relevant to wine.

    1. Winery: Weingut Von Winning, Chateau Ksara, Pierre Overnoy, etc.
    2. Country: US, France, Italy, Lebanon, Spain, Portugal, China, New Zealand, etc.
    3. Region: New York, Virginia, Douro, New Zealand North Island, Yunnan, etc.
    4. Appellation: Napa, Burgundy, Finger Lakes, Sardinia, Beqaa Valley, etc.
    5. Sub-appellation: Pouilly-Fumé, Oaksville, Vosne-Romanée, Barbaresco, etc.
    6. *lieu-dit* or *climat*: Le Tesson, Les Suchots, Rabaja, Monvigliero, Asili, etc.
    7. Soil: Kimmeridgian/Serravallian/Tortonian marl, chalk, sand, clay, limestone, schist, Silex (flint), gravel, granite, loess, loam, gneiss, etc.
    8. Grape Variety: Obaideh, Merwah, Rotgipfler, Negro Amaro, Nuragus, etc.
    9. Climate: hot Mediterranean, cool continental, moderate maritime.
    10. Winemaker: Ted Lemon, Cathy Corison, Paul Hobbs, Christopher Roumier, etc.
    11. Cooper: Damy, Minier, Chassin, Taransaud, François Frères, Rémond, Berthomieu, Stockinger, etc.

12. Organic/biodynamic certification: USDA Certified organic, Lodi rules, Demeter, etc.
13. Clone: Wädenswil, Pommard, Swan, Martini, Wente, Dijon;
14. Rootstock: AXR, 3309C (Courdec), 1103P (Paulsen), 16-16C (Courdec), 101-14 (Millardet et de Grasset), 110R (Richter), St George, etc.
15. Wine: 2018 Domaine Fabien Coche Meursault Gouttes d'Or, 2016 Cos d'Estournel, etc.
16. Closure: DIAM, screwcap (ROTE, ROPP, etc.), Vinolok, crown cap, Zork, etc.
17. Importer/distributor: Rosenthal Wine Merchant, Kermit Lynch, Becky Wasserman, Winebow;
18. Retailer: Flatiron Wine, Chamber Street Wine, Discovery Wine, Union Square Wine, etc.
19. Wine auctioneer: Sotheby's, Christie's, Zachy's K&L, Idealwine, winebid, etc.
20. Wine fund: Liv-ex, Wine Owners, WineDecider, WineDex, Vinfolio, vinovest, etc.
21. Wine critic/influencer: Jancis Robinson, Jasper Morris, Robert Parker, Jamie Goode, Antonio Galloni, etc.
22. Wine media: Wine Spectator, Wine Advocate, Vinous, Decanter, Wine Enthusiast, etc.
23. Wine association or promotional body: Wine of Australia, Wine of Portugal, Wine of Austria, etc.
24. Wine professional certification: Wine and Spirits Education Trust, Court of Master Sommelier, Wine Scholar Guild, Society of Wine Educators, etc.
25. Restaurant or bar: Noble Rot, The Fat Duck, Eleven Madison Park, Modern, Marta, etc.

- Links:

    1. Ownership: Charlie and Kareem Massoud are the owners of Paumanok vineyards, etc.
    2. Partnership: Jean-Nicolas Meo and Jay Boberg have enjoyed a long-term partnership in the establishment of Domaine Nicolas-Jay, etc.
    3. Friendship: Dominique Lafon, Patrick Bize, Christopher Roumier are all connected by friendship ties, so are Jean-Nicolas Meo and Jay Boberg, etc.
    4. Competitor: Corkbuzz, SommTime, Compagnie des Vins Surnaturels, are competitors in the Manhattan wine scene, etc.
    5. Subsumption: Calistoga AVA is subsumed by Napa Valley AVA, etc.
    6. Business relationship: importer Rosenthal Wine Merchant maintains a long-term business relationship with Domaine Forey in Vosne-Romanée, etc.

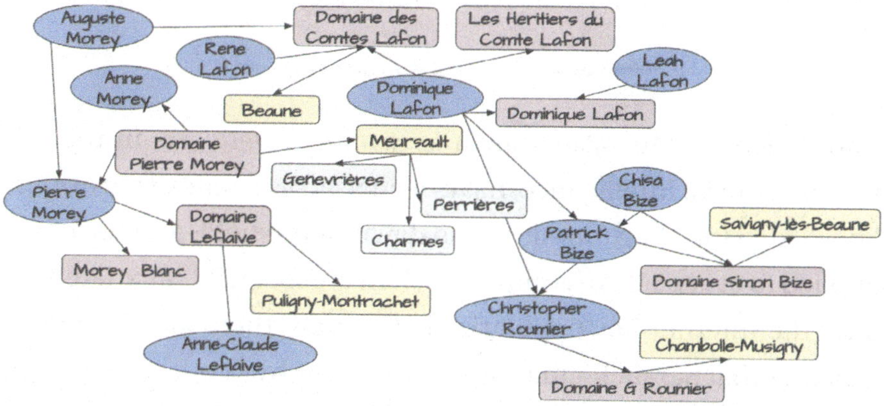

Figure 11: An illustration of (a part of) a wine knowledge graph. Blue oval boxes are nodes of individuals. Pale pink rectangles are nodes of wineries (estates). Pale yellow rectangles are nodes of communes. Pale grey rectangles are nodes of vineyards. Between different types of nodes are different types of edges too. Visit http://ai-for-wine.com/kg for dynamic and interactive knowledge graphs at a large scale.

For instance, in the following sentence —
"Pierre Morey, a living legend in Burgundy, was the *régisseur* (winemaker and vineyard manager) for the famed Domaine Leflaive for 20 years from 1988 to 2008. Pierre Morey's father, Auguste, was a share-cropper for Domaine des Comtes Lafon until 1984 when the Lafon family retook control of the parcels under the agreement, which included some of Meursault's best premier crus: Perrières, Charmes, and Genevrières. Today, Pierre is joined at his domaine by his daughter Anne Morey who is the co-manager of the estate. The 10 hectares domaine has parcels in the villages of Monthelie, Pommard, Puligny-Montrachet, and Meursault."
There are six types of nodes: *régisseur, sharecropper, region, appellation, vineyard,* and *winery*; and four types of edges: *is affiliated with, is located in, is sourced from,* and *produces,* all of which could be il-

lustrated as components as part of knowledge graph in Figure 11.

Knowledge Graphs, also known as *semantic networks* in the context of Artificial Intelligence, have been used as a repository of world knowledge for AI agents since the dawn of the field, and have been applied to every area of computer science, especially since late 1990s after the Internet has popularized. Granted, there are many other schemes that parallel semantic networks, such as conceptual graphs, rule languages, and probabilistic graphical models that could capture uncertainty around knowledge. The World Wide Web Consortium (W3C) standardized a family of knowledge representation languages that are now widely used for capturing knowledge on the internet. These languages include the Resource Description Framework (RDF), the Web Ontology Language(OWL), and the Semantic Web Rule Language (SWRL).
Such knowledge representation in AI has been driven in a top-down manner — we first develop a model of the world, and then use algorithms to deduce and draw conclusions from them. In contrast, there have been increasing interests in bottom up approaches to AI, that is, developing algorithms capable of processing the data from which algorithms can draw conclusions and insights. For the rest of the section, let me sketch out the role KGs are playing both in storing the learned knowledge, and in providing a source of domain knowledge as input to the AI algorithms for downstream applications.

Machine learning algorithms can perform better if they can incorporate domain knowledge. Knowledge Graphs are a useful data structure for capturing domain knowledge, but machine learning algorithms require that any symbolic or discrete structure, such as a graph, should first be converted into a numerical form. We can

convert symbolic inputs into a numerical form using a technique known as *embeddings*. Let us start with *word embeddings* and *graph embeddings* as an illustration of how *embeddings* work.
Word embeddings were originally developed for calculating similarity between words. To understand the word embeddings, let us consider the following set of sentences.

- I like knowledge graphs.
- I like drinking wine.
- I enjoy learning about AI.

Counts	I	like	knowledge	graphs	drinking	wine	enjoy	learning	about	AI	.
I	0	2	0	0	0	0	1	0	0	0	0
like	2	0	1	0	1	0	0	0	0	0	0
knowledge	0	1	0	1	0	0	0	0	0	0	0
graphs	0	0	1	0	0	0	0	0	0	0	1
drinking	0	1	0	0	0	1	0	0	0	0	0
wine	0	0	0	0	1	0	0	0	0	0	1
enjoy	1	0	0	0	0	0	0	1	0	0	0
learning	0	0	0	0	0	0	0	0	1	1	0
about	0	0	0	0	0	0	0	1	0	1	0
AI	0	0	0	0	0	0	0	0	1	0	1
.	0	0	0	1	0	1	0	0	0	1	0

Table 9: A matrix of co-occurrence counts.

In the above set of sentences, we could count how often a word appears next to another word and record the counts in a matrix. For example, the word I appears next to the word like twice, and the word enjoy once, and therefore, its counts for these two words are 2 and 1 respectively, and 0 for every other word. We can calculate the counts for the other words in a similar manner as shown in Table 9. Such a matrix is often referred to as word co-occurrence counts. The meaning of each word is captured by the vector in the row corresponding to that word. To calculate similarity between words, we calculate the similarity between the vectors corresponding to them.

In practice, we are interested in text that may contain millions of words, and a more compact representation is desired. As the co-occurrence matrix is sparse, we can use techniques such as singular value decomposition to reduce its dimensions. The resulting vector corresponding to a word is known as its word embedding.
A sentence is a sequence of words, and *word embeddings* calculate co-occurrences of words in it. I will delve into much greater details about the most recent advances in word embeddings in Section 7.4 on *contextualized word embeddings* and *language models.* Meanwhile, we could generalize this idea to *node embeddings* for a graph in the same spirit:

1. traverse the graph using a random walk generating a path through the graph;

2. obtain a set of paths through repeated traversals of the graph by random walks;

3. calculate co-occurrences of nodes on these paths just like how we calculated co-occurrences of words in a sentence for word embeddings, such that each row in the matrix of co-occurrence counts give us a vector for the corresponding node;

4. potentially reduce the dimension of the matrix to a smaller compact vector for each row, that is, a node embedding.

We can encode the whole graph into a vector which is known as its *graph embedding.* There are many approaches to calculate *graph embeddings,* perhaps the simplest approach is to add the vectors representing node embeddings for each of the nodes in the graph to obtain a vector representing the whole graph. While word embeddings capture the meanings of words and ease the calculation of similarity in-between, node embeddings capture the meaning of nodes in a graph and ease the calculation of similarity in-between. Many similarity functions for words or sentences could be readily generalized and applied to graph and node embeddings for calculating similarities.

Word embeddings and graph embeddings are common ways to give a compact symbolic input to a machine learning or AI algorithm. A common application of word embeddings is to learn a language model that can predict what word is likely to appear next in a sequence of words (see Section 7.4 for more in-depth reviews of recent advances). A more advanced application of word embeddings is to use them with a Knowledge Graph. For instance, the embedding for a more frequent word could be replaced with a less frequent word as long as the knowledge graph encodes that the less frequent word is its hyponym. A straightforward use for the graph embeddings calculated from a product graph is to recommend new producers to try out for a consumer. A more advanced use of graph embedding involves link prediction, for example, in a supply chain graph, we can use link prediction to identify potential new distributors for wineries or new restaurants for distributors.

Manual creation of knowledge graphs with a great of highly specialized domain knowledge is, in general, expensive. Therefore, any automation we can achieve for creating a knowledge graph is highly desirable. Until a few years ago, both natural language processing (NLP) and computer vision (CV) algorithms were struggling to do well on entity recognition from text and object detection from images. Because of recent progress enabled by deep learning, these algorithms are starting to move beyond the basic recognition tasks to extracting relationships among objects necessitating a representation in which the extracted relations could be stored for further processing and reasoning. Let me illustrate with some examples how the automation was made possible through NLP and CV techniques in automatically creating large-scale knowledge graphs.

Entity recognition and entity linking, or relation extraction from natural languages are among the most fundamental tasks in natural language processing. Methods for entity recognition and entity linking could be generally divided into rule-based methods, and machine learning approaches, the best performing ones are most likely based on deep learning nowadays. Rule-based approaches usually rely on the syntactical structure of the sentence or specify how entities or relationships could be identified in the input text, whereas machine learning methods leverage sequence labeling algorithms or language models for both entity and relation extraction.

The extracted information from multiple portions of the text needs to be correlated — termed as the task of co-reference resolution, which is another fundamental task in natural language processing that stems from the ambiguity of natural languages — and knowledge graphs provide a natural medium as a plausible solution. For instance, from the sentence shown in Figure 12, we can extract the entities *Didier Dagueneau, Pouilly-Fumé, Sauvignon blanc,* and *Loire Valley*; and the relations *situated in*, and *sourced from.* Once this snippet of knowledge is incorporated into a larger Knowledge Graph, we can use logical inference to get additional links (shown by dotted edges) such as a Sauvignon Blanc is a kind of vitis vinifera, *Silex* is his bottling of Sauvignon Blanc in Pouilly-Fumé (besides a flinty soil type the vines grow in), and that Didier also owns wineries in Jurançon, where he bottled *Les Jardins de Babylone made* from Petit Manseng grape, one of the signature grape varieties of Jurançon.

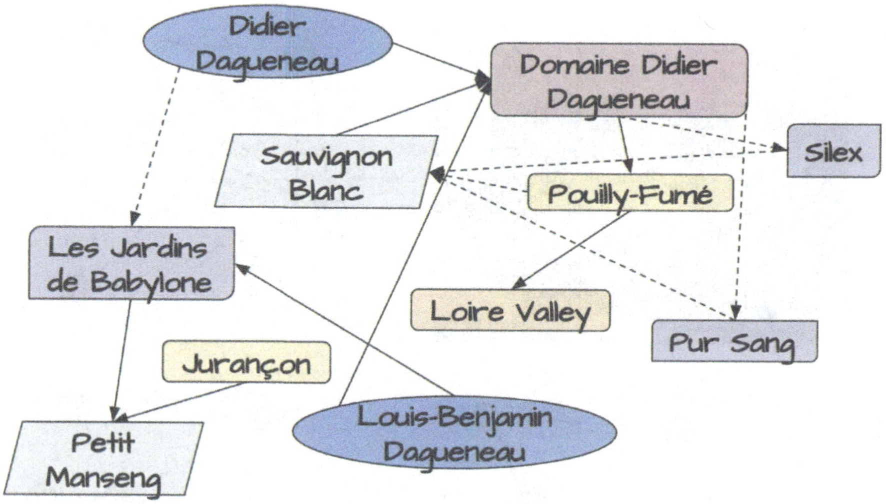

Figure 12: A knowledge graph created with entity and relation extraction from the following sentences: Didier Dagueneau was a winemaker in the Loire Valley who received a cult following for his Sauvignon Blanc wines from the Pouilly Fumé appellation.

A holy grail of computer vision is the complete understanding of an image, that is, detecting objects, describing their attributes, and recognizing their relationships. Understanding images would enable important applications such as image search, visual question answering, and navigation. Much progress has been made in recent years towards this goal, including super-human performances in tasks such as image classification and object detection. Modern large-scale computer vision systems reply on a variety of machines learning especially deep learning methods such as convolutional neural networks.

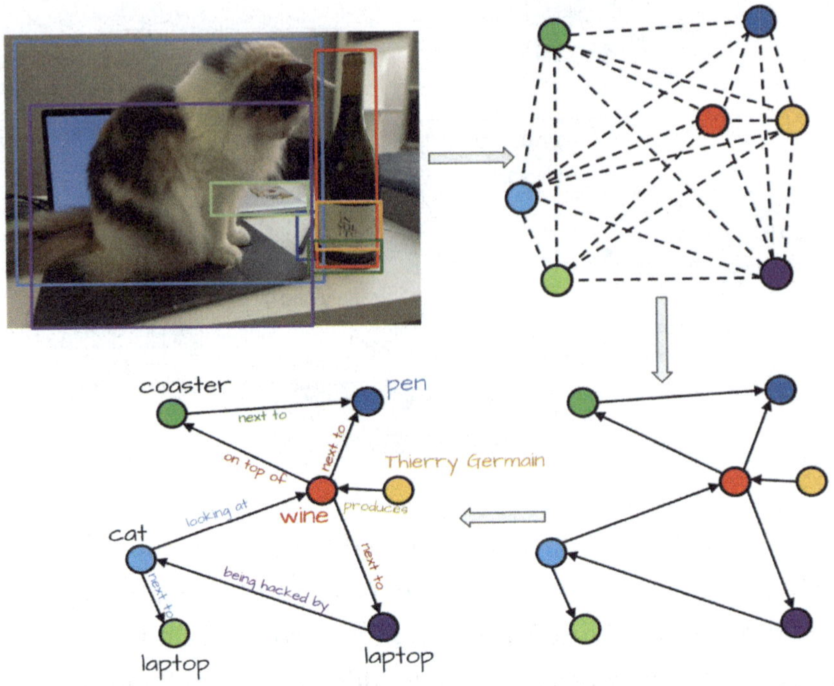

Figure 13: A knowledge graph (or scene graph) created with computer vision techniques such as object detection.

From the image on the left of Figure 13, a scene understanding system would produce a knowledge graph shown to the right. The nodes in the knowledge graph are the outputs of an object detector. More recent computer vision algorithms are capable to correctly infer the relationships between the objects, such as, a cat sniffing a bottle of wine, a cat standing on a laptop next to another laptop, etc. Therefore, given an image (top left), a set of objects visible in the scene could be extracted and all possible relationships between nodes considered (top right). Then unlikely relationships could be pruned with learned measures such as 'relatedness', resulting in a sparser candidate graph structure (bottom right). Finally, an attentional graph convolution network (details in Section 4.3) could be applied to integrate global context and update object node and relationship edge labels (bottom left). The knowledge graph shown on the bottom left is an example of a knowledge graph which provides foundation for tasks such as visual question answering.

3.2 Question Answering

Question answering (QA) systems aims to generate precise answers to users' questions in natural language, just like how sommeliers or wine specialists aim to answer any questions a customer might have. This is a long standing task in AI dating back to the early 1960s, when one of the earliest widely acknowledged QA system, **Baseball**, was designed to answer questions about American baseball games. In 1973, **LUNAR** question answering system was famously developed to assist lunar geologists in chemical analyses of lunar rocks and soils from Apollo moon mission. These early systems store all the relevant information in a structured knowledge base, and translate user questions into query statements using linguistic methods to extract answers from the knowledge base. This is what is commonly referred to as Knowledge Base-QA systems. As is illustrated in Figure 15a, a more practical and scalable type of QA system is textual QA systems which formulate answers from free-form text documents, since manual construction of knowledge bases is both time-consuming and costly, possibly requiring a certain level of domain knowledge, whereas a large amount of text documents on any topic are easily accessible online via popular search engines. In fact, many search engines like Google and Bing have incorporated question answering functionalities, with which they can provide precise answers to those queries entered as questions such as:

- Question: which rootstock grape species is native to deep limestone soils?
- Answer: vitis berlandieri.

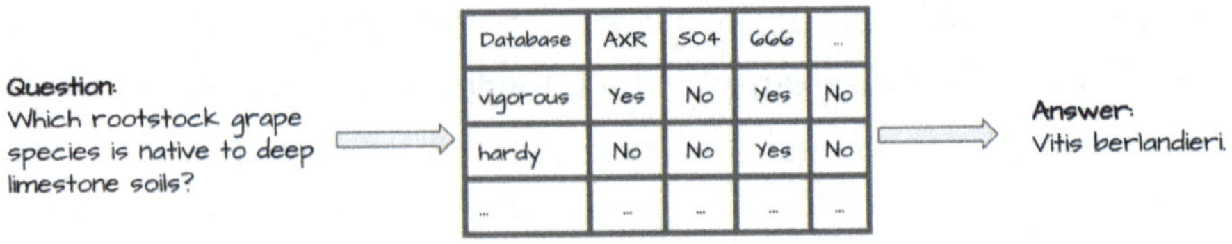

(a) Knowledge-based Question Answering system.

(b) Textual Question Answering system.

Figure 14: An illustration of the difference between knowledge-based and textual Question Answering systems.

Most modern QA systems are textual QA systems, even though knowledge bases such as Wikipedia are incorporated either explicitly as external knowledge enhancement, or implicitly baked into pre-trained language models (more details in Section 7.4). If given the question, we already know where exactly in the documents to search for the answers, the QA systems is essentially accomplishing the task of reading comprehension from any language proficiency tests, termed as *Machine Reading Comprehension* (MRC) in the field of *natural language processing*. However, in practice, hardly do we know in advance what the question is about, let alone a set of documents or web pages to skim through. Therefore, *Open-domain Question Answering* (ODQA), meaning answering questions without any contexts, is usually the focus of QA research development today. Compared to MRC, ODQA involved a first step of identifying relevant documents or web pages in which the corrects answers might reside based on the question given, and is therefore sometimes called *Machine Reading Comprehension at Scale*. In Figure 15, we illustrate the difference between Machine Reading Comprehension and Open-domain Question Answering as textual QA systems.

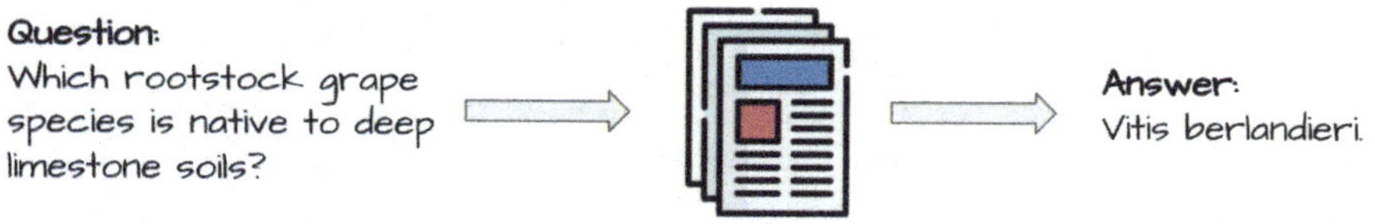

(a) Machine Reading Comprehension.

(b) Open-domain Question Answering.

Figure 15: An illustration of the difference between Machine Reading Comprehension (MRC) and Open-domain Question Answering (ODQA) systems.

A modern Open-domain Question Answering system is usually based upon a Retriever-Reader framework in which the Retriever module attempts to retrieve relevant documents or web pages given a question, whereas the Reader module is designed to obtain the final answer given the results returned by the Retriever. In essence, the Retriever is a modern information retrieval system whereas the Reader is a modern machine comprehension system, and it's only when the two join forces to maximize efficiency and improve iteratively can we achieve the optimal result for ODQA. Besides these two major components, auxiliary modules that are responsible for post-processing such as filtering and ranking in-between Retriever and

Reader, as well as drilling down to the final answer among several candidates returned by Reader, are sometimes necessary. In Figure 16, we plot the typical workflow of an open-domain Question Answering system based on a Retriever-Reader framework.

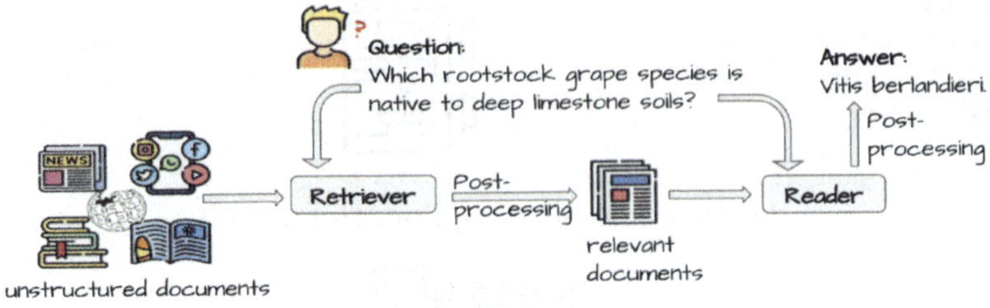

Figure 16: An illustration of the Retriever-Reader framework of Open-domain Question Answering (ODQA) systems.

With deep learning pushing the envelop of every front of AI, both Retriever and Reader modules of the state-of-the-art Open-domain Question Answering systems are based on deep neural networks nowadays. DrQA [Chen et al., 2017], which came out of the Stanford NLP group in 2017, was one of the pioneering frameworks that incorporated neural machine comprehension as the Reader into Open-domain Question Answering, establishing the Retriever-Reader framework that most later research efforts have emulated, and supplanting the traditional framework used to consist of at least three modules: question analysis, document retrieval, and answer extraction. Now with Retriever-Reader, the Open-domain Question Answering is more flexible with free-form text, without relying on additional linguistic heuristics and finer modular assumptions that plagued the traditional framework.

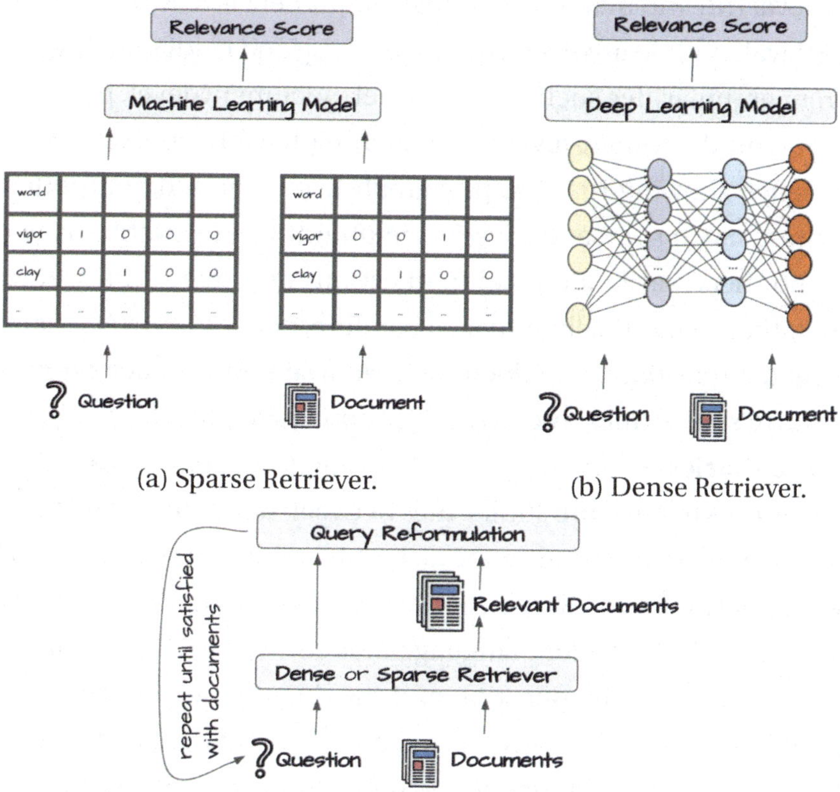

(a) Sparse Retriever.

(b) Dense Retriever.

(c) Iterative Retriever.

Figure 17: An illustration of three Retriever frameworks of Open-domain Question Answering (ODQA) systems.

Retriever is essentially an information retrieval system that aims to retrieve documents and paragraphs that are most likely to contain the correct answer to the question given in natural language, as well as ranking them according to their relevance. According to architectural details, modern approaches could perhaps be classified into three categories: sparse retriever, dense retriever, and iterative retriever, which are illustrated in Figure 17.

Sparse Retrievers refer to early methods that encode documents by sparse matrices, such as *tf-idf* and *bm25*. DrQA is regarded as the first modern ODQA system and it combines classical information retrieval (IR) and machine reading comprehension (MRC) where the Retrieval module involves bi-gram hashing and tf-idf matching. Different granularities such as word-level, document-level, paragraph-level, and document-level text matching have been explored with evidence showing that the paragraph-level matching outperforms the rest. Such sparse Retrievers are oftentimes restrictive as words are not necessarily identical in questions and relevant documents but rather semantically similar. Therefore, dense Retrievers that learn to match questions and documents in a semantic space often outperform sparse ones due to flexibility and generalization ability.

Dense Retrievers leverage deep learning to encode questions and documents to measure similarities between documents and the question. There exists various approaches to architecture design of deep neural networks for dense Retrievers. Two-stream dense Retrievers use two independent language models (e.g., BERT [Devlin et al., 2019]) to encode the question and the document respectively, and predict the similarity score between two embeddings. Two-stream methods vary by whether tailored pre-training processes are included, how the similarity score is calculated, and how training processes are carried out with diligent sample selection. This is similar to the idea of late fusion in multi-modal learning detailed in Section 4.2, which could suffer in performance as the interactions between embeddings of documents and the question are relatively limited compared to integrated dense Retrievers. These integrated dense Retrievers share the underlying idea with Generative Pre-trained Transformer (GPT) models (more details in Section 7.4). By concatenating sentences from the question and the document, coupled with attention mechanisms (details in Section 7.4) to allow word-level importance weighting, such integrated dense Retrievers are in general more flexible and effective than two-stream architectures or sparse matrices, with potential compromise on speed or efficiency. For instance, joint training of Retriever and Reader is made possible in this framework with multi-task learning (Section 2.3). More recent ODQA systems such as ColBERT-QA [Khattab and Zaharia, 2020, Khattab et al., 2020] and SPARTA [Zhao et al., 2020] combine two-stream encoding with word-level integration over document and question embeddings to predict similarity in-between, striking a balance of efficacy and efficiency.

Iterative Retrievers search for candidate documents in multiple steps, which are shown particularly effective when it comes to complex questions that require multi-hop reasoning to reach the final answer. There are at least three major sequential modules that multi-hop Retrievers involve every step of the way: *document retrieval, query generation,* and *stopping criteria.* Document retrieval step usually adopts either a sparse Retriever or a dense Retriever as introduced above. To gather enough relevant documents, search queries for more relevant documents are generated at each step based on retrieved documents and used queries from the previous step, whether it be of natural language (GOLDEN Retriever [Qi et al., 2019]), or a dense representation (MUPPET [Feldman and El-Yaniv, 2019]). The marginal benefit of extra steps of retrieval decreases with the number of steps and therefore, a stopping criteria is needed to balance efficiency and accuracy of the document retrieval process. Straightforward and easy to implement criteria include specifying a fixed number of steps, an upper bound on the number of retrieved documents, and the likes are efficient despite loss of effectiveness. Dynamically setting the number of retrieved documents for each question by either a heuristic threshold or a trainable regression learning model could prove a fruitful effort.

Document (re-)ranking as a post-processing step is sometimes included if the Retriever module does not include any ranking capability, even though recent ODQA systems tend to integrate ranking and retrieving processes such that a trainable retriever learns to rank and retrieve the most relevant documents simultaneously, eliminating the necessity of such document post-processing steps between Retriever and Reader modules. Various strategies have been explored and tested for document post-processing at different granularities, in different frameworks, for different objectives. R^3 [Wang et al., 2018b], for instance, jointly trains document post-processing with the Reader module with Reinforcement Learning, exploring different post-processing configurations according how Reader performs overall. By measuring the probability of each retrieved paragraph containing the answer among all candidate paragraphs, DS-QA [Lin et al., 2018b] removes documents with relatively more noise and less plausible informative to improve overall efficiency. Relation-Networks Ranker [Fornaciari et al., 2013] tests both semantic similarity and word-level similarity between retrieved documents and questions as ranking metrics, and finds that word-level similarity ranking boosts retrieval performance whereas semantic similarity ranking results in overall performance gain.

With such a document post-processing step in place, the objective of the Retriever module could be reasonably shifted to optimize for *recall* (such that no relevant documents are missed) over *precision* (such that all the retrieved documents are relevant), as opposed to both or precision over recall in many or even most scenarios.

Reader is as important a module as Retriever, if not more in modern ODQA systems, and often takes form of machine reading comprehension. However, it is more challenging than traditional machine reading comprehension tasks as it learns to come to the correct answer to the question from a set of ordered documents of paragraphs, as opposed to one paragraph. There are two kinds of Reader modules in prevailing literature: extractive and generative. An extractive Reader identified spans of texts in retrieved documents or paragraphs as answers whereas a generative Reader generates answers in natural language instead.

When correct answers do exist in retrieval results verbatim, extractive Readers could be efficient solutions to the machine reading comprehension tasks at hand. Extractive Readers generally learn to predict the start and end position of an answer within any one or more of the retrieved documents. Many such methods proceed as the following: rank the retrieved documents by the odds of including answers, if one hasn't already in previous steps, and then predict the answer span from the highest ranked documents. Some recent extractive Reader modules adopt graph-based learning principles. For instance, Graph Reader [Min et al., 2017], learns to represent retrieved documents and paragraphs as graphs and extracts the likely answer from them by traversing the graph. Joint extraction of answer spans from all the retrieved documents has proved to improve performance especially when different evidences from multiple long documents are required to form the correct answer. DrQA system [Chen et al., 2017] extracts from all the retrieved paragraphs various linguistic and syntactical features including part-of-speech, named entities, and term-frequency, with which its Reader module then predicts an answer span by aggregating all the prediction scores of different paragraphs in a comparable way. There are various follow-up works that provided non-trivial incremental improvement upon such a framework.

However when correct answers are nowhere to be found within the retrieved documents and at least some amount of semantic induction or summarization is required, generative Reader modules based on sequence-to-sequence neural networks are perhaps the solution. Sometimes proper extraction of potential answer spans could provide evidences or inputs to the generative Reader for the final answer (e.g., S-Net [Tan et al., 2018]). With the introduction of large-scale pre-trained language models (more details in Section 7.4) that excel in text generation tasks such as BART [Lewis et al., 2020b] and T5 [Raffel et al., 2020], recent ODQA systems quickly adopted these as Readers as well as text encoders. For instance, retrieved documents or paragraphs could be encoded with BART or T5 with attention mechanisms (detailed in Section 7.4 as well) placed on top of encoded outputs to identify the most important sections, which are then fed into BART-based or T5-based Reader to generate the final answer(s).

An additional post-processing module after Reader could be put in place to zoom in onto the final answer among the final set of answers extracted or generated by Reader. In its simplest form, it could be a rule-based module that calculates the likelihood of being or containing correct answers for every candidate answer without training processes. Recent answer post-processing modules are generally based on sequence-to-sequence neural networks that re-rank answers by aggregating features extracted from both retrieved documents, questions, and answer candidates, and thus the final answer is determined.

End-to-end ODQA systems have also been introduced with more streamlined training regimes that integrates training of Retriever and Reader together. Moreover, Retriever-only and Reader-only ODQA have also gained popularity due to greater efficiency.
Various recent Retriever-Reader ODQA systems are end-to-end trainable with deep learning frameworks such as multi-task learning (Section 2.3). For instance, Retriever and Reader could be jointly trained with multi-task learning that retrieves documents according to questions and identifies answer spans in parallel, as is demonstrated in ODQA systems such as Retrieve-and-read [Nishida et al., 2018], ORQA [Lee et al., 2019], and REALM [Guu et al., 2020].

Retrieval-only ODQA systems optimize for efficiency by eliminating Reader modules that could be time-consuming, despite oftentimes compromising performance with less contextual information that would be available from Retrieval. DenSPI [Seo et al., 2019], for example, constructs embeddings from concatenation of both tf-idf and semantics as candidates based on pre-specified document collections. Given a candidate question, the same tf-idf and semantic embeddings are extracted, after which FAISS [Johnson et al., 2019] is leveraged for a most efficient search for the most similar phrase as the final answer.

As the recent advances in pre-trained neural language models have revolutionized the natural language processing research field as a whole (detailed reviews in Section 7.4), it has been shown with various corroborating evidences that a large amount of knowledge learned from large-scale pre-training could be stored in their parameters, such that these language models are able to generate answers without accessing any additional documents or knowledge bases, making them Reader-only ODQAs. Famously, GPT-2 [Radford et al., 2019] has been shown to generate correct answers given a random question in natural language without additional finetuning, and GPT-3 [Brown et al., 2020] off-the-shelf has showcased remarkable zero-shot learning performance compared to then state-of-the-art methods that required finetuning. More comprehensive evaluations have also been attempted to reveal impressive performance gains on various ODQA benchmarks, perhaps retrofitting how ODQA systems could and should be built.

To really mimick what human sommeliers or wine professionals could offer in a conversation with consumers, **Conversational ODQA** systems are perhaps of the greatest practical relevance, and are capable of resolving gnarly challenges that remain with non-conversational ODQA systems. These challenges include ambiguity (e.g., how old is Dave Chappelle?), insufficient context (e.g., why are my vines dying?), and complex questions that require multi-hop reasoning (e.g., who is the second son of the proprietor of Domaine Lignier?), and ODQA systems stand better chances in solving them through user interaction.

Conversational ODQA systems enable interactive dialogues between human users and itself to exchange useful information. If an ambiguous question was detected, the conversational ODQA would raise a clarification question, such as "did you mean the French winemaker in Beaujolais, or the American comedian?". If a questions was posed with insufficient background knowledge, a follow-up question could play a central role in garnering more contextual information from the user and eventually arriving at appropriate answers. When a complex question was given like the one above, it could be decomposed into two simple questions sequentially: "who is the proprietor of Domaine Lignier?" followed by "who is the second son of him?". To make such a system happen, there are at least three challenges involved.

First, accurate classification of whether a question is ambiguous, lacking in contexts, or overly complex, is a necessity in conversational ODQA systems. Identifying unanswerable questions [Rajpurkar et al., 2018, Hu et al., 2019, Zhu et al., 2019] have been gaining traction in machine comprehension literature and could be incorporated for any conversational ODQA systems in practice.

Second, conversational ODQA systems necessitate an automatic question generation module to deal with situations where more follow-up questions are needed. Question generation as a part of QA systems has attracted notable research interests [Du et al., 2017, Duan et al., 2017, Zhou et al., 2017] in the past few years and such automatic question generation methods from raw texts could be tailored to conversational ODQA systems in particular domains such as vine and wine.

Third, leveraging conversation history to optimize both modules of Reader and Retriever for the conversational ODQA in a non-trivial task. Besides equipping the Reader module with both contexts and conversational history, the fundamental role of retrieval in conversational search could also be enhanced with open-retrieval conversational question-answering (OpenConvQA) systems (e.g., [Qu et al., 2020]) to enable evidence retrieval from a large collection before extracting answers, taking into account conversations, as a further step towards building functional conversational search systems. OpenConvQA attempts at answers without pre-specified contexts, thus makes for more realistic applications in alignment with human behaviors during real conversations.

SECTION 4

Wine Pairing

Wine is a multi-sensory experience. We see it glitter in the glass, we smell it in awe of all the possibilities, and we feel it racing through our palates, defying our imagination.

What shall we pair with wine, and how shall we pair with wine? What goes hand in hand with a cerebral Coulee de Serrant? What keeps the best company of a delightfully fizzy Getariako Txakolina? What reminds you the most of a Volnay Champans that exudes elegance and charm? Is it a hearty plate of Marcel Petite Comté with sunflower and thyme? Is it Liszt's rendition of Invitation to the Dance (Aufforderung zum Tanz)? Is it Frank Lyold Wright's Fallingwater on a late summer evening? Is it A Sunday Afternoon on the Island of La Grande Jatte? Or perhaps Georges Seurat himself sketching alone in the park?

For most, the phrase "wine pairing" perhaps conjures up pairings between food and wine.

For many Europeans, for people who have grown up in households where wine is a part of daily life, the notion of pairing food and wine is a familiar and happy one. But analyzing the fine details of what food goes with what wine with what sauces or condiments under what conditions and at what point of time could be overwhelming and all-consuming for wine professionals, let alone wine consumers.

Certainly there are the time-honored shortcuts to food and wine pairings providing some ease and comfort, such as the so-called classic pairings, whether it be Chablis and raw oysters, or Stilton cheese and tawny Port, and the "*what grows together goes together*" adage that readily applies to pairings like Sancerre and goat cheese, or Barolo and truffle.

But since both great food and wine could be diverse, ethereal, and evolving living things, pinpointing the exact pairings at the right time at the right place might as well strike one as rare to come by. It requires intimate knowledge of how a wine ages, its vintage or bottle variations, the style of the producer, and similarly how spices, ingredients, and preparation or cooking methods and duration affect a dish in terms of flavor and texture, and more importantly, how food and wine interact in the mouth either at the same time, or food before wine, or wine before food. A great deal of team work between chefs and sommeliers with trial and error.

A largely accepted — yet not often terribly scientific — theory of wine and food pairing, reiterated in numerous books and classrooms, breaks down both food and wine to basic tastes: sweetness, sourness, saltiness, and bitterness, all of which are present in food and wine at least to some extent. Different dishes and wines reveal various combinations of these basic tastes, and it's the combination of these basic tastes and the interaction that results when pairing food and wine that determines how the pairing turns out. Some generalization from such a principle for ease of mind perhaps manifests in common wisdom such as *similarities bind* (wines and foods pair well with those resemble each other), or *opposites attract* (wines and foods can harmonize despite seemingly disparate). I summarize this pairing principle on basic tastes in Table 10 and Table 11.

Wine Taste and Mouthfeel		Food Taste and Mouthfeel					
		Sweetness	Spiciness	Fat	Umami	Acidity	Salt
	Sweetness	Masks	Balances	Affinity	Balances	Caution	Balances
	Acidity	Caution	Balances	Balances	Balances	Masks	Balances
	Tannin (Bitterness)	Balances	Balances	Affinity	Affinity	Affinity	Neutral
	Alcohol	Balances	Caution	Balances	Aggravates	Caution	Aggravates

Table 10: Food and Wine Pairing by Basic Tastes.

Taste	Impact(s)
Alcohol	Matches wines and foods of equal weight.
Acidity	Cuts through rich, salty, oily, fatty, or mildly spicy dishes. Best for pairing with tart foods. Brings out the integrity of simple yet quality ingredients.
Sweetness	Counterbalances moderate levels of spicy heat. Complements a slight sweetness in food. Counterbalances saltiness. Takes the edge off tart foods. Dessert wines must be sweeter than the dessert itself.
Saltiness	Lessened by wine's acidity. Exaggerated by wine's tannin. Accentuates alcohol in wine. Counterbalanced by off-dry or sweet wines.
Tannin	Bitter foods pair well with bitter wines. Counterbalances fat and protein. Avoid fish oil with tannic wines.
Oak	Food could exaggerates oak flavors. Match cooking techniques to oak flavors (toast, char, smoke). Match food texture to the smoothness/roundness of oak.

Table 11: Food and Wine Pairing by Basic Tastes.

If such a principle holds true, then a simple rule-based AI system consisting three modules — one for breaking down each dish in terms of basic flavor compounds, one for breaking down each wine by basic flavor compounds, and a third implementing the rules specified by the interplay between these basic flavor compounds — would mostly likely be able to solve the food and wine pairing puzzle almost instantly and much better than human experts in terms of precision, accuracy, or cost, as such structured problems are the forte of AI systems with memory and computing powers no human being could possibly match. Let me illustrate such a rule-based food and wine pairing system in Figure 18.

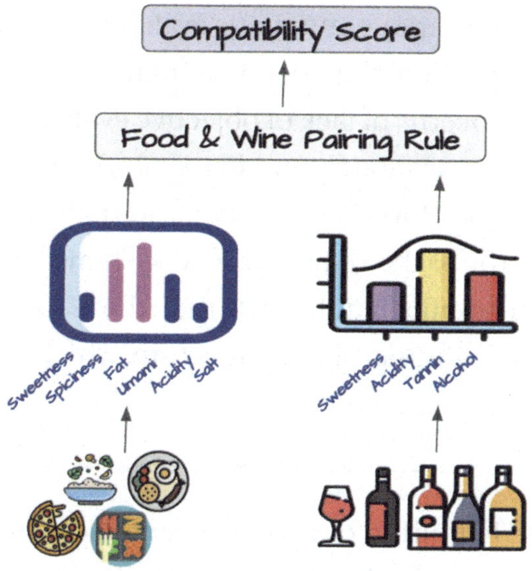

Figure 18: An illustration of a rule-based food and wine pairing system based on basic tastes.

However, the validity of such a principle is still up in the air, with various exceptions to the rules, which would make such a rule-based system prone to errors and thus requiring constant maintenance and manual intervention. And wine and food appreciation and enjoyment are personal, and more often than not even emotional. Eric

Ripert, chef of Le Bernardin, famously made a case in his video series of Perfect Pairings that Bordeaux wines can be paired with anything, and every wine and food book starts with a similar statement that it is such a subjective experience that you could pair any food with any wine in any form you would like. There are pairing believers who rare experience when the heavenly matched pairings strike, and non-believers like me. The problem with designing an AI system for such a subjective subject matter is the lack of objective evaluation metrics to tell the reliable and janky ones apart. This was a major point of criticism when *Style Transfer* (see Section 5.2) or *Image-to-image Translation* (see Section 5.1) techniques were used to generate artworks, even though over time, computer vision scientists did develop various automatic evaluation methods that align with human perception, together with manual human evaluations, to address the concerns of lack of objective evaluation.

But how does one accurately predict evoked emotions from food and wind pairings? How does one tailor to the right person, at the right time, and the at the right place? AI systems for such purposes would function not much differently than those for other wine pairings with music, painting, and architecture, which I will explore below.

The only sense left out in our wine experience is hearing, whereas the only sense through which transmission happens is when we experience music. Thus the bidirectional analogy between wine and music is essential to complete both experiences.

Music is beloved in the wine world. The champagne house Krug, with its well-deserved reputation as one of Champagne's best, perhaps is best known for comparing and pairing their Champagne to music. Olivier Krug, Directeur de la Maison Krug and a member of the Krug tasting committee, is fond of describing the house's cuvées as music. He compares Grande Cuvée, made from a blend of around two hundred based wines — *vins clairs* — from a dozen vintages to Tchaikovsky's Symphony No. 6, where many different individual musicians come together to create a harmonious and complete piece, something larger than each of them represents individually. Krug's vintage brut, which comes exclusively from wines harvested in the same year, is equivalent to a quartet, or chamber music, demonstrating the singular personality of the year. With an even finer delineation, Clos du Mesnil and Clos d'Ambonnay, two vintage-dated, single-vineyard Champagnes, are best described as soloists, highlighting the virtuosity of the performer — whether it's the producer or the site. As the Champagne specialist Peter Liem has put it eloquently: as with soloists and orchestras, a single-vineyard champagne is not necessarily better, or purer, or more expressive than a blended champagne, nor is a blended champagne necessarily more complex or complete than a single-terroir one. They simply express different things. For Olivier, the major grape varieties from which Krug Champagnes are made, showcase distinct musical characters. Chardonnay is more the violins, this backbone of freshness. Pinot Noir will be more the bass, the trombones giving the structure and maturity. And Pinot Meunier? It is from the funfair. "You hear a ting-ting-ting, or a trumpet from time to time." And Krug Echoes project, is indeed designed to translate specific Champagnes into pieces of music with artists devising soundtracks for Krug Grande Cuvée and vintage Champagnes, creating "3-D" music pairing experience for Krug visitors and consumers around the globe.

Wine is beloved in the world of music. Composers and performers savor wines, sometimes to the sparks that keep the creative juice flowing; and sometimes, to the detriment of their own health. Gioacchino Rossini was a notorious food and wine connoisseur of his time, and said to particularly love Bordeaux wines with exchanges of grapes and wines between him and Baron de Rothschild as proof. In an article published in 1866, it was told that Rossini would meticulously order wines to his liking to pair with each dish: Madeira with cured meat, Bordeaux with fried fare, Champagne with a roast duck, and Alicante or Lacrima with cheese and fruit. The deaths of Beethoven and Liszt were both at least partially attributed to their heavy alcohol consumption, or so I was informed. For Beethoven, it was Rhine Rieslings, nectars from Tokaji, and wines from Thermenregion in Austria — possibly Rotgipfler and Zierfandler that enjoyed their former glory on par with Mosel and Tokaji, that captured his body and soul till the last minute of life: "music is the wine which inspires one to new generative processes, and I am Bacchus who presses out this glorious wine for mankind and makes them spiritually drunken". For Liszt, it was probably claret, sometimes mixed with Cognac, and perhaps a short period of Absinthe, depending on how weak he felt and how his physician tried to keep him to wine diluted with water. Johann Sebastian Bach, Johannes Brahms, Franz Schubert, Richard Wagner, Igor Stravinsky, and Wolfgang Amadeus Mozart all had their own picks, whether it be Rhine Rieslings, Champagne, Marsala, or Italian wines such as Sicilian reds or perhaps Falernum?

In Bryce Wiatrak's minute piece on Music and Wine, he recollected how Stephanie Blythe, one of the most sought-after mezzo-sopranos today, once compared singing to drinking wine. She explained that a singer, much like a wine drinker, must explore the way the text feels on the palate. Some pieces may be languorous and chewy, others rapid and tempestuous. Above all, a singer should harness this experience to better recognize the true nature of a work and to then convey it before an audience. The parallels between music and wine are indeed both ample and profound.

Like music, wine holds the power of evoking some people's imaginations filled with colors. Maggie Harrison, partner and winemaker of Antica Terra and the Lillian wines in Willamette Valley in Oregon, having trained in the Sine Qua Non cellar for eight years, sees every wine and every parcel in colors — purple for Antikythera, orange for Botanica, and blue for Ceras Pinot Noirs. Franz Liszt, the greatest piano virtuoso of his time, was known to speak to fellow musicians in terms of the colours they needed to achieve in their performances, giving directions such as "A little bluer, if you please! This tone type requires it!" Alexander Scriabin, the composer very much influenced by his colour sense, went on to write Prometheus: The Poem of Fire, which featured the clavier à lumières, a keyboard instrument which emitted light instead of sound in correspondence to music scores.

Like wine, music evokes feelings and emotions out of people, whether it be in the forms of bursts or trickles, as both music and wine could trigger past memories by transporting us back to the scents and sounds of our childhoods, our memorable moments, and beyond. In *The Drops of God*[18], Shinzuki broke down weeping the moment he held upon his nose a glass of 1982 Mouton-Rothschild, the scent of the grapes brought him back to the summer of 1982 when he at the harvest of Mouton-Rothschild with his mother, who passed away soon afterwards the same year. When Lindy Novak and Beth Novak Milliken of Spottswoode in St. Helena Napa Valley opened their 2016 Mary's Block Sauvignon Blanc on a early spring afternoon in 2021, they almost teared up because it was the first vintage for this tiny production of estate bottled Sauvignon Blanc, made at their mother's Mary Novak's request for herself, who sadly passed away in the same year of 2016, after succumbing to cancer. It was Mary Novak, a widow after the sudden death of her husband due to a heart attack at the young age of 44, who persisted in their shared dream of making wine and decided to keep selling the fruit produced from their newly established vineyards.

[18]The manga series about two half brothers scouring the world to track down the 'Apostles' wines in a competition for the access to the million-dollar cellar of their late father, a world famous wine critic, that has swept the wine scene in East Asia by storm and gradually been gaining popularity in the West since its inception in 2004.

Like music, wine evolves with tempo, rhythm and dynamics. Underneath the layers of fruits, flowers, spices, and earthiness, what constantly moves us about wine is how it transcends time and space, constantly evolving in the bottle, if not on our tongue. A Chenin Blanc from Loire, Vouvray or Montlouis-sur-Loire, could perhaps be best described as a *crescendo* followed by a *thrill,* cast within Felix Mendelssohn's concert overture for A Midsummer Night's Dream. A Philipponat Clos des Goisses emitting a drifting sense of the rhythm of rocks, water, and love, while flowing consistently with a strong sense of direction and intention, could be perhaps best compared to Franz List's Liebesträum. A Gevrey-Chambertin 1er cru Lavaux St. Jacques from Denis Mortet, bright and vivacious, powerful yet lonesome, sensual yet troubled, stirring up a tinge of nostalgia, longing after a sweet past that will never return. Would it best paired with Slavonic Dances by Antonín Dvořák, or Fantaisie and Variations on The Carnival of Venice by Jean-Baptiste Arban?

Like wine, music takes on unique cultural expressions and interpretations wherever it goes. *Company,* the iconic musical by George Furth and Stephen Sondheim, would still sound as if it were for the New York City even if all New York references were striped away. The Well-Tempered Clavier, BWV 846–893, by Johann Sebastian Bach, just wouldn't shake off its Germanic structure and tone, however it's been rendered, adapted, or paraphrased. Just like how Zinfandel and Primitivo, despite being of the same grape variety with the same DNA markers, grow and adapt to their own home countries taking on distinct tastes that uniquely reflects the California sunshine with abundant ripeness and the dusty tannins of Puglia with a touch of Italian herbs, respectively.

The analogy between *art and wine,* or more specifically, *visual art and wine,* is a familiar one. Numerous artists and wine lovers have attempted to interweave wine and art into one single harmoniously unified experience, yet very few delivered. Among the very few, perhaps the works of Sarah Heller, the visual artist and Master of Wine based in Hong Kong, stood out to precisely capture the subjective experience of tasting wine and explore the synthetic work of imagination required to recreate and share that experience. Her visual art series of visual tasting focuses on individual wines and the pieces are meant to be read narratively from top to bottom, tracing the wine from initial impression to final aftertaste. Each one is a collage of hand painted, digitally painted and photographic fragments. Her visual interpretation of Biondi Santi Brunello Riserva 1971 features vibrancy and richness of fruit, undergirded by an almost mechanical precision that is nonetheless warm and human, unwinding to reveal layer upon layer of unexpected depth; whereas her Masseto 2006 gives off a much more rounder and sensuous vibe, showing off the wine's baroque and extravagant nose with an almost overwhelming richness and hedonistic wildness that then, on the palate, seems to be expertly hewn down to concise, flowing contours, all of its power compressed into a refined close. Her Le Pergole Torte 2001 piece perhaps sits somewhere in-between, alluding to the wine's return to classical form, with a wispy, shimmering texture woven around an elusive framework of aromas: sometimes floral and bright-fruited, next earthy and rich, then spicy and medicinal. Each layer emerges, half-seen, almost sharpening into focus before washing away again, finally coalescing into an unrelenting tannic grasp.

Like art appreciation, there perhaps is little other experience more subjective and personal than the appreciation and perception of wine. Perhaps it is the Whorfian theory — one's thought and even perception are determined by the language one happens to speak — kicking in, that how people perceive art or wine are deeply rooted in their language, which in turn is affected by culture. The appreciation for German off-dry and dessert wines appear to concentrate outside Germany with dry Rieslings or Kabinetts all the range within

Germany. Tasters with different cultural backgrounds could describe the identical aroma or flavor with completely different concepts and descriptors. Gerwürztraminer might be of roses and musk for western senses but perhaps lychee and curry for the eastern nose. A 15-year-old Chateau Montrose might exude blackcurrant, cassis, fig, and cigar box to the English, but perhaps symbolize social status, wealth, and cultural literacy to the Chinese, together with black grape, dried date, black raisins, tobacco.

Like art, the learning curve of wine could be steep [19] and a great wine experience is never all sunshine and roses. A great art piece is almost never all rainbows and butterflies — it puzzles you, provokes you, challenges you, and agonizes you. It takes you through an emotional roller-coaster and leaves you with trembling hands and racing hearts and a memory that never evades. To quote Henry James out of context: good wine is not an optical pleasure, it is an inward emotion. A great wine is never one hundred percent delicious either. It's sometimes even tainted with the flavors of things we'd never put in our mouths — graphite, petroleum, forest floor, pencil shavings, barnyard, leather belt. Just like fine art, it challenges us to ponder, through the mundane noises and evolving flavors and textures, we come to better appreciate what art and beauty really is. Which painting would you be reminded of while sipping on a 2000 Duckhorn Merlot? Would it be Vermeer's Milkmaid? Mild and mellow, and yet with inner strength not apparent at the first glance — layered with the familiarity of mundane life? Which wine would you pair with Klimt's The Kiss? Could it be a 2000 Henri Jayer Cros Parantoux that similarly conveys the sweet beguiling sensuality?

Like art, wine goes through cycles of fashion, witnessing bitter clashes between the modernists and the traditionalists in every culture. Yet the pendulum swings, and the wheel of history waits for no one. It

[19] Or flat, technically speaking, since a steep learning curve indicates that one could learn it rather fast.

is those who stayed true to their own beliefs and principles, and continued to quietly improve regardless of what fads and naysayers prescribe who shine through. Jean-Claude Fourrier of Domaine Fourrier famously evicted Robert Parker in the 1980s when he demanded a shift in winemaking to using 100% new oak, which in his opinion would make their wines far better. "Excuse me, my job is to make wine, and yours to describe it, not how to make it." Nonchalantly said Jean-Claude Fourrier, according to the recollection by Jean-Marc Fourrier, the son and current proprietor who took over in 1994. The Parker reviews that year came out denouncing Domaine Fourrier as the dampest and dirtiest cellar in all of Burgundy and thus made the family suffer economically for almost a decade — they became the domaine one should never even venture a taste. Despite the unfortunate turn of events, the family never caved in to Parkerization. Fortunately, in 1994, the bright-eyed American wine merchant Neal Rosenthal took a chance and the rest is history. The same tale is told in Napa, those who stood against Parkerization like Steve Matthiasson struggled in sales throughout the 90s and early 2000s when they stuck to the restraint low-alcohol style and ingenious Friuli varieties Ribolla Gialla, Tocai Friulano, Refosco, and Schioppettino. The market eventually diversified and as Kelli White, author of *Napa Valley Then and Now* has put it, it was such a relief to see Matthiasson wines on the wine lists of best restaurants in New York City at price points almost comparable to other icons around the world.

Like art, a great wine is the target of envy, conspiracy, and crime, requiring the most discerning eyes and meticulous minds to safeguard and preserve its authenticity. Benjamin Wallace's fascinatingly suspenseful book The Billionaire's Vinegar unfolds what is behind the veneer of the high-end wine collecting community of rich and powerful individuals who buy old and rare wines at auction, and their quest for the unforgettable get: mystery, competition, ego, wealth, cheating, lying, scandal, toxic masculinity, particle physics, and wine. It centered around the mysterious individual Hardy Rodenstock, allegedly a perpetrator of elaborate wine frauds that involve a trove of bottle that he believed to have belonged to Thomas Jefferson, the first president and serious wine connoisseur of United States; Maximillian Potter's Shadows in the Vineyard detailed the incredulous crime of poisoning vines in Romanée-Conti in 2010, which necessitated installation of preventative devices around the most coveted vineyard ever since; in Peter Hellman's In Vino Duplicitas and Sour Grapes, the masterful trickery of Ruby Kurniawan — the Dr. Conti and counterfeiter extraordinaire — was put under a microscope, despite being imprisoned, released after his term in November of 2020, deported to Malaysia early 2021, Rudy with some of his counterfeited bottles still circulating in the wild, are still constantly talked about and his detrimental impact on fine wine trading felt long after the reveal.

The analogy between architecture and wine, in my eyes, is much less far-fetched than many might anticipate, not (only) because numerous wineries around the world are architectural wonders themselves enlisting star architects from Renzo Piano, to Zaha Hadid and Frank Gehry, but (also) due to various fundamental principles and characteristics shared by the two equally mesmerizing worlds.

Like architectural design and construction, wine-making and vine-growing are long-term commitments that require sustained passion and dedication over years, if not decades. There are periods when you need to grub up old vineyards, either due to vine diseases and ailments, or simply as a natural course of action. It'd be much better if vignerons went back to leave it farrow for at least seven years, nourish it with cover crops, wildflowers, vegetables. Put in Nitrogen fixes, and plants that are good for killing off nematode worms that attack. In which case you wait at least ten years for a first crop, and twenty years for a marginally mature crop. The same applies to *massale selection* when it comes to vine materials. Those who bode the time are reaping the sweet benefits of patience and care, oftentimes generation after generation.

Like architecture, a great wine epitomizes both art and science where artistic juices run free within the boundaries delineated by scientific precision. Architectural design requires technical knowledge in the fields of engineering, logistics, geometry, functional design and ergonomics, among others. Being a broad and humanistic field, it also requires a certain sensibility to arts and aesthetics, with additional preoccupation for human inquiry and society. It is the same with making wine. To make a great wine, obsession with details and fussing over techniques however simple and primitive would not hurt, especially with precision viticulture and viniculture that have greatly improved the overall quality of wine since first adoption. Sensual and flamboyant, or delicate and elegant, that is an artistic choice of the designer or the vigneron, that more often than not reflects the personality of the man or woman at the helm.

Like architecture, the century-old maxim *form follows function* [Sullivan, 1896] rings true for wine at its very core: a beverage meant to be popped and enjoyed, preferably over a meal in the company of family and friends. David Lett, widely recognized as the father of Oregon's thriving pinot noir industry and a major force in winning worldwide respect for this state's wines, who had searched the world for a perfect place that resembles Burgundy to plant his beloved Pinot Noir grapes and settled down in Dundee Hills in Willamette Valley in the mid-1960s, had always felt strongly that in Pinot Noir, color and flavor exists in inverse ratio, despite how most Americans judge Pinot Noir by the color back then. He favored short cold fermentation as opposed to raising the fermentation temperature — one of the best ways to extract color, but the volatiles of aromatics would inevitably be boiled off by the heat. The same sentiment had and has been echoed in various respectable estates in Burgundy, in Central Otago, in Okanagan Valley, in Finger Lakes, and so forth. Like architecture, a great wine embodies the harmonious union of art and nature. Fallingwater, an exemplar of organic architecture was designed by Frank Lloyd Wright who deliberately chose to place the residence directly over the waterfall and creek creating a close and tranquil dialogue with the rushing water and the steep hillside. The horizontal striations of stone masonry with daring cantilevers of colored beige concrete blend with native rock outcroppings and the wooden environment, creating an intricate balance in color, lighting, natural sound, and structure. The similar ideology has been reiterated by various talented and accomplished vignerons around the globe: a great wine starts with a great vineyard with living soils within an entire regenerative self-sustained ecosystem, blessed by the delicate balance of Nature. Once you have good grape juice, the role of a winemaker is "not to screw it up".

In Section 4.1, I will detail how similarities or dissimilarities between two concepts or entities such as food and wine or music and wine, could be learnt by way of metric learning; in Section 4.2, various recent technical advances in how to combine different modalities such as sights and sounds or texts and visuals effectively to identify evoked emotions, corresponding colors, among other intangibles; in Section 4.3, let us recast wine pairings within the framework of personalized recommendation systems, just like how we select our movies from Netflix, and detail the various options to enable the best personalized wine recommender systems based on the exact dining experience.

4.1 Metric Learning

Metric learning is a machine learning approach based directly on a distance metric that aims to establish similarity or dissimilarity between data points by mapping them to an embedding space where similar samples are close together and dissimilar ones are far apart. Such a learning framework could be applied to wine pairing problems to learn a distance metric and an embedding space such that compatible pairings are close together and incompatible pairings are far apart.

In general, this can be achieved by means of embedding and classification losses[20].

Embedding losses operate on the relationships between samples in a batch, while classification losses include a weight matrix that transforms the embedding space into a vector that indicates class memberships.

Typically, embeddings are preferred when the task at hand is essentially *information retrieval,* where the goal is to return data that is most similar to a given query. An example of this is image search, where the input is a query image, and the output is the most visually similar images in a database. Some notable applications of this are face verification, person re-identification, and image retrieval (Section 6.1). There are also practical scenarios where using a classification loss is not possible. For example, when constructing a dataset, it might be difficult or costly to assign class labels to each sample, and it might be easier to specify the relative similarities between data samples in the form of pair or triplet relationships. Pairs and triplets can also provide additional training signals for existing datasets. In both cases, there are no explicit labels for classification,

[20]Loss functions are objective functions being minimized during the training processes of machine learning models. The better the model predictions align with the truth reflected from data samples, the smaller the losses.

so embedding losses remain an option.

More recently, there has been significant growing interest in self-supervised learning in the community, most notably advocated by Yan LeCun, the chief AI scientist of Facebook. This could be seen as a form of unsupervised learning where pseudo-labels are applied to data samples during training, often via ingenious data augmentations (Section 7.1.1) or signals from multiple modalities (Section 4.2). In this case, pseudo-labels indicate the similarities between data in a particular batch, and as such, they do not have any meaning across training iterations. Thus, embedding losses are favored over classification losses.

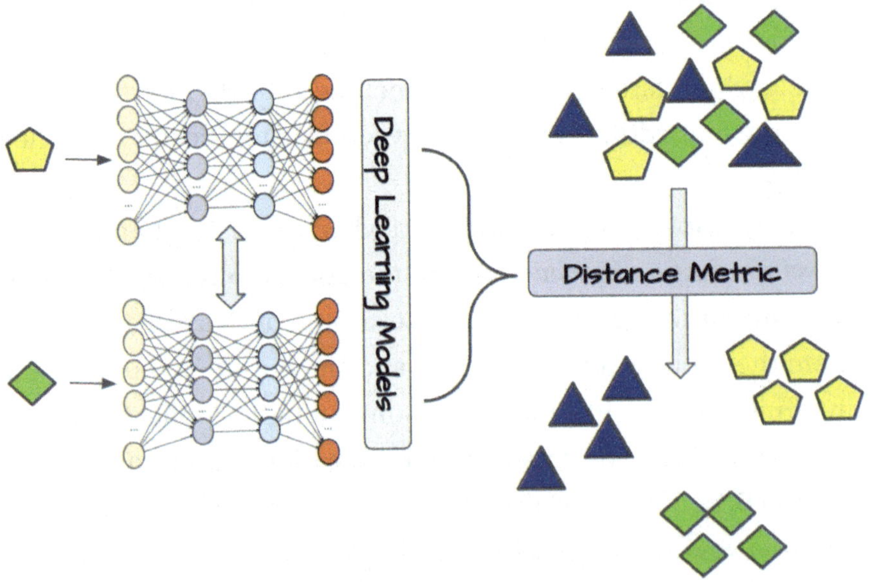

Figure 19: Deep Metric Learning.

In the last few years, deep learning and metric learning have been brought together to introduce the concept of deep metric learning. In 2017, [Lu et al., 2017a] summarized the concept of deep metric learning for visual understanding tasks. Let us illustrate the concept of deep metric learning in Figure 19. The choices of loss functions, sample selection strategies, training regimes, and network structures are critical towards an efficient deep metric learning.

4.1.1 Loss Functions

Pair and triplet losses provide the foundation for two fundamental approaches to metric learning.

A classic pair based method is the **contrastive loss**, which attempts to make the distance between positive pairs (similar samples) smaller than some threshold (often set to 0), and the distance between negative pairs (dissimilar samples) larger than some threshold [Hadsell et al., 2006]. The theoretical downside of this method is that the same distance threshold is applied to all pairs, even though there may be a large variance in their similarities and dissimilarities.

The triplet margin loss [Weinberger and Saul, 2009] theoretically addresses this issue. A triplet consists of an anchor, positive, and negative sample, where the anchor is more similar to the positive than the negative. The *triplet margin loss* attempts to make the anchor-positive distances smaller than the anchor-negative distances, by a predefined margin value. This theoretically places fewer restrictions on the embedding space, and allows the model to account for variance in inter-class dissimilarities.

A wide variety of losses has since been built on these fundamental concepts. For example, the angular loss [Wang et al., 2017] is a triplet loss where the margin is based on the angles formed by the triplet vectors, while the margin loss [Wu et al., 2017] modifies the contrastive loss by defining margins as learnable parameters via gradient descent. More recently, [Yuan et al., 2019] proposed a variation of the contrastive loss based on signal to noise ratios, where each embedding vector is considered signal, and the difference between it and other vectors is considered noise. Other pair losses are based on the *softmax function*[21] and *LogSumExp*, which is a smooth

[21]The softmax function is a generalization of the logistic function to multiple

approximation of the maximum function. For instance, the lifted structure loss [Oh Song et al., 2016], is the contrastive loss but with *LogSumExp* applied to all negative pairs, and the N-Pairs loss [Sohn, 2016] applies the softmax function to each positive pair relative to all other pairs. The recent multi similarity loss [Wang et al., 2019] applies *LogSumExp* to all pairs, but is specially formulated to give weight to different relative similarities among each embedding and its neighbors. The tuplet margin loss [Yu and Tao, 2019] also uses *LogSumExp*, but in combination with an implicit pair weighting method. FastAP [Cakir et al., 2019], in contrast to the pair and triplet losses, attempts to optimize for average precision within each batch, using a soft histogram binning technique.

Besides **embedding losses** detailed above, **classification losses** are based on the inclusion of a weight matrix, where each column corresponds to a particular class. In most cases, training consists of matrix multiplying the weights with embedding vectors to obtain logits, and then applying a loss function to the logits. The most straightforward case is the normalized softmax loss [Liu et al., 2017, Zhai and Wu, 2018], which is identical to cross entropy, but with the columns of the weight matrix L2 normalized. ProxyNCA [Movshovitz-Attias et al., 2017] is a variation of this, where cross entropy is applied to the Euclidean distances, rather than the cosine similarities, between embeddings and the weight matrix. A number of face verification losses have modified the cross entropy loss with angular margins in the softmax expression. SphereFace[Liu et al., 2017], CosFace [Wang et al., 2018a], and ArcFace [Deng et al., 2019] apply multiplicative-angular, additive-cosine, and additive-angular margins, respectively. The SoftTriple loss [Qian et al., 2019] takes a different approach, by

dimensions. It is used in multinomial logistic regression and is often used as the last activation function of a neural network to normalize the output of a network to a probability distribution over predicted output classes.

expanding the weight matrix to have multiple columns per class, theoretically providing more flexibility for modeling class variances. Table 12 aggregates all the loss functions we walked through above with a succinct summary, relevant topics, corresponding sample selection strategy, and references.

Metric	Sample Selection	Summary	Reference
Contrastive Loss	Hard negative.	Bring similar pairs close and dissimilar pairs apart.	[Hadsell et al., 2006]
Triplet Loss	Random sampling.	Brings anchor-positive pairs closer and anchor-negative pairs apart.	[Weinberger and Saul, 2009]
Angular Loss	Multiple negative.	Limiting the angle of negative sample formed by triplet vectors.	[Wang et al., 2017]
Margin Loss	Hard negative.	Adaptive margin learnable with SGD.	[Wu et al., 2017]
Signal-to-noise Loss	Distance weighting.	Weight pairs based on signal-to-noise ratio of informativeness.	[Yuan et al., 2019]
Lifted Structure Loss	Hard negative.	Lifting the vector of pairwise distances to matrix for efficiency.	[Oh Song et al., 2016]
N-Pair Loss	Multiple negative.	Pulls a positive sample away from multiple negative samples.	[Sohn, 2016]
Tuplet Margin Loss	Distance weighting.	Up-weights hard samples and down-weights easy samples with a slack margin in angular space.	[Yu and Tao, 2019]
Multi-Similarity Loss	Distance weighting.	Weight informative pairs on own and relative similarities.	[Wang et al., 2019]
FastAP	Random sampling.	Optimizing for distance ranking.	[Cakir et al., 2019]

Table 12: Loss Functions for Deep Metric Learning.

4.1.2 Sample Selection Strategies

Mining is the process of finding the best pairs or triplets to train models on. Broadly speaking, there are two approaches to mining: offline and online. Offline mining is performed before batch construction, so that each batch is made to contain the most informative samples. This might be accomplished by storing lists of hard negatives examples that the models frequently make mistakes on, doing a nearest neighbors search before each epoch or iteration. In contrast, online mining finds hard pairs or triplets within each randomly sampled batch. Using all possible pairs or triplets is an alternative, with at least two drawbacks: significant memory consumption, and indiscriminative sample selection that includes easy negatives and positives, causing performance to plateau quickly. Thus, one intuitive strategy is to select only the most difficult positive and negative samples, but this has been found to produce noisy gradients and convergence to bad local optima [Wu et al., 2017]. A possible remedy is semi-hard negative mining, which finds the negative samples in a batch that are close to the anchor, but still further away than the corresponding positive samples [Schroff et al., 2015]. On the other hand, [Wu et al., 2017] found that semi-hard mining makes little progress as the number of semi-hard negatives drops. They claim that distance-weighted sampling results in a variety of negatives (easy, semi-hard, and hard), and improved performance. Online mining can also be integrated into the structure of models. The hard-aware deeply cascaded method [Yuan et al., 2017], for instance, uses models of varying complexity, in which the loss for the complex models only considers the pairs that the simpler models find difficult. Recently, [Wang et al., 2019] proposed a simple pair mining strategy, where negatives are chosen if they are closer to an anchor than its hardest positive, and positives are chosen if they are further from an anchor than its hardest negative.

4.1.3 Training Regimes

To obtain higher accuracy, many recent papers have gone beyond loss functions or mining techniques. For example, several recent methods incorporate generator networks in their training procedure. [Lin et al., 2018a] use a generator as part of their framework for modeling class centers and intra-class variance. [Duan et al., 2018] use a hard-negative generator to expose the model to difficult negatives that might be absent from the training set. [Zheng et al., 2019] follow up on this work by using an adaptive interpolation method that creates negatives of varying difficulty, based on the strength of the model. Other more involved training methods include HTL [Ge, 2018], ABE [Kim et al., 2018], and MIC [Roth et al., 2019]. HTL [Ge, 2018] constructs a hierarchical class tree at regular intervals during training, to estimate the optimal per-class margin in the triplet margin loss. ABE is an attention-based ensemble, where each model learns a different set of attention masks. MIC uses a combination of clustering and encoder networks to disentangle class specific properties from shared characteristics like color and pose.

4.2 Multi-modal Learning

Multi-modal learning refers to the machine learning paradigm where information from different modalities are leveraged to improve learning outcomes. Just like how our wine experiences are oftentimes multi-sensory: the wine presents itself with a bright ruby color and an inviting bouquet and aroma of red berries and Asian five spices jumping out of the glass, and we praise it with our words — whether it be poetry or morse code, express it with colorful paintings, and pair it with music full of emotion; multi-modal learning incorporates information from different modalities — whether it be numeric, visual, textual, or acoustic.

Multi-modal learning as a research area has received increasingly more attention in the past few years, riding the waves off the tremendous growths of natural language processing and computer vision during the past decade, and therefore, the integration of vision and language has been on the forefronts of multi-modal learning efforts. Among the various multi-modal learning tasks explored within the research area, such as the most popular *Visual Question Answering, Visual Storytelling, Image Captioning, Visual Entailment, Multi-modal Machine Translation, Visual Reasoning, Multi-modal Navigation, Visual Dialog, Visual Text Generation, Multi-modal Verification, Visual Referring Expression,* etc., all of which are tabulated in Table 13 with brief descriptions and references to a selection of influential works therein, perhaps the most relevant to our context of wine pairing that's both personal and emotional is **Multi-modal Affective Computing**.

Affective Computing involves automatic recognition of affective phenomena resulting from emotions. Multi-modal Affective Comput-

Multi-modal Task	Description
Visual Question Answering (VQA)	Question Answering (Section) with questions that include images.
Visual Dialogue	Given an image, create natural and conversational dialogues about it.
Visual Referring Expression	Given a natural language expression and an image, identify the target region in the image that is referred by expression.
Visual Storytelling	Given a sequence of visual inputs, generate a narrative summary based on aligned texts.
Visual Description Generation	Given an image, generate a sensible text snippet to describe it.
Visual Entailment	Given a text and an image, determine if the text can be inferred from the image.
Visual Reasoning	Given an image of objects, generate a visual scene graph that describes relationships between objects in the image.
Visual Generation	Given a piece of text, generate an image accordingly.
Multi-modal Retrieval	Given a piece of text or an image, retrieval relevant texts and/or images.
Multi-modal Verification	Given one or more images and a natural language statement, judge the correctness or predict their semantic relationship.
Multi-modal Machine Translation	Translate between languages with additional visual content.
Vision-Language Navigation	Combine visual and textual instructions to navigate.

Table 13: Multi-modal Tasks with Descriptions.

ing seeks to combine cues or signals from multiple modalities such as texts, audios, images, and videos where emotions might be manifested. For instance, if a wine is invoking an image of a tropical beach side on a late summer Sunday afternoon with few people in sight except for yawning sea lions, a combination of such a textual description, a watercolor painting of such a scene, a soundtrack of soothing ocean waves, as well as the smell of ocean breezes mixed with Piña Colada, would definitely help with a better understanding of wine, either by human wine lovers, or multi-modal learning algorithms.

Multi-modal affective computing involves learning mappings from multi-modal input signals — whether it be text descriptions, visual designs or photographs, video contents, or music and sound, to the decision space of different emotions, sentiments, or other affective concepts. By fusing together information of different modalities in an intelligent way, a multi-modal system could achieve much better performance than one that sources from a single modality in automatic identification of evoked emotions, among others.

Multi-modal sentiment analysis with texts and images could be perhaps considered the precursor of multi-modal computing. Taking into account both texts and associated images in social media posts or news articles, sentiments such as positive, negative, or neural could be potentially determined at a higher level of confidence and accuracy if two modalities are fused properly. Tri-modal learning that involves textual (linguistic), visual, and acoustic-prosodic features such as facial expressions, gestures, poses, vocal features, textual descriptions, and transcriptions could prove even more fruitful if done judiciously despite of increased dimensionality and complexity in multi-modal fusion. Several works have leveraged visual cues from facial expressions, together with audio signals or textual transcriptions to learn correspondences between information from different modalities for fine-grained emotion classification.

One critical line of research within multi-modal affective computing, and multi-modal learning in general, revolves around optimal fusion techniques to cast multi-modal information into effective and integrated representations. Various methods have been proposed with different foci and applications:

- Early fusion of multiple sensory data into a single channel at the feature level.

- Late fusion of multiple sensory data with an additional neural network after blending multi-modal representations learnt separately.

- Hierarchical fusion that combines two modalities at one level to better capture semantic relationships.

- Multi-modal or cross-modal attention mechanisms that selectively focus on (ignore) modalities with high (low) fidelity or presence.

Another interesting line of work, in contrary to the fusion foci of multi-modal learning, stems from the fact that, sometimes multi-modal information is given in an integrated form and the first step of multi-modal learning could be to factorize or disentangle modality features in joint spaces. In addition, multi-modal information is oftentimes misaligned in that correspondences between textual transcriptions and audio signals are wacky or paired images and captions sometimes do not make much sense, in which case, alignment-independent or robust multi-modal learning techniques could greatly improve the practical relevance and boost accessibility and applicability of multi-modal methods in the wild.
In my multi-modal experiments with wine and artwork or music pairings, I fused together textual descriptions of wines with corresponding images or audio signals of music with different fusion techniques, and produced a multi-modal classification model that, given a pair of wine and image, or wine and music, would do the following:

1. Classify the relationship between the wine and the image or the music piece into one of the three categories: congruent, incompatible, neural, with one confidence score for each category.

2. Identify the evoked emotions by the wine and music, or the wine and image pair out of the eight primary emotions defined by Robert Plutchik: anger, fear, sadness, disgust, sur-

prise, anticipation, trust and joy, or out of the six basic emotions defined by Paul Ekman: fear, anger, joy, sadness, disgust, and surprise, again each of which is associated with a confidence score.

3. Track the temporal trajectory of detected sentiments and emotions, if available, of wine and music, or wine and image.

The second and third were used as auxiliary tasks to facilitate the first classification task of determining the compatibility score between wine and music pairing, or wine and image pairing. It could also help with interpretation of model results to improve transparency and explainability of the multi-modal and multi-task[22]) classification model for wine pairing. Let me illustrate this framework in Figure 20.

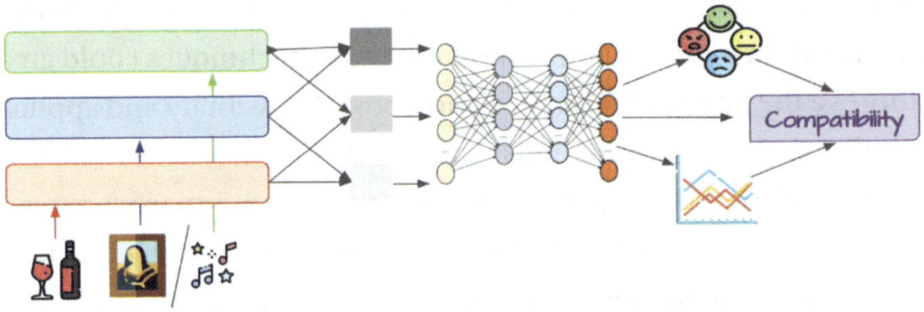

Figure 20: Multi-modal Learning for Wine Pairing.

Table 14 tabulates some of the results returned from my multi-modal models for wine and music pairings as well as wine and visual image pairings. These models will be made available as demos on the website.

[22] Please refer to Section 2.3 for an overview of multi-task learning.

Wine	Region	Vintage	Artist	Art	Compatibility
Joh. Jos. Prüm Auslese Goldkapsel	Mosel, Germany	2001	Johann Sebastian Bach	Goldberg Variations	High
Jamet Côte-Rôtie	Rhône, France	2007	Frédéric Chopin	Preludes Op.25 No.11	High
Pieropan Colvarino Soave Classico	Veneto, Italy	2016	Claude Debussy	La fille aux cheveux de lin	High
Jacques Selosse Cuvee Exquise	Champagne, France	NV	Felix Mendelssohn	String Quartet No. 2 in A minor	High
Masseto	Tuscany, Italy	2004	Niccolò Paganini	Carnival of Venice (Opus 10 MS 59)	High
Sylvain Pataille Bouzeron	Burgundy, France	2018	Aaron Copland	Four Piano Blues	High
Marcel Deiss Mambourg GC	Alsace, France	2011	Franz Liszt	Liebestraum No.3	High
Chardonnay, Au Bon Climat	Santa Barbara, US	2010	Johannes Brahms	6 Klavierstücke Op.118	Low
Henschke Hill of Grace	Eden Valley, Australia	2005	S. Rachmaninoff	Prelude Op.23 No.5	Low
Skouras Grande Cuvee	Nemea, Italy	2015	Wassily Kandinsky	Der Blaue Reiter	High
Jo Landron Les Houx	Loire Valley, France	2012	Katsushika Hokusai	The Great Wave Off Kanagawa	High
Trimbach Cuvée Frédéric Emile	Alsace, France	2011	Edgar Degas	Star Dancer	High
Gravner Bianco Breg	Friuli, Italy	2009	J.M.W. Turner	The Fighting Temeraire	High
G. Roumier Les Amoureuses	Burgundy, France	1999	Gustav Klimt	The Kiss	High
Bodega Garzón Reserva Tannat	Maldonado, Uruguay	2009	Henri Matisse	La Danse	High
Domaine des Baumard Quarts de Chaume	Loire, France	1985	Hieronymus Bosch	The Garden of Earthly Delights	High

Table 14: Results from multi-modal learning for wine pairings.

4.3 Recommender Systems

Recommender systems are ubiquitous in our daily lives to improve our user experience in the era of information overflow with overwhelmingly many available options for music, movie, online shopping, etc. Wine and wine pairing recommender systems are only one particular application of recommender systems, part of the fast evolving kaleidoscope of marketplaces vying for consumer attention and customer engagement.

Recommender systems infer user' preferences from user-item interactions or features, and recommend items that users might be interested in. Recommender systems as a research area has been popular for decades for its practical relevance and application value with plenty of opportunities and challenges still ahead. Recommender systems could be classified by tasks into **generic recommendation** and **sequential recommendation**.

Generic recommendation refers to static contexts where the recommendation algorithm aims to predict users' (assumed-to-be) static preferences based on historical user-item interaction data. For instance, given the historical records of a consumer's past wine purchases, what other wines might she be interested in? Sequential recommendation revolves around scenarios where users' preferences are best assumed dynamically evolving and the recommender systems aims to predict the next successive item(s) the user is likely to interact with, based on sequential patterns in the historical interaction data. For instance, given the historical records of sequences of what a consumer ordered at restaurants in the past, which wine(s) might he be ordering tonight at the restaurant or bar? **Session-based recommendation** is popular sub-category of sequential recommendation, where users are viewed as anonymous during engagement sessions, as opposed to identified with possibly user attributes in other sequential recommendation problems. For instance, a customer who is not one of the regulars of the bar showed up for a drink at the bar, given what he has already ordered (or maybe none ordered), what wine would he be most interested in ordering next? That would a session-based recommendation problem. Let us resume discussions about how solutions to generic versus sequential recommendation problems differ and have evolved over time towards the end of this chapter, after clarifying how and why wine recommendation is different from recommendation tasks in other widely adopted domains such as movies, products, hotels, etc., and familiarizing with widely adopted recommendation techniques and how they related to one another first.

In comparison to other domains where recommendations are widely deployed in practice, such as products (e.g., Amazon), movies (e.g., Netflix), jobs (e.g., LinkedIn), etc., recommendation in the wine industry features unique characteristics, some of which inform modifications of standard solutions, and others motivate new methods tailored for unique challenges.

First, the duration of the enjoyment of a glass of wine, whether it be out of a flight or in a dining environment, is usually much shorter than the duration of a movie, or product usage.

Second, with the ever-increasing variety and diversity the wines to sample from in the marketplace, coupled with the impressive quality of many wines at relatively low price points, it has become somewhat more forgiving with respect to wine recommendation especially when it comes to tasting flights, that one or two wines that do not perfectly fit the consumer's taste might not adversely affect user experience overall.

Third, repeated wine recommendations are sometimes appreciated especially when it comes to old favorites, as opposed to movies or durable products where recommending the same items should largely be avoided. Fortunately, deep learning frameworks are well suited for incorporating repeated recommendations due to its probabilistic nature.

Fourth, wines, just like music, paintings, and other art forms, could evoke intense emotions, oftentimes conditioned on the contexts. Therefore, context-aware and emotion-aware recommendation frameworks are perhaps highly relevant for building wine recommender systems.

Fifth, wines are often consumed in sequence, and accompanying food, typically as a flight that progresses with increasing intensity and complexity. Therefore, recommending a meaningful sequence of wines, in accordance with dishes in tandem is an important task in wine recommendation.

Lastly, wine consumption is sometimes passive, when the consumer does not pay much attention to it. It could be due to the fact that wine consumption often takes place in a social context where catching up with friends calls for full attention, or when ordering wine for a large group, usual considerations or preferences might not matter as much. This could be critical in optimizing for consumer data collection processes.

The recommendation algorithm is at the core of recommender systems, largely categorized into *collaborative filtering*, *content-based filtering*, and *hybrid* recommender systems.

Collaborative filtering (CF) approaches are based on the premises that users are likely interested in items (music, clothing, movie, wine, restaurant, etc.) favored by other people who share similar interaction patterns with them, such as having bought the same book or clothing before, having listened to the same album, liked the same restaurant or bottle of wine before, etc. For instance, if Dottie likes wines made from grape varieties Nerello Mascalese, Nebbiolo, Pinot

Noir, and Xinomavro, whereas Tootsie likes wines made from Pinot Noir, Gamay, Baga, and Nebbiolo, collaborative filtering methods would recommend Nerello Mascalese and Xinomavro to Tootsie, Gamay and Baga to Dottie. User-item interactions are usually divided into two types: explicit and implicit. Explicit interactions are perhaps considered more credible such as reviewing, rating, and liking, whereas implicit interactions such as viewing and clicking through are much more abundant than explicit ones but open to preference interpretations of user behavior and intention. CF methods require interaction traces from multiple users and items to estimate user preferences based on the similarity of users and recommended items independent of any information about users or items, thus suffering *cold start*[23] and *data sparsity* problems.

There are at least two types of collaborative filtering techniques widely used for recommendation — *neighborhood* and *latent factor* methods. *Neighborhood collaborative filtering* first learns to identify users who share similar interaction patterns with the focal user to whom recommendation is needed, and recommends to the focal user what similar users liked besides what the focal user had already experienced. The same goes for similar items. Neighborhood collaborative filtering method identifies items similar to what the focal user liked and recommends them to him or her. *Latent factor collaborative filtering* method learns unobservable (latent) factors for users and items and extrapolates to similar users and items that share latent factors for recommendation. For instance, in *latent factor collaborative filtering*, based on user-item interaction patterns, latent factors that might emerge to explain user preferences or item characteristics in the context of wine recommendation could be that some consumers appear to prefer wines that are light-bodied, flo-

[23]The cold start problem refers to when no user interaction data exists the vanilla collaborative filtering method would not be able to recommend meaningful items to users, especially when it comes to new users and items.

ral, red-berried, sometimes fizzy; whereas some prefer deep, ripe, tannic, and oaky characteristics in wine; some wines are perhaps funkier and more whimsical than others, whereas other wines are perfumy and decadent. *Latent factor collaborative filtering* methods learn to infer such latent factors first from user-item interaction data and leverage them to generalize and extrapolate for recommending items to users.

Content-based recommender systems, on the other hand, use content information extracted from users and items, such as synopses of movies, audio signals of songs, users' reviews and social networks, etc., to make predictions of user preferences over items *without* relying on any user-item interaction data. The assumption such content-based methods are based on is that users may be interested in items similar in content to what they interacted with in the past. Depending on the type of side information available for users or items, features are extracted and representations learnt, whether it be visual, textual, or graph-based. Based on how learnt feature representations of candidate items compare to those of items users had interacted with, recommendations are made, which usually lead to results similar to what the focal user liked in the past.

Hybrid recommender systems leverage both collaborative filtering and content extraction to obtain affinities between users and items at both the user-item interaction and content levels. Various external knowledge bases have been tapped, especially in content-based recommender systems, to infuse the recommender systems with rich background information, such as users' social networks demographics, interests and hobbies, item attributes (brands, categories), reviews, images, textual descriptions, audio signals, and video clips, circumventing sparsity and cold start problems common in collaborative filtering recommender systems.

During the past few decades, the paradigm of recommender systems perhaps have gradually shifted from neighborhood collaborative filtering to latent factor methods, further to content-based and hybrid methods with ever growing interests in and emphases on leveraging better representation learning to encode both users and items into a shared space. After matrix factorization methods, a class of latent factor collaborative filtering method, made headlines winning the Netflix Prize, various methods have been proposed to encode users and items to improve preference prediction, ranging from matrix factorization to deep learning.

Nowadays deep representation learning based methods have become the norm for large-scale recommender systems in academic and industry alike, due to their efficacy in capturing complex (non-linear) relationships between users and items as well as rich unstructured side information of users and items in forms of images, texts, audio signals, and videos.

To enable richly contextualized representation learning for recommender systems, especially relevant to subtly intricate domains such as wine and wine pairing, knowledge graphs (KGs, section 3.1) as side information have been shown to pay great dividends in improving recommender systems in recent years. To refresh our memory of Section 3.1, KGs consists of various types of nodes and edges. Nodes represent relevant entities such as grape variety, wine, vineyard, winery, winemaker, importer, distributor, region, country, etc., whereas edges represent various relations in-between nodes. Items and their attributes could be projected into a KG to put into perspectives their relations within the global structure. The same applies to users and their relations. Therefore a shared KG where both

users and items map to could accurately integrate information of both fronts, streamlining the estimation of more latent user-item relations that inform accurate recommendation predictions.
Greater interpretability has been cited as another reason why KG-based recommender systems are of practical relevance and efficacy. With knowledge graphs explicitly connecting users and items, it is straightforward to trace a path from an item recommended according to the recommendation algorithm to the focal use and identify the rationale.

Ever since the rise of deep learning, neural networks have become the mainstay for graph data and research development in graph neural networks (GNNs) gained tremendous momentum over the past decade. Among all the deep learning based recommender systems, graph neural network (GNN) is perhaps the most favored framework, best designed for learning from data structured as graphs, which is fundamental for modern recommender systems. Graph data is widely used to represent complex relations between concepts and entities such as social networks and knowledge graphs. In the context of recommender systems, user-item interaction data can be seen by a bipartite graph between users and items with edges representing interactions, side information conducive to recommendation quality of users and items are of naturally graph structures. For instance, user relationships can be represented as a social network, and item relations commonly represented as a knowledge graph (KG). For sequential recommendation, a sequence of items could be viewed as a sequence graph, where each item is linked to the next item(s), allowing greater flexibility and expressiveness of inter-item relations.
Not only do GNNs offer a unified graph-based framework to the recommendation applications integrating various graph structures associated with different interaction inputs and side information, but

also do they explicitly and naturally incorporate collaborative cues between users and items to improve joint representation learning through information propagation, the idea of which was pioneered in early efforts such as multi-faceted collaborative filtering [Koren, 2008], ItemRank [Gori et al., 2007], and factored item similarity model [Kabbur et al., 2013]. Multi-faceted collaborative filtering [Koren, 2008] and factored item similarity model [Kabbur et al., 2013] integrate item representations with user representations for knowledge enrichment yet ItemRank [Gori et al., 2007] rank items according to user representations using random walks along item graph representations. These early works essentially propose to use immediate neighbors' graph representations of items to augment and improve user representations, and GNNs-based recommendation methods could be viewed as generalizations to further incorporate more remote neighbors' representations into the framework, which have been shown to be rather effective for improving recommendation results.

The gist of GNNs could be perhaps summarized by the propagation process that involves aggregating feature information from neighboring nodes on the graph and integrating with the focal node representation for downstream applications. Propagation is operationalized by stacking multiple layers, each of which consists of neighborhood information aggregation and integration processes. When aggregating feature information from neighboring nodes, one could either treat all neighbors equally with *mean-pooling* [Li et al., 2015, Hamilton et al., 2017], or adjust the individual weights of neighbors based on importance with an *attention mechanism* [Veličković et al., 2017]. One could integrate the feature representations of neighbors into that of the focal node with sum operations [Veličković et al., 2017], or a Gated Recurrent Unit [Li et al., 2015], or nonlinear transformations [Hamilton et al., 2017], among various other options, depending on the specific task and context.

Graph neural networks (GNNs) could perhaps be categorized into the following groups based on architectural design and relevant data structure: recurrent GNN, spatial-temporal GNN, and graph autoencoder, and convolutional GNN. Recurrent GNNs learn aggregate representations by sharing parameters across recurrent nodes. Spatial-temporal GNNs are designed to capture both spatial and temporal dependencies of a graph simultaneously. Graph autoencoders were popular for learning compact graph representations without annotation. Convolutional GNNs, exemplified by graph convolutional networks (GCNs), are perhaps the most popular and widely adopted GNNs so far, especially in the field of recommender systems.

Graph convolutional networks (GCNs) [Kipf and Welling, 2016] encode the graph structure directly using a neural network by introducing a simple and well-behaved (linear) layer-wise propagation rule for neural network models which operate directly on graphs, motivated from a first-order approximation of spectral graph convolutions. GCNs can alleviate the problem of overfitting on local neighborhood structures for graphs with very wide node degree distributions, such as social networks, knowledge graphs and many other real-world graph datasets. Moreover, given a fixed computational budget, layer-wise linear formulations of GCNs [Kipf and Welling, 2016] afford one to build deeper models, a practice known to improve modeling capacity on a number of domains.

GraphSAGE [Hamilton et al., 2017] (SAmple and aggreGatE) is a node embedding method that extend GCNs to the task of inductive unsupervised learning and generalizes the GCNs approach to use trainable aggregation functions (beyond simple convolutions). Unlike embedding approaches that are based on matrix factorization, GraphSAGE leverages node features (e.g., text attributes, node profile information, node degrees) to learn an embedding function that generalizes to unseen nodes. By incorporating node features in the learning algorithm, GraphSAGE could simultaneously learn the topological structure of each node's neighborhood as well as the distribution of node features in the neighborhood. Instead of a distinct embedding vector for each node, a set of aggregator functions that learn to aggregate feature information from a node's local neighborhood is trained. Each aggregator function aggregates information from a different number of hops, or search depth, away from a given node. At test, or inference time, the trained system could generate embeddings for entirely unseen nodes by applying the learned aggregation functions.

Graph attention network [Veličković et al., 2017] differentiates the impact of neighboring nodes by leveraging attention mechanisms, the aggregate representations of which are integrated with the focal nodes. Such attention-based mechanism for graph representation learning is based on the assumption that the impact of neighboring nodes on the focal node is non-uniform and dynamic.

Gated Graph Sequence Neural Networks [Li et al., 2015] adapted the vanilla graph neural network [Scarselli et al., 2008] to output sequences instead of a single output. It is a typical example of recurrent GNNs, the typical propagation model is modified to use gating mechanisms like those in the iconic recurrent architectures Gated Recurrent Unit [Cho et al., 2014] and Long Short-term Memory [Hochreiter and Schmidhuber, 1997] models. After unrolling recurrence for a fixed number of steps, backpropagation could be then used through time with modern optimization methods to ensure convergence.

At the beginning of this section on *recommender systems*, we detailed how generic recommendation and sequential recommendations are different by the type of recommendation task they solve. Let us delve deeper into their respective challenges and existing solutions.

Generic recommendation assumes the users' preferences are static and estimates them based on either explicit (likes, ratings, etc.) or implicit (viewings, clicks, etc.) user interactions. A general framework for such a task is to reconstruct users' historical interactions with item and user representations. That is, given a learnt item representation and a learnt user representation, learn a preference score that describes the focal users' interactions with items most accurately. Various approaches have been proposed over the last few decades to tackle this task. Earlier works commonly take the perspective of matrix factorization where the user-item interactions are viewed as a matrix and the recommendation problem becomes a task of matrix completion. Matrix factorization methods cast users and items into a shared representation space to reconstruct the interaction matrix, enabling user preference estimation on new items. Ever since the era of deep learning, most recommendation algorithms are backed by deep learning. One line of research focuses on improving recommendations by integrating side information in forms of texts, images, audios, and videos, processed with deep learning methods. Due to the naturally graph-based structure of side information in many scenarios such as social networks as user side information, or knowledge graphs as item side information, the aforementioned graph neural networks (GNNs) are among the popular solutions to side information integration. Another line of research replaces the matrix factorization methods in early works with deep learning architectures, achieving remarkable performance boosts.

Sequential recommendation, which aims at predicting the next item(s) the focal user is most likely to engage with given sequential patterns in users' past interactions, assumes users' preferences to be context-dependent and dynamic. To further pare it down by user anonymity, session-based recommendation is a sub-category of sequential recommendation when users are considered anonymous. The major challenges of sequential recommendation problems lie in efficient learning of sequential representations that accurately describes users' preferences over time. Early works centered around Markov Chains for mimicking the dynamic transitions of users' states (mood, emotions, etc.) that manifest in preferences over options. Ever since the introduction and popularization of *recurrent neural networks (RNNs)* (mentioned in Section 2.1) for sequence learning problems, many recommender systems adopted RNNs to capture sequential patterns in user data. Likewise, *attention mechanisms* (more details in Section 7.4) have also been quickly assimilated into the sequence recommendation community to integrate the impact of entire sequences into predictions of the most likely item(s) to be chosen next. As Transformer [Vaswani et al., 2017] popularized the *self-attention mechanism,* among other groundbreaking contributions (covered in Section 7.4), some recent methods such as SASRec [Kang and McAuley, 2018] (self-attentive sequential recommendation) and BERT4Rec [Sun et al., 2019a] (sequential recommendation with BERT [Devlin et al., 2019], covered in Section 7.4) have also leveraged self-attention for better representations of item relations and greater flexibility of modeling transitions between items in sequence recommendation scenarios.

SECTION 5

Cartography

Maps are beloved in the wine world.

From my early exposure during the famed course Intro to Wine taught by the one and only Cheryl Stanley, instructor at the hotel school at Cornell, to later studies through the Court, Wine and Spirits Education Trust, and the upcoming MW program, map drawing as an effective strategy for studying wine theory has been consistently echoed by instructors along the way including Cheryl, various Master Sommeliers, Master of Wines, and other senior wine professionals.

Some (like me) leverage visual memorization by cramming all the information about a wine region into a map. For visual learners like myself, a colorfully annotated map coupled with a self-recorded wine podcast to listen to whenever and wherever is one of the most efficient ways of memorizing a large amount of factual knowledge.

Some draw wine maps and annotate texts right from scratch partly to further reinforce the geographical knowledge of wine regions, like what sommeliers Jane Lopes and Jill Zimorski have shared online. Such wine study efforts resemble what one could learn in a cartography course in college with a course project, designing and layering it up to create an informative map where a story could be readily told while picking up tidbits of geographical and geological knowledge along the way.

Some get into the art and science of cartography. Alessandro Masnaghetti, a nuclear-engineer-turned mapman who has literally put Italy's vineyards on the map, whether on paper or in a cellphone app. His maps excruciatingly details each and every parcel of wine producing regions, showcasing the elevation (especially the exquisite 3D versions), the soil type, the communes, the appellations, and other environmental elements. Having made groundbreaking maps of many wine regions including outside Italy such as Bordeaux, he is especially known for the MGA maps of Barolo and Barbaresco. Most excitingly, in 2020, he released his project Barolo MGA 360 that brought all of his work to its digital life online, where I have lost hours and hours exploring and being mesmerized while being thankful for the virtual tour around Brunate in the middle of the coronavirus (Covid-19) lockdown.

Another wine map project that has inspired me belongs to Deborah and Steve De Long, a textile designer and an architect, whose maps are a true labor of love. Steve De Long started wine blogging and turned his blog into De Long, their wine-related publishing empire of maps, charts, and accessories. I accidentally stumbled upon their Wine Grape Varietal Table many years ago and loved it so much that I immediately put it up in my living room and it followed me every time I moved over the years. It is such a wine reference chart disguised as a fine art print, organizing 184 grape varieties by body and acidity like a periodic table of elements. I happily obtained their

2020 release of an entire set of wine maps of the world after a successful crowdfunding on Kickstarter. This somehow complements Alessandro Masnaghetti's maps as even though it isn't as detailed in comparison (but that's too high a bar really), it does cover many new world wine regions not covered in Alessandro's maps, and the fine details of trees, mountains, combes (small valleys) and so forth tickle me every time I peruse.

Like many wine lovers, I greatly appreciate the exquisite pieces of wine maps with excruciating details of geology, geography, soil, vine growing, winery information, etc., and collect as many as I can throughout my wine study journey. Starting with the detailed professional maps from the World Atlas of Wine by the world famous wine writers Jancis Robinson and Hugh Johnson, produced with a team of professional cartographers, these are so comprehensive and detailed — altogether 230 of them in the eighth edition. In Jancis's words, wine, in its capacity to express a particular spot on the globe, is geography in a bottle, which makes the exceptionally detailed maps such useful and intriguing pieces of art.

As I indulged in more in-depth study on specific wine regions, I came across even more jewels of wine maps detailing each and every lieu-dit of wine lovers' favorite regions.

One of my favorite books on Champagne authored by Peter Liem includes reproductions of Louis Larmat's seven maps from the original print run back in 1944 from *Atlas de la France vinicole: Les vins de Champagne*, a fourth in a series of detailed maps of France's most notable vineyards. These remain the most detailed vineyard maps of the Champagne region publicly available.

Jasper Morris, the Burgundian wine expert and Master of Wine living in Haut Cote-de-Nuits, in his tome *Inside Burgundy*, encloses detailed maps of each and every lieu-dit of Burgundy, whether it be grand cru, 1er cru, or village. Even though Jasper himself has over time expressed dissatisfaction with the color scheme — one does occasionally find it slightly difficult to differentiate colors marking village versus 1er cru plots, I have thoroughly enjoyed learning my way through Cote d'Or with those maps where all the magical parcels scatter around conjuring up dreamy idyllic imagery of the French countryside permeated with the aroma of fermenting juice.

One could not not mention *Inside Bordeaux* by Jane Anson on this topic, released circa 2020. This beautifully crafted book reviews at length the recent evolution of economics and business, of regulation and classification, of viticultural and vinicultural practices in response to climate change, etc. But the real gems are the various visualizations — a.k.a. maps — of terroir in terms of climate (p.68-69), geology (p.75), soil (p.457), etc., accompanied by inputs from vintners verbatim informing why and how.

Lastly but not the least, the sommelier James Singh took wine map hand drawing up a notch and created the Children's Atlas of Wine, featuring these fabulous watercolor paintings of the world's wine regions.

Despite our appreciation for exquisite wine maps — especially those that perfectly combine dense, precise information and aesthetics, map making is a labor intensive and time-consuming process that requires extensive and in-depth knowledge of visual design, geography, perception, aesthetics, etc., even though the powerful modern softwares like arcGIS and Adobe Illustrator have indeed partially eased the process compared to manual map drawing. I've always lamented how few wine regions James Singh, wine map artist and sommelier, have covered so far with his masterful skills of watercolor mapping. What if, given a basic professional wine map of Burgundy, and a beautiful watercolor map (like Children's Atlas of Wine maps) of another region, say Bordeaux, we could automatically generate a beautifully rendered watercolor map of Burgundy in the style of the Bordeaux map!?

Luckily, computer vision researchers have been working hard on this exact problem — well, almost! — and with the era of deep learning, the subject of neural style transfer that exploded circa 2015 swept the field with breathtaking results, answering questions like, what would Monet have painted if he saw Degas's ballet dancers, and what Degas would have painted if presented with Monet's garden?

Figure 21: A Illustration of *Style Transfer*: given an image providing desired content, and an image providing desired style, *Style Transfer* algorithms produce images that combine the content from the content image and the style from the style image, just like how different styles of artistic paintings have been transferred to the original natural image on the top left.

Given the content image on the top left, and the three style images representative of the three artists — JMW Turner's The shipwreck of the Minotaur, 1805-1810..., Vincent van Gogh's Starry Night, and Edward Munch's The Scream, shown at the left bottom corners of the rest three images, as the respective style images, what L. Gatys and colleagues proposed as the neural style transfer algorithm generated the pleasing results of the accordingly stylized paintings. A brand new era of *(Neural) Style Transfer* thus started blooming...

How about applying it to wine maps? If only we could produce watercolor artisanal wine maps, in bulk! Turns out existing cutting edge computer vision research does have its own share of woes... And in most cases, the algorithm does not do well, especially when it comes to tiny blocks of texts intertwined with complex artistic patterns... But here is a promising first step — uCAST: unsupervised[24] CArtographic Style Transfer, by me:

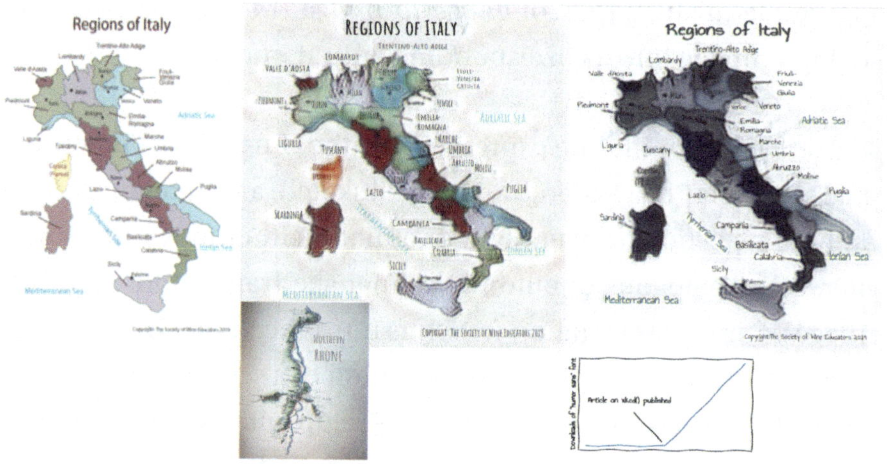

Figure 22: An Illustration of Cartographic Style Transfer. Large regional maps represent content, and the small images at the bottom represent respective styles.

We will discuss in-depth how to make it work, and what the field of neural style transfer, along with its close sibling image-to-image translation, is all about in the next few sections.

[24]Unsupervised in that we do not require paired images of identical content but different styles at the beginning for AI models to learn to make this happen.

5.1 Image-to-image Translation

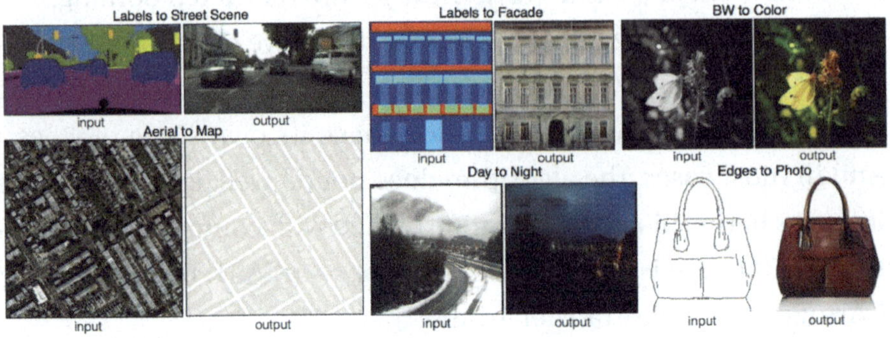

Figure 23: An illustration of *Image-to-image Translation*: translating an input image into a corresponding output image.

Just as a concept may be expressed in either English or French, a visual scene may be rendered as a pencil sketch, a watercolor cartoon, a photo realistic image at night or at noon either in winter or summer, etc. Analogous to automatic language translation, automatic image-to-image translation was thus introduced in 2018 as the task of translating one possible representation of a scene into another by then UC Berkeley researchers who came up with an all-purpose solution to unify a wide range of applications as is shown in Figure 23, widely endorsed by the online community who came up with even more creative applications like those in Figure 24.

Figure 24: Overwhelming community response to *Image-to-image Translation* generated even more creative applications.

Ever since then, image-to-image translation (sometimes abbreviated as I2I) methods have gained significant traction over the past few years, though the idea dates way back, at least to the studies of *image analogies*, introduced by Aron Hertzmann (and colleagues) at New York University and Microsoft Research back in the early 2000s, except that *image analogies* back then could be thought of as a simplified form of image-to-image translations that place various image filters on top the original image whereas image-to-image translation at its current state involves more aggressive transformation of the images as is shown in Figure 23 and Figure 24.

Such methods require image pairs each of which include one image of the original style, and the other of the desired style, sharing the exact same content preferably perfectly pixel-aligned. This is more often than not a rather restrictive constraint that could limits the practical application of such an amazing technology. Therefore, *unsupervised* image-to-image translation has been proposed to enable unpaired image datasets so that you only need two sets of images of different style to get it going. Researchers did it by introducing additional constraints in place of the pairing constraint. Some impose the aptly termed *cycle consistency* of images before and after translation: if you translate one image to another, and translate it back, it has to result in the same image. Some put on additional constraints on visual distance or geometry (*distance consistency* and *geometry consistency*, respectively), on the premise that images before and after translation should preserve the distance or geometric relationships.

All of these methods work great as long as within each set of styles — such as within a set of sketches or a separate set of watercolor paintings, the image styles are consistent and different sets of images don't differ by domain. For instance, transferring cats to dogs would probably work well whereas transferring cats to airplanes probably wouldn't. Therefore, another set of methods have been introduced to solve this *domain shift* problem and to enable AI models to generate diverse styles adapted to multiple domains, so that given an input image indicating desired content, and a set of images indicating desired styles, resulting images display a diverse set of styles.

Figure 25: An Illustration of An Image-to-image Translation Method for Multiple Modality from NVIDIA Research Lab.

What if we would like only a part of the image stylized rather than the entire image? Indeed, methods that focus image translation efforts on a patch or several patches of an image rather than the entire image have been developed to enable localized image-to-image translation. Fun applications of such methods include swapping garments in fashion images, replacing objects in either natural or synthetic images, and many more.

Figure 26: Image-to-image Translation at the Local Level. Research published by KAIST and POSTECH researchers. In the pair of images on the left, only the girls' pants are stylized into skirts; in the pair of images on the right, only sheep are stylized into giraffes.

5.2 Neural Style Transfer

Neural style transfer is a form of image-to-image translation by synthesizing a novel image by combining the content of one image with the style of another image with neural networks (hence neural). Ever since its genesis in 2015 when a paper titled "A Neural Algorithm of Artistic Style" authored by Leon A. Gatys and colleagues started circulating online, it has generated enormous interests in not only the AI research community but also the general public. Various commercial applications — Prisma, Ostagram, AlterDraw, Vinci, Artisto, Deep Forger, NeuralStyler, and Style2Paints — have since debuted and popularized by hundreds of thousands of users. With Prisma, you could easily upload an image you would like to stylize, choosing one of the hundreds of existing styles provided in the application, and get in return with a few seconds an image identical in content to the uploaded image but rendered in the style of the chosen image. It would not guarantee perfect stylization results in each and every combination but in general the outcomes are satisfying for many use cases.

Figure 27: An Illustration of Prisma Usage Before and After.

Follow up research improved the original method in terms of speed, accuracy, better application to photo-realistic images, better local stylization, enabling diverse styles, expanding to various domains, etc.
Now that image stylization has been well researched on, what about stylizing artistic fonts and texts with artistic effects?

5.3 Font and Text Effects Style Transfer

Neural font and artistic text synthesis studies apply the above-mentioned *neural style transfer* methods to generate new fonts and text effects with additional methodological modifications to deal with intricacies of texts and fonts. More recent published work addresses limitations the first few font style transfer models suffer from. For instance, previous models break down when there are any new alphabetical letters not included in the image provided as a style reference. In other words, given a stylized $\mathscr{B}$, how could we automatically produce a stylized $\mathscr{M}$? On the same note, font transfer methods between different languages especially those rather distinct like Japanese and English, have been developed.

Figure 28: An Illustration of Font Style Transfer. Given texts in a stylized font in one language (texts with a coral background), generate texts in another language with the same stylized font (texts with a robin blue background).

Figure 29: An Illustration of Text Effects Style Transfer. Given a background image, a style image, and textual content, the output is a stylized image that integrates texts in the desired style into the background image.

More seamless integration between stylized fonts and the visual background, between stylized texts and decorations dangling around artistic texts have been enabled as well by researchers at Peking University.

Now that we have stylized images and texts separately, could we combine them to stylize images that contain both visual patterns and stylized texts, such as posters, infographics, manga series, and... wine maps?

5.4 Cartographic Style Transfer

To properly style images that contain both texts and visual patterns, one plausible solution is to localize the text appearances (See Section 5.5), separate them from the visual patterns, stylize the remaining visual patterns and the text patches separately to desired styles respectively, and later combine the two back in a seamless manner. And this is exactly what I did to produce Figure 22.

5.5 Scene Text Detection and Recognition

But wait... How exactly does one automatically localize text appearances in images? The most standard methods to identify texts in images belong to the realm of *Optical Character Recognition*, which works the best when the texts are clean such as those in a scanned document or a screenshot of official documents. When it comes to stylized texts that warped, occluded, arbitrarily-oriented, or deformed, standard approaches break easily and this is where *scene text detection and recognition* methods really shine.

Scene text detection methods identify the location of the text appearances in the images, whereas *Scene text recognition* methods translate the texts in the image to plain texts as character strings.

Such models are indeed part of the backbones of wine label identification applications such as Vivino and Deletable, with which you can log your wine in terms of producer, region, and vintage automatically as soon as you upload an image of the bottle with labels visible. Challenging images usually fall into the following categories: (a) Difficult fonts, which are not uncommon on wine bottles; (b) Vertical texts; (c) Special characters. (d) Occlusion; for instance, if a bottle label is behind a wine glass not entirely visible; (e) Low resolution.

Figure 30: An Illustration of Scene Text Detection. Small texts were not captured.

Latest advancement in this realm usually revolve around improving performance in one or more of these challenging scenarios. In addition, there are also alternative modeling frameworks to tackle the wine labeling identification problem, some of which are similar to the popular face recognition frameworks, but that would be a whole other story.

Figure 31: An Illustration of Scene Text Recognition. Small texts were ignored.

To put things in perspective situated within the bigger picture, Scene Text Detection and Recognition are subsets of the more generally applicable and fundamental tasks *Object Detection* and *Image Recognition* where the object of interest was food. We will get into finer details about *Image Recognition* in Section 7.5 and Section 6.4.

6

SECTION

World of Wine

There appears a unanimous piece of advice passed on to (aspiring) wine professionals and enthusiasts about how to learn about wine. That is, to be on the road as much as possible, visiting vineyards and cellars in different continents and climatic zones, learning about various vine-growing and winemaking practices from local vignerons as well as the rationales thereof. Indeed, in this era of globalization, *flying winemakers* are increasingly the norm, rather than the exception. Despite the almost vilifying portrayal in the indie movie *Mondovino* of Michel Rolland , the famed Bordeaux-based oenologist having consulted with over two hundred wineries across thirteen countries, along side vividly featured personalities including Aimé Guibert from Mas de Daumas Gassac in Languedoc and Hubert de Montille from De Montille in Volnay as those who are adamantly against such phenomena of globalization and mechanization. *Flying winemakers*, Michel Rolland being an early exemplar of whom, are perhaps more likely lauded than frowned upon nowadays for more experience in diverse contexts, greater global exposure, and perhaps higher levels of engagement in the global information sharing network of the wine industry.

Among flying winemakers, there are the focused type, growing and vinifying roughly the same varieties in different parts of the world, with experience gained in-between perhaps directly applicable to another, thus creating synergies and accelerating experimentation. Perhaps one case in point is the ever growing connections between Burgundy and Oregon, the two heart lands of Pinot Noir. When the Steamboat Conference organized by Oregon to foster information sharing between Oregon and California started in early 1980s, it was the Burgundians who began attending this event that made a memorable impression on Oregon winemakers. Robert Drouhin of Domaine Drouhin, having visited Oregon as early as the 1970s became the first to settle down in Dundee Hills by establishing Domaine Drouhin Oregon, putting the limelight on the Oregon wine industry, and contributing to a long-lasting relationship between them. Michel Lafarge, Louis-Michel Liger-Belair, Dominique Lafon, Jean-Nicolas Méo, Matthieu Gille, Louis Jadot, Jean-Marc Fourrier, and the likes have all since participated with regularity in the Steamboat Conference as well as the International Pinot Noir Celebration (IPNC) shortly after every July. Some of them have been producing Oregon wine for more than a decade now. Oregon does offer plenty in common with Burgundy. The midpoint of the Willamette Valley lies at 45 degrees north latitude, the same as for Burgundy's Cote d'Or. Vintages in Oregon tend to parallel those in Burgundy. Oregon wineries have always been small, family-owned affairs, just like in Burgundy. The early clones such as Wädenswil[25] and Pommard[26] supposedly all came from Burgundy through UC Davis. And in the 1980s, thanks to Dr. Raymond Bernard, the Dijon clones finally came through from Domaine Ponsot's vines in Morey-St.-Denis. It is no wonder that, David Lett, the founder of the historic Eyrie Winery in Dundee Hill, searched the whole world for a perfect place outside Burgundy to plant his beloved Pinot Noir grapes, whether it be the south island of New Zealand, or Minho in northern Portugal, and finally settled down in Dundee Hill of Willamette Valley.

Dominique Lafon once contrasted Oregon against Burgundy, based on a decade's experience working with Evening Land and Lingua Franca: being the new world site with a much bigger acreage, Oregon allows much greater room for experimentation and exploration, compared to Burgundy, where, for instance, Volnay Champans affords you one single tank, leaving no room for trial and error, and thus perhaps much less risk taking ensued. Despite similar weather or climate, unlike Burgundy where frost damage has caused significant stress and crop loss in consecutive years in the last decade, there appears no ripeness issue in Oregon, nor do you have to worry about botrytis attack or downy mildew in general, if you pick early when bud breaks early and later when bud breaks late. In the cellar it is similar between the two, except perhaps slightly lengthier fermentation for reds, and maceration or extraction techniques have to be adapted to Oregon. Due to the differences of market competition and consumer profiles, sometimes it could be tricky to convince business partners and push for elegance and freshness in wine, as it could run counter to the expectation of American consumers whose palate might prefer greater power in Pinot Noirs than their

[25] It was brought in by David Lett of Eyrie Winery in 1965.

[26] It was brought in by Dick Erath and Charles Coury circa late 1960s, generally considered to be bolder in color, flavor, and structure than Wädenswil.

French counterparts. He relishes in the fact that his experience gained and techniques learnt in Oregon feed back to working in homeland for Domaine des Comtes Lafon, and his own labels Dominique Lafon, as well as Heritiers du Comte Lafon in Macon.

Similar stories keep repeating. Guillaume d'Angerville of the Volnay mainstay Marquis d'Angerville discovered the potential of Jura and established Domaine Pelican there, the beautiful name of which symbolized the link between Jura and Burgundy through an old tale of Arbois. He makes his Jura wine with a signature Volnay touch. This all started with a blind tasting he had in his usual restaurant in Paris when he was so convinced that the Jura Chardonnay was Burgundian. Jean-Baptiste Lecaillon, the *chef de cave* at Champagne Louis Roederer made sparkling wines around the globe — most notably at Jansz Winery in Tasmania — before settling down in Reims of Champagne. Christian Moueix, the former director of Château Pétrus in Pomerol for 38 years, searched around the world for the perfect terrior to grow Bordeaux varieties and stumbled upon the hillside Napanook vineyard in Yountville of Napa Valley. And the list goes on... For a Pinot purist who is always searching for a place around the globe that resembles, for instance, Chambolle-Musigny, how could one identify the most probable candidate regions among hundreds, if not thousands, of wine producing regions in the world with evolving climatic conditions in a most efficient way? Wouldn't it be awesome if we could automatically identify the places that look most similar to Chambolle-Musigny at a global scale? *What makes Burgundy look like Burgundy, and Chambolle-Musigny look like Chambolle-Musigny* anyway? Luckily, computer vision scientists have thought long and hard about such questions over the past few decades. In Section 6.1 I will illustrate how AI models could be used to quickly identify Burgundy look-alikes, or any [insert your favourite wine region] look-alikes. And in Section 6.5, I will detail ways to better understand Burgundy, or any of [your favourite wine regions], from a visual singularity point of view, by identifying signature or archetypal visual patterns that make Burgundy so unique.

Besides the purists who look over every corner of the world to find similar vineyard plots or the almost exact replica, there is another camp of *flying wine professionals*, or *flying wine enthusiasts* whose goals might appear orthogonal to those of the purists, which are, to experience as many as possible different vintages, climatic, geological and geographical characteristics, as well as grape varieties in terms of vine-growing and winemaking on the part of wine professionals, and tasting (drinking) or learning on the part of wine consumers. Such is a rather daunting undertaking, given everyone of us is constrained by limited amount of time, funding, and energy, in face of the vast wine world left to explore.

The life experience of Jean-Pierre de Smet, a co-founder and partner of Domaine de'Arlot in Nuits-Saint-George before his retirement in 2007, is perhaps one of those that best embodies the globetrotting lifestyle. Serendipitously, that led him to wine in the end.

Born in UK with a Belgium root, he moved to Nice soon after, and at the age of 20 years old in 1966, he left for Paris for education where he developed his long-lasting passion for skiing, racing, and other outdoor activities. This is how he met his wife, Liz, who is a close friend of Jacques Seysses of Domaine Dujac in Morey St Denis. The couple moved over to New Caledonia in the southwest Pacific Ocean, east of Australia, spending long hours at sea for years. They took a ten-year-long professional break from the accounting business in the late 70s till the 80s, indulging (in a great way) in various outdoor activities like sailing straight for three years, three times around the world! During this period, they, being close friends with

Jacques Seysses, visited Domaine Dujac various times, helping with the harvest. This is also where they formed connections with wine growers in other parts of France, such as the now-famed Alain Graillot whom Jean-Pierre helped with the first few vintages when Alain finally took the plunge to make wine in 1995 in Croze-Hermitage. It was this formative ten-year break that steered the course of Jean-Pierre towards a Burgundian winemaker forever. By the time to go back to work, it became obvious for the couple that winemakers like Jacques Seysses were what they ought to be, and the rest is history.

Benjamin Leroux, the former head winemaker at Comte Armand in Pommard for 15 years (1999-2014), and now the proprietor of Benjamin Leroux winery in Beaune, is another fine example whose critical thinking about vine-growing and winemaking practices over the past few decades and more importantly in the future where climate change is ever more imminent could at least be partially attributed to his extensive travelling and training experience at the beginning of and throughout his career in regions like South Africa, Bordeaux, Oregon, New Zealand, etc. outside Burgundy and besides Pinot Noir and Chardonnay grapes. To digress just a bit for a discussion on climate change, to be cycled back later as you will see: what are some potential answers to vine-growing and winemaking adaptations in Burgundy in face of climate change? With warmer and dried prospects in 50 years, more clay in soil that better retains water in droughts, higher density planting (up to 12,000 vines per hectare) of Aligoté, Chardonnay, and Pinot Beirout together and co-fermenting or blending into Chardonnay a bit of Aligoté or Pinot Beirout, grass cover, better sprayers and tractors, adjustment of trimming, hedging, and pruning strategies to be robust to extreme weathers, etc., require extensive experimentation and risk-taking to find answers in every aspect of the profession, ranging from new ways of grafting in the nurseries at the start, to reexamining harvest decision-making, from improvement in bottling processes to accommodate changes in the environment and in the bottle, to possible distribution logistical modifications as well as new rounds of consumer education about the changes in place. With warmer cellars, we are seeing shifts in malolactic fermentation practices in response to changes in the composition of acids along with pH: less lactic acids (milk cream) due to less malic acids (green apple) resulting in less coarse lees sediment thus mostly fine lees at the bottom, and more zesty tartatric acids. Much longer aging on fine lees, less racking, less time in barrels, more stainless steel usage, and more infusion rather extraction, are among the evolving practices seen in most recent warm vintages throughout Burgundy.

Such sentiments have been echoed in many other parts of the globe. For instance, Gaia Gaja of the iconic Gaja winery in Barbaresco of Piedmont shared similar vineyard management strategies in coping with warmer, drier and more intense sunlight over time. Her father, the legendary Angelo Gaja, an advocate of the artisan spirit distilled from his grandmother in the wise words of *fare, sapere fare, sapere far fare, far sapere* (meaning *to do, to know how, to teach, to broadcast knowledge*), emphasized their focus on *selection massale* to build greater resilience against the climate change. Angelo Gaja, the revolutionary and controversial figure featured in the documentary *Barolo Boys,* is another early example in the camp of globetrotters among Italian winemakers. It was after visiting Burgundy, seeing the drastic contrast in the financial and market situation in the that he decided to revolutionize with new cellar practices of shorter maceration and new French barriques. It was after visiting Robert Mondavi at the time of Zelma Long, and Hanzell winery helmed by James Zellerbach, being exposed to the large-scale experimentation with international grape varieties and sophisticated marketing programs, that he decided to cultivate international grape varieties Chardonnay, Sauvignon Blanc, and Cabernet Sauvignon back at home. To establish long-lasting business relationships with important distribution markets, he has travelled extensively to almost every corner of the globe, New York City being a most regular historical destination.

For newcomers to the wine scene (or experienced wine veterans alike), eager to learn in a most efficient way and constrained by time and money. How shall one select, for instance, twenty regions out of the hundreds of wine regions in the world to visit, such that we could maximize the amount of valuable information taken in, possibly by covering an optimal set of destinations that balances importance with diversity in terms of climates, geology, geography, vinegrowing, and winemaking? This problem is very much relevant to the field of **Active Learning**, where the active learner seeks out a small subset of data samples that is most valuable for maximizing learning potential. We will detail the principles of **Active Learning** in Section 6.2, its relevance in the era of deep learning today, and showcase how it could be applied to our search for a diverse set of wine regions in practice.

For an experienced world traveller who frequent vineyards and cellars like those mentioned above and many others, it takes a mere split second to identify what the region and which vineyard or cellar is if given an image of the place. Imagine you are walking inside the vineyard pictured in Figure 32 right now, surrounded by rows of Riesling vines on vertical shoot positioning (VSP) training systems with fertile clay and slate soils underneath, breathing in the chilly and humid spring air. Where exactly do you think it could possibly be?

VINEYARD GUESSR

Figure 32: The Vineyard Guessr game.

Another great memory of yours perhaps took place in the cellar in Figure 33. It was one of the most incredible sensory experiences — the unique mix of fragrance in the air permeated with fresh sea breezes, crushed grapes, and cherry blossoms. You indulge in the bouquet of the glass just thiefed out of the old neutral barrels and handed over to you by the proprietor, while feel amazed by walls of stacked barrels that surround you. Where in the world is this and which cellar does all of this belong to?

Let us introduce the wine lover version of the beloved *Geo Guessr* game: *Vineyard Guessr* and *Cellar Guessr*. *Geo Guessr* places the player on a series of semi-random locations around the world. And the rule of the game is to guess the geo-location of the environment the player is placed in. In *Vineyard Guessr* and *Cellar Guessr*, however, a player is placed in a series of different vineyards and cellars, and the goal is to guess as many as possible the associated regions or parcels, and the wineries correctly, respectively. Figure 34 and Figure 36 show collages of vineyards and cellars with Figure 35 and Figure 37 zooming in on parts of Figure 34 and Figure 36, respectively. Some of the vineyards are distinctly different than the rest:

the ash crate of the canary islands, the old gnarly vines on a barren sandy plateau of Yecla, the basket vines of Santorini... These are indeed the softballs whereas others, especially those with the universally adopted vertical shoot positioning trellising systems, not so much...

Figure 33: The Cellar Guessr game.

This setting happens to coincide with a classic computer vision problem — Image Geolocalization or Place Recognition, about which many researchers in the fields of computer vision, machine learning, and robotics have developed various approaches over time. In Section 6.3 and Section 6.4 let us review this line of efforts in the AI community and explore how it could be applied to vineyards and cellars.

Figure 34: A photo-mosaic collage of a vineyard with vineyard images around the world included in the Vineyard Guessr game.

Figure 35: Zooming in on the bottom left corner of Figure 34, a photo-mosaic collage of a vineyard with vineyard images around the world included in the Vineyard Guessr game.

Figure 36: A photo-mosaic collage of a cellar with cellar images around the world included in the Cellar Guessr game.

Figure 37: Zooming in on the bottom left corner of Figure 36, a photo-mosaic collage of a cellar with cellars images around the world included in the Cellar Guessr game.

But how would you go about figuring it out? What are the visual clues you would be looking for to get a better chance of correct answers? To circle back to the quintessential question raised earlier in this section, what exactly makes Burgundy look like Burgundy? Or what makes [*insert your favorite vineyard or cellar here*] look like [*insert your favorite vineyard or cellar here*]? In Section 6.5, let us detail ways to better understand a place by its unique visual patterns that distinguish it from everywhere else in the world.

6.1 Image Retrieval

Image retrieval refers to the task of searching for similar images to a given query image from the user in a large image database by analyzing their visual content. An efficient and accurate solution to such a long-standing research topic in the field of computer vision has never been more important and sought-after with the exponentially increasing amount of images and video data online. Image retrieval algorithms have already penetrated many aspects of the society and our lives by enabling medical image search, face re-identification, product recommendation, etc., and here we are applying it to search for similar vineyards around the globe.

Searching for the desired images could feel like finding the needle in a haystack, especially in large-scale image databases of millions, if not billions of images. Searching efficiently is therefore, no less critical than searching accurately. At the core of image retrieval systems lies in compact and yet rick *visual feature representations*, which has been what a majority of technical advances in image retrieval methods focused on.

Before deep learning revolutionized the field of machine learning in the early 2010s, image retrieval methods were dominated by feature engineering, symbolized by various visual feature descriptors such as Scale-Invariant Feature Transform (SIFT), Speed-up Robust Features (SURF), Binary Robust Independent Elementary Features (BRIEF), Oriented FAST and Rotated BRIEF (ORB), Histogram of Oriented Gradients (HOG), GIST, etc. many of which are still widely in use today.

Ever since 2012 when AlexNet [Krizhevsky et al., 2012] re-ignited the potential of convolutional neural networks with deep learning and ImageNet [Deng et al., 2009], feature representation learning with deep convolutional neural networks has become the default approach for not only image retrieval, but various other computer vision tasks such as image classification, object detection, and semantic segmentation. The name "convolutional neural network" indicates that the network uses a mathematical operation termed *convolution*, a specialized kind of linear operation. And convolutional networks are neural networks that use convolution in place of general matrix multiplication in some of their layers [Goodfellow et al., 2016]. The past decade has witnessed tremendous progress towards more efficient and accurate image retrieval systems built with deep convolutional neural networks. The proliferation of technical methods could be roughly summarized into the following categories based on causes of algorithmic improvement:

Neural Network Architectures: from LeNet [LeCun et al., 1998] to AlexNet
[Krizhevsky et al., 2012], from GoogLeNet (Inception) [Szegedy et al., 2015] to ResNet [He et al., 2016], from DenseNet [Huang et al., 2017a] to EfficientNet [Tan and Le, 2019], ... What made a difference is not only going deeper and wider, but also a great deal of scientific and engineering ingenuity;

Visual Feature Extraction: how to extract rich yet compact features from deep neural networks and how to combine them most efficiently for image retrieval involved lots of experimentation with trials and errors, the results of which benefited not only image retrieval, but all around;

Visual Feature Fusion: the question of how to efficiently fuse extracted feature representations from multiple sources, tailored to various tasks, datasets, and contexts, that has taken center stage in multi-modal (Section 4.2) and multimedia research domains to some extent;

Neural Network Fine-tuning and **Domain Adaptation**: either fine-tuning or domain adapting a pre-trained large-scale convolutional neural network for image classification tasks greatly improves model performance on a different domain, which perhaps appears serendipitous and the exact reason why is yet to be fully understood;

Metric Learning (detailed in Section 4.1): an approach based directly on a distance metric that aims to establish similarity or dissimilarity between data points by mapping them to an embedding space where similar samples are close together and dissimilar ones are far apart. The idea dates back at least to Siamese Networks [Hadsell et al., 2006], has shown promisingly scalable results for image retrieval.

Within this first category, let me detail the architectural improvements over time, which not only enabled tremendously more efficient and powerful image retrieval systems, but also boosted the performance of computer vision algorithms on a wide range of vision tasks.

Figure 38 visualizes the major milestones in terms of architectural advances in convolutional neural networks (CNNs) over time, and Table 15 summarizes each one of them in terms of scientific contributions, model parameters or model capacity that signals efficiency or learning capability, as well as corresponding references.

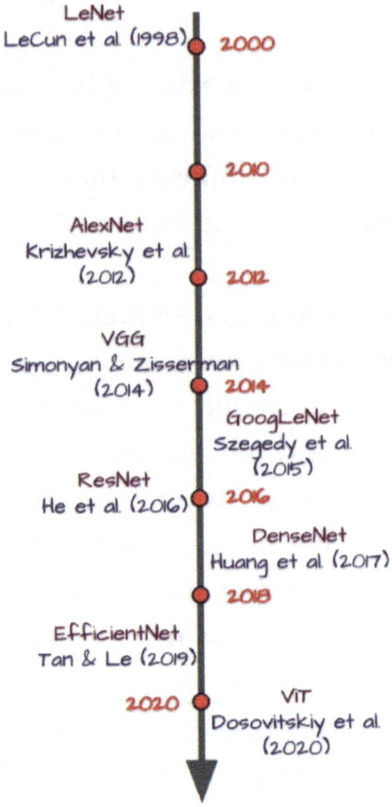

Figure 38: A timeline of major architectural milestones of convolutional neural networks in Computer Vision.

LeNet [LeCun et al., 1998], best known as the first convolutional neural networks, was proposed by Yan LeCun in 1998 for handwritten digit recognition to showcase the advantage of convolutional neural works operated directly on pixel images over hand-crafted feature extraction of the past. It was one of the few research efforts that demonstrated the traditional way of building recognition systems by manually integrating individually designed modules can be replaced by a unified and well-principled design paradigm, even though the lack of computing power or large-scale image datasets at the time largely stifled its scalability and practical applications.

It wasn't until early 2000s, with the introduction of graphic processing units (GPUs)[27], the release of large-scale visual recognition datasets and more efficient training regimes that deep neural networks — and deep convolutional neural networks — were brought back into the limelight with the revival of deep learning.

Architecture	Year	Summary of Main Contributions	Parameters	Reference
LeNet	1998	First popular convolutional neural net.	0.06M	[LeCun et al., 1998]
AlexNet	2012	Deeper and wider than LeNet with ReLU, Dropout...	60M	[Krizhevsky et al., 2012]
VGG	2014	Simple yet deeper topology with 1x1 convolution.	138M	[Simonyan and Zisserman, 2014]
GoogLeNet	2015	Inception block that splits, transforms, and merges.	4M	[Szegedy et al., 2015]
ResNet	2016	Skip connections, Residual learning.	6.8M	[He et al., 2016]
DenseNet	2017	Cross-layer information flow.	14M	[Huang et al., 2017a]
EfficientNet	2019	Efficient model scaling with a compounding factor.	(b0) 5.3M (b6) 43M (v2) 24M	[Tan and Le, 2019]
Vision Transformer	2020	Transformer [Vaswani et al., 2017] architecture for vision tasks.	86M	[Dosovitskiy et al., 2020]

Table 15: A Summary of Recent Architectures of Deep Convolutional Neural Networks.

AlexNet [Krizhevsky et al., 2012] came along at the cusp of the deep learning renaissance and marked the beginning of deep convolutional neural networks, with image classification and recognition results that dwarfed shallow machine learning models (reducing the

[27]NVIDIA launched the CUDA platform, the current mainstay for deep learning workstations, in 2007.

error rate by around 10% when previous improvements had been incremental around low single digit), having leveraged parallel computing with GPUs and a deeper architecture than LeNet [LeCun et al., 1998] while averting overfitting with Dropout [Hinton et al., 2012] regularization technique.

Ever since then, the field has exploded with new neural architectures every year, some of which rose up to the top in image recognition competitions. After AlexNet [Krizhevsky et al., 2012], a number of research works devoted to improving the performance of convolutional neural networks with parameter optimization and restructuring. VGG [Simonyan and Zisserman, 2014] from the Visual Geometry Group of Oxford was one of them. VGGNet investigated the effect of the convolutional network depth on its accuracy for large-scale image recognition problems, and concluded that a significant improvement on the prior-art neural network architecture configurations could be achieved by pushing the depth to 16-19 layers, which also generalizes well to a variety of datasets.

Soon after, GoogLeNet [Szegedy et al., 2015] (paying tribute to LeNet), codenamed Inception, which derives its name from the idea of network-in-network in previous literature [Lin et al., 2013] in conjunction with the infamous "we need to go deeper" internet meme, further reduced the computational cost with a wider and deeper architectural design by a carefully crafted design, the hallmark of which is the improved utilization of the computing resources by multi-scale and multi-level transformation such that both local and global information are captured and subtle details of images noted.

Perhaps the watershed moment of deep convolutional neural networks came around in 2015 when Kaiming He and his colleagues at Microsoft came up with ResNet [He et al., 2016] in which residual blocks were introduced to drastically deepen the network architecture (20 times AlexNet and 8 times VGG) with even less computational complexity, achieving impressive performance improvement as much as 28% on object detection tasks. Even though the idea of cross-layer connectivity was not new, it was ResNet that pioneered within-layers shortcuts to enable cross-layer connection without additional data or parameters, effectively solving the notorious problem of diminishing gradient and speeding up training with faster convergence.

As a followup to ResNet, DenseNet [Huang et al., 2017a] out of Cornell University took this line of research even further by connecting each layer to every other layer. For each layer, the feature-maps of all preceding layers are used as inputs, and its own feature-maps are used as inputs into all subsequent layers. By doing so, they alleviated the vanishing-gradient problem, strengthened feature propagation, encouraged feature reuse, and substantially reduced the number of parameters.

In 2019, with automatic search of optimal neural architecture all the range for a while, EfficientNets [Tan and Le, 2019] once again upped the game over DenseNet by systematically scaling and carefully balancing network depth, width, and resolution that lead to better performance in terms of higher accuracy yet much faster inference time relative to previous generations of deep convolutional networks at different scales.

At the same time, the parallel field of natural language processing was also going through a series of transformations with the Transformer [Vaswani et al., 2017] architecture being one of the milestone discoveries of the generation. Having been dancing around each other as two closely intertwined research fields as computer vision and natural language processing (exemplified in multi-modal learning covered in Section 4.2), it did not come as a surprise as Vision Transformer (ViT) [Dosovitskiy et al., 2020] showcased how Transformers could replace standard convolutions in deep neural networks on large-scale computer vision datasets by applying the original Transformer architecture meant for natural languages (with minimal changes) on a sequence of image patches (just like a sequence of English words in a sentence) and achieving results comparable to ResNet.

All of these architectural advances spilled over to large-scale image retrieval systems which rely on the architectural backbones, enabling performance boosts regardless of specific application contexts, datasets, or targeted domains.

Feature extraction from deep convolutional neural networks could take on various forms, depending on characteristics of the neural architecture in use, diversity of input data, major challenges and objectives of task at hand, to name just a few. Let us compare and contrast the following strategies from the perspectives of global versus local features, single-scale versus multi-scale features, and strategic selection processes.

- Feature extraction from the last fully-connected and/or convolutional layer: since fully-connected layers do not capture spatial information within images, the last convolutional layer could be extracted instead or at the same time to capture geometric variances that could matter for image retrieval tasks. These features, after normalization and possibly dimension reduction with whitening, could be used directly for similarity measurements between query images and references images in image retrieval tasks.

- Feature extraction from various layers of convolutional neural networks: since it has been shown with convolutional network visualization research that the later or deeper layers capture more global and semantic information while earlier or shallower layers capture finer and more local details such as texture, sampling from not only the last layers but also early or intermediate layers sometimes lead to a more comprehensive understanding of images.

- Multi-scale feature extraction: rather than a single image as a whole, multiple image patches of different scales could be selected and processed for visual feature representation before being encoded as a final global feature, such a strategy could lead to high retrieval accuracy due to paying attention to different scales that might matter in image retrieval tasks, despite sacrificing retrieval efficiency.
- Strategic choices of which image patches to focus on: instead of generating multi-scale image patches randomly or densely, region proposal methods introduced a principled way to choose patches that contain salient objects to direct attention to, improving scene understanding capabilities of the algorithm in various contexts and applications including image retrieval.

After efficient extraction of visual features from deep convolutional neural networks, **feature fusion** based on extracted deep visual feature representations could be done at different stages of the pipeline and in different forms:
Within-model fusion: there exists various methods to fuse together features from different neural network layers depending on the number and nature of the layers. One could fuse features from multiple different fully-connected layers with an optimal aggregation strategy with different balancing weights. When multiple fully-connected layers run in parallel on top of a ResNet architecture as the backbone, one could concatenate the global features from all these layers to obtain combined global features. Features from fully-connected layers (global features), and those from convolutional layers (local features), could complement each other to improve image retrieval

systems to some extent. To account for both textual and semantic information in images, one could concatenate both global and local features, or adopt more strategic fusion approaches to leverage local features to distinguish subtle feature differences after filtering first with global features when it comes to finalizing the candidate list of image retrieval. Lastly, the optimal selection of which layer combination is better suited for fusion could also result in noticeable improvement in the accuracy of image retrieval systems in the end.

Between-model fusion: multiple models could be selectively aggregated as an ensemble to allow for greater generalization to new contexts or domains. The wildly popular Dropout regularization technique could be interpreted as an ensemble of randomly chosen subnetworks, whereas in VGGNet [Simonyan and Zisserman, 2014] , the authors showed that two different architectures VGG-16 and VGG-19 could be fused to further improve feature learning. Selective ensemble of different ResNet architectures have also been explored to showcase promising accuracy improvement in image retrieval. Furthermore, concatenating feature representations from ResNet and Inception, or VGGNet and AlexNet, or an even wider range of convolutional models with some parameter tweaking has all shown improvement in image retrieval applications.

According to fusion timing and mechanism, we could perhaps further illustrate by the following categories:

- *Early Fusion*: when combining features from two separate models, one could concatenate the immediate feature representations first before passing on to further similarity learning modules, and such could be considered an early fusion strategy;
- *Late Fusion*: instead of fusing feature representations immediately after separate convolutional models, one could apply

similarity learning modules separately to generate final scores from which image retrieval results could be derived directly, and such a method would be considered a late fusion strategy;

- *Feature projection (embedding)*: instead of simple concatenation of feature representations from different models, one could also project them to a common feature space for feature alignment, reducing potential feature redundancy in terms of either local textures or global semantics, thus conducive to better feature selection for the purpose of image search or image retrieval;

- *Attention mechanism*: more recent advances in feature fusion and feature space embedding come from attention mechanisms, one of which the Transformer [Vaswani et al., 2017] architecture is known for. The core of attention mechanism, inspired by how human perception works, is to highlight the most relevant features while downplaying irrelevant feature activations. One could learn the attention map signalling feature importance by pooling features across RGB channels or by patch. Alternatively, a prior belief about which parts of the image could result in more important features could also be incorporated. Perhaps a more principled approach is to learn attention maps of feature importance from deep neural networks themselves, with the inputs being image patches, or features learnt from previous convolutional layers, or even an entire image;

- *Image hashing*: applying hashing methods to feature representations to transform deep features into more compact codes has been widely used for large-scale image search due to benefits of computational and memory efficiency.

Just like many other applications and tasks in computer vision, **domain adaptation** (e.g., given a classification model working perfectly on daytime images, make it work perfectly for nighttime images too) or *fine-tuning* (given a classification model working perfectly to distinguish between cats and dogs, make it work perfectly to distinguish between bears and bunnies too) are standard approaches to adapt to specific contexts, datasets, and tasks in practice. A classification model domain-adapted or fine-tuned on specific datasets similar to what one wishes to apply the algorithms to eventually could generally improve the generalizability and robustness of the deep learning model, possibly mitigating the issue of knowledge transfer for image retrieval tasks, but not without limitations such as requiring (probably costly) cleanly annotated images, or error prone at fine-grained classes.

Given extracted visual features from deep neural networks, an efficient alternative to an image retrieval framework based on classification is **metric learning**, which we have introduced in Section 4.1 when learning which wine pairing works the best. The same framework has long been applied to image retrieval tasks in that with metric learning, one strives to learn how to accurately measure the distance between two images based on their feature representations. To avoid repeating ourselves, please refer to Section 4.1 for a review of fundamental methods in the realm of *metric learning*.

After experimenting with and applying various image retrieval frameworks described in this chapter to identify vineyards around the world that look the most similar to Gevrey-Chambertin, Central Otago, Alsace, and Finger Lakes, I tabulated the top five regions returned for each of the four queries in Table 16, most of which perhaps do not come as a surprise after all.

Query	Top 1	Top 2	Top 3	Top 4	Top 5
Gevrey-Chambertin, France	Morey-Saint-Denis, France	Savigny-Lès-Beaune, France	Chambolle-Musigny, France	Chassagne-Montrachet, France	Thermen-region, Austria
Central Otage, New Zealand	Columbia Valley, US	Nelson, New Zealand	Simikame-en Valley, Canada	Marlborough, New Zealand	Lake County, US
Alsace, France	Franken, Germany	Barbaresco, Italy	Barolo, Italy	Pfalz, Germany	Alto-Adige, Italy
Finger Lakes, US	Okanagan Valley, Canada	Lake Erie North Shore, Canada	Niagara Peninsula, Canada	Tasmania, Australia	Geelong, Australia

Table 16: Top five image retrieval results for Gevrey-Chambertin, Central Otago, Alsace, and Finger Lakes.

However when applied to Jumilia, Ningxia, Beqaa Valley, and Swartland, the results in Table 17 might look more interesting (especially to those not terribly familiar with these terrains).

Query	Top 1	Top 2	Top 3	Top 4	Top 5
Jumilia, Spain	Yecla, Spain	Utiel-Requena, Spain	Toro, Spain	Valdepeñas, Spain	Calatayud, Spain
Uco Valley, Argentina	Vayots Dzor, Armenia	Maipo Valley, Chile	Luján de Cuyo, Argentina	Ningxia, China	Breedekloof, South Africa
Beqaa valley, Lebanon	Campo de Borja, Spain	Yunnan, China	Rio Negro, Argentina	Elqui, Chile	Aconcagua Valley, Chile
Swartland, South Africa	Franschhoek Valley, South Africa	Paarl, South Africa	Macedonia, Greece	Bierzo, Spain	Grampians, Australia

Table 17: Top five image retrieval results for Jumilia, Ningxia, Beqaa Valley, and Swartland.

What if we set out to search anywhere in the opposite hemisphere, rather than the entire globe? For example, a winemaker in the northern hemisphere might want to focus on winemaking during and after harvest time at his or her own home estate or country in the second half of a year, therefore prefers to seek winemaking opportunities in the southern hemisphere at harvest in the first half of a year when he or she is free from obligations at his own estate in the home country. Vice versa for a vintner based in the southern hemisphere. Here in Table 18 are the top five image retrieval results if we hypothetically constrain ourselves to the opposite hemisphere.

Query	Top 1	Top 2	Top 3	Top 4	Top 5
Gigondas, France	Itata Valley, Chile	Robertson, South Africa	Malleco Valley, Chile	Cape Town, South Africa	Eden Valley, Australia
Central Otage, New Zealand	Columbia Valley, US	Simikameen Valley, Canada	Lake County, US	Puget Sound, US	Horse Heaven Hills, US
Hawke's Bay, New Zealand	Santa Barbara, US	Rutherford, US	Petaluma Gap, US	Vancouver Island, Canada	Santa Lucia Highlands, US
Finger Lakes, US	Tasmania, Australia	Geelong, Australia	King Valley, Australia	Auckland, New Zealand	Gippsland, Australia

Table 18: Top five image retrieval results in the opposite hemisphere for Gigondas, Central Otago, Hawke's Bay, and Finger Lakes.

All the above retrieval results are based on visual patterns alone, which is probably not enough if one sets out to identify a place that resembles a particular *lieu-dit* (named place) in practice, since a multitude of other factors such as climate, soil, elevation, irrigation, aspect, proximity to water body, etc. matter even though sometimes such information could be inferred from images. Therefore, *multi-modal information retrieval* that would enable the global search by taking in account all these important factors besides visual features could prove even more practical and relevant. This is still a relatively nascent research area and leveraging multi-modal information retrieval algorithms with multi-modal knowledge graphs for wine is certainly one of the exploratory research projects I am looking forward to taking on in the near future.

6.2 Active Learning

Assume that we are faced with a large pool of potential wine region destinations that we are unfamiliar with, active learning, a sub-field of machine learning, which aims to boost AI model performance with the least amount of data, would then select the most useful samples from the pool of destinations for us to visit and examine such that by only visiting a small set of carefully chosen destinations well within our budget, we in fact learn no less, if not more than visiting every destination in the original pool.

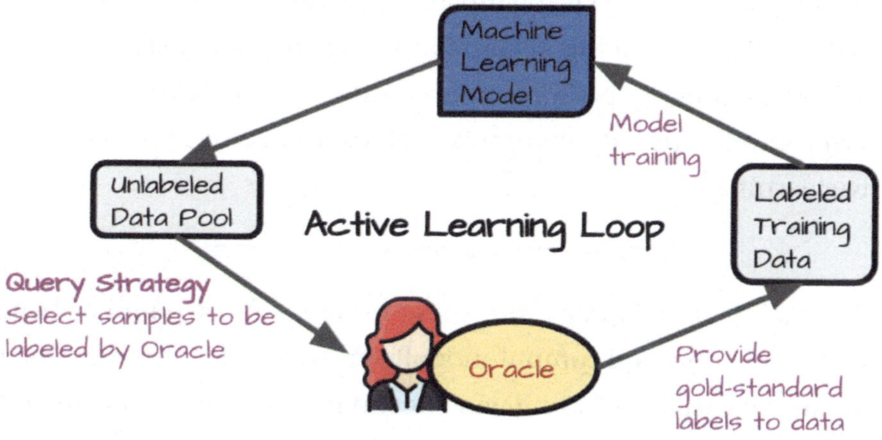

Figure 39: A Pool-based Active Learning Cycle.

Figure 40 illustrates the iterative process of such pool-based active learning. Initially, we could select one or more samples (destinations) from the unlabelled pool, give this sample to the Oracle (us human) to get the labeled dataset (visit and examine the region), on which we train a machine learning model (learn wine knowledge by visiting the region). Next we use our newly-gained knowledge to choose the next most valuable sample to be labeled (choose the next wine destination to visit based on gained knowledge such that the next one could provide the most valuable information), and continue with another iteration of model training with the chosen sample (visit the next chosen destination and learn). The process continues until our labeling budget is exhausted or a satisfying model performance is reached (we stop visiting when we run out of money or time, or when we are satisfied with the amount of wine knowledge we gained already).

In other words, active learning starts with a pool of unlabeled dataset, and largely through the design of how to select the best samples — let's call it *a query strategy* — from the unlabeled pool for the Oracle to judge, reduces the labeling cost as much as possible while maintaining or exceeding the overall model performance. Hence, the *design of query strategies* is the bread and butter of active learning. Let us delve into later in this section, most existing query strategies can be seen as either one of or a combination of two major camps: *uncertainty* and *diversity,* commonly referred to as the two faces of active learning.

Uncertainty-based query strategies are by far most popular, being relatively simple and computationally inexpensive. Intuitively speaking, in the case of selecting wine destinations for best learning opportunities, with an uncertainty-based query strategy, we would choose the wine regions the least familiar to visit such that we could take in the maximum amount of information by visiting and studying it. This might as well work out just fine, especially if our choice is small to begin with. Nonetheless, one of the major pitfalls of uncertainty-based query strategies is that it could easily lead to insufficient diversity of selected samples. For example, if we were to choose five destinations for our month-long field trip for the first time, and the wine countries we know least about are indeed, Chile, Argentina, Brazil, Uruguay, and Peru. However, if we did end up visiting these five countries, we might find out they are relatively similar in terms of terrior, viticultural or vinicultural practices, and wine distribution, compared to an alternative set of countries that we might be slightly more familiar with but much more diverse: Australia, Chile, Austria, Lebanon, and Portugal, which we are likely to gain more insights by not entirely relying on uncertainty as a selection criterion.

Diversity-based query strategy complements uncertainty-based strategies by making sure the chosen set of samples is as diverse as possible in terms of all sorts of characteristics. Most of the diversity-based strategies use a variety of clustering methods to identify similar data clusters and choose from each cluster respectively.

Density-based query strategies are similar to diversity-based strategy except that the aim is to select *a* ***core set*** that is most representative of the original unlabeled dataset, just like how data compression works in practice. However, diversity or density-based strategies do not work perfectly for all scenarios, especially when both our choice set and budget are limited to begin with. For instance, if we only have enough budget for two destinations, and we know more about Australia, Austria, China, and Portugal than Chile and Argentina, then if we chose Australia and Chile based on diversity, we might end up learning less than if we chose Chile and Argentina in this particular example. In addition, understanding and quantifying diversity or density are typically more complex and computationally expensive than uncertainty, therefore diversity or density-based strategies usually require more resources, which might as well pay off when faced with a rich set of content. Sometimes it could be challenging to measure similarity between sample points especially when we are faced with particularly unstructured, noisy, high-dimensional and even multimodal (for instance, including texts, images, videos, audios, etc. all at once) data, then diversity-based query strategy might prove thorny.

In Figure 40, let us visualize side by side the selected choice landscape if we were to go with uncertainty-based strategy or diversity-based strategy when choosing a sub-sample. Each dot is in fact an image and the closer an image is to another image in the visualization, the more similar the two images are. The two graphs clearly show that with an uncertainty-based query strategy on the left, we end up with a set of images that look much more similar than that chosen by a diversity-based query strategy on the right, where the dots representing images are much more diffuse, signaling more dissimilar images overall.

More often than not, most state-of-the-art active learning strategies strike an automatic balance between uncertainty and diversity simultaneously either explicitly or implicitly. We call these strategies hybrid strategies in that they combine the best of both worlds with uncertainty and diversity, thus achieving notably superior performance more robustly across different tasks and contexts. Ensemble methods are another type of hybrid methods that aggregate advice from multiple uncertainty-based or diversity-based strategies in a way that maximizes overall performance by, for example, focusing on disagreement between different query strategies.

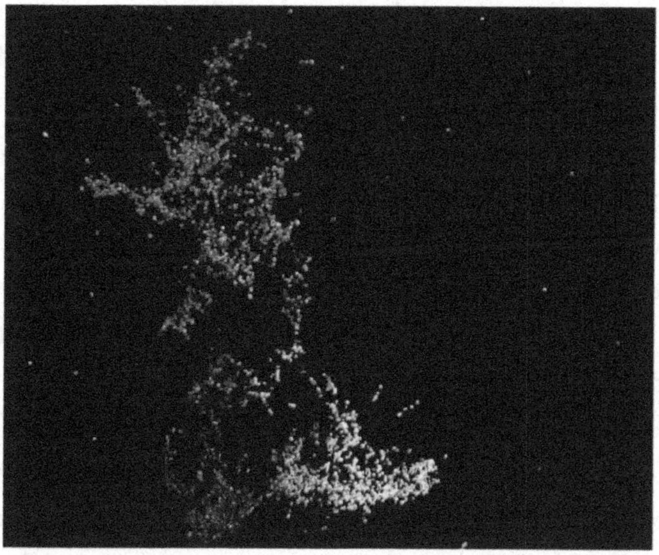

(a) Uncertainty.

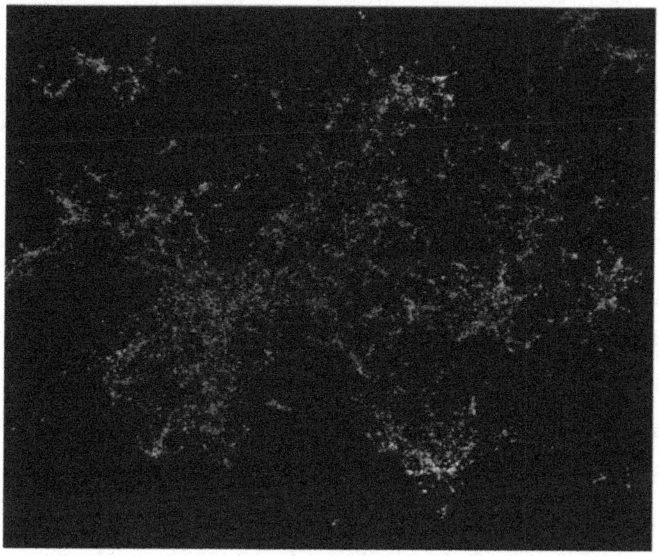

(b) Diversity.

Figure 40: A side-by-side comparison of visualization results from uncertainty-based and diversity-based active learning query strategies.

Active Learning (AL) aims to maximize a model's performance with as little human-annotated data as possible. Deep learning, on the other hand, usually requires a large amount of annotated data to estimate a large number of model parameters to achieve impressive performance, sometimes seemingly surpassing human capabilities. Therefore the combination of active learning and deep learning, which we call deep active learning (DAL, hereafter), offers promising horizons where performance is maximized with the least amount of necessary human annotation, saving on human resources, time, and monetary costs. It is wildly fitting in our case where we aim to learn as efficiently about wine as possible while expending the least amount of time and money. However, since active learning itself wasn't initially designed for deep learning models, integrating them naively would surely bring challenges:

1. Conflicting data principles. Traditional active learning was designed for relatively simple machine learning models to learn from a small amount of labeled data, whereas deep learning is notoriously data hungry.

2. Unreliable uncertainty. Uncertainty-based query strategy is one of the most popular strategies in active learning. But deep learning models are notorious for coming up with unreliable uncertainty metrics — it has been widely shown that AI models with some popular architectures and configurations are frequently overconfident about their incorrect judgments [Hein et al., 2019, Lokhande et al., 2020]. Therefore, if an active learning query relies heavily on such shaky grounds, its performance will inevitably suffer.

3. Inconsistent training paradigms. Traditional active learning is designed for hand-engineered static feature representations, most suited for traditional machine learning methods such as naive Bayes and support vector machine. Deep learning thrives on the principle of representation learning that does

away with feature engineering and fixed representations, but rather learns feature representation automatically and continuously, which runs counter to what traditional active learning is capable of.

With challenges, came solutions out of scientific ingenuity. AI researchers have proposed a large pool of solutions to address each of these challenges.

To solve the potential problem of data insufficiency resulting from the conflicting data regimes of active learning and deep learning, some deep active learning methods leverage generative adversarial networks (GANs) [Goodfellow et al., 2014] for data augmentation or automatic sample labeling with high confidence.

Adversarial active learning methods generate synthetic samples along the decision boundaries where algorithms have the most problems, and examples may help to considerably decrease the number of annotations (e.g., [Ducoffe and Precioso, 2018, Tran et al., 2019a]). Other active learning strategies in natural language processing such as **ALPS** ([Yuan et al., 2020]) (Active Learning by Processing Surprisal) extract existing knowledge from pre-trained language models like BERT [Devlin et al., 2019] (details in Section 7.4) to augment training data, thus alleviating the data insufficiency problem, especially valuable in a cold-start[28] setting. In addition, batch optimization, as opposed to the one-by-one sampling strategy prevalent in traditional active learning literature, has been exploited to the benefit of deep active learning (e.g., [Ash et al., 2019, Kirsch et al., 2019]).

To alleviate the problem of unreliable uncertainty resulting from neural networks, **Bayesian active learning** (e.g., [Gal et al., 2017, Kirsch et al., 2019, Tran et al., 2019b]) has been explored to accommodate samples of high dimensions with fewer queries per batch, mitigating the issue of overconfidence on the part of deep learning models.

[28] Lack of labeled training data at the beginning of the training process.

To integrate the disparate training regimes of active learning and deep learning, frameworks that iterates between active learning and deep feature learning have been propose for various tasks in an end-to-end fashion. In particular, research efforts that focus on robustifying and generalizing active learning approaches such that they could be readily adapted to various domains have led to promising results. For example, **Learning Loss for Active Learning** [Yoo and Kweon, 2019] (**LLAL**) introduces a task-agnostic architecture design that works efficiently with deep neural networks[29]. **Discriminative Active Learning** views active learning as a binary classification task, and designs a robust and easily generalizable query strategy that aims to select samples such that they are indistinguishable from the unlabeled dataset. Because it samples from the unlabeled dataset in proportion to the data density, it avoids introducing selection biases that could favor sample points in the sparse popular domain.

Circling back to the classic dichotomy of active learning, and deep active learning — uncertainty-based query strategies and diversity-based strategies, even though diversity-based strategies have shown remarkably good performance, they are not necessarily the best for all datasets, tasks, and AI models. More specifically, in general, the richer the dataset content, the larger the batch size, the better the effect of diversity-based methods; whereas an uncertainty-based query strategy will likely perform better with smaller batch sizes and more uniform datasets. These characteristics depend on the statistical characteristics of the dataset, the contexts of the task, and the model specifications.

[29] More specifically, they attach a small parametric module, "loss prediction module", to a target network, and learn it to predict target losses of unlabeled inputs. Therefore, this module could predict which data samples would likely cause the target model to produce a wrong prediction. This method is task-agnostic as networks are learned from a single loss regardless of target tasks.

	Fast	Uncertainty + Diversity	Task-Agnostic	Relatively Robust	Scalable	Cold Start
Uncertainty	✓		✓		✓	
EGL					✓	
Adversarial			✓	✓		
Bayesian	✓		✓	✓		
Core-set			✓	✓		
BADGE		✓	✓	✓	✓	
DAL		✓	✓	✓		
LLAL		✓	✓	✓	✓	
ALPS	✓	✓	✓	✓	✓	✓
Ensemble		✓		✓		

Table 19: Comparisons of major deep active learning strategies.

In practice, sometimes the dataset at hand could be unfamiliar and unstructured, making it difficult to choose between active learning query strategies. In light of this, Batch Active learning by Diverse Gradient Embeddings (**BADGE**) [Ash et al., 2019] samples point groups that are disparate and high magnitude when represented in a hallucinated gradient space, meaning that both the prediction uncertainty of the model and the diversity of the samples in a batch are considered simultaneously. It strives to strike a balance between predicted sample uncertainty and sample diversity without resorting to hyperparameter engineering. Various other followup methods have been proposed along the same vein of balancing sample uncertainty and diversity (e.g., **ALPS** [Yuan et al., 2020]).

Table 19 provides an overview of how different deep active learning strategies compare with respect to the following aspects: speed ("Fast"), whether it combines both uncertainty and diversity ("Uncertainty + Diversity"), applicability with respect to different tasks ("Task-Agnostic"), performance robustness across applications ("Relatively Robust"), ease of scaling it up to perhaps 1,000 times more data ("Scalable"), and whether it requires initial annotated data to kickstart ("Cold Start").

6.3 Image Geolocalization

Image geolocalization (or sometimes called visual place recognition) is the task of predicting the geographic location of image (recognizing the place in an image) based on the image alone. Geolocalizing images is a challenging task since input images often contain limited visual cues informative or representative enough of their locations. To master this task, whether it be for human beings or AI algorithms, a firm and comprehensive grasp of visual cues of the globe is perhaps a necessary prerequisite.

There are two major research streams addressing this challenge: one formulates it as an image retrieval task (Section 6.1), the other, an image classification task. As an image retrieval task, an extensive collection of image database of places around the globe embody our extensive prior knowledge of all places of interest where each image in the database is associated with a known location. When a new image comes in, the image-retrieval-based geolocalization system searches for images that look similar to the new image in our extensive database and assign its location based on locations associated with retrieved images that look alike. On the other hand, image-classification-based approach divides the global map into many fine-grained categories, each of which is associated with a geo-location. When a new image comes in, this classification based geolocalization system categorizes it into one or several of the pre-specified categories together with the associated geo-location(s). Thanks to advances in deep learning, simple image classification methods are able to handle such complex visual understanding problem rather competently, usually exceeding human capabilities especially when domain expertise is required.

Image retrieval-based methods for geolocalization have been explored extensively as the mainstream solution, where a query image is matched to the most similar reference images in a large image database of tens of thousands, if not millions or billions of images, and the geo-location is determined based on the existing geo-locations of similar images, that is, if similar images do exist in the database. Such a retrieval process could be divided into the following three major steps, which I will elaborate on one by one:

1. A pre-processing ("encoding") stage in which our computer vision algorithm learns to present all the images in the large reference database in an efficient manner to ease the effort involved in later stages;

2. A image search stage where the new image is compared against each and every image in our reference database efficiently, and best matches are returned;

3. A post-processing stage that refines the results from the image search process in the previous step.

Prior to the era of deep learning, the first step of pre-processing in the image retrieval pipeline involves a great deal of hand-crafted visual features designed to be discriminative with respect to places. These visual features could be roughly divided into local versus global descriptors.

Various standard computer vision feature descriptors that operate on small patches of images to identify and characterize key points, edges, corners, etc., have been adopted. Multi-class classifiers have been used to identify useful features for geo-localization tasks on top of local feature extraction and aggregation. One important idea emerged regarding the scalability and effectiveness of this approach was that it was not enough to simply match images on individual local features, but rather on how global views of similar local features differ or converge. For instance, if two images both show a 5 : 3 : 2 ratio of three pre-specified shared local features, they are more likely to be visually similar than two images that coincide perfectly on five specific local features. This is the so-called Bag of Words (BoW) approach widely used in computer vision research before the era of deep learning. Many other approaches have improved upon BoW over the years by weighting different local features more strategically, compressing the number of visual words (i.e., local visual descriptors), etc. Some later methods try to project all the visual features to a single representation space and aggregate them in an logical and efficient manner to preserve their visual relationships in-between, for the ease of image search and post-processing steps later on. Other works in the same vein have strove to preserve some desirable properties of many early visual descriptors that could get lost in large-scale visual representation learning, such as being robust to cropping, viewpoint alteration, scaling, etc., easing the image search process later on.

Besides aggregating local visual feature descriptors to obtain a global representation of an image, global feature descriptors that encode holistic features of an image could also be extracted directly. Without fine-grained computing on local patches of images, global visual descriptors are relatively less computationally expensive. These include some computer vision mainstays such as Histogram of Oriented Gradients (HOG) and Gist[30], along with their improved variants in terms of efficiency and robustness, even though their performance could suffer from excessive viewpoint variations and object occlusions (scene obstructed by other objects), among others.

Ever since deep learning revolutionized the field of machine learning, convolutional neural networks have shown tremendous potential for computer vision problems, the evolution and ingenuity of which were reviewed in Section 6.1.

What is even more remarkable about this series of convolutional neural networks lies in their unexpectedly exceptional ability to transfer knowledge from one generic vision understanding task to many other visual tasks. It is these groundbreaking findings that have spilled over to the application field of image retrieval, inspiring deep-learning-based applications to image retrieval tasks, where they have blown the traditional methods out of water in terms of performance accuracy.

To reduce the footprint of the above mentioned image retrieval methods, enabling them to run faster sometimes even on edge devices, more followup works have experimented with dimension reduction and model compression methods with promising results.

The second and arguably the most critical step of image retrieval is image similarity search, which is usually framed as a $k-$nearest neighbor search problem in which k images in the reference dataset

[30]Gist: aptly named, expressing the gist of a scene, and designed to match human visual concepts with respect to features in images.

are identified as closest to the query image. Efficient implementations of several approximate nearest neighbour algorithms are publicly available and notably, FAISS — A library for efficient similarity search — that came out of Facebook AI has been relatively widely adopted both in academia and industry. The similarity search for image geo-localization can also be implemented by matching multiple features within a single image, using a nearest neighbour algorithm for each individual local feature in the query image, which are then clustered and filtered to shortlist the results of matched images from the reference image database.

Besides viewing each image as a stand-alone entity and coming up with similarity measures for each pair of disjoint images — one being the query image, the other from the large reference database. The mindset of everything grounded in a contextual network could be adopted and have proved greatly beneficial. This is the *diffusion* method of image search, where each image is embedded into a universal graph where links in between represent visual similarities. Such a method provides a more holistic view of similar images that takes into account the contexts around images at higher dimensions. Recent advances in this research stream resulted from the wide adoption of graph convolutional networks (GCN), shown to be rather effective in encoding each and every node (image) within the large graph with contexts.

After the step of image search, a set of potentially similar images from the large reference image dataset are retrieved as a consideration set of final candidates for the query image in question. At this point, there could still be some incorrectly retrieved images included due to limitations of the last two steps of image retrieval and the reference dataset itself. On the flip side, some relevant images that should have been included might have been missed. Therefore, this post-processing step provides one last opportunity to ensure the validity of our results as much as possible. Here are several techniques commonly drawn upon to improve the quality of the shortlisted image candidates:

1. *Spatial verification* is one of the most widely adopted and studied method in computer vision, which detects feature correspondences between two image pairs and verifies the validity of the matching by evaluating the spatial consistency in-between. Based on how reliable the matching turns out to be based on spatial verification, images returned from the last step are ranked with the more reliable ones at the top concluding the image retrieval pipeline.

2. Besides spatial correspondences, other *non-spatial methods* have been proposed *for ranking* candidate images, such as matching scores based on similarities between regional maximum activations of convolutions of each pair of the query and the reference image, similarity of labels assigned to the images by k-nearest neighbor search with voting mechanisms, and more hand-crafted feature matching.

3. *Query expansion* is another wildly popular technique to improve retrieval results in both computer vision and natural language processing. By looping the set of images returned from image search back into the image search step to surface an even richer set of image candidates, it significantly lowers the possibility of missing any relevant images in the image search step. However, its effectiveness hinges upon the quality of the initially returned candidate set, as with unreliable candidates one could only introduce more noise or irrelevant images into the final mix. Therefore, query expansion is usually applied after spatial or non-spatial verification to ensure the quality of input images for reliable expansion.

Even though image geolocalization is commonly addressed as an image retrieval task, there are several major challenging aspects that distinguish it from an image retrieval task alone:

1. Places that look alike might be correctly retrieved in an image retrieval task, but result in incorrect results in an image geolocalization task. For two hospitals or chain restaurants in different parts of the same country might look very similar inside due to the standardized equipment, interior design, and uniforms. This is exactly why I referred to *identifying Burgundy or Beaujolais look-alikes* as an image retrieval task but *Geo Guessr* or *Cellar Guessr* as image geolocalization tasks in the introduction part of this section.
   Feeding the image search model with auxiliary information that could help differentiate finer details is one potential solution. Semantic information could also be leveraged to emphasize more informative and distinctive features. For instance, man-made structures might be more useful to enable clearer differentiation between New York and Philadelphia. As I will detail in the next few pages, image-classification based geolocalization methods could prove particularly effective in resolving this problem, especially when coupled with scene recognition, which treats different scenes — natural landscape, building interior, highway, etc. — separately.

2. On the other hand, visually dis-similar images could be of the same geo-location due to different viewpoints, weather patterns, or lightings, and such images would likely not be captured by standard image similarity search processes, resulting in sub-optimal retrieval outcomes.
   Common solutions to this problem come from *image synthesis*, closely related to what we introduced in Section 5.2 and

Section 5.1, by generating synthetic images of the input image with altered viewpoint, illumination, scale, warping, and other environmental contexts. By augmenting the original reference database with these synthetically generated images, our image search algorithm could better learn to bypass dissimilarities in illumination or viewpoint or others when it comes to images of the same place.

3. Temporary objects or instances within an image could be misleading when localizing without additional information on the relative importance of objects or instances in a scene. For instance, a Google StreetView image is likely to include FedEx trucks or Starbucks storefront as well as pedestrians dressed in a certain style of clothing, however there is absolutely no guarantee that a Google StreetView image taken at the same place on another day would include a FedEx truck, the same storefront (you know how fast stores open and close), or the same pedestrians. If we search for images by focusing on these clues rather than more permanent ones, our algorithm is very much doomed in such applications.
   Various solutions have emerged to guide the image retrieval pipeline to focus on the most informative parts of the images and avoiding elements that might cause confusion or distraction, including extracting regions of interest by cropping and zooming in on region proposals, incorporating attention mechanism to strategically and empirically select relevant information from input images without cropping, and so forth.

Image-classification-based approaches divide the globe into a set of fine-grained categories, each of which is associated with a geolocation. When a new image comes in, a classification-based geolocalization system categorizes it into one or several of the pre-specified categories, with the associated geo-location(s) assigned accordingly. This idea stems not only from the impressive results deep-learning-based image classification systems have achieved at a large scale, but also from the observation that human beings are able to estimate the location of a photo as a whole without singling out particular elements, which could be particularly efficient at a global scale.

Classification-based image geolocalization techniques, provides a more (memory and disk) efficient and faster alternative to image retrieval-based solutions. No image reference databases are required, which would have taken up at least hundreds of gigabytes, if not terabytes, of storage space. Nor do we have to search over the entire image database in search for similar images as in retrieval-based methods, saving time and computing resources in practice, especially at scale. Such an edge in speed is even more prominent when multiple answers to one query image is required to sometimes hedge the bets or when there exists multiple correct answers.

This line of work was initiated by Google researchers and published [Weyand et al., 2016] in the year of 2016. They partition the surface of the earth, or area of interest, into non-overlapping cells and each cell corresponds to a class in the classification problem. The partitioning process is done according to the the number of available images that fall within each cell in an adaptive way such that in the end each cell contains a similar number of images available in our dataset used for training the classification algorithm. There exists a performance trade-off that is baked into the design of this approach. The finer the partitioning, the smaller the individual cells, the more accurate the classification algorithm could potentially achieve and the more useful it would be in practice, but at the same time, the more difficult it would be for the algorithm to learn and improve its performance due to more classes and the greater complexity and subtlety it needs to comprehend.

There are at least two limitations to this approach. First, any correlation that could potentially make the task easier is overlooked, as assigning a photo of Beaujolais to Mâconnais, both of which are in Burgundy, is considered equally incorrect as assigning it to Central Otago in New Zealand. Second, such geographic partitioning could create artificial demarcation where the two regions on both sides are almost the same, creating false signals for the algorithm to learn, which could cause the training process to progress slowly and begrudgingly. This problem could be mitigated if we were to increase the number of cells by resorting to even finer-grained partitioning, which unfortunately could create even more problems for training as the effective number of images available for each class or cell is even smaller, falling short of the increasing complexity of the classification algorithm required to deal with finer-grained classes. It's a vicious cycle.

The same authors [Hongsuck Seo et al., 2018] came up with a solution two years later in 2018 of a combinatorial partitioning algorithm to generate fine-grained cells. It combines distinctive coarser cells such that a general and more lightweight framework could be used to learn how to achieve accurate coarse-grained classification, the results of which when combined efficiently would lead to accurate fine-grained classification results. This greatly improves the scalability of classification-based image geolocalization methods, readily applicable at a global scale. At the same time, researchers at the Leibniz Information Centre for Science and Technology [Muller-Budack et al., 2018] proposed to complement classification-based approach with additional contextual information and more specific visual features for various environmental settings such as indoor, natural, or urban settings. They demonstrated the effectiveness and efficiency of this classification-based method that combines scene recognition and place recognition, even though it might not be easily scalable due to algorithm architecture hand-engineering tailored to specific environments that rely on human inputs.

Now that we have detailed the mainstream approaches based on image retrieval, as well as more recent state-of-the-art approaches based on image classification, a natural question to ask is how the two streams of disparate approaches stack up against each other. There exist a few studies that compared and contrasted the two. Even though no extensive or thorough comparison exists, nor does a fair comparing regimen exist so far since the two methods leverage different resources and are set up in non-overlapping ways, some insights do seem to emerge from existing partial comparisons. First, retrieval-based methods appear to perform better at finer scales in general, whereas classification-based methods remove the constraint necessary for image retrieval that a large and diverse image database covering every region of interest is required, affording it greater flexibility and generalizability when it comes to new environments and viewpoints. On the other hand, the performance of classification-based methods is contingent on the region partitioning in the first place, which makes it less robust with respect to algorithm specifications than retrieval-based methods.

Naturally, one might ask, what if we could combine the retrieval-based and classification-based image geolocalization methods to enjoy the best of both worlds? It does not come as a surprise that some recent research efforts were indeed devoted to combining the two. For instance, researchers [Vo et al., 2017] at Georgia Institute of Technology estimate the geographic location of an image by matching it to its closest counterparts in the reference database, that is, an image-retrieval based method, but using visual features learned from image classification. They found that such a combination greatly improves geolocalization accuracy with significantly less training data than classification-based methods.

6.4 Fine-grained Image Classification

Figure 41: An illustration of the difference between generic image classification and *fine-grained image classification.*

Fine-grained Image Classification, alternatively, *Fine-grained Image Recognition* or *Fine-grained Visual Categorization (FGVC)* refers to the problem distinguishing between images of closely related entities. In other words, in fine-grained visual categorization tasks, one strives to differentiate between subtle subcategories of objects, such as different species of birds, breeds of dogs or cats, models and makes of cars or aircrafts, species of plants or insects, types of food, styles of fashion clothing, castles around the world, consumer product packaging, among many others.

Recent efforts have been made to create challenging datasets that are both fine-grained and large-scale, leveraging recently digitized rich resources and tailored to the practical needs and wants of various organizations, such as a large, long-tailed collection of herbarium specimens collected by the New York Botanical Garden and an enormous collection of artworks by the Met (Metropolitan Museum of Art) in New York City.

Figure 41 further illustrates what differentiates *fine-grained image recognition* from generic image recognition tasks, one only needs to be able to tell the difference between object classes in broad strokes, just like a five-year-old first learning about the world in coarse terms — dogs, cats, bunnies, trees, flowers, etc., whereas as one delves deeper into one particular category to appreciate the finer details and nuances, one could potentially tell the differences between visually similar sub-categories such as cat breeds like Ragdoll, Ragamuffin, Maine Coon, and Norwegian forest cats, the process of which oftentimes requires expert-level domain knowledge.

Being such a fundamental, practical and yet challenging problem, it has drawn a great deal of research interests and efforts over the past decades, most notably after *deep learning* revolutionized machine learning as a field, such that the Fine-grained Visual Categorization (FGVC) workshop became one of the long-running workshops in the computer vision community. Backtrack over ten years ago when the first ever FGVC workshop was held in 2011 in Colorado Springs, this subfield of fine-grained visual classification was still nascent, and very few fine-grained datasets existed. The only ones that existed, such as the Caltech-UCSD Birds (CUB) Dataset consisting of 200 bird species, posed a daunting challenge to then state-of-the-art image classification algorithms. Each year new datasets and challenges of fine-grained visual categorization were introduced and so did more exciting prediction results that followed. Over the past decade, the computer vision landscape has undergone breathtaking changes — deep learning based methods boosted the prediction accuracy of this first CUB dataset of 200 bird species to skyrocket from 17% to 90%. Many more new datasets have proliferated, coming from a diverse array of organizations and institutions, such as universities, museums, companies, farms, and government agencies. Tabulated in Table 20 by dataset, release year, classes, number of sub-classes, and number of images indicative the scale of the challenge, etc., are existing benchmark datasets and challenges for fine-grained image classification.

Dataset	Year	Class	Sub-classes	Images	Accuracy	Reference
Oxford Flower	2008	Flower	102	8,189	0.73	[Nilsback and Zisserman, 2008]
CUB-200	2011	Bird	200	11,788	0.90	[Wah et al., 2011]
Stanford Dog	2011	Dog	120	20,580	NA	[Khosla et al., 2011]
Stanford Car	2013	Car	196	16,185	0.76	[Krause et al., 2013]
Aircraft	2013	Aircraft	100	10,000	0.49	[Maji et al., 2013]
Birdsnap	2014	Bird	500	49,829	0.67	[Berg et al., 2014]
Fru92	2017	Fruit	92	69,614	0.88	[Hou et al., 2017]
Veg200	2017	Vegetable	200	91,117	0.84	[Hou et al., 2017]
iNat	2017	Plant, animal	5,089	859,000	0.95	[iNaturalist]
iNat	2021	Plant, animal	10,000	2.7 Mil	0.94	[iNaturalist]
iMaterialist	2017	Apparel object Apparel part Apparel attribute	27 19 294	50,461	(0.72)	[iMat]
Fungi	2018	Mushroom	1,500	100,000	0.79	[Fungi]
iWildCam	2019	Camera location	65	106,428	0.93	[iWildCam]
iWildCam	2020	Camera location	441	217,959	0.91	[iWildCam]
iCassava	2019	Cassava disease	5	20,000	0.94	[iCassava]
RPC	2019	Retail product	200	83,739	0.57	[Wei et al., 2019]
iFood	2019	Food	251	120,216	0.94	[iFood]
iDesigner	2019	Fashion designer	50	50,000	0.99	[iDesigner]
Fieldguide	2019	Butterflies & Moths	5,000	530,000	0.95	[Fieldguide]
iHerbarium	2019	Vascular plant	680	46,000	0.90	[iHerbarium]
iHerbarium	2020	Vascular plant	32,000	1 Mil	(0.84)	[iHerbarium]
iMet	2019	Art (attribute)	1,103	109,274	[0.67]	[iMet]
iMet	2020	Art (attribute)	3,474	168,000	(0.74)	[iMet]
Plant Pathology	2020	Foliar disease	11	3,645	(0.98)	[Thapa et al., 2020]
Castle	2021	Castle	2,412	772,927	0.83	[Anderson et al., 2021]
Hotel-ID	2021	Hotel	8,000	100,000	0.86	[Hotel-ID]

Table 20: A summary of existing fine-grained visual categorization benchmark datasets. Additional information included are release years, class categories, the number of sub-class categories, the total number of images included, the documented classification results in terms of accuracy, (F1 score in parentheses), [F2 score in square brackets], with pointers to references.

Some of the most exciting recent challenges in the running that continue to attract and excite respective domain experts and computer vision scientists in its current edition include:

- *iNaturalist*: jointly developed by the California Academy of Sciences and the National Geographic Society and has emerged as a world leader for citizen scientists to share observations of species and connect with nature since its founding in 2008. The computer vision iNaturalist challenge initiated in 2017 aims to classify images into 5,000 natural species in its current edition.

- *iMaterialist* and *iMaterialist - Fashion*: with the ever growing popularity of online shopping, being able to recognize products from pictures is an important but challenging problem. The initial iMaterialist challenge in 2017 aims to classify product images into 2,019 different products at the stock keeping unit (SKU) level. In its current edition *iMaterialist - Fashion* in 2021, participants are expected to perform apparel instance segmentation and fine-grained attribute classification by localizing apparel in fashion images and classifying into 46 apparel objects, and 294 attributes.

- *iWildCam*: initiated in 2018 and based on data from camera traps used by biologists to study animals in the wild, paired with remote sensing imagery to assist in generalization to unseen cameras in the training dataset. This challenge aims to predict if camera trap images contain animals.

- *iMet*: developed with the Metropolitan Museum of Art based on its diverse collection of over 1.5 million objects of which over 200,000 have been digitized with imagery. Participants are challenged to develop fine-grained attribute classification algorithms on these digitized art objects catalogued by subject matter experts with respect to artist, title, date, medium, culture, size, provenance, geographic location, etc.

(a) Stanford Cars

(b) Stanford Dogs

(c) iFood

(d) iNaturalist

Figure 42: Samples of existing benchmark datasets for *fine-grained image classification.*

- *Herbarium*: based on a large, long-tailed collection of herbarium specimens supplied by the New York Botanical Garden. The challenge aims to identify up to 32k vascular plant species based on over one million images of herbarium specimens.

- *PlantPathology*: as foliar diseases are major issues in agriculture and current disease diagnosis in apples is based on expensive and time-consuming human manual scouting, this challenge aims to provide plant disease diagnosis of apples using a reference dataset of expert-annotated diseased specimens in three steps: first, distinguish diseased leaves from healthy ones; second, distinguish between many plant diseases, sometimes more than one on a single leaf; third, asses the severity of the disease.

- *Hotel-ID*: human-trafficking victims are often photographed in hotels and participants are challenged to accurately identify up to 8,000 hotels based on over 100,000 images to help combat human trafficking.

Figure 42 showcases some sample images randomly drawn from these major fine-grained visual categorization datasets.

To contribute to this line of academic research as well as the wine industry, I created four challenges with associated datasets curated with the wine industry in mind, the details and motivations of which have been introduced throughout different sections of this book, tabulated in Table 21 with some samples visualized in Figure 43, Figure 44, Figure 61 (in Section 7.5), and Figure 62 (in Section 7.5):

Dataset	Year	Class	Sub-classes	Images	Accuracy	Reference
iCellar	2021	Winery cellar	773	68,157	0.87	Section 6.4
iVineyard	2021	Vineyard	327	29,166	0.85	Section 6.4
iGrapevine	2021	Grapevine	153	13,550	0.92	Section 7.5
VinePathology	2021	Vine diseases, pests, weeds, other hazards	42	5,894	0.95	Section 7.5

Table 21: New challenges and datasets for fine-grained visual categorization of wine and vine.

Major challenges of fine-grained visual categorization lie in the subtle differences between sub-categories that distinguish one from another, which oftentimes require a great deal of domain knowledge. For accurate recognition, one sometimes has to separate and analyze different parts to make informed decisions. For instance, in order to distinguish a Ragamuffin cat from a Ragdoll cat, one might need to pay close attention to ears, eyes, neck floofs, and color patterns. Knowing what exact features to pay attention to for each pair of sub-classes among all sub-classes, and what features are distinctive to a particular sub-class but not the other, are the keys to making accurate predictions. To summarize, subtle differences between every pair of sub-classes, compounded by the scale of such datasets, makes it a challenging task not only to AI algorithms, but also to human experts.

To effectively and efficiently address these challenges, various fine-grained image recognition methods have been proposed in the field of computer vision. These approaches could be categorized into three camps:

1. Fine-grained recognition with sub-modules that localize and classify distinctive parts that are conducive to clear differentiation between similar sub-classes: quite a few standard computer vision algorithms as sub-modules can be applied to zoom in on parts of images that are most discriminative, mimicking how human experts differentiate between visually confusing sub-classes. For instance, an insect or animal's head or ears could be segmented out (with polygons) or detected (with bounding boxes), and an object's key points (contour, edge, etc.) could be detected. With further higher-level feature extraction based on such localized information, final recognition accuracy could be significantly boosted with enhanced fine-grained feature learning;

Figure 43: A photo-mosaic collage of sample images from iCellar for *fine-grained image classification* of winery cellars.

Figure 44: A photo-mosaic collage of sample images from iVineyard for *fine-grained image classification* of vineyards around the world.

2. Fine-grained recognition with tailored architecture and training regime: various integrated architectures (as opposed to modular as in the first camp of methods) and training regimes have been proposed to increase the diversity of relevant features for better classification results, either by removing irrelevant information (such as background) by better localization, or supplementing features with part and pose information, or more training data. Some other methods focus on modifying the objective of model training to tailor for more discriminative fine-grained feature learning in order to boost the final accuracy[31];

3. Fine-grained recognition with auxiliary information: yet another camp of methods emphasize complementing existing models and data samples with easily obtainable external information, whether it be additional web search results to augment model training, geo-locations of images taken which could be informative in contexts such as native plant or animal species, relevant text information or knowledge base (Section 3) entries. Such additional information sources could be especially

---

[31] *Technical note for end-to-end fine grained image recognition just for researchers*: Bilinear pooling which combines pairwise local features to improve spatial invariance has been critical. It has been extended by Kernel Pooling with higher-order interactions instead of dot products proposed originally, and Compact Bilinear Pooling that speeds up the operation. Alternatively, one could predict an affine transformation of the original image, which was introduced in Spatial Transformer Networks. Local features could also be boosted by part-based Region CNNs with local attention. Additional information such as pose and regions have also been explored, along with robust image representations such as CNN filter banks, VLAD, and Fisher vectors. Supplementing training data and model averaging have also had significant improvements. Another recent study by MIT researchers focuses on the classification task after obtaining features (and is hence compatible with existing approaches), by selecting the classifier that assumes the minimum information about the task by principle of Maximum-Entropy.

valuable if they provide critical information for classification that were missing in the original datasets.

In my experiments with fine-grained visual categorization for vineyards, cellars, grapevine clusters, vine leaves, and vine diseases, I found by combing methods from the second and the third camp the best classification results could be achieved at over 90%, way above what a non-expert in wine could do in such tasks. How about comparing it to human experts — wine professionals and enthusiasts? I have set up online quizzes at http://ai-for-wine.com/fgvc for you to challenge AI algorithms if you are interested. Welcome to quiz yourself and find out if you beat AI algorithms in this challenging task — have fun and good luck!

6.5 Object Discovery

What makes Burgundy look like Burgundy, and Piedmont look like Piedmont? What makes Paris look like Paris but not London or New York? Carnegie-Mellon University researchers (now at Google Research) have collected evidence that human beings are remarkably sensitive to geographically-informative features within the visual environment. But what are those features? The ones so localized and distinctive that immediately give away the identity of a place? For New York, things like brownstone buildings with black fire escapes, yellow school buses and red sightseeing buses, the distinctive skylines, etc. could be particularly helpful. Finding such features can be challenging, since every image could contain hundreds of thousands local patches, and millions of images could be available for every region of interest, within which only a small fraction might be truly distinctive.

How could we find such geo-informative visual features automatically at a large scale, from a large image database of natural photographs? To put it more precisely, given a large image dataset consisting natural images bucketed into different geographical regions such as Piedmont, Friuli, Sicily, Rioja, Douro, Jura, Champagne, Xinjiang, Margaret River, Marlborough, etc., at the scale of hundreds of thousands, if not, millions of images, how could be find a few hundred visual elements per region that are both repeating and geographically distinctive? That is, visual elements that not only occur frequently in a particular region but also much more frequently than any other regions.

Such a task could not only help cognitive scientists with better understanding which visual elements are fundamental to our perception of complex visual concepts, but also, in more practical terms, facilitate generating the so-called *reference art* of a region by providing a *stylistic narrative* for a visual experience. Such describes the research stream of **computational geo-cultural modeling**, and is highly related to a line of work on **object discovery**, in which one attempts to discover features or objects that frequently occur in many images and are useful as meaningful visual elements.

The major challenge of this task lies in the fact that the majority of our data samples are likely uninteresting, making the discoveries of rare and distinctive elements more like finding the needle in a haystack.

Let me describe such a well-known algorithm proposed by researchers at Carnegie-Mellon University. As a preparation step, let us divide the large image reference dataset into two parts:

1. the positive set comprising images from the region whose visual elements we wish to discover (e.g. Alsace);

2. the negative set comprising images from the rest of the world excluding the region of interest.

A basic idea is to cluster all the images on both visual features and geographic information, extracting elements both frequently appearing and distinctive at the same time. One straightforward intuition is that visual patches portraying non-discriminative elements tend to be matched with similar patches in both positive and negative sets, whereas patches portraying non-repeating or infrequent patterns (like landmarks such as Times Square, or Eiffel Tower) will match patches in both positive and negative image sets in a randomly fashion. Operating on such an intuition, let me sketch the steps in the algorithm as the following:

1. Randomly sample a large subset of high-contrast patches as initial candidates;

2. Estimate the initial geo-informativeness of each patch candidate by finding the top 20 nearest neighbor in the full image reference dataset of both positive and negative parts;

3. Retain the candidates with the highest proportion of their nearest neighbors in the positive set while rejecting as well as near-duplicate patches;

4. Gradually build clusters by applying iterative discriminative learning to each surviving candidate patch:

    (a) In each iteration, a new binary classifier is trained for each visual element to differentiate between positive and negative samples using its top k nearest neighbors from the positive set from the last round of iteration as positive training samples and all negative patches from the last round as negative training samples;

    (b) Stop iterations until most good clusters have stopped changing;

    (c) After the final iteration, return rank the resulting classifiers based on accuracy — the percentage of top positive predictions of patches that are in the positive set (belonging to the region of interest);

(d) Return the top hundred patches as geo-informative visual elements that are both repeated and distinctive to the region of interest.

In the following series of figures, let us plot the resulting visual elements from applying such an algorithm to our wine region image dataset to identify geo-informative visual elements of Gevrey-Chambertin (Figure 45), Canary Island (Figure 48), Santorini (Figure 46), and Finger Lakes (Figure 47).
As is clear from distinctive visual elements discovered within a few minutes of running the algorithm, Gevrey-Chambertin appears to be defined by the visually distinctive crimson-roofed houses with thin windows, country roads snaking and winding its way through vineyards, and brick walls; Santorini seems to be characterized by white domed single-storey buildings, baskets woven by branches — *Kouloura*[32] on barren land, bush vines with stony crates; Canary Islands are noted for the mountain skyline, bush vines inside crescent stony crates as well as black ash crates; and the Finger Lakes by vertical shoot positioning trellis systems with prominent timber poles, vigorous tree-like vines, and various waterfronts.

[32] Kouloura or *Gyristo*, alternatively, *Kladeftiko* or *Amolyto*.

Figure 45: Visual elements of Gevrey-Chambertin.

Figure 46: Visual elements of Santorini.

Figure 47: Visual elements of Finger Lakes.

Figure 48: Visual elements of Canary Islands.

SECTION 7

Grape Varieties

Admittedly and arguably, the fascination with grape varieties — most likely, *vitis vinifera* — was more of an American cultural trend than the rest of the world. It wasn't until fairly recently that a wine's place appeared far more important than the grape. For centuries, it wasn't Chardonnay, the wine was called Meursault. People did not ask for Riesling, they wanted a wine from the Rhine region. It was not Garnache, it was a wine from Châteauneuf-du-Pape, or Priorat.

This mental model of American consumers categorizing wines primarily based on grape varieties could be perhaps partly explained the pioneering practice of putting varieties on wine labels by Californian vintners, especially the famed Robert Mondavi, dating back at least to the 1960s, as opposed the time-honored tradition of labeling wines with the region name, appellation, or winery such as those still in practice in France. For instance, best wines are labelled by *terrior* in Burgundy, by brand in Bordeaux, etc., with the exception of Alsace, where wines have been labelled with varieties due to political uncertainty over time in history.

To grab a glimpse of the world of wine in terms of flavor and structure (aspects of acid, tannin, body, etc.) in the sense that one could identify similar wines and form general impressions of representative characteristics of similar wines, clustering the world of wines by grape varieties, is no worse a starting point than soil types, climates, or geographical features. After all, wine grapes appear to follow the ubiquitous 80\20 rule, if not having taken it to greater extremes: out of almost 1,500 known varieties of wine grapes in the world, around 20 grape varieties — that is less than 2% as opposed to 20% — are responsible for 80% of wine we imbibe. If you understand the most popular 20 grape varieties, you already stand a fat chance of 80% knowing at least something about whatever wine coming your way at random throughout your daily life.

But what about the rest of 20% from over 1,000 possible grape varieties? The Robert Parker tirade about consumers' irrational chase after *godforsaken* grapes driven by obsession of novelty spurred waves of discussions on both sides. Jancis Robinson took issue with Parker's assertion that "godforsaken grapes" like Trousseau or Savagnin are not capable of producing wines that "consumers should be beating a path to buy and drink." But to many people's surprise, she did side with him on celebrating the classics of the wine world, agreeing that some tastemakers appear to have taken it to extremes to seek obscurity as the only determinant of a wine's worth. Jason Wilson, on the other hand, in a cocky mock salute to the furious Parker, wrote the book Godforsaken Grapes with gusto and fanfare, about all these godforsaken grapes that the Bordeaux King is disdainful of. I, for one, whole-heartedly embrace both classics and novelty: the nuances of Brunate versus Rocche dell'Annunziata in La Morra bring me as much joy as what a well-made Rotgipfler or Zierfandler from Thermenregion in Austria does. Just like almost everything else in life, a customizable balance in-between is perhaps the answer. Within the reach of familiarity, we have learnt to appreciate nuances that could spark the greatest joy and delight in place of complete novelty. No matter how knowledgeable or experienced one is in wine, there are always moments when unfamiliar varieties or familiar varieties in unfamiliar regions spark curiosity and excitement.

But how does one learn about unfamiliar grape varieties? Given the familiar grape varieties we have internalized and archetyped (detailed in Section 2 as the first step of deductive tasting), one of the efficient ways to internalize an unknown variety we are encountering is to associate it with each of the grape varieties we are familiar with: for instance, some referred to Albariño as Viognier on the nose but Riesling on the palate when it started to gain traction, so was Grüner Veltliner as a hypothetical baby of Viognier and Sauvignon Blanc, and Nerello Mascalese has been frequently described as the combination of Nebbiolo and Pinot Noir ever since the explosion of Etna Rosso in the global wine scene. Regardless of how accurate such associations scientifically, the unfamiliar variety is now tightly knit into the network of familiar grape varieties and made stick to one's memory. Alternatively, with all the familiar varieties, we have internalized a systematic way to evaluate any given grape variety regardless of one's familiarity, according to which every familiar variety is positioned in this grape universe. Whenever a new unfamiliar grape comes along, we could evaluate it in the same systematic way and embed it into its own place in our grape universe alongside other familiar ones. Think of the deductive tasting method or any tasting method you'd prefer, you might encode Muscadet (Melon de Bourgogne) as a neutral white grape with searing electric high acidity, texture from phenolic bitterness, and aromas of white peach, sea salt, tons of stony minerality, and white flowers. When you run into Zierfandler or Obaideh for the first time, in a similar way, you might register it in your mind as a semi-neutral white grape with piercing acidity, pithy texture, and aromas of lemon, quince, apricot, spices, and stony minerality. You might also tentatively lump it together with Chenin Blanc, Timorasso, and Romorantin, perhaps, in terms of flavor and structure profile. The next time you taste a Zierfandler from Thermenregion or Obaideh from Beqaa Valley, you might be able to recognize it blind based on such associations or characteristics. For an ampelologist discovering new varieties, the same process and logic apply except that familiar grapes could be internalized not only by taste, but also by grapevine and viticultural characteristics such as thick and pink skin, pointed leaf ends, being early budding or late ripening, susceptibility to fungal diseases like downy mildew and botrytis rot, prey to European grape moth and other pests, to name just a few. Such a learning process towards recognizing more and more rare wine varieties is the exact process widely studied in Machine Learning called **few-shot** or **zero-shot Learning**, depending on the number of encounters it takes you to recognize the new variety the next time around. In **Section 7.1** and **Section 7.2**, let us highlight some major results in this body of AI research and how to apply them to wine grapes to assist in discovering unknown wine grapes.

As part of the learning process traversing through the universe of wine grapes, we could think of all the distinctive grape varieties as situated in a shared high-dimensional space. For instance, if we think of an archetypical variety along three possible dimensions: the level of acidity, the level of aromatic intensity, and the level of tannin (or phenolic bitterness), every variety can be positioned into a 3D plot (or cube) with these three measures as axes.

But three is too restrictive, as we need all the information available about a variety to make the best-informed decisions and judgements. Therefore in the same way as the 3D scenario, we could cast all the grape varieties into a shared high-dimensional space encapsulating all the useful and available features about them, such that we have a much better understanding of every variety relative to others in the universe of grape varieties. Then with dimension reduction and visualization techniques such as t-SNE [Hinton and Roweis, 2002] or UMAP [McInnes et al., 2018], we could cast them back into two-dimensional spaces for ease of interpretation as in Figure 49.

In addition, the same grape variety grown in a different growing environment and cultivated in the hands of different vintners could come off as completely distinctive. Domaine de la Romanée-Conti Montrachet towers so definitively over Yellow Tail Chardonnay, and Robert Mondavi Fumé Blanc is so distinctively different than François Cotat Sancerre, despite being made from the same ubiquitous grape variety. Therefore perhaps contexts should be included as important features besides all the varietal features as well. But still, coming up with a list of comprehensive features or dimensions is no simple task itself, nor can we guarantee whichever feature we decide to include is indeed essential in deepening our understanding.

What if we could find a way to automatically identify the critical features towards our learning goal? Ultimately, a better grounding of every variety in the universe grape varieties could inform answers to curious yet critical questions. For instance, what are the white grape varieties that most closely resemble red grape varieties? Which grape varieties share similar viticultural features that might be better planted in similar climates? Which grape varieties are the closest or the most distant to Furmint in terms of flavor profile, and which in terms of preferred growing environment?

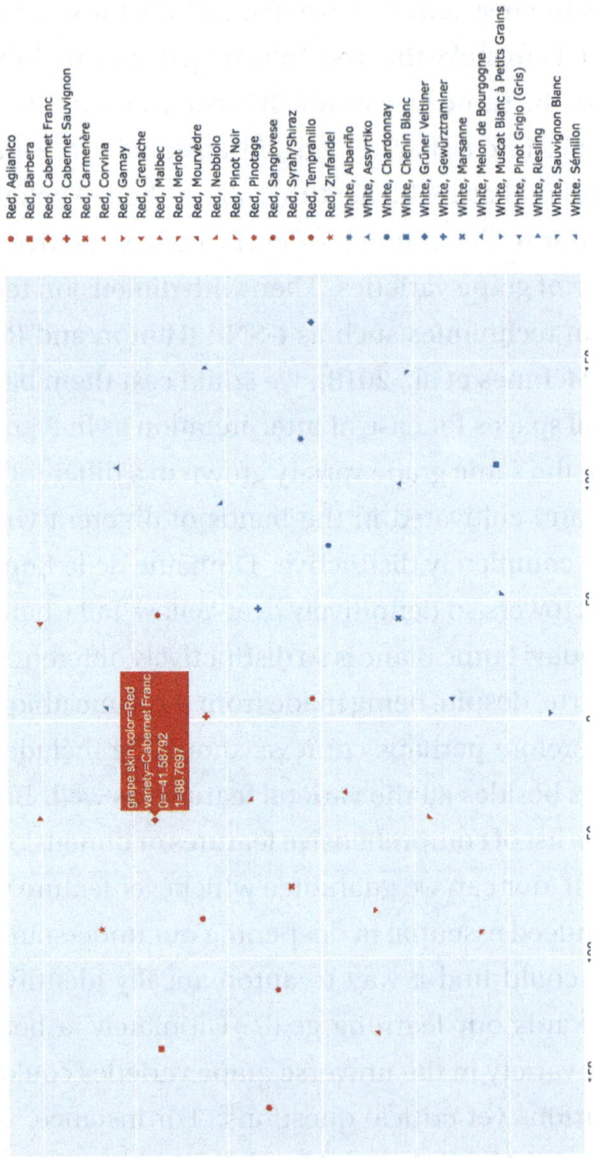

Figure 49: Plotting grape varieties in a two-dimensional space reduced from a high-dimensional space that encodes a variety of varietal characteristics in terms of color, aroma, and flavor. More comprehensive and interactive visualizations at http://ai-somm.com/grape/.

In Section 7.4 of Contextual Embedding, let us discuss a series of major breakthroughs in the field of Natural Language Processing that swept the AI community by storm, revolutionizing many ways we solve problems, which enabled with remarkable results what we have described and aspired to achieve in this paragraph.

Just like many other scientific discoveries, identifying new grape varieties, or new links between known grape varieties, sometimes require not only valid methods and hard work, but also a streak of luck. It was Carole Meredith, the professor Emeritus in viticulture and ecology at University of California Davis and winemaker of Lagier Meredith in Mount Veeder District of Napa Valley, together with her then PhD student John Bowers, now a professor of viticulture at University of Georgia, who first uncovered the parentage links between Cabernet Sauvignon, Sauvignon Blanc, and Cabernet Franc, as well as those between Chardonnay, Pinot Noir and Gouais Blanc, alongside more than a dozen grapes who share the same parents of Pinot Noir and Gouais Blanc with Chardonnay including Aligoté, Aubin Vert, Auxerrois, Gamay Blanc Gloriod, Gamay Noir, Melon, and so forth. What was perhaps an even more fascinating discovery of hers was the identity of American Zinfandel and its links between the Croatian varieties Crljenak Kaštelanski and Tribidrag, as well as to the Primitivo in Puglia of Italy. In Carole Meredith's humble words, it was truly a streak of luck. It all started with a seminar at the UC Davis medical school, given by Dr. Eric Lander, who is one of the pioneers in genomics and DNA markers. In his talk, he introduced a then new method of micro-satellite markers used for studying hypertension in rats by localizing the genes shown to be important for hypertension. It was such micro-satellite markers that could help mapping out inheritance and parentage. Wouldn't it be great to do that in grape? The light bulb sparked and it spawned research efforts of several decades down the path, connecting researchers from around the globe in an concerted effort to document, trace, and preserve grape varieties. Lagier Meredith winery at the southern end of the Mount Veeder district, where cooling afternoon breezes from the San Pablo Bay helps retain fresh acidity and bring out complexity, now produces complexly delicious Syrah, Malbec, as well as Tribidrag and Mondeuse, whose parentage identification marked the highlights of Carole Meredith's academic career.

Similar illuminating discoveries by vintners have also surfaced nuances about existing grape varieties, solving long-term puzzles and connecting dots along the way. Trebbiano Abruzzese from Trebbiano d'Abruzzo is one of them. In the best vintners' hands, it can showcase crystalline acidity, a honeyed mouthfeel with a mineral edge, peppered with mint and acacia, and juicy pomaceous fruit, and just as long-lasting as the fine white Burgundys. It is no wonder Valentini's Trebbiano d'Abruzzo, cultivated in Loreto Aprutino on the gentle rolling hills close to the ocean, with plenty sunlight interception and air circulation that keeps the fungal diseases at bay, is widely considered of Italy's greatest whites of all time. However, it had long been a puzzle to many why the late Edoardo Valentini, the mysterious producer of Valentini's Trebbiano d'Abruzzo chose to cultivate the Trebbiano grape, widely believed to be unremarkable and ordinary at best and raised it to such an unreachable height. "It is with the white, made from the usually ordinary Trebbiano grape, that Valentini stakes its claim to greatness." As Eric Asimov, the wine writer for New York Times, has put it. Many had assumed it is Valentini's green fingers and masterful winemaking skills that have made Valentini's Trebbiano d'Abruzzo great. True. But what most don't realize, including many wildly knowledgeable wine professionals like Eric Asimov, is that Trebbiano d'Abruzzo is but one of the Italy's many Trebbiano varieties, and for the longest time, it was thought to be a poor-quality variety because it was confused with the likes of

Trebbiano Toscano, Bombino Bianco, and Mostosa. Therefore uninformed the growers were unknowingly co-planting different varieties in their vineyards and treating them identically despite the fact that different varieties excel in different conditions regarding soil type, sunlight exposure, training and trellising, etc. Because of its finicky nature, full of vigor and susceptible to powdery mildew and likely to suffer in windy locations, if not cared for in its own right, its high acidity could drop rapidly overnight and the must would oxidize easily, wasting away the hidden potential. Whereas in Valentini's vineyards, it is 100% Trebbiano Abruzzese, not mixed in with other lower quality Trebbianos. In the best hands that treat the variety where it grows best, it makes truly magical and unforgettable wines.

A similar tale could be told about Aligoté, the younger sister of Chardonnay who shares the same parents of Pinot Noir and Gouais Blanc, the underdog of white Burgundy. Chardonnay seems to have inherited the superstar qualities of Pinot Noir now both planted and praised everywhere. Gouais Blanc was the workhorse grape in the middle ages, enjoyed among the masses, but not really considered to be a fine high quality grape, and had long faded into obscurity today. In this tale of two siblings, Chardonnay prevailed in part because of bureaucracy. While Burgundy's AOC system has revolutionized around the wine world, it has a chilling effect on Aligoté, relegating the grape to regional wines, barring Bouzeron. Since Aligoté can not carry the name of a village, 1er cru, or grand cru site, but rather the basic Bourgogne Blanc no matter how good a site they hail from, the owner of better site is better off the market planting Chardonnay or Pinot Noir to claim the land's status and investment. The Matthew effect kicks in, and Aligoté is pushed to the fringe. This unfortunate chain of events in turn sends the subcultural message that because Bourgogne Aligoté is named by variety, not a village, a *climat* or a *lieu-dit*, it can not transmit terrior — the root of its inferiority to Chardonnay. To make it even worse, Aligoté is often produced from vines cloned from the 1970s, with yields over 80 hectoliters per hectare. It's no wonder that Aligoté has acquired a bad rep. But not all Aligotés are created equal: Aligoté Vert, the modern clonal selection, is the high-yielding version usually considered thin and uninteresting, whereas Aligoté Doré, the pre-clonal version, is in another completely different league altogether. There is a complexity to the acidity, seamlessly wrapped in the fruit of Aligoté Doré, bursting with electric energy, tension, and precision. Jean-Charles le Bault de la Morinière who only makes grand cru on the hill of Corton at Bonneau du Martray wishes that he still had Aligoté Doré in his Corton-Charlemagne. The domaine had about one hectare until it was uprooted in the 1960s. Becky Wasserman had shared a few bottles of these old-aged Corton Aligotés at her events with vintners, surprising many people who blind tasted them alongside serious Premier and Grand Cru Chardonnays, and inspiring some to start cultivating it themselves. Because its rarity, without a single nursery proposing, the only people who have Aligoté Doré are those who have very old vines. De Villaine, Comte Armand, Michel Lafarge, Pierre Morey, Nicolas Faure, and Jean-Marie Ponsot in his Premier Cru Monts Luisants, are a few of the domaines who produce it. But its greatest champion, with four single-vineyard bottlings, is without doubt Sylvain Pataille in Marsannay. He is one of the newer generations who is treating Aligoté Doré like a rockstar in a way it deserves, making beautiful terrior-driven expressions ever since the vintage of 2013.

Nuances apart, what about native grape varieties of extraordinary quality potential that were simply eclipsed by international grape varieties to the point of extinction or at the very least forgotten, possibly due to being finicky and difficult to grow? In the 1950s, Fiano, one of the greatest white wines in Italy, was almost extinct. Back in 1978, plantings in Fiano di Avellino DOC were down to only 4 hectares. Mastroberardino family, the most historic wine estate in Campania ever since 1878, had and has been a real champion for the native grape varieties of Campania such as Fiano, Greco, and Aglianico. When Antonio Mastroberardino, now widely referred to as the Grape Archaeologist, took over the family business in late 1950s, everything was in shambles after the devastation of World War Two. It was a daunting task to rebuild the viticulture and the winery to restore its former glory at the beginning of 1900s. Taking a leaf out of his grandfather Angelo's and father Michele's books, literally[33], Antonio started once again traveling overseas to open export foreign markets, except that everywhere he went, no one had ever heard of Fiano or Greco. Taking a decision as brave as to focus on such obscure native grape varieties, to identify, preserve, and bring them back to the limelight, rather than taking the safe route like everyone else of planting international grape varieties, was no was no easy feat. It must have taken him an incredible amount of bravery, hard work, and faith to push it through and fortunately it panned out. He was the absolute leader, a lone wolf at the time if you will, as there were simply no others. Had it not been him, Fiano or Greco might not have been restored to such popularity and high esteem as it is now.

Now with such a long-winded digression at my own risk of burying the lead... Wouldn't it be awesome if we could provide scientists and vintners with tools that consolidate knowledge and automatically identify grape varieties based on previously fragmented knowledge about existing varieties leaf pattern, viticultural features,

[33]The Mastroberardino family are apparently fond of keeping journals of their extensive travel history to pass on for future generations to peruse in awe and nostalgia.

etc. that could potentially accelerate the rate of such discoveries? In Section 7.5 let us detail how AI models could enable universal large-scale fine-grained identification of grape varieties and grape diseases to assist in ampelographical scientific discovery.

7.1 Few-shot Learning

Few-shot learning refers to the learning scenario where despite an abundant set of samples covering a large set of categories, for some particular categories there exists only a few samples, and few-shot learning strategies aim at efficiently grasping the essence of such categories with very limited samples. For instance, a wine professional working in an Italian fine-dining restaurant might frequently sample Italian wines, and could comfortably ace any Italian wines in a blind tasting. However, his or her exposure to Lebanese wines might be limited and had only tasted a few samples from Chateau Musar and Domaine des Tourelles in the past, which is a shame. How could he or she still manage to identify Lebanese wines in a blind tasting? Few-shot learning solves exactly this.

Traditionally, to grasp a new subject or area of interest, one needs to learn from a set of data samples as large as possible to identify hidden truths or common patterns about it. With limited resources or time constraints, how shall one extrapolate and learn about a new subject with only a few samples? Let us explore two possibly feasible routes:

- Augmenting the few limited samples to include more plausible samples, called *Data Augmentation*.
- Revising our learning strategy to suffice with only a few limited samples for the particular task. Most notable examples of such learning strategies include *Multi-task Learning* (covered in Section 4.2) and *Meta Learning*.

7.1.1 Data Augmentation

Data augmentation is a widely used machine learning technique as a solution to limited data, operated on the assumption that more information could be extracted from the available data samples by enriching it with augmentation. For instance, one typically augments one sample into multiple additional samples of various forms without changing the core content of the sample, so the original labels associated with the original single sample could be broadcast to all the augmented samples with confidence. Sometimes one could augment by combining several original data samples with known logics that would naturally inform the associated labels for the augmented samples. Data augmentation was perhaps mostly commonly applied to computer vision problems at least at the very beginning, but has been assimilated rather quickly by various other machine learning fields such as speech and natural language processing to augment datasets of all forms.

There are at least three major methodologically representative data augmentation methods that have permeated not only the field of computer vision, but various other fields as well: rule-based techniques, sample interpolation techniques, and model-based techniques. Let me walk you through each of them by detailing how they manifest in the fields of computer vision and natural language processing.

The relatively intuitive and straightforward data augmentation techniques revolve around **rule-based manipulation**s. These are data augmentation primitives that use easy-to-compute and pre-specified transforms agnostic of whatever AI models one might use.

- In computer vision, various geometric or spatial transformations of images had long been established as standard augmentation practices. Consider a standard computer vision task such as image classification or object detection, an image of cats that's been horizontally flipped, or rotated, or shifted slightly to the left, etc., still remains an image of cats.

Color space manipulation, blurring and sharpening, and noise reduction or injection are common image augmentation strategies widely used in practice as well, as oftentimes a picture of cats in a full scale of colors remains a picture of cats when converted black and white, or decorated with a purple tint, when cats' edges are blurred or sharpened, or when the image quality improves or degrades. Even though in particular applications, such augmentation strategies might not work any more. For instance, if the task at hand is image sentiment or emotion classification, which classifies an image into invoking either positive or negative emotions, then a different color scheme is very likely to change the corresponding labels, thus color space manipulation as a data augmentation strategy would probably compromise the validity of corresponding labels. In another case, when reducing the pixel values of an image to simulate a nighttime environment, it might become too dark for any objects within the image to be legible. However, for many other tasks, color, blurring, or image quality manipulations could prove fruitful in improving the generalization ability of resulting algorithms.

Some other rule-based manipulations take the form of *feature space augmentation* with image analogy — given an image of a dog under a tree, and an image of a mountain top, generate the image analogy of a dog on top of a mountain. Such analogies were largely exploited with rule-based computer graphics techniques in the early days before neural style transfer (covered in Section 5.2) or image translation (covered in Section 5.1) came along circa 2015, when the switch to neural style transfer or image translation for effective image augmentation resulted. We will go into greater detail in model-based techniques of data augmentation below.

- Likewise in natural language processing, a set of insertion, deletion, and swap operations could be randomly applied randomly to texts, without altering the message therein, therefore increasing the size of data samples at one's disposal and improving the algorithm performance at low cost. For paraphrase identification tasks, a signed graph could be constructed over the textual documents with sentences as nodes and pair labels as signed edges indicating which two sentences could be paraphrased back and forth. With logical deduction over the constructed graph based on balance theory and transitivity, one could infer additional sentence pairs as valid augmented data for this task. Moreover, taking hints from image cropping and rotation, dependency tree morphing has been proposed to effectively rewrite any given sentence syntactically to generate more textual data. For instance, for dependency-parsed sentences, children of the same parent could be swapped or deleted without altering the gist of the sentence.

Sample interpolation techniques comprise another class of data augmentation methods, first introduced independently around the same time in 2017 by different research groups including Facebook AI, IBM, and University of Tokyo, largely designed for computer vision applications.

- *SamplePairing* [Inoue, 2018] technique for image augmentation synthesizes a new sample from one image by overlaying another image randomly chosen from the training data (i.e., taking the average of two images for each pixel) while preserving the original associated labels. Between-Class learning [Tokozume et al., 2018] generates between-class images by mixing two images belonging to different classes with a random ratio and trains the model to learn to output the mixing ratio. At the same time, the later-widely-adopted *mixup* method [Zhang et al., 2018a] was proposed to mix two randomly selected samples by applying an identical linear function to both the samples and the corresponding labels to create virtual training samples. All three methods have been shown to result in remarkable performance boosts in results with varying levels of robustness and generalization ability, despite being perhaps not terribly sensible to human eyes.

Random erasing [Zhong et al., 2020] is another augmentation technique especially effective to cope with image occlusions which usually make visual tasks more challenging (for example, a cat whose body is largely blocked by a big box is harder to make sense of by computer vision algorithms). By randomly selecting a patch within an image and masking it to be all white or all black or any random colors, it forces the computer vision model to learn more descriptive features about an image, improving its generalization ability.

- What had delayed the adoption of sample interpolation in the field of natural language processing was due to the fact that such methods require continuous inputs like pixels when natural languages are discrete. It wasn't until 2020 that padding and mixing embedding (embeddings were covered in Section 7.4) or hidden layers in deep neural networks were proposed to tailor this idea to natural language texts. Later variants proposed similar strategies for augmenting speech signals accordingly. Notably, *seq2mixup* [Guo et al., 2020] further generalized *mixup* for sequence transduction tasks in two ways — one being sampling a binary mask and picking from one of two sentences while generating each word within a newly augmented sentence; and the other more lax version being interpolating between two sentences based on a coefficient, which appeared to outperform the former.

With deep learning penetrating every corner of machine learning and AI communities, **model-based data augmentation** techniques are the most recent innovations (as of 2021) within this line of research. Model-based techniques include:

- Two classes of image generation techniques *neural style transfer* (covered in Section 5.2) and *image-to-image translation* (covered in Section 5.1) have proved effective when used as image augmentation strategies. By transferring different styles to original content images, semantic information is preserved and a large amount of image samples could be augmented for tasks that focus on semantic content or relationships within images. Such model-based image augmentation techniques could be traced back to image augmentation with generative models such as generative adversarial networks (GANs) notoriously capable of generating realistic images. This class of augmentation aims to create artificial yet realistic looking samples from a dataset such that they retain similar features to the original set and has shown remarkable potential in performance improvement in model training.

- In natural language processing, sequence-to-sequence text generation models have also been used for data augmentation. An early yet popular approach is *backtranslation* [Sennrich et al., 2016, Edunov et al., 2018] which generates valid new sentences by translating into another language and back into the original language. Pre-trained language models such as Transformers [Vaswani et al., 2017] have also been leveraged similarly by reconstructing parts of original sentences. Better variants popped up over time, one of which, for instance, generates augmented samples by replacing words with other words at random but drawn with probabilities according to the contexts. Another approach called "corrupt-and-reconstruct" uses a corruption function to mask an arbitrary number of word positions and a reconstruction function unmasking them using BERT language model [Devlin et al., 2019] (covered in Section 7.4), which appears to work well where *domain shifts* (training models in one context but applying to another) are present.

Besides augmenting samples from available samples, some other approaches use generative language models like GPT [Radford et al., 2018] (covered in Section 7.4) conditioned on available or potential labels to generate candidate samples. Another classifier trained on the original dataset is then used to select the best ones to include for augmentation.

With such a wide range of augmentation strategies at our disposal, one could certainly mix and match different strategies, and the resulting augmentation space could be enormous, which could lead to compromised performance in the end if applied blindly. This naturally begs the question of when and how to apply different augmentation techniques laid out above? Which tasks, datasets, and contexts are best suited for which techniques? This is exactly where augmentation optimization strategies such as *AutoAugment* [Cubuk et al., 2018] enters the picture. It introduced an automated approach to identify optimal data augmentation policies from data, being inspired by research advances in architecture search that discovers optimal model architectures from data. It adopts a reinforcement learning framework that searches for an optimal augmentation strategy within a constrained set of geometric transformations with miscellaneous levels of distortions. Evolutionary algorithms or random search were also cited by authors of *AutoAugment* as effective search algorithms for finding optimal augmentation strategies. This line of work was further improved with respect to computational efficiency with various search strategies.

7.1.2 Meta Learning

To solve a new task with very limited examples, meta learning is designed to build efficient algorithms capable of learning the new task quickly by leveraging learning experience from a variety of other tasks with rich annotated samples such that few examples are needed for the new task. Therefore meta learning is another popular machine learning paradigm for few-shot learning problems.

In contrast to traditional learning processes where we treat each data sample point as a training example of a specific learning task, meta learning treats each task as a training example and in order to quickly learn how to solve a new task, a variety of tasks are gathered and a meta model is trained to adapt to all the available tasks, while optimizing for the expected performance on the brand new task.

This might sound somewhat similar to *multi-task learning* which was detailed in Section 2.3. In *multi-task learning*, a model is jointly learned to perform well on multiple pre-specified tasks, whereas in meta learning, a meta model is trained on multiple tasks to be able to adapt to new tasks quickly. In a meta learning paradigm, one doesn't necessarily learn how to solve a specific task but rather learns to solve many tasks in sequence. Each time our meta learner learns a new task, it gets better at learning new tasks — it learns to learn with past experience of previous tasks whereas a multi-task learner does *not* necessarily improve as the number of tasks increases.

Let us illustrate the difference between multi-task and meta learning with Figure 50.

Figure 50: An illustration of the difference between multi-task and meta learning.

One fairly accepted taxonomy of meta learning techniques proposed by Google DeepMind researcher Oriol Vinyals in 2017 divides the space into three categories, which we will expand on in the following texts one by one:

1. metric-based meta learning (or simply *metric learning*, covered in Section 4.1);

2. model-based meta learning;

3. optimization-based meta learning.

Metric-based methods in essence aim to acquire meta knowledge in the form of a good feature space that can be used for various new tasks. New tasks are learned when we compare new samples with existing samples that we are certain about in the learned feature space. The more similar they appear to be, the more likely the new samples are associated with the same outcome labels as existing samples. Therefore, the goal of metric learning lies in how to learn an accurate and generalizable similarity function capable of correctly associating similar samples and telling dissimilar samples apart. To that end, task-agnostic metric-based meta learners are trained on a range of different tasks to learn a good similarity function, which facilitates task-specific learning done through pairwise sample comparisons with the similarity function. Therefore, the fact that one learns a similarity function across tasks to boost performances on individual tasks embodies the essence of meta learning: learning to learn.

Siamese networks [Koch et al., 2015] marked the beginning of deep-learning-based metric learning (a.k.a. deep metric learning) by initiating the idea of learning similarities between and comparing query and reference samples.

Matching networks [Vinyals et al., 2016] that came along soon after inherited the same idea of comparing inputs for making model predictions, except with a new proposal of a direct training paradigm tailored for few-shot learning upon a variety of tasks.

Prototypical networks [Snell et al., 2017] further improved upon Siamese and Matching networks by reducing the number of candidates for comparison to a selection of representative prototypes, which significantly sped up and robustified the algorithm.

Relation networks [Sung et al., 2018] improved the flexibility of similarity functions by replacing pre-specified static metrics in earlier works with deep neural networks that could be tailored for new tasks.

Graph networks-based methods [Satorras and Estrach, 2018] generalized earlier works such as Siamese or prototypical networks to learn efficient and flexible information transfer within a directed graph that subsumes earlier structures.

Inspired by biological underpinnings that humans compare similar objects by constantly shifting attention back and forth, the *attentive recurrent comparator*s framework [Shyam et al., 2017] compares by taking multiple interwoven glimpses at different parts of samples being compared.

Metric learning techniques for few-shot learning applications in general boost straightforward concepts, and fast inference at relatively smaller scales. However when it comes to greater domain shifts between novel tasks and existing tasks or learning a large number of tasks at a large scale, metric learning approaches could suffer from expensive computational costs due to pairwise comparisons.

Model-based meta learning techniques are more task-adaptive alternatives to metric-based ones, as dynamic hidden representations of tasks are maintained throughout, despite being less straightforward conceptually therefore perhaps relatively less interpretable. Several pioneering works took the approach of sequential learning for dynamic representations with available data samples such as memory-augmented neural networks and recurrent meta-learners. Meta networks strove to tailor to every task with generative models of custom model parameters.

Simple neural attentive meta-learner (SNAIL) improved the memory capacity of the learner as well as its ability to siphon out specific memory according to new tasks, which previous works suffered from, with attention mechanisms.

Neural statistician and *conditional neural process (CPN)* both attempted more integrated frameworks for meta learning, with neural statisticians adopting distances between curated meta features to make predictions for new tasks and conditional neural processes conditioning classifiers on such meta features.

Compared to metric learners, model-based meta learners are generally more flexible, therefore more applicable to a broader context. But it has been documented that oftentimes model-based meta learners are worse than metric learners, especially those based on graph neural networks, and could still suffer from a large set of tasks in large scale applications or when novel tasks are rather distant from existing tasks, at least compared to optimization-based meta learning methods.

Optimization-based meta learning techniques differ even more from metric-based or model-based approaches in concept. Most methods in this class view meta learning as a hierarchical optimization problem where at the base level, each learner makes task-specific learning progress with certain optimizers while the performance across various tasks higher up the hierarchy is optimized.

[Andrychowicz et al., 2016] first introduced the idea of replacing hand-crafted optimizer with a trainable deep learning model in 2016, which perhaps marked the start of optimization-based meta learning techniques. Soon after the neural network as optimizer approach was tailored for few-shot learning settings by not only learning the optimization procedure, but also an optimal initialization, which enabled it to be applied across tasks.

Model-agnostic meta-learning (MAML) [Finn et al., 2017], for one, received considerable recognition within the meta learning community, inspiring many other works down the path. The premise of MAML is that the process of training a model's parameters such that a few steps of model training can produce good results on a new task can be viewed from a feature learning standpoint as building an internal representation that is broadly suitable for many tasks. If the internal representation is suitable for many tasks, simply fine-tuning slightly can produce good results. The reason partly lies in the fact that some internal representations are more transferrable than others. For example, a neural network might learn internal features that are broadly applicable to all tasks, rather than a single individual task. To encourage the emergence of such general-purpose representations, MAML adopts an explicit approach to find sensitive model parameters such that small changes in the parameters will produce large improvements on model performance of any task. Various followup works extended the MAML framework in different directions: incorporating meta learning of learning rate alongside initializations (Meta-SGD [Li et al., 2017]), adopting active learning (covered in Section 6.2) frameworks (e.g., active one-shot learning [Woodward and Finn, 2017]), adapting to multi-modal (Section 4.2) settings (MMAML [Vuorio et al., 2019]), improving robustness and relieving computational burdens, and so forth.

Optimization-based meta learning, being a rather nascent and active area of research, is definitely fast evolving with increasingly more new innovations proposed every year. Optimization-based meta learning methods in general are more generalizable and robust than meta learners based on metrics or models, perhaps better suited for a wider range of distinct tasks, despite being more computationally expensive, which might as well be addressed soon in upcoming research works.

7.2 Zero-shot Learning

Zero-shot learning refers to the learning scenario where despite an abundant set of samples covering a large set of categories, for some particular categories no samples exist whatsoever, most likely due to rarity, expensive acquisition cost, or fast evolution and mutation, and zero-shot learning strategies aim at efficiently grasping the essence of such categories with no samples at all. For instance, a wine professional working in an Italian fine-dining restaurant might frequently sample Italian wines, and could comfortably ace any Italian wines in a blind tasting. However, he or she might have never had any Lebanese wines, which is a shame. How could he or she still manage to identify Lebanese wines in a blind tasting? Zero-shot learning (ZSL) solves exactly this.

ZSL was first proposed for image classification problems in the computer vision community [Palatucci et al., 2009]. A typical scenario is recognizing grapevines for which no training images exist by leveraging their semantic relationships to grapevines with training images via *side information* such as textual descriptions, visual anno-

tations, and a grapevine taxonomy. Since then, ZSL has been applied to various tasks in other fields of AI such as text classification, event extraction in natural language processing (NLP) and link prediction in knowledge graph (KG).
One popular way to understand categories and characteristics of mainstream methods for ZSL is to bucket them into a few groups that are not necessarily mutually exclusive: attribute prediction models, compatibility models, hybrid models, transductive models, generative models, graph models. Since side information or external knowledge is such a critical aspect in ZSL, another plausible perspective is to categorize based on the nature or type of side information: text, attribute, knowledge graph, rule and ontology. Let me walk you through both taxonomies in the rest of this section.

Intermediate attribute prediction: [Lampert et al., 2013] introduced the concept of attributes as critical information for ZSL to make decisions, upon which two classic ZSL methods are based — the direct attribute prediction method (DAP) and the indirect attribute prediction method (IAP). Given an unknown image of a grapevine, ZSL methods predict the attribute of its species and then selects the most likely species according to the similarity of the attribute to the attributes of the known species. Direct attribute prediction methods (DAP) train a group of binary classifiers from image-attribute pairs, one individually for each attribute. During the test stage, the learned classifiers are applied to predict which subset of attributes the input image may have. Even though these methods achieve a relatively good performance in predicting attribute and recognizing unseen categories, limitations include untapped information of correlation between attributes, difficulties in predicting non-visual attributes, negative attribute correlation between object and scene that might set back learning, positive attribute correlation that might result in information redundancy and poor performance, different visual attribute manifestations across categories, unreliable human labeling of visual attributes, etc. To tackle these issues, indirect attribution prediction methods have been proposed to indirectly predict attributes by transferring knowledge between categories which can infer some attributes that are unable to detect directly.

Compatibility: compatibility methods learn a mapping from an image feature space to a semantic space, and evaluate the compatibility of the rendered image feature and output category vectors in the subspace to predict the category label. Some well-known contributions along this line of research include linear compatibility methods such as:

- SOC [Palatucci et al., 2009] (Semantic Output Code) classifier maps the image features into a semantic space and searches the nearest class label embedding therein;
- ALE [Akata et al., 2013] (Attribute Label Embedding) model learns a bilinear compatibility function between the image and the attribute space with a ranking loss function. It averts solving any intermediate problem (as in intermediate attribute prediction) and learns the model parameters to optimize directly the class ranking. Flexibility is improved as labeled samples can be added incrementally to update the embedding; Additionally, the label embedding framework is generic and not restricted to attributes therefore other sources of prior information can be readily combined with attributes;
- DeViSE [Frome et al., 2013] (Deep Visual-Semantic Embedding) model leverages textual data to learn semantic relationships between labels, and explicitly maps images into a rich semantic embedding space;
- An embarrassingly simple approach to zero-shot learning (ES-

ZSL) [Romera-Paredes and Torr, 2015] introduces a method that could be implemented with one line of code, outperforming then state-of-the-art methods. Based on a more general framework which models the relationships between features, attributes, and classes as a two linear layers network, where the weights of the top layer are not learned but are given by the environment, it learns a bilinear compatibility function with explicit regularization.

And nonlinear compatibility methods such as:

- LATEM [Xian et al., 2016] (Latent Embedding Model) extends a bilinear compatibility method SJE [Akata et al., 2015] to be (nonlinear) piecewise linear by learning multiple linear mappings with the selection of which being a latent variable. By incorporating latent variables in the compatibility function, the method achieves factorization over possibly complex combinations of variations in pose, appearance and other factors, therefore consistently improves upon linear compatibility models that were the state-of-the-art;

- Cross-modal transfer method [Socher et al., 2013] adopts a two-layer neural network to learn a nonlinear projection from image feature space to word embedding space. Most previous zero-shot learning models can only differentiate between unseen classes. In contrast, CMT can both obtain state-of-the-art performance on classes that have thousands of training images and obtain reasonable performance on unseen classes. This is achieved by first using outlier detection in the semantic space and then two separate recognition models without any manually defined semantic features for either words or images;

- [Lei Ba et al., 2015] trains a deep convolutional neural network (CNN) while learning a visual semantic embedding. Textual features are used to predict the output weights of both the convolutional and the fully connected layers of CNN. By leveraging the architecture of CNNs and learning features at different layers, rather than just learning an embedding space for both visual and textual modalities, as is common with other ZSL approaches, the method affords automatic generation of a list of pseudo-attributes for each visual category with of words from Wikipedia articles where textual embeddings are derived;

- Despite the success of deep neural networks that learn an end-to-end model between text and images in other vision problems such as image captioning, deep ZSL models show little advantage over ZSL models that use deep feature representations not learnt in an end-to-end manner. In [Zhang et al., 2017], the authors argue that the key is to choose the right embedding space. Instead of embedding into a semantic space or an intermediate space, the visual space might as well be used as the embedding space. This is because that in this space, the subsequent nearest neighbour search would suffer much less from the hubness problem (a few unseen class prototypes will become the nearest neighbors of many data points, i.e., hubs, since the embedding space is of high dimensions where nearest neighbor search is to be performed) and thus become more effective. This model design also provides a natural mechanism for multiple semantic modalities (e.g., attributes and sentence descriptions) to be fused and optimised jointly in an end-to-end manner;
- [Changpinyo et al., 2017] introduces a simple method that takes advantage of clustering structures in the semantic embedding space. It projects class semantic representations into the visual feature space and carries out nearest neighbor classifiers among projected representations. The key idea is to impose

the structural constraint that semantic representations must be predictive of the locations of their corresponding visual exemplars, thus reducing the ZSL problem to training multiple kernel-based regressors from semantic representation exemplar pairs from labeled data of the seen categories.

Hybrid: hybrid methods combine feature space mappings that correspond to the training class labels to represent the mapping of the testing samples in the feature space, and then obtain the class label estimation of the testing sample based on the similarity between the sample mapping and the testing class label mapping. In principle, hybrid methods embed both the image and semantic features into another shared intermediate space.

- SSE [Zhang and Saligrama, 2015] (Semantic Similarity Embedding) method views each source or target data as a mixture of seen class proportions, based on the assumption that the mixture patterns have to be similar if the two instances belong to the same unseen class. This perspective leads to learning both the source and target embedding functions that map an arbitrary source or target domain data into a same semantic space where similarity can be readily measured;

- Following SSE, joint latent similarity embedding method [Zhang and Saligrama, 2016] learns a joint latent space for both visual and semantic features using structured learning. The learned joint space is used not only to fit each instance well with dictionary learning, but also to enable recognition by bilinear classifiers during test;

- Multi-cue ZSL [Akata et al., 2016] jointly embed multiple text representations and semantic visual parts to ground visual attributes on image regions for fine-grained zero-shot recognition;

- Both SYNC [Changpinyo et al., 2016] (Synthesized classifier) approach and semantic manifold distance approach [Fu et al., 2015b] both tackle the ZSL problem from the perspective of manifold learning, by exploiting the class label relationship as a graph and aligning the semantic space that is derived from external information to the model space that concerns itself with recognizing visual features;
- LAGO [Atzmon and Chechik, 2018] (Learning Attribute Grouping) is a zero-shot probabilistic model that leverages and-or semantic structure in the attribute space, combining direct attribute prediction method (DAP) [Lampert et al., 2013] and the embarrassingly simple approach to zero-shot learning (ES-ZSL) introduced earlier.

Transductive: attribute prediction and semantic embedding methods however suffers from a projection domain shift problem — the visual feature mapping (embedding) learned from the seen class data may not generalise well to the unseen class data, which is an implicit assumption for semantic embedding based ZSL. Transductive embedding frameworks are among the possible solutions to mitigate such an issue, as well as another potential problem with transfer learning and domain adaptation style style methods for ZSL that lie in the sparsity of class prototypes for each target class: only a single prototype is available for zero-shot learning given a semantic representation. Unlike the opposite inductive methods for which only data of the source categories are available during the training phase. For the transductive ZSL methods, both the labeled source data and the unlabeled target data are available for training. The transductive setting refers to using the unlabelled test data to improve generalisation accuracy. Transductive methods use the class labels of the training classes and the side information of the testing classes to determine the class labels of the testing samples, which are then used to augment the labeled training data for training. And such a process continues in iteration until all the testing samples are labeled. However, since such transductive methods involve the data of unseen classes for learning the model, which many argue, breaches the strict ZSL settings, at least to some extent.

The transductive multi-view approach [Fu et al., 2015a] represents each unlabelled target class instance by multiple views: its low-level feature view and its (biased) projections in multiple semantic spaces such as visual attribute space and word space. To rectify the domain shift between side information and target datasets, a multi-view semantic space alignment process is specified to correlate different semantic views and the low-level feature view by projecting them onto a common latent embedding space learned using multi-view Canonical Correlation Analysis (CCA), with the intuition being that when the biased target data projections (semantic representations) are correlated or aligned with their (unbiased) low-level feature representations, the bias resulted from domain shift is then alleviated. Furthermore, after exploiting the synergy of different low-level feature and semantic views in the common embedding space, different target classes could become more compact and separable, making the subsequent zero-shot recognition task easier. Meanwhile, prototypes in each view are treated as labelled 'instances' and the manifold structure of the unlabelled data distribution in each view is exploited in the embedding space via label propagation on a graph, thus alleviating the other class prototype sparsity issue not uncommon in ZSL settings.

Shared model space (SMS) learning [Guo et al., 2016] is another transductive ZSL method for image recognition to enable efficient knowledge transfer between classes using attributes. With the shared model space and class attributes, the recognition model which directly generates labels for target class can be effectively constructed without any intermediate attribute learning.

Generative: Generative Adversarial Networks have been adopted as well to synthesize data for unseen categories based on side information such as semantic embeddings, such that the training data is augmented and ZSL converted to conventional supervised learning problems with a reasonable amount of labelled — albeit artificially — data for both seen and unseen categories. To improve synthetically generated sample points, some research efforts have ensured the synthetic samples to be almost indistinguishable from real samples, while others strive to preserve the inter-class relationships in synthetic samples in the semantic embedding space, with for instance, CycleGAN, StackGAN, as well as other generative models such as Variational Autoencoders (VAE) and ensembles of GANs and VAEs.

Another perhaps cleaner taxonomy is to categorize external knowledge or side information, essential in zero-shot learning frameworks, into *texts, attributes, knowledge graphs, ontologies, and rules.*

Side information in the form of **texts** refers to unstructured textual information of the categories such as descriptions, definitions, and names, ranging from single words to long documents. For instance, categories names and their word embeddings have been used to facilitate image classification in the early years of ZSL, sometimes boosted with descriptions from Wikipedia entries and crowdsourced descriptions for greater customization and granularity for fine-grained classification contexts.

To encode textual side information in terms of semantic meanings, one conventional approach is to use its contextualized word embeddings from a pre-trained language model (Section 7.4), which could suffer from misaligned optimization objectives since the two processes — semantic encoding and zero-shot prediction — are detached. An integrated approach would involve joint learning of zero-shot prediction and semantic encoding at the same time. For instance, DeViSE [Frome et al., 2013] jointly trains an early generation word embedding model (*skip-gram*) and an image classifier with finetuning. Besides textual names of different classes (or labels, or prediction targets), longer descriptions and even relevant documents have been used as potentially more detailed yet noisy side information. Additional feature learning and selection processes could be leveraged for such side information, sometimes at word or character level, and the same argument for joint learning applies regardless.

Attribute external knowledge, echoing the early and perhaps most well-known ZSL techniques of intermediate attribute prediction, refers to specific properties associated with each category that we try to learn about. As is included in Figure 51, for instance, if we are classifying grape varieties with zero-shot learning, relevant attributes could categorical, numerical, or binary ones such as color of the grape skin and pulp, cluster tightness, thickness of the grape skin, timing of budding or ripening, prone to reduction or oxidation or not, characteristic aromatics, disease resistance, preferable soil type, etc. Attributes could also be relative, conducive to comparison and distinction between different classes. For example, Syrah is perhaps more prone to reduction compared to Grenache, which is more prone to oxidation, which is part of the reason why, according Philippe Guigal of the Guigal estate in Ampuis in the northern Rhône Valley, their Côte-Rôties spend years aging in their in-house own dry aged French oak barrels and foudres (old and new) to counter reduction with slow micro-oxygenation. Attributes could also be applied in zero-shot link prediction in graphs where node attributes are used to predict unseen nodes without any pre-established connections to the original graph. Direct attribute prediction methods directly represent attributes with one-hot vectors (for instance, 1 for prone to reduction, 0 for otherwise). Indirect attribute prediction methods take a step further by encoding attributes with semantic embeddings, whether it be visual, textual, or graph-based, to which learned mapping functions or generative models could be applied. Compared to textual side information, attributes, despite being less noisy and more expressive, are perhaps much less available due to sparsity and costly manual annotation. Additionally, a zero-shot learning framework for fine-grained visual categorization (Section 7.5 and Section 6.4) [Huynh and Elhamifar, 2020] leverages a dense attribute-based attention mechanism that for each attribute focuses on the most relevant image regions, obtaining attribute-based features. The attribute-based attention model is guided by each attribute semantic vector, therefore, building the same number of feature vectors as the number of attributes. Instead of aligning a combination of all attribute-based features with the true class semantic vector, an attribute embedding technique aligns each attribute-based feature with its attribute semantic vector. Therefore, a vector of attribute scores is computed, for the presence of each attribute in an image, whose similarity with the true class semantic vector is maximized. Each attribute score is curated with an attention model over attributes to better capture the discriminative power of different attributes to enable differentiation between classes that are different in only a few attributes.

Knowledge graphs (Section 3.1) could serve as a semantically rich source of side information for ZSL, encompassing both texts and attributes as external knowledge. Considering the classification problem of grape varieties or even clones, a knowledge graph could express different kinds of semantics for the inter-varietal relationship, such as the grape family by DNA (Schiava Grossa crossed with Muscat of Alexandria produces Malvasia del Lazio and Muscat of Hamburg, Pinot crossed with Schiava Grossa produces Madeleine Royale, which is a parent of Müller-Thurgau, when crossed with Riesling, Touriga Nacional and Marufo the parents of Touriga Franca, etc.), frequent co-planting, co-fermenting, or blending relationships (Syrah or Shiraz and Viognier are commonly co-fermented, Touriga Nacional and Touriga Franca are commonly co-planted, Corvina, Corvinone, Rondinella, Oseleta, and Molinara are commonly blended, etc.), and varietal affinity for a particular soil type (Merlot perhaps does better in clay-rich soils, Gamay enjoys living in granite soils, and loess appears to work wonders for Grüner Veltliner, etc.).

To automatically construct domain-specific knowledge graphs (KGs) such as wine KGs, one could leverage knowledge or information extraction and integration tools and techniques. To extract relevant wine knowledge, the relevant documents or articles that include relevant wine concepts and entities could be matched with KG entries using either existing associations (such as information of nodes and links already included in KG) or mapping in-between such documents and KG entries by (fuzzy) string matching. Once we have constructed the initial KG, the node semantic vectors could be readily learnt with a *KG embedding method* based on either Graph Neural Networks (GNN) like Relational or Attentive Graph Convolutional Networks (GCN), or machine translation and factorization (such as TransE, DistMult). Compared to texts and attributes, KGs are perhaps more structured and informative, despite being even more costly and challenging to construct, curate, and maintain. KGs with specific knowledge are more often than not hard to come by for a ZSL task in practice.

Rules and ontologies could be particularly valuable as side information for ZSL as they house structured logical relationship information between seen and unseen classes. Rules could be prescribed to associate seen classes with unseen ones with logical deduction. For instance, an associative rule could apply to (1) Cabernet Franc, Cabernet Sauvignon, and Carménère are all known to contain pyrazine; (2) Pyrazine as a chemical compound is usually responsible for aromas of green bell pepper, reaching the deduction that Cabernet Franc, Cabernet Sauvignon, and Carménère are all known for aromas of green bell pepper. One example of a rule-based ZSL pipeline could include matching all the potential relations with Wikipedia relations, constructing a KG from them, learning the KG embeddings, and calculating the unseen relations' embeddings with compositional relations specified by the defined rules.

An ontology represents structured knowledge such as concepts and entities as well as their relations, annotations, properties or attributes, and sometimes respective constraints and additional meta. Ontologies by Web Ontology Language (OWL) further include logical relationships. Approach for integrating ontology into zero-shot learning pipeline include using ontology to guide [Geng et al., 2021] or enhance [Chen et al., 2020] the learning process, where semantic vectors of seen and unseen classes could be learnt by KG embeddings derived from ontologies and then a ZSL method based on a generative model could be applied.

In (conventional) ZSL settings, the algorithms are expected to deploy to work on samples that contain exclusively the unseen classes or categories, which could be rather unrealistic in practice, since examples of the seen classes on which the algorithms were trained on are more common than the rare long-tailed classes left unseen. Therefore, recognizing both seen and unseen classes at the same time is perhaps of much greater practical relevance, and this is exactly what **generalized zero-shot learning** (GZSL) is called for. Figure 51 helps illustrate the key differences between ZSL and GZSL.

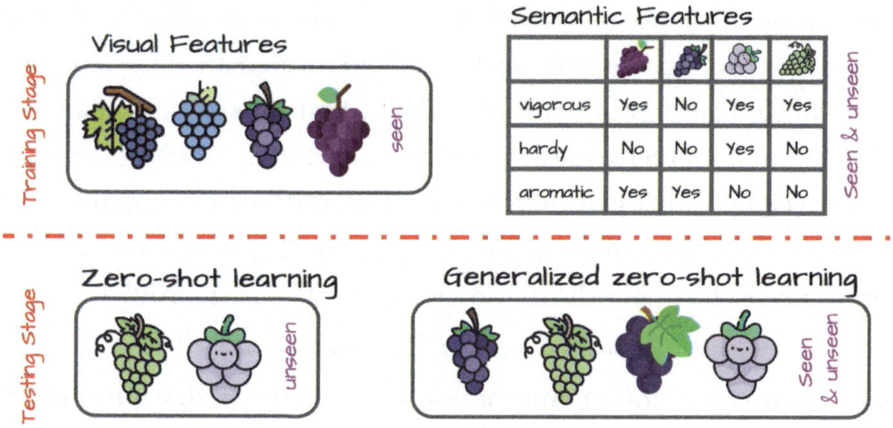

Figure 51: An illustration of zero-shot Learning (ZSL) and generalized zero-shot learning (GZSL).

7.3 Generalized Zero-shot Learning

The same wine professional working in a fine-dining restaurant might frequently sample French, Italian, and American wines, and could perhaps comfortably ace most French, Italian or American wines in a blind tasting if we constrain our blind wines to be from France, Italy, or US. However, he or she might have never had any Armenian wines, which is a shame. How could he or she still manage to identify Lebanese or Armenian wines in a blind tasting of Armenian wines? This is the problem zero-shot learning solves. How will he or she be able to tell the differences between Armenian wines and those from France, Italy, or US in a blind tasting where any wine could be poured? This is where generalized zero-shot learning enters the picture and how it differs from zero-shot learning: in zero-shot learning, one is searching for the new category knowing that it has never shown up before or it is definitely not what have been learnt or known, whereas in generalized zero-shot learning, whatever new sample we are faced with could fall within a category we are already familiar with or something completely new to us. The onus is on us to tell them apart, which makes generalized zero-shot learning problems more challenging, and more realistic in real life. Generalized zero-shot learning (GZSL), first introduced as a solution to open set recognition [Scheirer et al., 2012] problems in computer vision, didn't gain much attention or interests of many until 2016, when empirical evidences [Chao et al., 2016] showed that ZSL methods perform poorly on the more realistic GZSL problems.

GZSL poses a unique combination of challenges: first, the model has to learn effectively for classes without samples (zero-shot). It also needs to learn well for classes with many samples. Finally, the two very different regimes should be combined in a consistent way in a single model. The fact that existing ZSL methods perform much worse in GZSL than ZSL settings was documented in multiple studies including [Chao et al., 2016] in which a simple but effective calibration method *calibrated stacking* that downweights seen classes to balance two conflicting forces: recognizing data from seen classes versus those from unseen ones was introduced as well as a modified performance metric Area Under Seen-Unseen accuracy Curve (AUSUC) to characterize such a trade-off and examine its utility in evaluating various ZSL approaches. Various similar alternative solutions to mitigate biases towards the seen classes include *scaled calibration, probabilistic representation*, and *temperature scaling*. Another class of solutions treat unseen classes as outliers and apply outlier (or anomaly, or novelty) detection algorithms, whether it be probabilistic-based, entropy-based, or clustering-based, to separate seen and unseen classes first. In addition, GZSL could also be decomposed into two tasks: *open set recognition* (OSR) which recognizes the seen classes but not the unseen ones, and ZSL which identifies the unseen classes left from OSR.

At least three specific phenomena have been shown to make GZSL challenging: *biases towards seen classes, hubness*, and *domain shift.*

One vital factor accounting for the poor performance of ZSL techniques on GZSL problems could perhaps be explained as follows. ZSL achieves the recognition of new categories by establishing the connection between the visual embeddings and the semantic embeddings. However, a strong bias could stem from bridging the visual and the semantic embeddings. During the training phase of most existing ZSL methods, the visual instances are usually projected to several fixed anchor points specified by the source classes in the semantic embedding space. This leads to a strong bias when these methods are used for testing: given images of novel classes in the target dataset, they tend to categorize them as one of the source classes. In light of that, quasi-fully supervised learning [Song et al., 2018] proposes to map labeled source images to several fixed point points specified by the source categories in the semantic embedding space, and the unlabeled target images are forced to be mapped to other points specified by the target categories. On the other hand, the adaptive confidence smoothing (COSMO) approach [Atzmon and Chechik, 2019] consists of three classifiers: A "gating" model that makes soft decisions if a sample is from a "seen" class, and two experts: a ZSL expert, and an expert model for seen classes. These modules share their prediction confidence in a principled probabilistic way in order to reach an accurate joint decision during inference. Various other approaches are available for mitigating such biases including meta learning (Section 7.1.2).

One of the challenges that early generations of ZSL and GZSL methods focused on is the *hubness problem.* It largely results from the curse of dimensionality. The early paradigm that maps visual features into a high-dimensional semantic space where one searches for the nearest neighbor easily leads to too many sample points close together and difficult to distinguish, thus forming a hub especially when common items cluster.

The notorious *domain shift* issue remains as well with GZSL and ZSL. It comes in multiple forms, with one referring to the gap between visual and semantic space, and the other the domain gap between seen and unseen classes. The domain shift problem is perhaps generally more severe in GZSL than ZSL since seen classes do appear side by side with unseen classes in the final prediction, and more likely to occur in inductive settings than tranductive settings since no signals or traces of data belonging to unseen classes are included in inductive, unlike transductive paradigms. To clarify, Figure 52, Figure 53, and Figure 54 illustrate the differences between transductive and inductive GZSL settings. In short, visual and semantic features of the unseen classes — assuming a canonical image classification task at hand though generalizable to other types of tasks too — are still accessible in transductive settings whereas no such information of unseen classes remains accessible in inductive settings. Therefore, as a solution, some inductive GZSL methods introduce side information from the unseen classes, which makes it semantically transductive, sitting somewhere in-between inductive and transductive regimes.

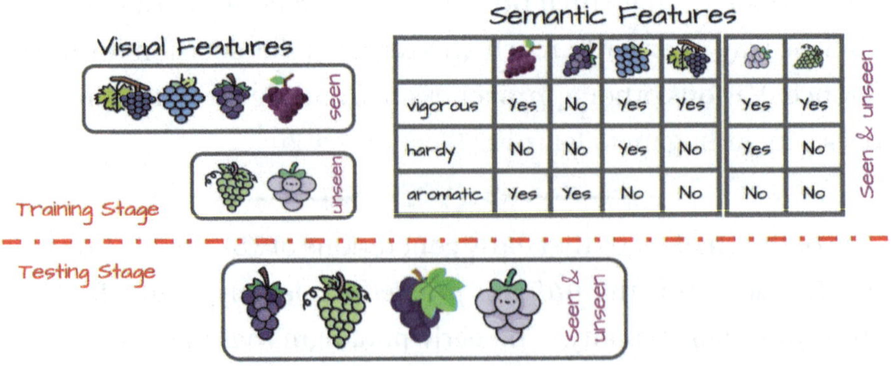

Figure 52: Transductive generalized zero-shot learning.

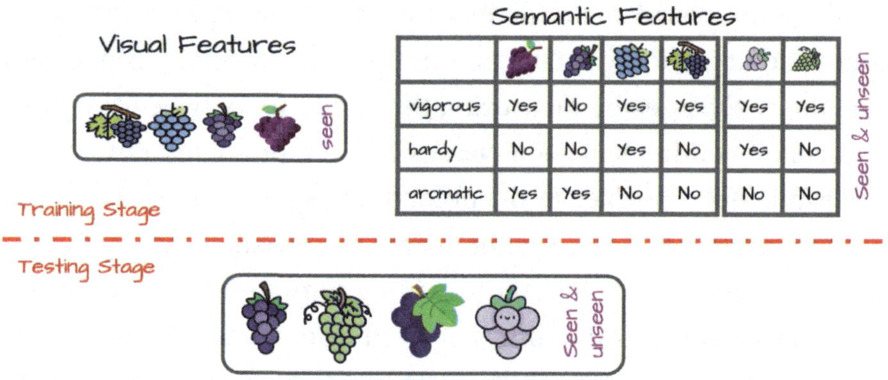

Figure 53: Transductive *semantic* generalized zero-shot learning.

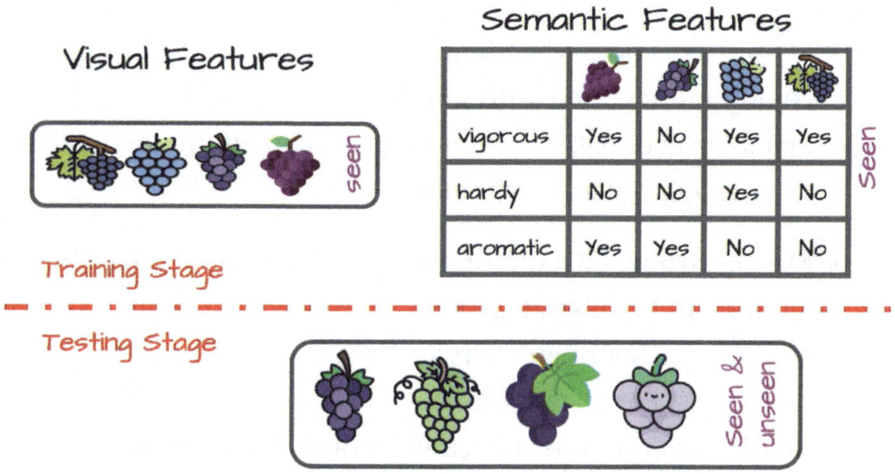

Figure 54: Inductive generalized zero-shot learning.

Beside the distinction between inductive and transductive GZSL methods, another dimension along which one categorizes GZSL is perhaps embedding-based versus generative-based methods.

Embedding-based methods learn to project visual features to semantic embeddings, and the learnt projection is then used to identify unseen classes by measuring the similarity between the prototypical embeddings of seen classes and the predicted embeddings of testing data samples in the embedding space. Generative-based methods instead learn to generate images or visual features for each of the unseen classes based on training samples of the seen classes and the semantic embeddings derived from both seen and unseen classes. A GZSL task could be converted to a supervised learning task with generated samples for unseen classes.

Among embedding-based GZSL methods, the following categories based on specific techniques are perhaps the most popular:

- KG-based: knowledge graphs (KGs, detailed in Section 3.1) could be integrated with graph neural networks (GNNs, detailed in Section 4.3) especially graph convolutional networks (GCNs) to build a classifier for GZSL.

- Meta Learning (detailed in Section 7.1.2): meta learning or learning to learn strategy aims to extract transferable knowledge from a set of auxiliary tasks to enable efficient learning with GZSL. For instance, one could train various tasks by randomly selecting the classes from both the seen and the unseen, thus transferring knowledge from seen to unseen classes and alleviating prediction biases towards seen classes.

- Attention mechanism (detailed in Section 7.4: attention-based ZSL and GZSL methods could focus on learning the important image regions, especially effective for identifying fine-grained classes (detailed in Section 7.5 and Section 6.4) or relevant attributes as oftentimes fine-grained classes are sensitive to discriminative information about specific attributes only in a few regions.

- Dictionary Learning: the goal of dictionary learning, a subfield of representation learning, is to learn an empirical basis from the data that best summarizes it. For instance, CDL [Jiang et al., 2018, Wang et al., 2020b] (**coupled dictionary learning**) jointly aligns the visual-semantic structure to construct a class representation between the visual and semantic spaces. This is done by obtaining the class prototypes in both the visual and semantic spaces and exploring the most informative empirical bases in each space to represent each class. Domain adaptation methods are then applied to mitigate potential biases towards the seen classes.

Generative models are applied to GZSL to generate samples for the unseen classes given their semantic representations and relationships relative seen classes. Generated samples that augment unseen classes should ideally satisfy at least two conditions to ensure efficacy: class distinctive such that from a classifier could be reasonably trained, and realistic in the sense that they are at least semantically associated with real data. When it comes to generative-based GZSL methods, perhaps generative adversarial networks (GAN)-based and (variational) autoencoder (VAE)-based approaches are among the most popular.

GANs leverages the game-theoretic aspects of two counteracting parties pitted against each other and improves together as training proceeds. It consists of a generator that generates visual features with semantic attributes and Gaussian noises, and a discriminator that distinguishes real visual features from those generated by the generator. The generator is trained to generate data samples on the seen classes and extrapolates to generate for the unseen. Over time, a multitude of GAN variants and improved frameworks have been proposed and widely adopted to boost the training efficiency by solving the notorious mode collapse problem and other wacky behaviors of the original, e.g., CGAN [Mirza and Osindero, 2014], WGAN [Arjovsky et al., 2017], WGAM [Gulrajani et al., 2017], CWGAN [Xian et al., 2018], StackGAN [Huang et al., 2017b], CycleGAN [Zhu et al., 2017], to name just a few.

VAEs, concerned with learning how data relates to its latent representations, comprise of an encoder that translates data into latent representations, and a decoder that translates latent representations back to data. Similar to GANs, VAEs have been used to augment data samples for unseen classes by generating visual features in the context of GZSL. VAEs tend to generate blurry images that are much less realistic than those from GANs in general whereas GANs are perhaps more challenging to train. Somehow by combining both VAE and GAN architectures, both limitations are somewhat alleviated. VAE-GAN [Gao et al., 2018] and Zero-VAE-GAN [Gao et al., 2020a] both manage to generate better data samples for unseen classes with the discriminator learning for visual similarities between real and generated samples.

7.4 Contextual Embeddings and Language Models

The year of 2018 (though some perhaps credit the year of 2019 instead) had been a major watershed in the field of natural language processing in terms of natural language understanding. Those like me who graduated from phd programs in 2018-2019 shared the same shock back then: the frameworks we learnt and used in graduate school became obsolete overnight the moment we graduated. Prior to 2018, whenever attempting to tackle a natural language understanding task — for instance, given a passage, determine the correct answers to questions, given a sentence about an event, identify what, when, where, who, and possibly why of it, etc. — we flex our muscles by designing a custom model or architecture for each task, sometimes using static *word embeddings* such as *word2vec* [Mikolov et al., 2013] or *GloVe* [Pennington et al., 2014].

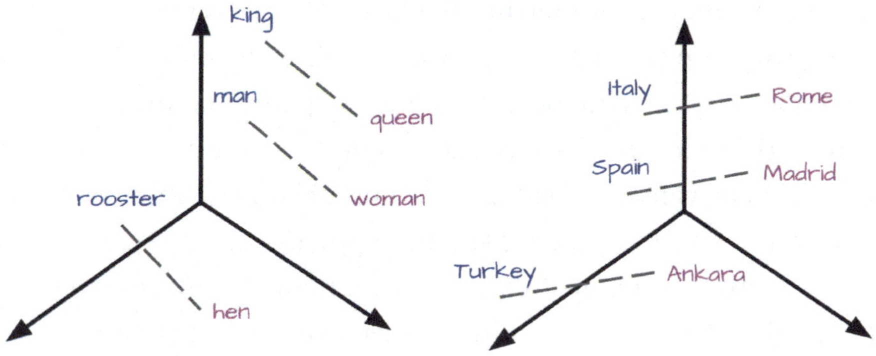

Figure 55: An illustration of static word embeddings.

Word embeddings map words into a high-dimensional space while preserving the semantic structure in-between, as is depicted in Figure 55. For instance, the distance between man and woman would be identical to king and queen, so that one could easily find out what the capital city of Turkey is by calculating the distance between Italy and Rome, and trace that from the word Turkey, using word embeddings.

Over the last few years after 2018, as is shown in Figure 56, large-scale language models have completely revolutionized the field of natural language processing, rendering those custom models obsolete, because such pre-trained — meaning a large amount of plain texts were used to train the model — general purpose language models have been shown to blow custom models out of the water on a wide variety of natural language understanding tasks. But why language models? To begin with, language models are probabilistic distributions of text strings, which you could estimate with existing text documents. Most language models break down the overall probability into probabilities of each individual word conditioned on some other set of words. It's like finishing your partner's sentence automatically because you are so familiar with the context.

Before 2018, there had already been a rich body of research on language modeling. However, these were mostly applied to a subset of natural language understanding tasks — text generation, where text strings are produced as outputs such as machine translation (given an English sentence, generate its Spanish counterpart) and summarization (given a passage, generate a summary). In other words, there were no broad applications of language models to various other aspects of natural language processing, like question answering (like how Quora operates), sentiment classification (given a tweet, classifying it into positive or negative sentiment), etc.

It was not until 2018, the idea of apply general purpose language models to a wide range of tasks caught on, despite of the fact that the very same idea had been around circa 2008 when Ronan Collobert (now at Facebook) and colleagues proposed unified architectures for natural language processing. Part of it was perhaps because the computing power and data availability were rather lacking in order to realize the full potential of such an idea, which, even though we are by no means there yet, could be signaling that solving the language model would potentially solve every natural language processing problem under the sun. How exciting!

Now that we are in the new era of natural language understanding post-2018. Figure 56 plots various high-profile groundbreaking language models ever since on a grid of time and scale. While it is indeed true that over time these models kept scaling up with more compute and data, achieving even greater performance overall, they are also packed with human ingenuity in terms of clever formulations and innovative ideas.

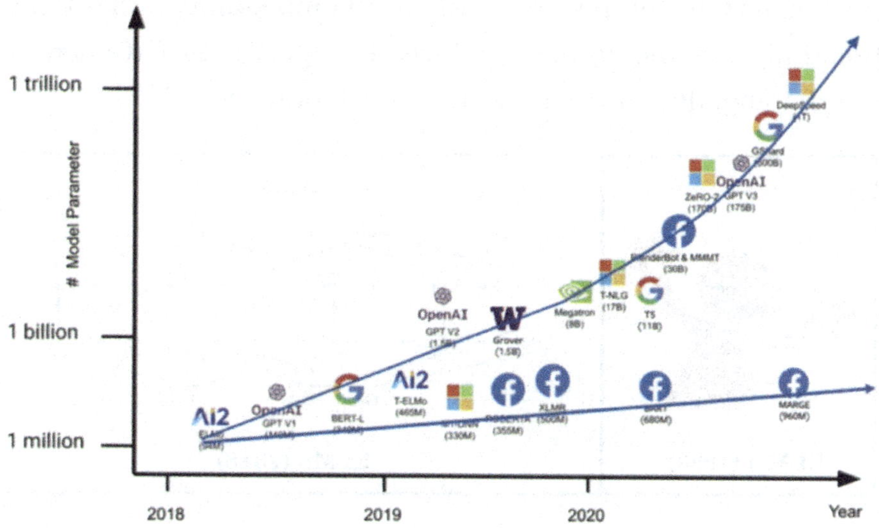

Figure 56: The Evolution of State-of-the-art Pre-trained Language Models.

In 2018, Allen AI Institute introduced the first contextual word embedding ELMo [Peters et al., 2018] (Embeddings for Language Models) to resolve one of the long standing problems with static language models, that is, inability to resolve word ambiguities. For instance, the word *play* assumes very different meanings in the following two sentences, which would be rendered the same if we used last-generation static word embeddings:

- My cats like to *play* with the new cat toy I bought them.
- The Broadway *play* To Kill a Mockingbird is one of the best I have ever seen.

In addition, ELMo advocated for bi-directional training in the sense that we stand a better chance of figuring out the meaning of *play* if we look at both words occurred both before (*my cats like to*) and after (*new cat toy...*), as opposed to only before (*my cats like to*). However, ELMo, in hindsight, was still pigeonholed into this old framework of training custom models tailored to different tasks while improving its one component — the word embedding, rather than a brand new regime, to be introduced by OpenAI' GPT (Generative Pre-training) [Radford et al., 2018] model soon after.

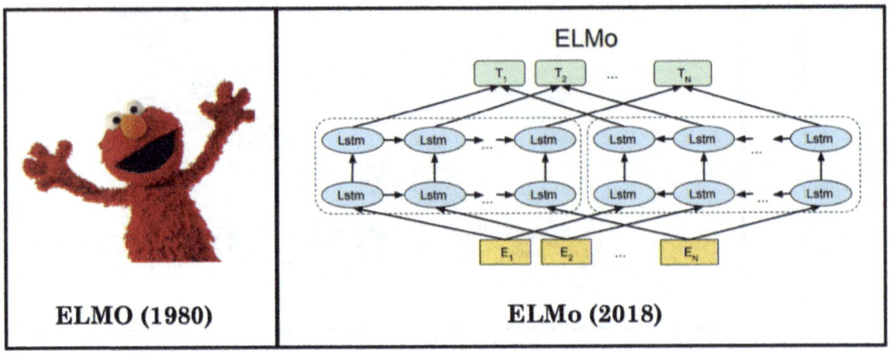

Figure 57: An illustration of ELMo [Peters et al., 2018]

The original GPT model (GPT-1) challenged the notion of word embeddings and custom architectures by converting every natural language understanding task into a language model problem, paving the way towards a general purpose model that solves it all. For instance, for text classification problems, you concatenate the sentence and the sentiment together separated by some token in-between and feed into a Transformer model to extract representations; for text entailment problems (if sentence 1 implied sentence 2), you concatenate two sentences separated by a token, and feed into a Transformer model for feature extraction; for a text similarity problem, you concatenate two text strings in opposite orders and feed to two Transformers in parallel, etc. In this way, you change very small changes to this general purpose language model to perform a large set of natural language understanding problems.
As transformative as GPT has been, it did not incorporate the idea of bi-directional training — looking at the contexts both left and right as opposed to just left. BERT (Bidirectional Encoder Representations from Transformers) [Devlin et al., 2019] therefore came along, exploiting what GPT excels at while incorporating the idea of

bi-directional training, along with other brilliant ideas such as introducing pre-training tasks like Masked Language Model, and Next Sentence Prediction, establishing generalization far beyond just text classification. The researchers showcased its capability with extensive comparisons with previous generation models, blowing people's mind with the drastic improvements, thus completely changing the mindset of the field. Since then BERT has quickly become the focus of intensive and extensive studies in the realm of natural language processing while spilling over to almost every other field of AI, most notably computer vision, information extraction, speech, recommender system, you name it.

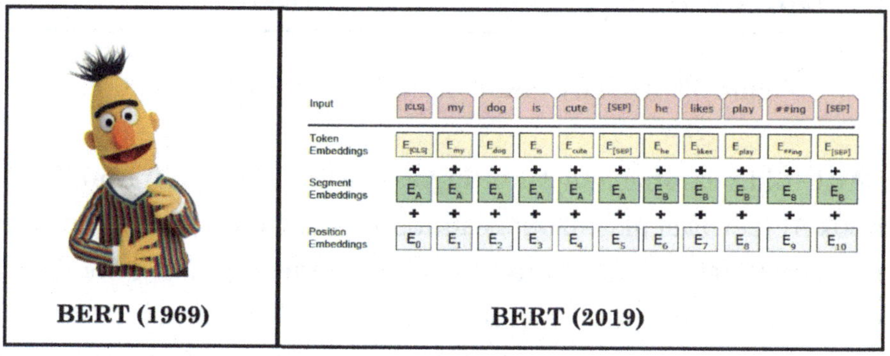

Figure 58: An illustration of BERT [Devlin et al., 2019].

Facebook AI researchers replicated BERT with more compute without scaling up the model parameters, but rather simplifying and streamlining it. They came to the surprising discovery that the real potential of BERT is much greater than originally documented — at least twice as good. They released their implementation as RoBERTa (a Robustly Optimized BERT Pretraining Approach).

Google AI introduced T5 model [Raffel et al., 2020] in 2019 that up a bi-directional model and unified all the tasks into a single sequence-to-sequence (*seq2seq*) framework, posing everything as a machine translation problem: given a sentence missing some information, generate the information again at both pre-training and finetuning.

GPT-3 came out in the year of 2020, building on top of its earlier versions GPT and GPT-2, scaling up to be one of the largest and densest models to date, exemplifying surprisingly great few-shot performance (fine-tuning with limited data), among others.

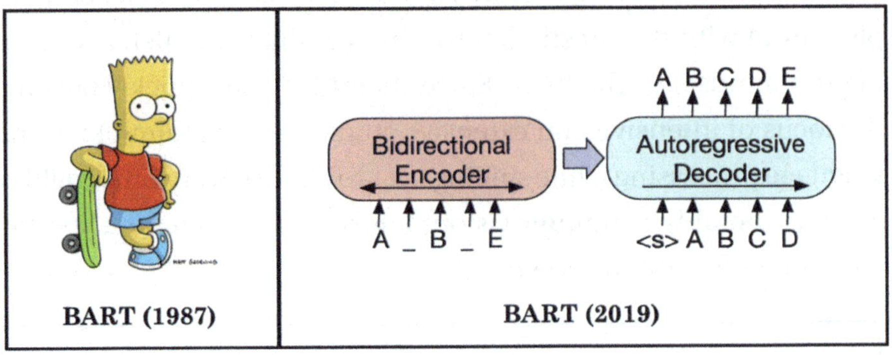

Figure 59: An Illustration of BART [Lewis et al., 2020b].

BART (Bidirectional and Auto-Regressive Transformers) from Facebook AI [Lewis et al., 2020b] is another widely recognized improvement on BERT that came out around the same as T5 from Google AI, with similar motivations. In BERT and RoBERTa, it was still not directly applicable to one particular type of task: text generation, and the proposed self-supervised pre-training procedures like Masked Language Model and Next Sentence Prediction tasks were soon challenged in terms of efficiency in later analyses. Therefore BART seeks answers to *How to support more tasks such as text generation? What are principled ways to self-supervise in this context?* BART attempted to combine the bests of both worlds of BERT and T5, by injecting noise into a sentence and asking the model to regenerate the original sentence without noise as a pre-training task, thus enabling the pre-trained sequence-to-sequence model for both text generation and classification tasks. The real trick here is to allow any possible noise function for the entire sentence — masking or deleting words, rotating or permuting sentences in documents, masking text spans, etc., as opposed to just masking words or word spans in early versions like BERT and T5, which greatly improved generalizability across text generation tasks and different languages while matching the performance of RoBERTa.

The same authors of BART (Michael Lewis at Facebook AI) further explore new sources of supervision for pre-trianing in their MARGE model [Lewis et al., 2020a]. In MARGE, you learn to paraphrase — rewriting documents with the same semantic meanings but very different words and syntax, the idea being. By first retrieving similar documents that are semantically similar, then discovering similarities and differences in-between these corresponding documents, MARGE is able to pick up enough signals to improve the performance of pre-trained language models.

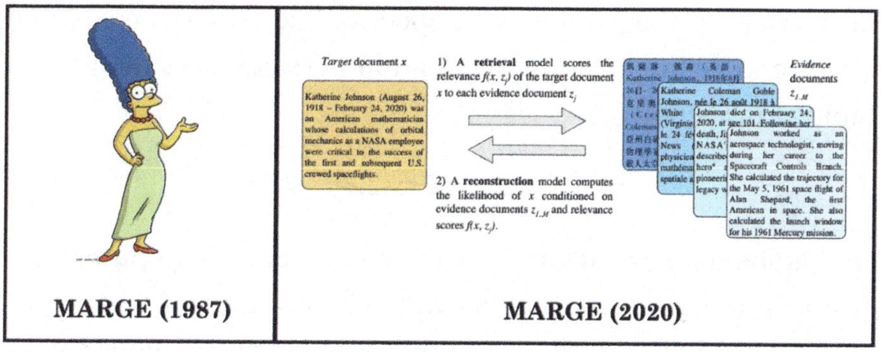

Figure 60: An Illustration of MARGE [Lewis et al., 2020a].

In awe of what all these large language models have achieved and could do, we ought be aware of their limitations and inherent costs thereof. For starters, the current evaluation benchmarks have been shown to be somewhat lacking and claims about these language models enabled general language understanding are probably overstated, especially when it comes to common sense reasoning. Secondly, training these models requires a large amount of compute resources, restricting them to large industrial AI labs only. Both training and running these models incur high levels of carbon footprints, which runs counter to environmental sustainability. In addition, pre-training requires a huge amount of data and whatever societal biases existing in human online conversations could only magnify in these large-scale language models if not handled properly.

7.5 Fine-grained Visual Categorization

As was introduced in Section 6.4, fine-grained image classification as a sub-field in computer vision has evolved for over a decade with impressive progress, and the techniques developed could be readily applied to viticultural problems. For grapevine identification specifically, I have introduced two fine-grained datasets **iGrapevine** and **VinePathology** with respective baseline classification models for the purpose of automatic visual identification of grape variety or cultivar, as well as vine pathology. Respective images are shown in Figure 61 and Figure 62 and classification performances tabulated in Table 21 in Section 6.4.

Fine-grained image classification as a sub-field of computer vision has been rather focused on accurate classification of what it is in the image over the past decade. While it might appear impressive to enable the computers to identify particular cultivar of grape variety or plant pathology is present in an image, some recent studies have reminded us of the fact that when working with domain experts or scientists working in the domain, correct identification of species (or grape variety, or plant pathology) is not terribly impressive or informative since most likely it's something they already know of, and such AI classification algorithms could help speed up their work at best. What experts are more interested in are downstream tasks. In terms of modern computer vision and machine learning, we would think of this as learned representations and how useful are those learned representations for different downstream tasks.

Figure 61: A photo-mosaic collage of sample images from iGrapevine for *fine-grained image classification.*

Figure 62: A photo-mosaic collage of sample images from VinePathology for *fine-grained image classification.*

For example, given an image of a grapevine in terms of leaves or clusters, besides training a fine-grained visual classification algorithm to recognize the grape variety, viticulturists are perhaps more interested in automatic assessment of vine age, vine health, potential pathology, current level of water stress, environmental information that could be derived from the grapevine image such as the soil type, or the macro-, meso-, and micro-climate the vine is cultivated in, etc. Answering questions such as how effective learned representations learned for the classic fine-grained visual categorization problem could be used for attacking a myriad of downstream tasks, perhaps with the help of contrastive learning (Section 4.1) could indeed accelerate the adoption and penetration of state-of-the-art AI algorithms in various scientific domains such as viticulture or biodiversity.

[Van Horn et al., 2021] presented one of the first few steps in such directions. And there exists many open problems in this exciting domain of fine-grained image analysis yet to be addressed:

- Formal characterization of the problem: what exactly does "fine-grained" mean and how to define or disambiguate a potential definition of granularity?

- Data and label efficient approaches to fine-grained image analysis: how to design efficient approaches of targeted engagement with human expertise in mind?

- Self-supervision in the fine-grained setting: perhaps data augmentation (detailed in Section 7.1.1) could be leveraged for contrastive learning (see Section 4.1);

- Going beyond static images: how should we incorporate multimodal datasets such as combining video clips and spectrogram data (or audio data in general)?

Some of these problems and their manifestations in viticulture and agriculture are indeed on our agenda for future work, hopefully to be published and introduced in future editions of this book.

SECTION

8

Craft Cocktails

There appears no definite or universally acknowledged definition of cocktail, even though some define it as any drink made by mixing two or ingredients together. For instance, John deBart, a mixologist formerly at Please Don't Tell (PDT) and Momofuku in Manhattan, started off the topic with "that's right, coffee with milk and sugar, that's cocktail right there in your morning cup of joe" in his hilarious book Drink What You Want.

A firm grasp of knowledge in cocktails, spirits, and mixology could pay good dividends at some point of one's career as a beverage professional, a. It may as well involve learning classic cocktail recipes by heart (how to make The Last Word?), understanding the making as well as the flavor profiles of each and every ingredient (what is Drambuie made of?), and perhaps being able to explain the history, cultural references, and tales around iconic creations like Sazerac or Vesper. As a sommelier or beverage director gets more involved in putting together a beverage program, one might start experimenting with new alcoholic concoctions that best suit the restaurant, the consumer base, or even the occasion. Such begs the questions, how shall we create new craft cocktails? And what makes a cocktail creative?

There exists this popular misconception that a great recipe strikes from out of the blue, when in fact, almost every idea, however groundbreakingly creative, depends closely on what came before. Coming up with an idea for a recipe, or any idea, whether it be for new cocktails or building new rockets, can be summarized as combining existing ingredients or modifying a recipe to come up with something new. But is there a way to determine which set or arrangement of ingredients will make a greatly creative cocktail recipe?

To answer this question, let us look to social psychology research on creativity that have enjoyed decades of scholarly interests and devotion in various domains ranging from scientific discovery [Uzzi et al., 2013], to linguistics [Giora, 2003]. One of the robust conclusion from this line of research is that *creativity results from the optimal balance between novelty and familiarity.* For instance, in an influential *Nature* article [Uzzi et al., 2013], a link was established between the impact of scientific papers and the network of journals cited in these papers. It was found that papers are more likely be impactful if they cite papers from publication outlets that are commonly cited together, with unusual combinations that are rarely seen. In other words, papers or ideas are more likely to have an impact if they "reflect a balance between novelty and a connection to previous ideas" [Ward, 1995]. Therefore, in order to understand what makes a creative cocktail recipe in a practical and precise manner, perhaps clear and actionable answers to the following questions could help us pare down what it takes to generate a creative cocktail recipe:

- First, how should we *define novelty* and *familiarity* in the context of a cocktail recipe?
- Second, how could we measure or *quantify novelty* and *familiarity*?
- Third, what makes *an optimal balance* between novelty and familiarity?

First, let us take the view of social networks and present cocktails as a network of ingredients and preparations, analogous to how friends, family, and colleagues form a social network. If we look at each recipe as a sub-network of ingredients, illustrated in Figure 63, situated within the network of the world of cocktails. Then every ingredient of a cocktail recipe could be associated with one another either in one recipe or another. When two ingredients occur frequently together with each other, for example, lemon juice and simple syrup perhaps, they are common associations; if two ingredients rarely or even never occur with each other they are uncommon associations. Then it's only natural to relate novelty to uncommon associations of ingredients, and familiarity to common associations. For instance, novelty does not necessarily come from choosing novel ingredients for the recipe, but rather from choosing ingredients that do not often appear together. Chili and matcha are common and familiar ingredients in recipes, but the combination of the two less so, therefore could be considered novel.

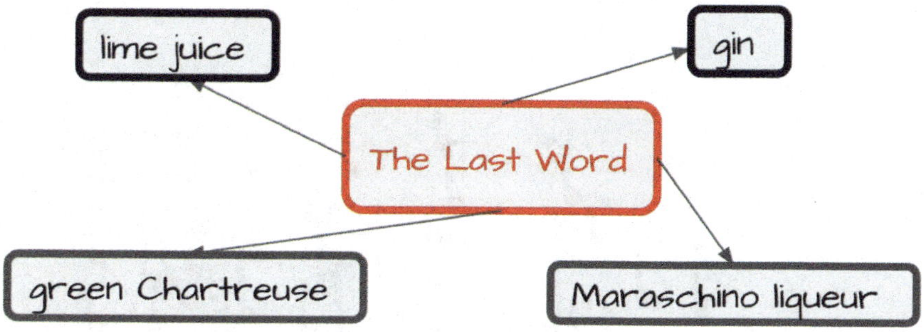

Figure 63: The Last Word recipe represented as a sub-network of ingredients. For more comprehensive and interactive cocktail recipe visualizations, please visit http://ai-somm.com/cocktail/.

Now that we have a clearer idea of what novelty and familiarity could mean in this context, let us construct a network of ingredients where each node is represents by an ingredient, and each edge between two nodes is assigned a value that indicates how common is the combination of these two ingredients in the world of classic cocktail recipes. More specifically, we calculate the ratio between

1. the number of existing cocktail recipes that contain both ingredients;
2. the number of existing cocktail recipes that contain either ingredient.

The more frequently tonic tags along gin in recipes, the higher our indicator value of familiarity is, and the less novel the combination is. In this way, the balance between novelty and familiarity is now embedded in the values of the edges of any sub-network that represents a cocktail.
Figure 64 illustrates a semantic network of all the IBA cocktail recipes.

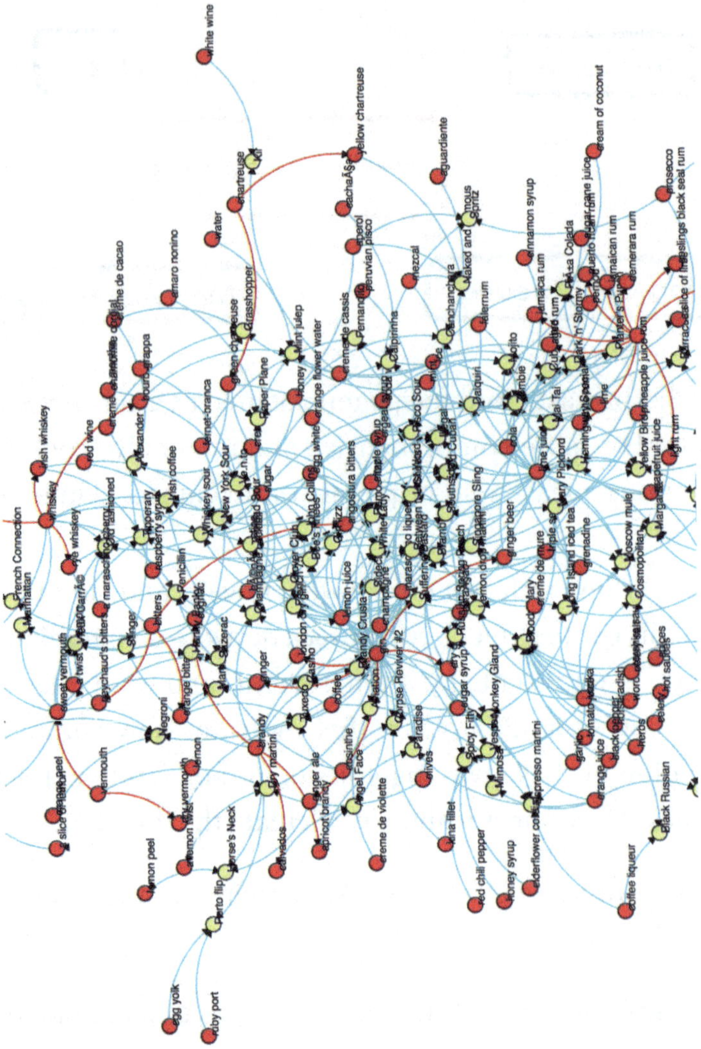

Figure 64: A Semantic Network of IBA Cocktails. Red nodes represent ingredients, and yellow nodes cocktails. Red edges represent relationships between ingredients, e.g., rye whiskey belongs to whiskey. Cyan edges represent compositions. More comprehensive and interactive visualizations at http://ai-somm.com/cocktail/.

Each recipe involves a subset of the nodes (ingredients) in the general network, which form a semantic sub-network where the weight of each edge captures the strength of association between two ingredients (nodes) in the network representing the world of cocktails. Familiar combinations of ingredients have higher edge weights, indicating that they are commonly found together in cocktail recipes whereas novel combinations of ingredients have lower edge weights, indicative of the more unusual combinations thereof.

Given our network of IBA classic cocktails, we could describe a recipe based on any representative metric that involves its nodes and edges, for instance, the average weight of its edges, or other statistics such as the minimum, maximum, variance, and median of included nodes. But to leverage the robust finding that creativity lies in the optimal balance between the novel and the familiar, and to capture the balance between novel and familiar combination, we need to perhaps take a more comprehensive look at the semantic sub-network of a recipe. Given that we have defined and quantified novelty versus familiarity, how could we identify *the optimal balance* in-between novelty and familiarity that is perceived to be creative?

Let us perhaps take a step back and explore first the cognitive process of generating an idea. From a cognitive point of view, idea generation is hinged upon this premise that generating ideas involves retrieving knowledge from long-term memory. An early milestone in this line of research, Geneplore [Finke et al., 1992] framework suggests that the generation of creative ideas involve two iterative phases: a generative phase during which mental representations of concepts are initiated and constructed, and a exploratory phase when the constructed concepts are then modified and combined in meaningful ways. Importantly, it raised the awareness that new ideas do not spring out of the blue in a vacuum, but rather are based upon basic building blocks — the pre-inventive concepts typically retrieved from long-term memory. The apparent analogy between creative mixology and creative cooking perhaps helps illustrate the process: for a home chef looking to cook dinner, a set of ingredients and preparation methods, whether it be celery, gnocchi, eel, and deep-frying, or yuzu, Crème fraîche, chocolate, and sous vide, will form pre-inventive concepts as basis for a potentially creative cooking solution.

Whatever pre-inventive concepts retrieved during the initial generative phase will certainly impact the generated ideas in terms of quality, creativeness, or originality. How could identify the link between the type and form of retrieved concepts and the resulting ideas? To put it more concisely, what combinations of pre-inventive concepts contribute to the perceived creativeness of the resulting idea? To put it more concretely, how could we combine ingredients and preparation methods, and possibly other relevant elements to make a cocktail creative?

Echoing the gist of Geneplore [Finke et al., 1992] that outlined the idea generation process, let us draw from a large body of research spanning psychology, biology, art, and behavioral science for insights on this topic.

It has been shown that *prototypes* — averages — have inherent qualities and properties that make them appealing. This phenomenon is perhaps most well-known when it comes to human faces. A multitude of research studies have shown this robust finding that humans find faces with *average* features more beautiful and attractive. It is also widely and robustly demonstrated in various domains. Paintings, sculptures, and musical creations. Poetry and linguistics. Economics and business.Several explanations based on biology, evolutionary theory, and psychological fluency have perhaps garnered attention and acceptance. Some associate it with the "wisdom of the crowds" phenomenon. It does appear across various domains that this so-called "beauty in averageness" effect holds where quality relies on the *optimal balance* between various features or the optimal distribution of important resources across multiple dimensions. A beautiful piece of musical performance is one in which the keystrokes are neither too heavy nor too light. A creative idea is one that is neither too radical nor too banal. Each composition could be seen as an attempt to strike an optimal allocation of different pitches, tempos, rhythms, and dynamics. Averaging a large set of elements could cancel out noises and surface an allocation closer to the optimal. By the same token, taking the average of edge weights across ingredients could be indicative of an optimal allocation of ingredients that balance out novelty and familiarity, and such a balance is perhaps likely seen as creative.

To test such an hypothesis, let us aggregate all the edges for each cocktail recipe in Figure 64 and identify the recipes whose edges are most and least similar to what the averaged out version turned out to be, which we tabulate in Table 22. Don't they appear more creative or banal than other recipes in the graph of Figure 64?

Most		Least	
Prototypical Cocktail Recipes			
Rank	Recipe	Rank	Recipe
1	Aviation	1	Bull Shot
2	Sidecar	2	Rob Roy
3	Last Word	3	Blood Mary
4	Adonis	4	Grasshopper
5	Coffee Cocktail	5	Golden Dawn
6	Clover Club	6	Long Island Iced Tea
7	Blood and Sand	7	Black Velvet
8	Paper Plane	8	Singapore Sling
9	Sazerac	9	Kamikaze
10	Naked and Famous	10	Vieux Carre

Table 22: Ten most and least prototypical cocktail recipes in the recipe dataset.

8.1 Recipe Generation

Now that we have explored what makes creative cocktails, how could we incorporate such insights into our design of automatic generation processes of cocktail recipes?

Let us start with practical scenarios where we might wish for such an automatic recipe generation system.

Perhaps on a Thursday evening we found ourselves at home with a bar tool set and some fresh lemons, a quarter bottle of Riesling-infused Gin, a new bottle of Mezcal, some leftover Absinthe[34], Drambuie[35], and Kahlúa[36]. How could we design an automatic cocktail recipe generation framework that would output a cocktail recipe that best suits our mood — whether we are feeling lazy or fancy, festive or desperate, classic or adventurous — using all or a subset of the ingredients at hand? Let us call such a framework a **controllable recipe generation** system (for now).

Perhaps on random Monday night, you are browsing social media and a post caught your eyes: a blue-streaked lemonade-looking highball topped with herb-like glitter and curly lemon peels with the caption “a thunderous bolt of liquid lightning”. You are intrigued. Besides immediately replying to the thread and asking directly for the specific recipe, how could you automatically generate a cocktail recipe based on simply the picture? Let us call such a recipe generation tool an **inverse mixology system**, in the sense that it enables us to infer ingredients and preparation instructions from images.

Fortunately, similar AI systems have attracted widespread research interests and attention in several communities such as natural language processing and computer vision, within the realm of *food com-*

---

[34] An anise-flavored spirit infused with wormwood (Artemisia absinthium), green anise, sweet fennel, and other herbs.

[35] A liqueur made from Scotch whiskey, heather honey, herbs, and spices.

[36] A coffee liqueur.

puting[37]. Even though to the best of my knowledge there exists no exact systems as described above available for cocktails, similar systems have indeed been proposed and implemented for cooking and foodstuff in general. Despite some nuanced differences between cooking recipe generation and cocktail recipe generation, we could readily adapt existing *controllable text generation* systems and *inverse cooking systems* for the purpose of generating cocktail recipes, as we will explore below.

Controllable recipe generation systems aim to generate cocktail recipes given a list of ingredients and some contextual (e.g., feeling fancy, boozy, lazy, etc.) or dietary (e.g., non-alcoholic, low sugar, no cherry) constraints. Research interests and efforts on recipes have been around in the natural language processing community for almost a decade, with early efforts centering around recipe parsing and retrieval and more recent works on generation. A majority of recipe generation systems developed over the past decade generate recipes in a way that covers the entire set of input ingredients, thus sometimes compromising the quality of resulting recipes when some ingredients are better left out. Nor was personalized recipe generation with customizable constraints possible with most (early) systems. We could adopt selective routing algorithms [Yu et al., 2020b][38]to identify an

[37]Food computing is an inter-disciplinary subject area that involves the acquisition and analysis of food data with computational methods where quantitative methods in fields such as computer vision, machine learning, and data mining, meet conventional food-related fields such as food science, medicine, biology, agronomy, sociology, and gastronomy.

[38]A brief overview of the evolution of literature: transformation matrices that learn to encode intrinsic spatial relationship between a part and a whole viewpoints were introduced circa 2011 [Hinton et al., 2011], upon which interactive routing-by-agreement mechanisms [Sabour et al., 2017] were use to learn inter-layer relationships within neural networks, an alternative approach [Hinton et al., 2018] based on EM (Expectation Maximization) algorithm was investigated too.

optimal set of ingredients within the input list, based on which a hierarchical attention mechanism (details about attention mechanism in Section 7.4) could be coupled with a text generation system backed by a large-scale pre-trained language model (surveyed in Section 7.4). The hierarchical attention mechanism would factor in structures of cocktail recipes (title, ingredient, different parts of instructions) in both the training and generation processes such that resulting recipes would turn out more fleshed out and detailed component by component.

Let us illustrate the intuitive *controllable recipe generation* framework in Figure 65.

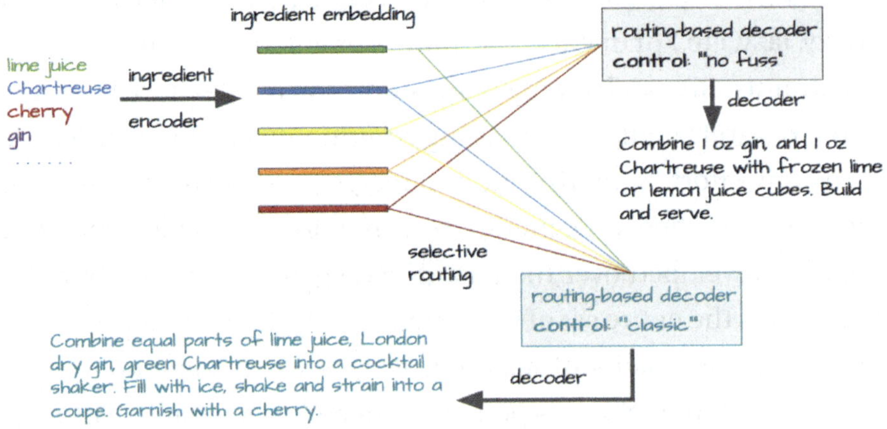

Figure 65: A Controllable Recipe Generation System with Dynamic Routing and Structural Awareness.

Let us term the task of generating a cocktail recipe — title, ingredients, and instructions — given an image as *inverse mixology*. Generating a recipe from a single image is a challenging task as it demands semantic understanding of the ingredients as well as the preparations they went through, e.g. slicing, blending or mixing with other ingredients. Despite the fact that computer vision techniques have made remarkable progress in natural image understanding that sometimes surpasses human capability, beverage (or food recognition) poses additional challenges, due to the fact that the ingredients of food and beverages could become hardly recognizable as they go through the preparation process. Ingredients are frequently occluded in a beverage or food item and come in a variety of colors, forms and textures. Therefore, visual ingredient detection from images requires human-level reasoning and prior knowledge (e.g., there is likely sugar in cakes, and butter in croissants).

Instead of obtaining the recipe from an image directly, various research works have shown that a recipe generation pipeline would benefit from some intermediate steps such as predicting the ingredients (e.g., lemon, simple syrup, Vermouth, gin), identifying preparation processes (peel, zest, pour, build, etc.), and generating a template or structure for the recipe (e.g., a tree structure that bifurcates into a lemon preparation branch, a simple syrup branch, and a Vermouth or gin branch). The sequence of instructions would then be generated conditioned on both the image, its corresponding list of ingredients, and the identified structure of the potential recipe, where the interplay between image and ingredients or preparation processes could shed light on how the template or structure could be filled to produce the resulting beverage. Let us illustrate the overall *inverse mixology* framework in Figure 66.

An alternative approach to coming up with recipes is perhaps to curate a large-scale comprehensive recipe database, and devise an effective and efficient *cross-modal recipe retrieval* framework to identify recipes that would best suit our needs given a specific context.

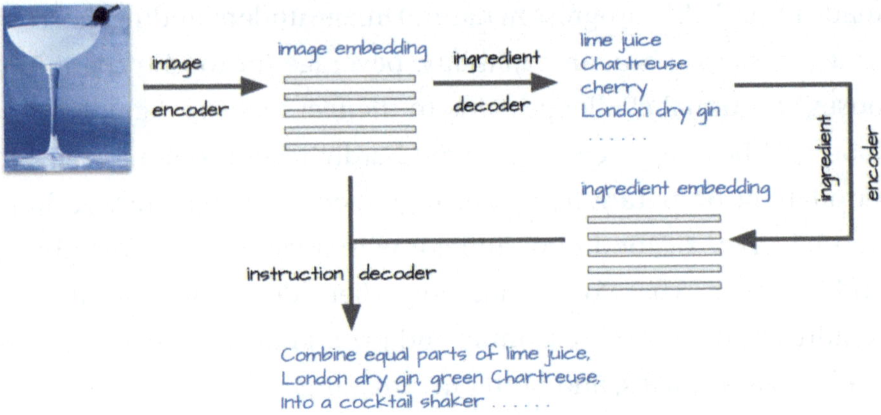

Figure 66: A Modular Recipe Generation Framework for Inverse Mixology.

The goal of cross-modal recipe retrieval is to design systems capable of finding relevant cocktail recipes given an image of a cocktail. This framework is cross-modal because it requires developing models in the intersection of natural language processing and computer vision. As is common with cross-modal scenarios, such frameworks also require sufficient robustness with respect to handling unstructured, noisy, and incomplete data to afford large-scale adoption in practice.

Therefore, learning joint representations for textual and visual modalities in the context of cocktail recipes is crucial. Various existing research studies on cross-modal recipe retrieval have introduced approaches for learning representations or embeddings for recipes and images separately, which are then projected into a joint embedding space. A proliferation of methodological contributions followed, proposing complex models and loss functions[39] to improve the efficacy of projection and the joint representation learning process, such as cross-modal attention (more background information and details in Section 7.4, generative adversarial networks (Section 5.1

[39] Loss functions are objectives with which models are trained towards.

provides examples of alternative popular applications), the use of auxiliary semantic losses (more background information and contexts in Section 2.3), and reconstruction losses (commonly used in models and applications detailed in Section 5.2).

To obtain strong representation for recipe texts, we could encode texts in recipes hierarchically based on pre-trained large-scale language models such as Transformers and the likes (detailed in Section 7.4) to align with the structured nature of recipes (i.e. titles, ingredients, and instructions). For instance, instead of encoding texts in recipes uniformly, we could encode lists of ingredients and instructions by extracting sentence-level embeddings as intermediate representations, while learning relationships within each intermediate module. In addition, training joint embedding models usually requires paired data, i.e., each cocktail image must be associated to its corresponding recipe texts, which are often not available when dealing with large-scale datasets gathered from the Internet where unpaired cocktail images and recipes are abundant. Therefore, even though most cross-modal retrieval systems discard unpaired data sources, *self-supervision strategies* could be incorporated to make use of both paired and text-only data that could result in improving retrieval efficacy. Such self-supervision strategies could be tailored for text-only recipe learning based on the intuition that while the individual components of a particular recipe (title, ingredients, and instructions) provide complementary information, they still share strong semantic cues that can be used to obtain more robust and semantically consistent recipe embeddings. Therefore, by constraining recipe embeddings during training such that intermediate representations of individual recipe components are closer if they are of the same recipe, and farther apart otherwise. Let us illustrate such cross-modal recipe retrieval systems with Figure 67.

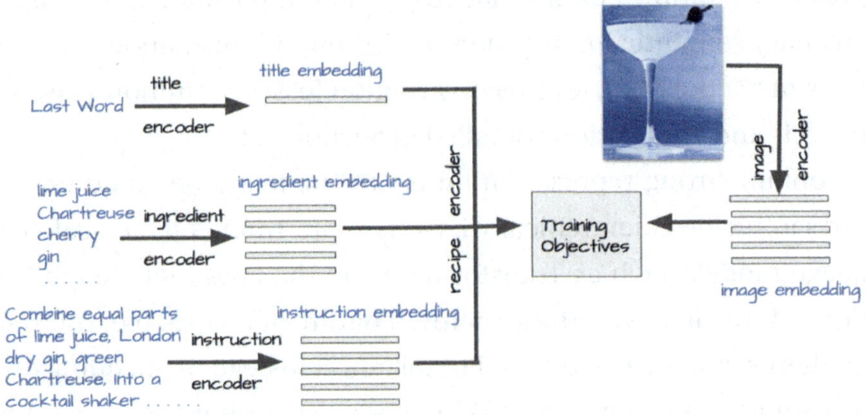

Figure 67: A Cross-modal Recipe Retrieval Framework for Inverse Mixology.

9

SECTION

Wine Lists

What makes a great wine list?

This is by no means the first time it has been asked. A precursor to that question is perhaps how wine lists started and evolved to what they are today. A scan through the major wine publications and organizations could perhaps point us to some clues — best wine list awards, top sommelier lists, best wine service awards, best wine restaurants list, star wine lists, and the list goes on.

One of the first, if not the first, widely recognized wine list awards was initiated by *Wine Spectator* in the early 1980s, at the dawn of the rise of the sommelier profession, even though the idea of a wine collection as the centerpiece for a restaurant was still perhaps in its infancy. The original award was rather different from what it is to-day — back then, restaurant candidates were nominated by wine writers, consultants, importers and distributors. Each wine list was supposedly reviewed for its quality of selection, breadth and depth, value and presentation with editors personally visiting the final candidates to evaluate inventory and storage, service and ambience, as well as the quality of the restaurant's cuisine. Only 13 winners in the United States were selected for the Grand Award in the inauguration year of 1981. The scale and expanse of the program steadily grew over time, and it was not until 1985, the Award of Excellence and Best of Award of Excellence categories debuted to complete the three-tiered award system that it is today, with each tier targeting wine lists of different sizes: short (over 90 selections), medium (over 350 selections), and long (over 1,000 selections).

Various wine-oriented publications such as *Food & Wine*, *Wine & Spirits*, and *Wine Enthusiast* have followed over time, each with their own foci. For instance, *Food & Wine* established their Best New Wine List Award back in the late 1990s, and pivoted to the annual Best New Sommelier Award, thus gaining some serious following and recognition. Award finalists are nomination-based, with winners in previous years voting on the next generation of rising stars. *Wine Enthusiast* introduced their Best Wine Restaurant List Award in the summer of 2011. Their finalists are mostly nominated internally by editors based on their own dining experiences, with an ever-expanding international reach. Perhaps the most serious contender against *Wine Spectator*'s Grand Award with the most comprehensive and international emphasis was launched by the London-based *World of Fine Wine* magazine in 2014. Described by the late Gerard Basset MS, MW, OBE as "rapidly becoming as coveted as Michelin stars," the World's Best Wine Lists awards have since attracted establishments with serious wine programs with a wide range of award types including a star-rating system and category awards. Unlike *Wine Spectator*, *World of Fine Wine* assembles a judging panel with a much broader international focus including notable wine critics and writers, Masters of Wine, Master Sommeliers, and other award-winning sommeliers, even though the two major publications do agree on application-based entries as opposed to nominations. Despite the proliferation of such awards with their respective followings and sizable trade-wide impacts, the judging process across the board remains rather vague, if not opaque, not unlike many other aspects of the wine industry. General guidelines are along the lines of diversity, depth, etc., while some might look for how well wine is integrated into the overall dining experience the establishment delivers. Hence, after my long digression of wine list awards that might provide some pointers as to the most accepted essential traits of great wine lists, the answers to the opening question remain rather elusive. After collating various discussions between wine professionals and the opinion pieces of well-known wine writers such as Jancis Robinson, Alder Yarrow, Jamie Goode, and the likes on this topic, here are nine desirable traits of great wine lists that are perhaps very likely to resonate with many wine professionals curating or judging a wine list:

Accuracy. In Court in Master Sommelier's written Theory exams at the certified and advanced level, there is this frequent question where a mock wine list is given and you are asked to circle the mistakes therein. There are often mismatches between producer and region, between grape variety and cuvée, typos, incorrect organization of wine, missing information, etc. Such is not entirely uncommon in practice. Inaccuracies in wine lists, just like typos in articles and mispronunciation of common words, could cause confusion and turn off customers regardless of how excellent the wine list really is.

Breath/diversity. A common theme of a great list echoed by many professionals centers around breath (for a long list) or diversity (for a short or medium list), with the goal being ensuring there exists something on the list for every customer, whether it be a buttery

Chardonnay, a Kiwi Sauvignon Blanc, or something geeky like a Blanc de Noir from Chisa Bize (Simon Bize), an orange wine from Claude de Nicolay (Chandon de Briailles), or a Juhfark from Béla Fekete (Fekete Pince).

Depth. This is probably more applicable to long lists with over five hundred or even a thousand entries for a large wine-centric establishment where muscles could indeed flexed by showing a wide horizontal variety of producers for a given style or region, as well as vertical variety when it comes to different vintages of classic producers.

Focus. Whether it be a regional emphasis, a stylistic highlight, or a suitable complement to the cuisine, focus, for lack of a better word, would make a list feel not of a random collection thrown together, but rather one of sensibility and intention. On the other hand, focus does not mean over representation of single regions or the sommelier's preferences, therefore, a balanced sweet spot is probably somewhere in-between.

Rarity. This perhaps mostly applies to expansive wine lists with ambitions to be of world-class caliber in mind. It may well be just me biased towards mature and rare wines, whether it be a 1984 Chateau Musar, a 1921 Madeira, or a 1928 Ruinart. World-class wine lists certainly would include at least a few for the wow factor.

Readability. This is perhaps the only trait that is divorced from its content, and that lies in its presentation. Typeface, font, layout, and organization, when done right, all add to the readability of a wine list immensely, making ordering wine an even more pleasing experience.

Originality. Most wine lists read the same and look the same after all, with minor differences in typography, formatting, and style. The lack of originality that stirs up the tradition makes wine lists from places like Terrior in TriBeCa of Manhattan stand out with loads of personality however opinionated it might be, even though it might not be appropriate for many places and occasions.

Value. Those who don't know much about wine look at a wine list and hatch onto any familiar name, if any, at an acceptable price. Those who love it know very well what a premium they are paying for the privilege of drinking wine in a restaurant rather than from their own cellar. A reasonable yet sustainable markup goes a long way in attracting return customers and building reputation.

All of the existing wine list award judgment processes are manual, to the best of my knowledge, however, as I will detail in Section 9.1, all of the above essential traits could be automatically extracted with methods grounded in the fields of **Knowledge Graphs** (covered in Section 3.1), **Natural Language Processing** and **Computational Linguistics**, oftentimes with super-human precision, without introducing or easing the elimination of human biases such as being subconsciously influenced by well-known names like Eleven Madison Park in the process.

If creating a grand by-bottle wine list is like curating an art museum or a library, creating a by-glass wine list is perhaps akin to curating a music playlist that could be tailored to a theme, a mood, or one's taste. Just like how a thoughtfully curated music playlist could help listeners sift through their choices in a breeze, a by-glass short showcase list could alleviate consumer confusion and indecision, possibly intimidated by an enormous wine list.

Music playlists, the modern counterpart of traditional broadcast radio, affect music consumption behavior in at least two main ways: discovery of new music, and repetition of old favorites. Creating a great by-glass shortlist is the same, it should offer both the option of a voyage of discovery, and the comfort of holding onto old classics. Put another way, if you had a favorite musician and you would love to turn someone onto their music, would you play them something obscure that took you a while to appreciate, or would you play them

the less compelling songs that are more in tune with what the individual is comfortable with? Or perhaps both in a carefully curated sequence that would facilitate the seamless transition in-between?
To put it more concretely, if you were to try to get someone interested in Broadway musicals and you only played for them cast recordings of musicals like *The Great Comet of 1812*, or *Hamilton*, you would likely be doing just as much of a disservice as if you only played *Cats* or *The Phantom of the Opera*. They are by no means lacking in pleasure or technique, it's just some are simply more interesting than others, perhaps. Would you be doing someone a favor when you share something you deeply love, or did you forget that you also have to start somewhere?
Wine lists are like playlists, or old-school mixtapes. Is there something that would take your breath away and get your mind blown, or is it but a collage of toe tappingly good nothingness?
With the extreme success of on-demand music streaming services such as Spotify or Apple Music in the past two decades, playlists curation at a large scale has been increasingly leveraging the power of AI with deep learning to cater to millions of active users who interact with personalized playlists on a daily basis. For instance, Spotify's Discover Weekly boosts its big AI-driven personalization as a huge hit that witnessed 40 million users in the first year since its launch in 2015; Apple rolled out personalized playlists Discover Mix as part of Apple's iOS 10 update, taking on Spotify. In Section 9.2, let us recount how the rich knowledge and research progress in building AI algorithms for personalized music playlist generation could be transferred to automate wine list curation, with controlled processes tailored to restaurant themes, customers' or sommeliers' mood, or the taste profile of each and every individual.

9.1 Automatic Evaluation

To automatically evaluate wine lists, there are two commonly used frameworks we could try. The first framework focuses on coming up with a list of important and informative features that we could extract automatically from every wine list to help inform how great a wine list is. The second framework focuses on making sure a large dataset of both great and awful wine lists are available, upon which a selection of AI models could be learnt to distinguish the greats automatically. Let us start with the first framework that had prevailed in the machine learning field before the deep learning era, still useful and relevant sometimes and possibly seeing a comeback.

Accuracy. To identify factual mistakes on a wine list such as mismatches between producer and region, between grape variety and cuvée, typos, incorrect organization of wine, missing information, etc., a straightforward and sometimes brittle way is to leverage our multilingual and multimodal knowledge graph that houses all the wine information accurately. For every line of text in a wine list, one would automatically parse and use tailored **named entity recognition**[40] to retrieve corresponding information of producer, vintage, wine, parcel, style, if applicable, and match to the entry in the knowledge graph for accuracy verification. Such a relatively manual approach could suffer from inflexibility or lack of robustness when new terms or concepts are encountered and not yet incorporated into the knowledge graph, as well as error propagation that occurs when the wine-focused NER model makes a mistake, further mag-

[40]Named entity recognition, oftentimes abbreviated as NER, is a fundamental problem in natural language processing that aims to automatically identify and classify components of a sentence into categories such as person, location, organization, etc. Our wine-focused NER models would automatically tag words in a sentence and classify into the following wine-related categories: producer, region, country, vintage, vineyard, parcel, appellation, quality classification, grape, wine (name), practice, etc.

nified by the retrieval process through dedicated knowledge graphs. An alternative approach is to adopt open-domain question generation and answering systems (see Section 3.2 for overview), along the lines of recent studies [Wang et al., 2020a] that ensure the **factual consistency** of text summarization systems. The idea is that if we ask questions about a wine and its closest match in the knowledge graph about vintage, producer, etc., we will receive similar answers if the wine is factually consistent with the information associated with it on the wine list.

Breath/diversity. Textual diversity is nothing new to the field of natural language processing and measuring diversity of the wine list at a global level, a country level, or a region level, is akin to measuring topic diversity at different granularity levels, with various methods being proposed and accepted such as Proportion of Unique Words [Dieng et al., 2020], Pairwise Jaccard Diversity [Tran et al., 2013], Inverted Rank-Biased Overlap [Bianchi et al., 2020a], Embedding-based Centroid Distance
[Bianchi et al., 2020b], etc.

Depth. This is probably more applicable to long lists where depth could be demonstrated with a wide horizontal variety of producers for a given style or region, as well as vertical variety when it comes to different vintages of classic producers. Therefore, measuring depth of a wine list is largely measuring diversity within a region or even a producer and the aforementioned methods for breath and diversity could be readily applied to an even narrow set of a particular region or producer for depth measurements.

Focus. Focus could take on various interpretations: a regional emphasis (e.g., ancient yet upcoming wine countries like Armenia, Croatia, Georgia, etc.), a stylistic highlight (e.g., small production, organic, natural biodynamic), a suitable complement to the cuisine (Lebanese/Italian wine for Lebanese/Italian restaurants), or simply a good balance somewhere between a diverse set of randomly put together toe-tappingly good nothingness and over representation of single regions or the sommelier's preferences. Therefore, to evaluate focus, or how balance the wine list is, the balanced entropy of the distribution of the wine list in terms of vintage, region, style, producer, variety, etc. could be a good start, since a high entropy likely means that the wine list appears randomly thrown together without much effort, whereas a low entropy hints at over representation of one's preference for a particular style or region, which sometimes is not necessarily a bad thing either.

Rarity. How difficult it is to obtain the wine could be the ultimate calling card of how awesome a wine list is, especially when it comes to expansive wine lists where wine collectors and connoisseurs frequent. To measure the rarity of wines on a wine list, automatically or manually, an external knowledge graph that collates accurate information of market accessibility of every wine such as the number of bottles or cases produced, and the number of bottles still in circulation versus the number of bottles being cellared, is essential. Such a knowledge graph can be perhaps constructed with information obtained through APIs by Wine Searcher[41] and Cellar Tracker[42]. Given such a knowledge graph of wine market, rarity scores of any wine list would be easily calculated by aggregating the rarity of each wine on its list in various ways such as averaging, taking the maximum rarity scores, collating the top 10 rarest scores, etc.

Readability. Predicting readability of text documents has been studied extensively in the field of natural language processing for over a decade, where readability refers to this important aspect of a document — whether it is easily processed and understood by a human reader as intended by its writer. Readability in the context of natural language processing involves many aspects including grammaticality, conciseness, clarity, and lack of ambiguity. Various auto-

[41] wine-searcher.com
[42] cellartracker.com

matic. Various methods have been proposed, largely sophisticated combination of linguistic features derived from various syntactic parsers and language models and more recently, direct predictions from language models (Section 7.4), with excellent results that prove more accurate than the predictions of naive human judges when compared against the predictions of linguistically-trained expert human judges. Such a natural language definition of readability perhaps covers but one aspect of readability in our context of wine lists, where besides textual readability, visual readability also matters a great deal. The choice of typeface, font, layout, and spacing could also matter to whoever browsing and looking for the next bottle to pop open. Predicting subjective aesthetic judgment of visual designs has drawn considerable research attention and interest in the field of computer vision in the past few years, which led to workshops such as Understanding Subjective Attributes of Data at premier conferences of computer vision (e.g. CVPR). One could treat each page of a wine list as an image and learn a computer vision pipeline either in a modular way that chains separate modules of font detection, spacing/margin detection, clutter detection, typeface detection, structured prediction of layout, etc., or in an end-to-end way that learns the image as a whole with perhaps more attention paid to particular parts of the image of wine lists. In the end, one could fuse the textual readability extracted with natural language processing methods, and the visual readability extracted with computer vision methods, multi-modally to incorporate both aspects of readability in our context of wine lists. One could learn such a multi-modal model tailored to one's target consumers to gauge which aspect — textual or visual — matters more to the target audience. Perhaps in a neighborhood where consumers are relatively more sophisticated wine drinkers, the textual aspect could outweigh the visual aspect, whereas in an area where there is not much of a wine drinking culture, the visual aspect matters more to leave good first impressions on patrons.

Originality. The lack of originality in most wine lists makes wine lists from places like Terrior in TriBeCa of Manhattan stand out like no other. What makes a wine list original and how to automatically measure originality could easily be someone's doctoral dissertation that takes five years to finish. One shortcut would be rephrasing the problem as identifying the unusual wine lists from the most, which makes it an anomaly detection problem with clustering algorithms being possible solutions. The more a wine list is predicted to deviate from most wine lists we have seen, the more original it might be. Anomaly detection with Gaussian Mixture Models for clustering is perhaps one of the most widely used and fundamental machine learning methods, and one could tailor it for either natural language or visual image with respective feature extractors.

Value. To measure the markup of a wine list requires an accurate knowledge graph that houses the real-time market price, either the most recent auction hammer price or retail price, of each wine on the wine list. Given such a knowledge graph, constructed with Web Crawling, Wine Searcher API and the likes, it is straightforward to calculate an average markup or the spread of markups of all the wines across all categories of any given wine list. Such could be the value indicator of a wine list.

9.2 Playlist Generation

In many ways, the task of playlist generation, or recommending music in a sequential and context dependent manner, sits at the intersection of recommendation (detailed in Section 4.3) and text generation (Section 7.4 provides a review).

Over the past decade, various machine learning approaches have been proposed to create meaningful song sequences. A sizable body of studies approach the task of playlist generation with an information retrieval framework: given a query indicative of user preferences or contextual cues, retrieve a list of items from the large music repository that will most likely satisfy. Songs observed to co-occur with the query are relevant, and all other songs are irrelevant. For example, [Platt et al., 2001] observe a subset of songs in an existing playlist (the query), and the algorithm predicts a ranking of all songs and the quality of the algorithm is then determined by the position within the predicted ranking of the remaining, unobserved songs from the playlist. [Maillet et al., 2009] similarly predict a ranking over songs from a contextual query, evaluated by comparing the ranking to one derived from a large collection of existing playlists. One of the drawbacks of information-retrieval types of solutions lies in the sparsity of samples, i.e., rare co-occurrences of songs in a playlist relative to the size of the entire music repository. In even moderately large music databases on the order of thousands of songs, the probability of observing any given pair of songs in a playlist becomes fairly small, thus an overwhelming majority of song predictions are considered incorrect. In this framework, a good prediction may disagree with observed co-occurrences (thus deemed to be incorrect), but still be equally enjoyable to a user of the system. The information retrieval approach — and more generally, any discriminative learning approach — is only applicable when one can obtain negative examples, i.e., bad playlists. In reality, negative examples are difficult to define, let alone obtain, as users typically only share playlists that they like.

In favor of generative learning over discriminative frameworks[43] for

[43]Generative and discriminative are two major modeling frameworks in machine learning. The fundamental difference between them is that generative models focus on learning the data distribution (how data could be generated) whereas discriminative models focus on learning the decision boundaries. Take binary classification as an example, generative models (e.g., naive bayes) focus on learning how data of both classes are distributed whereas discriminative models (e.g., support vector machine, decision tree (Section 2.2)) focus on learning how to distinguish one class from the other.

playlist compositions, [McFee and Lanckriet, 2011] examined playlists as a natural language model (Section 7.4) induced over songs, and trained a simple yet effective *bigram* model[44] for song transitions. [Chen et al., 2012] took a similar Markovian approach to modeling song transitions by treating playlists as *Markov chains* in the latent space, and learning a metric representation (more details in Section 4.1 on metric learning) for each song. [Zheleva et al., 2010] adapted a *topic modeling* framework to capture music taste from listening activities across users and songs. [Wang et al., 2014] frame it as a *multi-armed bandit* problem and solve by efficiently balancing exploration and exploitation in the novelty discovery process of playlist generation. Similarly, [Xing et al., 2014] strive to strike the balance between novelty and diversity as concurrent objectives of generating quality playlists. [Logan and Salomon, 2001, Logan, 2002] quantify musical novelty in song trajectories with a similarity measure. With contextual cues, [Lehtiniemi, 2008] tailor a mobile music streaming service to user needs better, showcasing the impact of contexts on increased song novelty experienced by users. Moreover, graph-based methods (e.g., Section 4.3) have also been used to more efficiently search for diverse playlists, mitigating user fatigue or disinterest ([Taramigkou et al., 2013]).

In summary, Figure 68 visualizes and Table 23 aggregates major camps of techniques for automatic playlist generation with examples, advantages, and limitations, respectively.

[44]A simplistic bigram language model where sentences are generated by pairs of words based on empirical distribution and/or co-occurrences of word pairs.

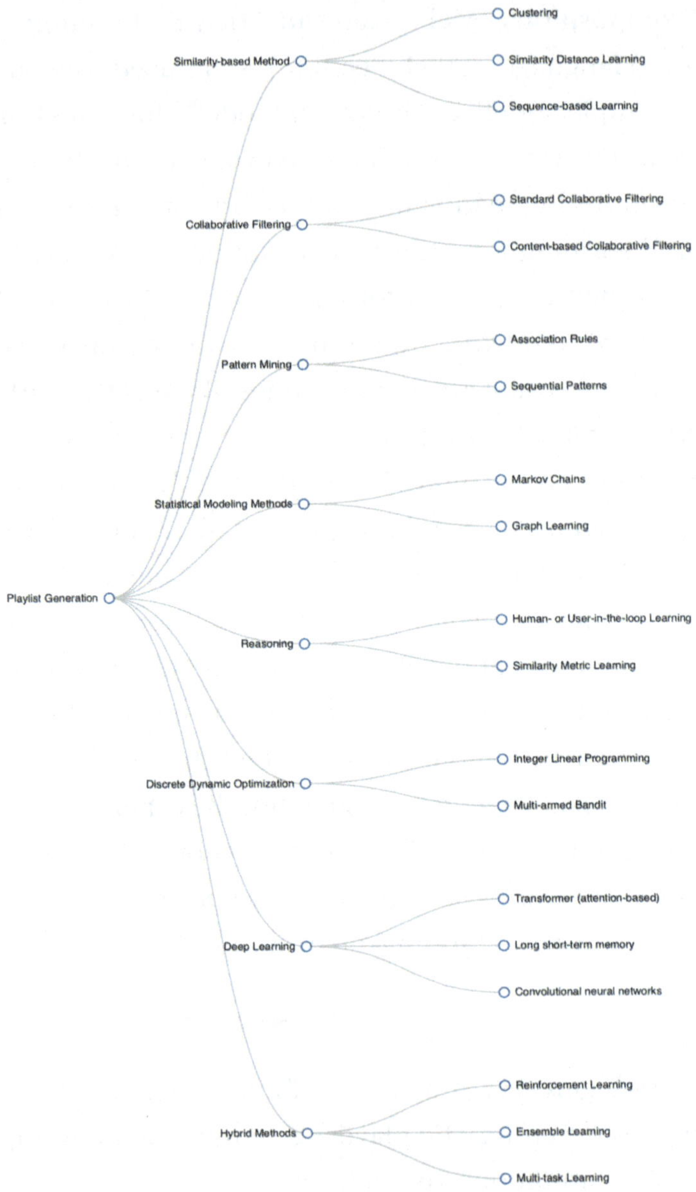

Figure 68: A treemap visualization of different automatic playlist generation techniques.

Out of the ocean of viable methods, I experimented with a personalized sequential recommender system [Wu et al., 2020] (for more details on recommender system, please refer to Section 4.3) based on

Techniques	Advantages	Limitations
Similarity-based	Scalability, consistency.	Lacking in diversity or user exploration.
Collaborative Filtering	Extensive research available.	Data hungry.
Pattern Mining	Reproducibility, ease of integration with human curation.	Lacking in robustness or consistency.
Statistical Modeling	Extensive research available.	(Lack of) Scalability.
Reasoning	Generalization ability.	(Lack of) Scalability.
Optimization	Interpretability. Transparency.	(Lack of) Scalability. Lacking in robustness.
Deep Learning	Overall performance. Extensive research available.	Data hungry. Potential lack of transparency or interpretability.
Hybrid	Adaptivity. Robustness.	(Lack of) Scalability.

Table 23: Automatic playlist generation approaches with respective advantages, and limitations.

Transformer [Vaswani et al., 2017] (more details in Section 7.4) with a knowledge base of available wines constructed from a snapshot of tasting notes of Jancis Robinson's purple page[45], which produces seemingly plausible results. More experiments are in progress to incorporate inventory constraints and controllable generation modules (e.g., Section 8.1). Demos will be made available at ai-for-wine.com.

[45]jancisrobinson.com

SECTION 10

Terrior

How and whether the tastes of the soil, the stones, the flowers, the herbs, the spices, the orchard fruits, grandmother's garden or kitchen, and favorite childhood desserts snuck into the wines we love are endlessly debatable among wine lovers. Being able to taste the vineyard geology in the wine — a *goût de terroir*, or the gushing Mistral wind, the morning fog, and the afternoon breezes, is perhaps more of a romantic notion that makes for an effectively engaging pitch of content marketing than a purely scientific one.

Some of the well-trained could ascertain different soil types rather than grape varieties in a blind tasting. The sandy soil in Cannubi was commonly attributed to the gracefulness in wines of Barolo Cannubi, whereas volcanic wines such as those from the Pantelleria Island, Forst in Pfalz, or the The Rangen de Thann vineyard in Hengst of Alsace supposedly produce some of the most powerful wines around the world. One of the easiest geological elements to distinguish in a glass is perhaps fruit that comes from a fertile site with heavy clay, where there's often a chunky quality. What about gravel? There is perhaps a mineral spine racing through. And the highly sought-after limestone? It's been said that there exists some palpable sugar from ripe fruit and acid structures that stand out from the rest. How about basalt? A smoky and almost ashy undertone flirt in the background. The iron-rich terra cotta (terrior rouge)? The rustic streak is sometimes unmistakable. Last but not the least, the well-loved granite? There is perhaps some textual breath showing its presence especially on the finish, a salty mineral edge.

These romantic associations between the *terrior* where the vine is grown and what is perceived in our glass are subjective and contextual, by no means a consensus by any stretch of imagination, and a further cry from scientifically proven *causal* links between *terrior* and wine. They are, perhaps (sometimes spurious) *correlations* between soils and subjectively perceived wines traits at best.

Why do *causal* links between *terrior* and wine matter, as opposed to *correlation* or *association* between them?

A best case in point is perhaps the dreaded topic of what *causes* premature oxidation, or premox, which refers to the phenomenon that wines age before their time[46]. Even though it is a wide-spread phenomena that affects all white wines[47] in all regions — I have had my own shares of premox'ed Condrieu, Verdejo, Etna Bianco, Hermitage Blanc, and Burgundy — everything seemed to have fallen a

[46]For instance, a typical white Burgundy at the village level is best at 8-10 years old with 1er crus and grand crus expected to last longer.

[47]According to researcher Valerie Levine and her colleagues at University of Bordeaux, premox affects all white wines, still and sparkling, dry and sweet, all grape varieties, and all origins.

cliff with white Burgundy wines starting late 1990s.

What could have *caused* the sudden surge starting 1995-1996? Various hypotheses and theories have been proposed and circulated:

- Better vineyard management with regular ploughing and sometimes grass cover, which does compete against vines for nitrogen.
- Global warming with riper grapes of lower acidity levels.
- Less crushing the grapes before pressing, thus less skin contact than the old times, which might have provided a phenolic foil.
- The introduction of horizontal pneumatic presses which reached majority adoption among Burgundians in 1996.
- After pressing, until recently, most would have put the juice into the barrel and let the fermentation happen, after the thick layers of solids (dirt, yeast, grape skin paste, etc.) had settled overnight.
- Timing of malolactic fermentation: malo used to be delayed until the following Spring whereas now it is mostly happening around Christmas, as long periods of unsulfured juice could induce premox.
- Lees stirring as an anti-oxidant strategy, which some had taken to extremes at both ends.
- Automatic bottling lines were introduced and it wasn't until recently that constant tests for dissolved oxygen were administered at bottling. François Jobard found that contrary to their full bottles, their half bottles were unaffected as the size didn't fit the machine and they had to hand bottle them back then.

- Sulphur usage both at bottling, during maturation, and throughout the process ebbed and flowed over time and in the 1990s the trend was to limit sulphur usage due to sulphur legislation.

- Quality degradation of cork closure became an issue as demand for cork exploded with that for wine.

- Changes in cork treatment such as hydrogen peroxide that had been used to treat cork to get rid of possible TCA taint, introducing chlorine flavor, as well as paraffin, which usually sticks to the side of bottle, and silicon, which is slippery.

Nonetheless, there appear no definitive conclusions regarding the exact *causes* of premox, and without which, no solutions could guarantee the eradication of premox and the problem remains unsolved, which is where we stand now in the course of history.
Here is another concrete albeit slightly involved example as to why we care about causal inference, and why identifying the exact causes matter for wine. As we are aware that global warming results in the acceleration of berries reaching physiological (sugar) ripeness ahead of phenolic ripeness, especially when it comes to young vines, in which case winemakers used to include stems are now likely destemming, which would supposedly result in fruit purity in the final wine, whereas stem inclusion is usually associated with complex aromatics such as spicy pepperiness and crushed strawberries. Due to the high level of fruit ripeness (i.e. sugar ripeness), the amount of malic acid would decrease during fermentation, resulting in less lactic acid, since malic acid gets converted into lactic acid via malolactic fermentation, and thus less gross lees would be left at the bottom of the fermentation vessel and the wine would aged on fine lees. Destemming practices and lower levels of malic acid are therefore likely correlated but not necessarily causal. If we only observe destemming and lack of malic acid and mistakenly thought destemming causes the reduction of malic acid, then switching to destemming

from whole cluster or stem inclusion for the purpose of reducing malic acid would likely be in vain.

Just like how a medical researcher might be determined to find out whether a new drug is effective in treating a disease, or an economist interested in uncovering the effects of family income on children's personality development, a conscientious winemaker perhaps would like to know the exact causes of premature oxidation (premox) in his or her own wines, as much as a forward-looking viticulturist who wishes to know the effect of climate change on vine-growing. In all of these scenarios, a simple correlation instead of causal effect would not suffice, since if the new drug did not necessarily lead to the cure of the disease, if increasing family income did not consistently affect children's personality development positively, and if no particular viticultural or vinification processes appeared to robustly lead to premox, then none of the relevant policy or procedural changes would lead to desired outcomes, nor would we be able to understand how things work, not until we were able to cleanly tease out different confounding factors and pinpoint the exact causes of observed phenomena.

What exactly amounts to establishing a causal link between *terrior* and wine? In contrast to descriptive or predictive tasks, causal inference aims to understand how intervening on one variable affects another variable. Specifically, many applied researchers aim to estimate the size of a specific causal effect, the effect of a single treatment variable on an outcome variable. However, a major challenge in causal inference is addressing *confounders*, variables that influence both treatment and outcome. For example, consider estimating the size of the causal effect of organic and biodynamic viticultural practices (treatment) on wine quality (outcome). Fungal disease pressure could be a potential confounder that may influence both the propensity to adopt organic biodynamic practices and wine quality. Estimating the effect of treatment on outcome without accounting for this confounding could result in strongly biased estimates and thus invalid causal conclusions. To eliminate confounding bias, one approach is to perform randomized controlled trials (RCTs) in which researchers randomly assign treatment. Yet, in many research areas, randomly assigning treatment is either infeasible or unethical. The economist studying the causal effect of family income on children's personality development might find it challenging to identify opportunities to randomly assign twins to both poor and rich families. And the viticulturist investigating the potential causal effect of climate change on vine-growing cannot simply randomly assign plots to different climate conditions since it is beyond human control. In such cases, researchers instead use observational datasets that are more available yet not well-controlled at first glance, and adjust for the confounding bias statistically with methods that we will detail in Section 10.1 through Section 10.5 of this chapter.

Identifying the effect of *terrior* (or *vigneron*) on wine quality is no easy undertaking. Randomized controlled trials (RCTs) are oftentimes infeasible, as most likely one simply could not *randomly* assign different climates, soil types, and elevations (or vignerons) to the same vineyard plot, holding various other factors constant such as weather, vintage, vinification, operational factors, market condition, etc. Moreover, when gauging the causal effect of *terrior* (or *vigneron*) on wine quality especially that perceived by consumers, one ought to tease out the reputation effect of a particular lieu-dit or climat and vigneron from the geographical or vinicultural effects. However, there are indeed rare occasions where cleanly controlled field experiments were carried out, in alignment with particular causal inference objectives, whether it be intentionally or inadvertently. In these scenarios that we are about to venture a discussion on, perhaps relatively straightforward comparisons of outcomes could provide at least some close approximations of the causal effects of interest.

How could we identify the causal impact of the lieu-dit or climat on the final wine? It is almost an impossible mission that would require holding everything else equal except the lieu-dit or climat in question. That means, the same vigneron, the same vine material, the same vine age, the same trellis and training systems, the same planting density, the same vineyard practices, as well as the same vinification processes, regardless of which and where the particular vineyard plot is. Even though it is perhaps indeed impossible to find such circumstances as plot-by-plot or precision viticulture is gaining traction, and tailoring viticultural and vinicultural strategies to different terriors are becoming the norm, close approximations could perhaps be found with vignerons like Frederic Mugnier of Domaine Jacques-Frederic Mugnier, a former engineer whose principle is somewhat unusual in that he persists in making wine strictly the same way across all his vineyards regardless of quality levels. According to him, It's tempting for a winemaker to adapt to specificity of any vineyards: one could think that this plot produces grapes with less tannin thus there must be more extraction to balance the wine and less is needed in the other wine. Frederic thinks it's a mistake, and that in being consistent in his approaches tending vines and making wines, he lets terrior speak without interfering.

By the same token, how could we possibly identify the causal effects of soil types and other geological characteristics on the final wine? As difficult as it might sound when it comes to holding everything else identical such as exposure, vineyard, elevation, viticultural and vinification practices, etc., the wine world's fascination of geology did help immensely in this regard, even though the task is still challenging because the ubiquitous single vineyard bottling nowadays usually happens with vineyards far apart with distinctive characters where other factors are not well-controlled any more. Perhaps the monopole[48] of Domaine George Roumier, the premier cru Clos de La Bussière in Morey-Saint-Denis is one exception where within the two and a half hectares there are a diversity of limestones and other geological features due to several faulting lines situated in the center of the lieu-dit where the rocks were bent during multiple turmoils of ancient geographical movements. A thick layer of clay on stones that is believed to translate to the broader structure and slow-maturing nature of the final wine; a plot that's particularly iron-rich comparable to Pommard (especially its premier cru Rugiens) and La Montrachet that is believed to impart power and weight. If Christopher Roumier tended to vines of similar vine materials, if not identical, in these different parts of the monopole and vinified them separately with identical processes, the resulting wine could be perhaps some of the closest estimates of how geological features shape the final wine.

Around ten degrees of latitude south on the other side of the Atlantic Ocean, all the way to the west of the North American continent, Diamond Creek Winery in Calistoga of Napa Valley was one of the first in the region to bottle separately three wines made from grapes grown on three distinctive soil types 60 feet away from one another. It could be perhaps cited as a new world example for such a thought experiment of causal identification of soils on wine in the valley. Al Brounstein's legacy as the strong-headed proponent of separate bottlings of micro-parcels within an already relatively small vineyard will continue to provoke intellectual conversations of terrior among next generations of Napa vintners. The friable gray volcanic ash in Volcanic Hill, the more iron-rich volcanic ash in Red Rock Terrace, and the alluvial fan of sand and gravel in Gravelly Measure were all planted with the same varietal composition, dry-farmed,

[48]Monopole refers to a lieu-dit owned entirely by one single estate.

and vinified in a similar fashion, despite notable differences in exposure, aspect, and elevation. Therefore, even though the three different labels could perhaps provide a hint of the causal effects of soils on wine, additional techniques detailed in Section 10.1 through Section 10.5 would be needed for more scientifically sound conclusions.

How could we identify the causal impact of different grape varieties on the final wine? Mondeuse, the grape native to the Savoie region in the French Alps, usually comes across as a light-bodied, red-berried, floral, yet spicy summer quaffer. But grape DNA analysis has shown that it is the closest relative (half-sibling or grandparent) of Syrah, which conjures up a drastically different image: inky dark purple, meaty, leathery, dark and red plums, black peppercorns and violets, with a great structure and a full body. But are these stereotypes indeed what Mondeuse and Syrah bring to the table as their own varietal traits, or are they simply different terrior expressions of Savoie in the foothills of the Alps and the roasted rolling hill of Cote Rotie in the northern Rhone? Luckily, a well-controlled field experiment where Mondeuse and Syrah were side-by-side in the same terrior, treated in the same way, and tended by the same hands, had teased out — as best as it could have been done — the causal effect of grape variety versus terrior on the final wine. They are the Syrah and Mondeuse bottlings of Lagier Meredith Vineyard on Mount Veeder in Napa Valley, the labor of love of professor emerita Carole Meredith and her husband, the Robert Mondavi veteran winemaker Steve Lagier.

Identifying the causal effect of grape variety on wine is also at the center of the debate on the quality of Aligoté Vert versus Aligoté Doré. Aligoté Doré appears to have been revered by producers working with these vines and many of them are wary of Aligoté Vert. The differences between them? According to Anne Morey of Domaine

Pierre Morey where both Aligoté Doré and Aligoté Vert are cultivated in different parcels. Aligoté Doré vines are of denser bunches with pink- or golden-colored smaller berries than green Aligoté Vert, perhaps partially because the contrasting common vine ages of the century-old Aligoté Doré from massale selection versus the twenty-something Aligoté Vert from mono-clonal plant materials from modern nurseries. Without pitting Aligoté Doré against Vert side-by-side on equal footing, meaning similar vine material in terms of quality, age, source, etc., in similar growing environments to begin with, no scientifically sound conclusions could be drawn on the intrinsic quality of the two clonal variations without being biased by the various confounding factors such as vine age, site selection, growing conditions, and viticultural practices.

Another curious yet topically opposite thought we might flirt with, for instance, is to identify the causal effect of domaine reputation on secondary market pricing or perceived quality of wine. One would have to alter only the domaine on the label, while holding everything else equal, including terrior, vine material, vine-growing and winemaking practices and individuals, and so forth. Luckily, albeit rare, there are indeed various such occasions in history where everything except the labels and the domaines on the label is identical and the resulting prices and wine reviews tuned out drastically different for different labels, highlighting the causal effects of domaine reputation and labels, independent of any vine-growing or winemaking factors, on consumer perception and demand.

Louis-Michel Liger-Belair of Domaine du Comte Liger-Belair, detailed how he gradually took over the family domaine and started estate bottling rather than selling wine to their long-term family-tied negociant partner Bouchard after being back from the engineering school in 1991. During the gradual transition between 2002 and 2005, Louis-Michel made Vosne-Romanée premier crus that were split in half: half were labelled as Bouchard La Romanée and half were labelled as Domaine du Comte Liger-Belair, even though the wines were the same, except for the bottling processes. However when both wines were being auctioned side-by-side almost thirty years later, with explicit confirmation by Louis-Michel Liger-Belair to auction participants that they were the same, the Domaine du Comte Liger-Belair bottlings still fetched hammer prices three times more than Bouchard ones.

Another similar tale takes us back to the founding moments of modern Priorat over three decades ago when "a group of romantics full of enthusiasm for a project" came to rescue a historic appellation, blessed with faith, volition, and perhaps a streak of luck.

René Barbier, who had been growing vines since 1978, was the one of the first to recognize the potential of Priorat, with its ancient bush vines, steep slopes and *llicorella* soils. He was joined by the enology professor José Luiz Pérez, and a few other bright-eyed "hipsters" like Alvaro Palacios and Daphne Glorian, to produce one wine in the first vintage of 1989 under ten different labels. "Critics said they preferred some to others," called Barbier, "but it was all the same stuff." The wine was an intriguing, one-off cuvée of Pinot Noir, Tempranillo, Merlot, Cabernet Sauvignon, Syrah and at its core, Grenache and Carignan. On a rare occasion in 2019 when the wine was opened, it was still alive, with mushroomy and slightly balsamic notes rightfully so after the thirty years over which Priorat grew into such a vibrant and well-celebrated wine producing region in the world.

The arguably easier-to-estimate causal effects of various viticultural and vinification practices on the final wine are perhaps indeed what experimental trials of conscientious vignerons are designed for. The effect of organic and biodynamic practices in the vineyard? Cultivate similar plots next to each other at the same time for a run of different vintages with traditional, organic, and biodynamic practices respectively and compare. Pioneers everywhere around globe went through such processes: Nicolas Joly of La Coulée de Serrant in the Loire Valley, Lalou Bize-Leroy of Domaine Leroy and Anne-Claude Leflaive of Domaine Leflaive in Burgundy, the OGs of the natural wine movement — Jules Chauvet, Marcel Lapierre, Jean Foillard, Guy Breton, Jean-Paul Thevenet, and Joseph Chamonard — in Morgon of Beaujolais, Pierre Overnoy in Jura, Eric Pfiferling in Tavel. Fast forward thirty or forty years in the new world, Randall Grahm of Bonny Doon in the Santa Cruz Mountains, Randall Robert Haas of Tablas Creek in Paso Robles, Maher Harb of Sept Winery in Lebanon, Frederick Merwarth of Hermann J Wiemer in Finger Lakes, ...What about the effect of fermentation or aging vessels? Subject the same batch of harvested grapes to identical treatment in the winery except for fermentation or aging vessels. I am convinced that the greatness of some of the world's best known vignerons lies in, to some extent, the non-stopping experimental trials they almost fanatically carry out, year in, year out. Jean-Marc Roulot of Domaine Roulot in Meursault has a mix of glass globes, cooked earth vessels, a steel barrel and Stockinger casks as well as the oak pièces traditional in Burgundy to experiment with for the same wine. He keeps track of what is where and its performance on a spreadsheet. Similar story goes for the experimentalists around the globe: Chateau Pontet-Canet in Pauillac on the right bank of Bordeaux, Meinklang in Burgenland south of Austria, Zorah in the volcanic Vayk mountain range where Vayotz Dzor of Armenia is, the Zuccardi family in Mendoza of Argentina, Bodega Garzón along the Atlantic coast of Uruguay, ...

10.1 Causal Inference

Two predominant causal inference [Pearl, 2009b] frameworks are structural causal models [Pearl, 2009a] and potential outcomes [Rubin, 1974, Rubin, 2005], which are complementary and connected [Pearl,

2009a, Morgan and Winship, 2015] in theory. While the two frameworks share the same goals of estimating causal effects in general, they do focus on separate aspects of the inference process: structural causal models tend to emphasize conceptualizing and reasoning about the effects of possible causal relationships among factors (variables), while methods from potential outcomes put more emphasis on estimating the size or strength of causal effects. With more in-depth discussions on the two frameworks in Section 10.1.1 and Section 10.1.2, in the following sections of this chapter, causal inference methods will be introduced in the order of the number of assumptions from the most to the least with the latter ones most similar to true randomized experiments which are considered the gold standard of causal inference.

10.1.1 Potential Outcomes Framework

In the ideal causal experiment, for each each unit of analysis, for instance, a grape vine, one would like to measure the outcome, for instance, a measure of vine health or vine balance, in both a world in which the unit received treatment, such as the vine being cultivated in limestone soil, as well as in the counterfactual world in which the *same* unit did not receive treatment, that is, the same grape vine did not grow in limestone soil, but rather the default, say, clay soil[49]. A fundamental challenge of causal inference is that one cannot simultaneously observe treatment and non-treatment for one single unit. The most common aggregate estimand of interest is the average treatment effect (ATE). In the absence of confounders, this is simply the difference in average outcome measures between the treatment group (average vine health in limestone soil) and the control group (average vine health in clay soil). However, such a simple estimation will be biased if there are confounders that influence both treatment

[49]This is an example of binary treatment. Multi-value treatments are also available and widely studied.

and outcome at the same time, such as elevation, gradient of the slope, etc.

10.1.2 Structural Causal Models Framework

Structural causal models (SCMs) use directed graphs that depict nodes as random variables and directed edges as the direct causal dependence between these variables. The typical estimand of choice here is the probability distribution of an outcome variable given an intervention on a treatment variable, which is similar to the estimand in the potential outcomes framework but different in that the latter (potential outcome framework) concerns the point estimate of the treatment effect on a sub-groups whereas the former (structural causal model) is interested in the full distribution of treatment effects that could be changing via intervention.

For this reason, there is a legitimate concern of how to generate causal inferences using standard conditional methods based on structural causal models. This concern is often not precisely articulated, but rather, in the form of a concern for endogeneity bias. For instance, great lieux-dits such as Burgundy Grand Crus, Germany Grosses Gewächses, and Barolo MGAs (Menzione Geografica Aggiuntiva), are widely believed to contribute to the quality and aging potential of the resulting wines. However, the vignerons working these parcels are also the ones with the most intimate knowledge of the land, the best viticultural and winemaking skills, the best winemaking equipments, as well as the most resourceful social networks to bounce off ideas with. Therefore, the quality of vigneron becomes a confounding factor that makes the causal estimation of the effect of lieu-dit on wine *endogenous* due to the selection bias cause by intrinsic quality of the vigneron that's strongly correlated with the quality of the final wine.

The ideal solution to the endogeneity problem would be to conduct an experiment in which superior sites are *randomly* assigned to growers regardless of their knowledge or skills. Short of this ideal, for observational studies that lack exogenous intervention, one needs an *identification* strategy in order to represent the probability distribution of an outcome variable given an intervention on a treatment variable, in terms of distributions of observed variables. One such identification strategy is the backdoor criterion which applies to a set of variables, if they block every backdoor path between treatment and outcome, and none of the variables could result from treatment. The intuition is that if these paths are blocked, then any systematic correlation between treatment and outcome reflects the effect of treatment on outcome.

One traditional solution under the umbrella of the backdoor criterion is to use Instrumental Variable (IV) methods.

10.2 Instrumental Variable

Instrumental Variable (IV) methods, by definition, do not use all of the variation in the data to identify causal effects, but rather, partition the variation into that which could be considered as clean or as though generated via experimental methods, and that which is contaminated and could result in endogeneity bias.

To take a step back, let us assign the structural model a rather generic form of equation that assumes that the outcome variable is equal to a particular functional transformation of weight sums of the treatment variable and observable control variables, together with some noise term that accounts for other factors unaccounted for. The endogeneity problem is perhaps best understood as arising from an unobservable that is correlated with the noise and the treatment variable (and possibly other control variables too) in the structural model equation. Regression methods were originally designed for experimental data where the treatment variable was chosen and randomly assigned as part of the experimental design. For observational data, that is not true and there is always the danger that there exists some unobservable variable that has been omitted from the structural model, thus a generic criticism of endogeneity almost always applicable.

The ideal solution to the endogeneity problem would be to conduct an experiment where the treatment is uncorrelated with any unobservable variables by design via randomization. Short of randomized experimental design, we could partition the variation in the endogenous variable into two parts: variation orthogonal or unrelated to the noise term of the structural equation (or intuitively, the outcome variable), and variation possibly correlated with the noise term. Such a partition arguably always exists, even though the real question lies in the accessibility of it via the introduction of an observable variable, which is our aptly termed Instrumental Variable. Specifically, to resolve endogeneity, we are in search of Instrumental Variables that are correlated with the treatment variable, but independent of the treatment outcome variable, given the treatment.

For instance, in the earlier example of estimating the effect of the best vineyard parcels on the quality of final wines where the best vignerons are confounding factors because due to historical reasons the best vignerons are also more likely to own the best parcels. In a unique setting of Germany in the 1950s, a potential Instrumental Variable to tease out the effect of Terrior versus Vigneron could be *Flurbereinigung*, roughly translated as land reform or land consolidation. It was with the intention to correct the situation where after centuries of equal division of the inheritance of small farmers among their heirs and unregulated sales, most farmers owned many small non-adjacent plots of land, making access and cultivation difficult and inefficient. Even though it cause wide-spread criticism not only in the German wine industry but also agriculture in general. After criticism about loss of biodiversity caused by large-scale land reforms began to be voiced in the late 1970s, restoring the natural environment became another objective. Despite the controversies and ramifications of *Flurbereinigung*, it could serve as an exogenous shock to the structural equation, essentially breaking the correlational link between vigneron and terrior to some extent, thus causal inference in this scenario could be done in a cleaner manner. Caveats are in order that are sometimes convincing enough to steer researchers clear of the IV method. While endogeneity bias is defined as the asymptotic bias for an estimator that uses all of the variation in the data — almost always, IV methods are only asymptotically unbiased if the instrument variables are indeed *valid*, which is in essence unverifiable. Even if validity stands, the estimator of the outcome effect of specific treatments based on the Instrumental Variable could still suffer from poor sampling properties such as distributional fat tails, high root mean square error, and statistical bias, which are perhaps not well appreciated among econometricians.

One of the main obstacles to reliable causal effect estimation with observational data is the reliance on the strong, untestable assumption of no unobserved confounding. To avoid this, only in very specific settings (e.g., instrumental variable regression) it is possible to allow for unobserved confounding and still identify the causal effect. Outside of these settings, one can only hope to meaningfully bound the causal effect [Manski, 2009]. The existence of an Instrumental Variable can be used to derive upper (lower) bounds on causal effects of interest by maximizing (minimizing) those effects among all IV models compatible with the observable distribution. In a recent work, algorithms to compute these bounds on causal effects over "all" IV models compatible with the data in a general continuous setting were introduced by [Kilbertus et al., 2020] exploiting modern optimization machinery. The burden of the trade-off is put explicitly on the practitioner, as opposed to embracing possibly crude approximations due to the limitations of identification strategies. While this addresses an important source of uncertainty in causal inference — partial identifiability as opposed to full identifiability — there is also statistical uncertainty: confidence or credible intervals for the bounds themselves, an important matter perhaps for future work.

10.3 Matching

Matching methods aim to create treatment and control groups with similar confounder assignments; for example, grouping units by observed variables (e.g., in the setting of a vine, age, rookstock, scion, variety, trellis, training, pruning method, timing of budbreak or flowering, berry size, skin thickness), then estimating effect size within each stratum [Stuart, 2010]. Exact matching on confounders is ideal but nearly impossible to obtain with high-dimensional confounders. A framework for matching requires choosing:

1. (optional) a feature representation;
2. a distance metric;
3. a matching algorithm.

The matching algorithm involves additional decisions about:

1. greedy (local search) vs. optimal matching;
2. number of control items per treatment item to match for;
3. using calipers (thresholds of maximum distance to cut off matching at);
4. matching with or without data sample replacement.

Coarsened exact matching(CEM), one of the most widely adopted matching algorithms, matches on discretized raw values of the observed confounders [Iacus et al., 2012]. Instead of directly matching on observed variables, *stratified propensity-score matching* [Caliendo and Kopeinig, 2008] partitions propensity scores into intervals (strata) and then all units are compared within a single strata. Stratification is also known as interval matching, blocking, and subclassification. Once the matching process is done, counterfactuals (estimated potential outcomes) could be readily obtained from the matches for each sample. Such counterfactuals would enable us to answer a myriad of "what-if" questions without carrying out the corresponding experiments that could be all-consuming: what if we planted this rootstock in limestone-rich soils versus clay-rich soils? What if we moved the vine up slope where it's much windier and where soils erode much faster?

Despite the fact that matching could be viewed as a method to reduce model dependence because, unlike regression, it does not rely on a restrictive parametric form, estimated causal effects may still be sensitive to other matching method decisions such as the number of bins in coarsened exact matching, the number of controls to match with each treatment in the matching algorithm, or the choice of caliper. Therefore, the robustness and sensitivity of the causal estimators becomes a critical bottleneck and room for improvement.

In the past few years, as causal inference as a research topic has finally grabbed the interest and attention of machine learning researchers, a lieu of machine learning research has proliferated to incorporate such traditionally econometrician causal inference methods into the machine learning model training paradigm. [Agarwal et al., 2019] was one of the first few to integrate propensity score matching methods to learning-to-rank (LTR, hereafter) problems in the context of information retrieval. In their earlier work [Joachims et al., 2017], they showed counterfactual inference methods provide a provably unbiased and consistent approach to LTR despite biased data. The key prerequisite for counterfactual LTR is knowledge of the propensity of obtaining a particular user feedback signal, which

enables unbiased effect estimation[50] via Inverse Propensity Score (IPS) weighting. This makes getting accurate propensity estimates a crucial prerequisite for effective unbiased LTR. The algorithms proposed in [Agarwal et al., 2019] improved information retrieval performance and user experience while eliminating the need for inquiring for additional user interaction or feedback.
Both [Schnabel et al., 2016] and [Liang et al., 2016] adapted the propensity-score matching approach for causal inference to recommendation systems learning unbiased estimators from biased user rating data. [Schnabel et al., 2016] based propensity weights on user preferences, either directly through ratings or indirectly through user and item features or feature representations, whereas [Liang et al., 2016] also take into consideration exposure data — information about items or services users discover rather than explicitly like.

10.4 Doubly-robust methods

Unlike most methods that model only treatment or only outcome, doubly robust methods model both treatment and outcome, and have the desirable property that, if either the treatment or outcome models are unbiased, then the effect estimate will be unbiased as well. In practice these methods have been shown to really shine [Van der Laan and Rose, 2011]. For instance, Adjusted inverse probability of treatment weighting (A-IPTW) combines estimated propensity scores and potential conditional outcomes, while the more general targeted maximum likelihood estimator (TMLE) [Dorie et al., 2019] updates the conditional outcome estimate with a regression on the

[50] By way of Empirical Risk Minimization (ERM), a principle in statistical learning theory which is used to give theoretical bounds on their performance. The core idea is that we cannot know exactly how well an algorithm will work in practice because we don't know the true distribution of data that the algorithm will work on, but we can instead measure its performance on a known set of training data, which is the empirical risk.

propensity weights and counterfactual outcomes.

10.5 Causal-driven Representation Learning

The application field of natural language processing is perhaps one of the first where causal inference with machine learning starts to catch on. Several research efforts design representations of text specifically for causal inference. These approaches still initialize their models with representations of text that recover latent confounders, either by way of pre-specifying the confounders of interest and measuring them from text, or by learning confounders inductively and using a low-dimensional representation as the confounder in downstream causal estimations. But then the representations are updated with machine learning architectures that incorporate the observed treatment assignment and other causal information.

[Johansson et al., 2016] leveraged multi-task learning (Section 2.3) to aim for low prediction error for the conditional outcome estimates, and minimizes the discrepancy distance between potential outcomes given different treatment in order to achieve balance in the confounders. [Roberts et al., 2020] combined structural topic models ([Roberts et al., 2014]), propensity scores, and matching. They use the observed treatment assignment as the content covariate in the structural topic model, append an estimated propensity score to the topic-proportion vector for each document[51], and then perform coarsened exact matching on that vector. 12-in-1 [Veitch et al., 2019] fine-tune a pre-trained BERT [Devlin et al., 2019] network (more details in Section 7.4) with a multi-task learning framework (refer to Section 2.3) that jointly learns:

- the language model BERT with its original masked-language modeling objective;

[51] A document could be seen as a distribution over topics, according to the topic modeling framework.

- propensity scores;
- conditional outcomes for both the treatment group and the control group.

They use the predicted conditional outcomes and propensity scores in regression adjustment[52] and the targeted maximum likelihood estimator (TMLE) (Section 10.4) formulas.

Such methods could be particularly useful when we set out to identify potential outcomes regarding perceived wine quality or wine characteristics by wine critics or consumers using wine reviews and articles as data. However, these methods have yet to be compared to one another on the same benchmark datasets and tasks for fair comparisons. In addition, it remains future work for us to investigate if and when causal effects are sensitive to network architectures and hyperparameters used in these methods, as well as potential mitigation strategies if sensitivity is indeed an issue.

10.6 Regression Discontinuity

Absent of randomized controlled experiments due to time, monetary, or ethical constraints, econometricians often rely on "natural experiments", which are fortuitous circumstances of quasi-randomization that can be exploited for causal inference. Regression discontinuity designs (RDDs) are such a technique. RDDs use sharp changes in treatment assignment[53] for causal inference.

For example, it is often difficult to assess the effect of organic or biodynamic certification on wine quality since certified wineries may

[52] Regression adjustment fits a supervised model from observed data about the expected potential outcomes conditional on the treatment variable and covariates. The learned conditional outcome then could be used to derive counterfactual outcomes for each sample point in either the treatment group or the control group.

[53] Treatment assignment in the language of the potential outcome framework refers to the presence of the effect under investigation for causal inference.

systematically differ from others to start. Yet, if certification bodies grant certification to wineries based on a relatively objective evaluation score, that is, those who received an aggregate score higher than a threshold get certified whereas those fell below the same threshold didn't, then wineries with scores just above or below the threshold are not systematically different and effectively receive random treatment. That threshold induces an RDD that can be used to infer the effect of the intervention of organic or biodynamic certification.

The essential element of a regression discontinuity design lies in the discontinuity, or "unexpected jump" in the outcome variable, as is illustrated in Figure 69. The model approximates the data well except for the two regions of deviation of opposite directions and possibly different magnitudes, on both sides of the discontinuity.

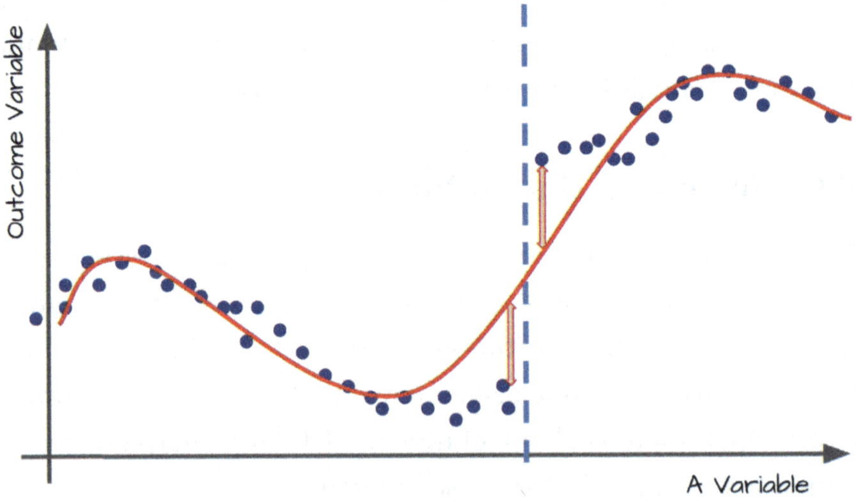

Figure 69: Illustration of a one-dimensional regression discontinuity design (dashed vertical line). Navy dots are data samples and the red curve is a fitted model. The gap between the two vertical two-sided arrows (and including the two arrows) is the *unexpected jump* identified by the regression discontinuity design, thus the causal treatment effect.

RDDs require fewer assumptions than most causal inference techniques and are arguably most similar to true randomized experiments [Lee and Lemieux, 2010]. However, identifying RDDs could be painstakingly manual as it requires human intuition and construction, and thus limited by human biases. Indeed, many academic studies reuse the same or analogous RDDs (e.g., discontinuities at geographic boundaries, or test score cutoffs for school admission) and most of these RDDs are single-dimensional, represented by a threshold value for a single variable. Finally, RDDs often rely on the human eye to verify their validity. The tinkering that is often done in practice implies that RDDs discovered by humans are subject to multiple testing issues.
Machine learning techniques could be used to aid in discovering, quantifying, and validating RDDs in data. Automatic Local Regression Discontinuity Design method [Herlands et al., 2018] could be used to discover new RDDs across arbitrarily high dimensional spaces, expanding human capability to tap the full potential of RDD methods, with interpretability enabled by a simple mechanism for ranking how (observed) factors influence the discovered discontinuities.

SECTION 11

Trust and Ethics

Trust is an essential element in all aspects of life including professional interactions and economic transactions. The wine industry is no exception.

A particularly relevant setting is that of a wine supply chain, in which interdependent parties or stakeholders — growers, winemakers, importers, distributors, retailers, etc. — with potentially conflicting incentives need to coordinate information and actions to satisfy consumer demand for wine. However, when and how much to trust are no simple decisions. A lack of trust or overoptimistic trust can both be detrimental.

This is especially true when it comes to the supplier-buyer or winemaker-importer relationship where trust plays an important, if not the most important role in the constancy of the mutual relationships that preserve through difficult vintages, dismal economic times, and the stresses from greater competition in the market.

Neal Rosenthal in his memoir Reflections of A Wine Merchant revealed one of his best decisions and one of his serious mistakes in his decades-long career. One is a tale about unwavering loyalty and trust, the other about overoptimistic and misplaced trust, both of which happened in Burgundy.

Burgundy as a region, perhaps to a greater extent than many others, suffers from fickle weather patterns and natural hazards that frequently wreck havoc in the vineyards, whether it be frost, hail, fungal diseases, or insects and animals that feed on grapes, and the fragility of Pinot Noir doesn't help. Therefore Burgundian growers were perhaps more sensitive and stressed, than those in other regions, having been through the vicissitudes of it all, plus the elasticity of the demand that could cause the market to shut down entirely when the wine is expensive and the wine critics are not singing about a certain vintage, at least back in the early 1980s when Neal Rosenthal just started the business.

Over the course of the eight years from 1977 to 1985, weathers had been largely abysmal and the resulting wines arguably lackluster, with notable exceptions of vintages 1978 and 1985. For any "savvy" importer, it is in his best economic interest to say no to the troubling and almost forgettable 1983s and 1984s, while sealing the deals as much as possible for the 1985s. This was not uncommon and only human nature. But a grower's fate is perennially tied to the weather, and Neal Rosenthal understands all too well that a grower needs a proper partner who could prevail the vicissitudes standing behind the grower no matter what. This was exactly what he did for the growers in his portfolio, buying up the 1984s just as he had purchased the preceding vintages, despite a great deal of financial pain, when others were shunning the vintage of 1984 and then showing up at the cellar for the very fine 1985s as if 1984 had never happened. Words went around Burgundy, and Neal Rosenthal's credibility with growers soared, and the access to growers' finest wines assured for decades to come. The other side of the same tale was a sad one, even though it did come full circle in the end. One of Neal Rosenthal's first suppliers in Gevrey-Chambertin was Georges Vachet who owned some of the best parcels such as Mazis Chambertin and Lavaux Saint-Jacques through his wife's family lineage of Rousseau. But things quickly took a dramatic turn as Georges' son Gerard took over, who decided to take shortcuts in winemaking in favor of profitability while sacrificing quality. Neal Rosenthal wasn't willing to abandon this domaine that satisfied his own customers for years and helped build the credibility of his importer business, and begrudgingly stuck with them for another few years until it became too painfully clear that the domaine was no longer what it used to be. Years later, Gerard gave up his winemaking career and rented out their stellar vineyards to a neighboring grower Gerard Harmand, who after a serendipitous turn of events became Neal Rosenthal's client afterwards. It was a story running full circle.

The other tale was not an uncommon one, as trust is a two-way street. While growers or suppliers select wine merchants or importers who they can trust, they also need to establish their own trust-worthy reputation for the business relationship to continue to blossom. One of Neal Rosenthal's early sources in Vosne-Romanée with access to the highly coveted 1er cru "Les Suchots" stealthily shipped him cases of 1977 Vosne "Suchots", when the procurement agreement was initially placed for the 1979 vintage right after Neal tasted through the vintages in the cellar and passed on the 1977s. The same shenanigan was pulled by Robert Sirugue, when he swapped out the cuvée made from old vines for another cuvée from young vines. In the early 1980s, Neal Rosenthal, due to financial constraints had to decide from whom to buying wines between Robert Sirugue and Jean Faurois, both of whom with access to some of the best lieux-dits and climats in Vosne with Robert's holdings more wide-ranging and prestigious. The commercial instinct got the better of him and he cut ties with Jean Faurois, an unassuming gentleman born into the winemaking family and tradition. This is what Neal Rosenthal refers to as one of the serious mistakes he ever made in his professional life, because the relationship with Sirugue quickly ruptured after even more conflicts over wine quality and he humbly begged for recommence with Jean Faurois who graciously agreed.

From the perspective of growers, trust certainly plays an essential role in selecting whom to sell their finest wines to. It is especially true when it comes to the most sought-after domaines whose wines fetch extraordinarily high yet ever-increasing prices in the secondary gray market. Guillaume d'Angerville, the former JP Morgan executive and owner of the iconic Volnay producer Domaine Marquis d'Angerville once shared his concerns towards the possibility of the price of their wine being forced up as land prices rise and speculators rage the market: "It's painful to see your wines in a virtual market at prices many times what you know you're going to be selling them for. To get a hold on the prices, I try to put my wines in the hands of people that I trust. Every year I eliminate people from the client list. The goal is to have perhaps 50 clients that I trust entirely." Such a sentiment is shared and reiterated by numerous other growers, as well as buyers looking for trustworthy and reliable growers to source from. This is especially true for natural wine merchants and sommeliers who advocate for natural wines. When asked about how did they choose which natural wine producers to work with, Pascaline Lepeltier, partner of Racines wine bar and well-known sommelier and educator, and David Lillie, partner of Chambers Street Wine, focused on naturally made wines from artisanal small producers, both cited trust as a top criterion and factor in their decisions where and from whom to source the wines in the store or in the restaurant.

Besides the supply chain relationships between sellers and buyers, trust and ethics permeate almost every other corner of the wine business as well: wine legislation, wine writing, wine education and certification, and the list goes on.

One such example revolves around the conundrum of "natural wine". Despite the prominent rise of the modern natural wine movement that started with several bright-eyed winemakers in the 1970s in Morgon, and trickled to every major hub of the world during the past decade, the widespread confusion among consumers around natural wine is palpable and not unwarranted. Reasons abound ranging from lack of legislation around terminology, to widespread misconception between being natural and organic biodynamic, from various certification bodies and associations clamouring for authority, to the general consumer unawareness of disparate marketing foci regarding sustainable vine-growing and winemaking, among others. Therefore, there comes the long-standing conundrum in the center of this movement. On one hand, earnest natural winemakers try to make across to consumers with labeling or marketing how they differ from large-scale industrial producers who adopt different philosophies of vine-growing and winemaking for disparate end goals. On the other hand, authoritative legal bodies, given no legal definition of natural wine, punish winemakers for putting unverifiable terms on labels that could potentially mislead consumers and hurt other producers, whereas letting loose those who abuse the term and hype of "natural wine" by putting on a natural wine facade while deviating from its philosophy that even the most savvy consumers sometimes let it slip.

Free wine trips for wine bloggers and wine influencers paid for by associations of a wine region for the purpose of promotion, free wine dinners and tastings hosted by wineries to woo over wine critics and wine journalists for raving reviews and positive ratings, generous sponsorship of wine events and wine challenges for potential favoritism behind the curtains, among others, do not come as a surprise to most industry professionals, not unlike many other industries in the world. Just like the prevalence of Amazon fake reviews and sock puppets that flooded social media, insincere endorsement of wine regions, producers, restaurants, bars, wine books, and other wine products permeate the space, making honest and independent voices all the more cherished and rare. As we will detail in Section 11.1, computer scientists have long started assisting in the society's battle against insincerity and deceitfulness with automatic methods for detecting deception in various contexts for various stakeholders, with proven evidence that AI-backed methods do excel and outperform most human beings by a large margin.

In 2018, a cheating scandal broke out at the Master Sommelier exams administered by the organization the Court of Master Sommelier — one of the world's notoriously difficult verbal exams for wine professionals — and shook the global wine industry. Answers were found leaked by one examiner to some candidates beforehand and all the results were invalidated. Candidates were required to take the exam a second time. Those who took it honestly and passed were now stripped of their hard-earned title and being questioned for their integrity. Sommelier Jane Lopes detailed some of the chaos in her memoir Vignette, while several others bit the bullet and went with the drill all over again to prove their honesty and capability. Such blatant leaking and cheating are not uncommon in education, and I myself had also been a victim to the same dilemma when I took my first Graduate Record Examinations (GRE) when applying to graduate school, the results of which were invalidated and

I was forced to take it a second time after half a year's delay and stress. Such nasty unfolding of events with no one admitting any mistakes or taking any responsibilities broached the trust between the organizations and the exam takers, the victims. As I will detail in Section 11.2, machine learning or deep learning, speech and natural language processing could prove especially conducive in sussing out whoever concealing the information and putting on a veer of naivety and honesty, as well as shedding light on what acoustic-prosodic and linguistic cues to look for when trying to distinguish between information concealers and truth-tellers.

11.1 Deception Detection

Deception is a rather common occurrence in our daily lives, and there have been sustained interests in understanding and accurately detecting detection throughout human history.

Deception is an act or a statement intended to make people believe something other than what the speaker believes to be true, or even partially true, excluding unintentional lies such as honest mistakes, or mis-remembering.

Deception detection has long been extensively studied in multiple disciplines such as cognitive psychology, computational linguistics, paralinguistics, forensic science, etc., with growing interests from fields where its applications might be very much in demand, such as business, jurisprudence, law enforcement, and national security. Deception and detecting deception is a complex psychological phenomena that speak to cognitive processes or mental activities. Therefore, psychology as a field has been one of its first strongholds of research development. It has been a robust finding that most humans do no better than chance in detecting lies of others, with detection accuracy increasing to over 80% in groups of people with special training or relevant life experiences.

Early work by psychologists such as Paul Ekman, whose work inspired and led to the wildly popular TV series Lie To Me, documented behavioral measures such as micro-expressions and pitch increases as informative indicators of deceptive speech.

Why might these indeed be useful for detecting lies?

One widely cited explanation is when individuals are telling lies, which often requires making up a story about an non-existent experience or attitude, they experience greater cognitive load to keep their logic straight, in fear of being debunked, especially when the stakes are high and the expectations are great. Psychologists have long demonstrated a general relation between the amount of stress that a speaker is experiencing and the fundamental frequency of his or her voice, as well as changes in facial expressions linked to the amount of internal debate.

In addition, the made-up stories or sentiments could also be qualitatively and quantitatively different from true stories, which social psychologists (such as James Pennebaker and Jeffrey Hancock), computational linguists (such as Yejin Choi and Claire Cardie), and speech scientists (such as Julia Hirschberg) have all shown great interested in and devoted years of research on, discovering statistically significant differences linguistically, acoustically, and prosodically between truthful statements and lies, but not without mixed evidence and context dependency. For instance, liars were found to show lower cognitive complexity, use fewer self-references and other references, and use more negative emotion words. On the other hand, Joan Bachenko and colleagues identified a mixture of linguistic features including hedging, verb tense, and negative expressions to be predictive of truthfulness in criminal narratives, interrogation, and legal testimony.

More recently, computer scientists have investigated deception detection in various contexts, identifying cues from texts, speech signals, gestures, and facial expressions in video clips.

Language-based indicators of deception have been widely identified in various online platforms that have permeated our everyday lives.

Myle Ott and Yejin Choi investigated online deceptive opinion spams by crowdsourcing a dataset of fake hotel reviews, and found deceptive spams exhibit more positive emotions, first-person singulars, concrete expressions, and fewer spatial configurations. Jeffrey Hancock and colleagues revealed in their conversational studies that liars produce more words, more sense-based words (seeing, touching), and use fewer self-oriented but more other-oriented pronouns when lying than when telling the truth, all of which was corroborated in various other studies. What appeared more interesting was the finding that motivated liars avoided causal terms when lying whereas unmotivated liars tended to increase use of negations.

Lies also altered how the liars conversational partners' behaviors despite being blind to the lies being told. More questions with shorter sentences were asked when they were being lied to, matching the liar's linguistic styles. Rada Mihalcea found that besides greater detachment from self references, words related to certainty are more dominant in deceptive texts, which likely means that liars tend to explicitly use truth-related words as a way to emphasize the fake truth and conceal the lies. On the contrary, belief-related words such as I think, I believe, I feel, are more frequently found in truthful statements where no additional emphasis is needed for the truthfulness. Yejin Choi and her colleagues also looked at syntactic stylometry for detecting deception, demonstrating the presence of hidden information of deception in complex syntactical structures of texts.

Online dating websites are one of the major sources of lies about oneself. Catalina Toma and Jeffrey Hancock closely examined the role of online daters' physical attractiveness in how they self-present with or without exaggeration or blatant lies. The results were not pretty: the lower online daters' attractiveness, the more likely they were to beatify their online photographs and lie about physical descriptors (height, weight, age), which, perhaps surprisingly, is found to be unrelated to other non-physical elements such as income or occupation. That is to say, online daters' intentional deceptions were within bounds and strategically aimed at elements they lack or essential. Researchers pointed to as explanations evolutionary theories about the importance of physical attractiveness in the dating market as well as recent technological advancements that make such strategic online representation possible.

There has also been much progress in identifying cues of deception in speech signals.

Sarah Levitan and Julia Hirschberg at Columbia Speech Lab collected a large-scale corpus of cross-cultural speech of deception and truth-telling, coupled with individual features such as personality traits. They found that gender, native language, and personality information significantly improves accuracy of detecting deception along with acoustic-prosodic features. They further combined acoustic-prosodic, lexical, and phonotactic features to automate deception detection and outperformed human performance by a large margin. Statistically significant acoustic-prosodic and linguistic indicators of deception detection were also extensively tested. The researchers observed that increased pitch maximum is an indicator of deception across all speakers, the significance is even stronger in deceptive speech for male speakers and for native Chinese speakers, but diminished for female speakers or native speakers of English.

Another universal indicator of deception was increased maximum intensity of speech, but it was found to not necessarily hold for native speakers of Chinese. Increased speaking rate is also an interesting find as an indicator of truth telling in native Chinese speakers speaking English, which is consistent with the line of thinking that lying consumes extra cognitive load. But such an effect appears to be significant only in non-native speakers, suggesting that the fact of conversing in a second language makes the effect of increased cognitive load more apparent for observers. Increased jitter in speech was also identified as a strong signal of truthful speech in females. Interestingly, people were also shown to believe those who speak fast are telling the truth, when in fact, there was no significant differences between lies and truth-telling except for non-native speakers.

When it comes to linguistic cues to deception, Sarah and her colleagues found that the longer total duration of response, the longer the average response time, the more words per sentence, the more filled pauses, the more interrogatives or words indicating influence or power, the more hedging and self-distancing, and the more vividly detailed descriptors, the more statistically likely a speech was deceptive, which is consistent with the explanation of increased cognitive load when lying resulting in difficulties of speech planning and overcompensation in words, details, and feigned confidence.

Videos of deceptive and non-deceptive speech have also been collected to leverage the visual cues for automatic detection. [Pérez-Rosas et al., 2015a, Pérez-Rosas et al., 2015b] collected real-life trial videos and applied image processing methods to extract gestures and facial expressions on top of linguistic analyses of texts, and showcased how such multimodal deception detection systems outperform the human capability of identifying deceit. They found that spontaneous lies often include negation, certain, and you words, consistent with a large body of previous work on domain-specific deception detection, meaning that liars would try to enhance their lies by using stronger words and detaching from oneself. On the other hand, researchers found people are less likely to lie about family, religion, and positive experiences. When it comes to gender differences in lying tendencies, men lie more about friends and others, whereas women lie more about money and the future. Truth-telling females also appear to use more metaphors in their speech whereas males are more likely telling the truth when talking about music and sports. Things get even more interesting when it comes to age differences in liars' word usage patterns. Older liars appear to refer to anxiety, money, and motion related words more likely when deceiving, whereas younger ones more likely reference anger, negation, and death related words when telling lies. The researchers also closely examined how different aspects of facial expressions are indicative of lying behaviors, and identified the five most predictive features to be: the presence of side turns, up gazes, blinking, smiling, and lips pressing down, thus demonstrating that gestures associated with human interaction to be important components of human deception.

11.2 Information Concealment Detection

In 2018, a cheating scandal [Mobley, 2018] at the world's most notoriously difficult verbal exam for wine professionals shook the global wine industry — answers were found leaked by some examiners to candidates beforehand — and all results were invalidated; in 2016, with questions leaking ahead of political campaigns [Wemple, 2016], CNN faced a grave scandal from which only more controversies ensued; in 2000, the notorious debate leak [Bruni and Van Natta, 2000] in-between the Bush and the Gore campaigns drew the attention of F.B.I. investigators. What all of the three scandals share in common is the fact that it had been difficult to accurately identify who and to whom leaked the critical information, because the party who unfairly obtained the information tried their best to conceal and pretend otherwise.

Despite the importance and potential impact of detecting concealed information, research on detecting concealed information has been scarce. It is partly because large-scale datasets with ground truth labels of information concealment are difficult to come by, because it is only in rare cases can we verify the existence of concealed information in the wild.

From the perspective of information attainment and revelation, deception and concealing information are correlated ambiguously. In Table 24, let us clarify the difference between the two important concepts with an information grid. When we possess the critical information but appear not in possession, we are concealing information; whereas when we do not possess the information but pretend we are in the know, we are deceiving. Despite the proliferation of deception detection studies in text and speech, research on the closely related problem of detecting concealed information has been sparse.

The Information Grid		Appearance	
		Information	No Information
Truth	Information	Honesty	Concealed Information
	No Information	Deception	Honesty

Table 24: The Information Grid: Concealed Information vs. Deception

In my own research on detecting concealed information in text and speech, published in the 2019 proceedings of Association of Computational Linguistics Annual Conference, I asked and addressed various questions on this topic, including the following:

1. How good (or bad) are humans at detecting concealed information in technical settings?

2. Can we improve on human performance, with a new multimodal dataset, a better understanding of individual differences, and tailored classifiers for audios and texts?

3. How are indicators of concealed information related to those of deception?

4. When are Machine Learning models better (or worse) than human domain experts?

Why would concealed information be detectable? There exist at least two counteracting factors. First, consistent with deception, when individuals are concealing information, they experience greater cognitive load to keep their logic straight, in fear of being caught, especially when the stakes are high, and the expectations are great. Second, contrary to deception, because of the endowment with critical information, the individual candidates also experience more confidence, less fear, and lighter cognitive load, because they have informational advantages. All of these possible offsets make it particularly challenging to control for potential indicators of concealing information.

Curiously, I collected a speech dataset of wine professionals practicing for blind tasting exams, in which for each round, some knew the true identity of the particular wine being poured whereas some didn't. Those who were informed were incentivized to intentionally conceal the information by pretending not knowing in advance at all.

After analyzing the data I got, I found that across all speakers, an increase in maximum pitch, intensity, and speaking rate for those who conceal information, suggesting that speakers on average tend to speak with higher maximum pitch, intensity, and rate when concealing information.

To further drill down on individual differences in speech with concealed information, I found that maximum pitch is significantly increased in information concealment for male speakers but not for female speakers, and that increased speaking rate in information concealment for speakers with lower skill levels. These results largely echo the results in recent deception detection studies in interview dialogues at Columbia Speech Lab, except that here the total duration was longer for truthful speech than speech with concealed information. The finding about increased speaking rate in relatively lower-skilled professionals perhaps signals that the extra information boosts confidence level and outweighs the effect of increased cognitive load when concealing information.

When comparing these results with those from Columbia Speech Lab on deception detection, such as [Levitan et al., 2016] and [Levitan et al., 2018], from a linguistic perspective, I found that, inconsistent with earlier verdicts on filler pauses — more filler pauses more likely deceiving, the rationale being liars undertake a greater cognitive processing load, I found that the use of filler pauses such as "um" were correlated with truthful speech. On the other hand, words indicative of cognitive processes (e.g., "think", "know"), certainty, positive emotions, negation, and assent were significantly more frequent in speech with concealed information, in line with what Sarah and her colleagues found in [Levitan et al., 2018], possibly indicating that cognitive load, as well as confidence level, increases with the pressure of concealing information.

I also found words that make comparisons, express feelings, are verbs and express hedging (perhaps, maybe, probably), as well as the length of sentences significantly more frequently associated with speech without concealed information, suggesting an interesting balance of more visceral responses and deliberation associated with truth-telling.

Other significant indicators of concealed information include syntactical distinctiveness (sentence structures are more complex and unusual), specificity (specific terms like botrytis or lychee rather than more generic terms such as fruit and spices), clout (showing off confidence and dominance), discrepancy (expressing something being different than another), and disparity between speech and written text (when what individuals wrote contradicts what they say). Among these results, the ones regarding clout (confidence) and discrepancy (expressing differences) are consistent with what were found in deception detection [Levitan et al., 2018].

Long story short, in this project I explored acoustic-prosodic and linguistic indicators of information concealment by collecting a unique corpus of professionals practicing for oral exams while concealing information. I revealed subtle signs of concealing information in speech and text, comparing and contrasting them with those in deception detection studies, uncovering the link between concealing information and deception. I then tested with a series of experiments that automatically detect concealed information from text and speech. I compared the use of acoustic-prosodic, linguistic, and individual feature sets, using different machine learning models. Finally, I presented a multi-task learning framework (See Section 2.3) with acoustic, linguistic, and individual features, that outperforms human performance by over 15%.

SECTION 12

Wine Auction

On October 13, 2018, a new Guinness world record (as of August 4, 2021) for the hammer price of a bottle of wine sold at auction broke out at one of Sotheby's auctions in New York. A bottle of 1945 Romanée-Conti was sold for $558,000 (£422,801; £481,976) buyer premium included. A few minutes later, at the same auction, another bottle of 1945 Romanée-Conti was auctioned for $496,000, establishing the second highest price ever seen at auction for wine. The 73 year old French Burgundy bottle, part of a 600 batch produced by DRC (Domaine de la Romanée-Conti) in 1945, just before the domaine uprooted and replanted the vines, was sold more than 17 times the original asking price of $32,000 (£24,246; £27,640). The markup in the bottle's value is suspected to be a result of the Chinese market's interest in Burgundy. In addition, the bottle was sold by Robert Drouhin, patriarch of Maison Joseph Drouhin. Besides this new world record, earlier records and other headline worthy auction sales in recent years include three bottles of 1869 Château Lafite Rothschild that went up for auction in Hong Kong in the year of 2010, with an asking price in the range of $8,000 each. After a heated bidding war that sent the price through the roof, a single buyer bought all three bottles at $232,692 each. Later in the same year, a Cheval Blanc vintage 1947 was purchased at an auction in Geneva for $304,000.

What has propelled such a chain of events? What would have happened if the settings were slightly altered? Would the hammer price be even higher if more potential bidders were present? Would the process be even longer if every potential bidder was well-informed of each and every aspect of the wine being auctioned? What would have resulted if instead of such an openly bidding auction with increasing prices and a soft stopping rule, a sealed-price with a hard stopping rule was in place? Could auctioneers achieve better gains with optimal designs and strategies, if any? In contrast, could bidders do better in the sense of winning the lot at the lowest price possible, and avoid post-auction regrets as much as possible? These are among the questions addressed in this chapter. For instance, Section 12.1 reviews the time-honored auction theory by introducing different auction mechanisms and their relationships. Section 12.2 refreshes our memory about the classic results informing auctioneers of the optimal design strategies for auctions that could generate the most revenue possible. Further, we will be acquainted with how AI or deep learning helped tremendously in solving the problem of choosing the optimal auction strategy for multi-item auctions.

The fine wine market has evolved with the arrival of auction houses, wine brokers and wine investment service providers operating on all continents. Many auction houses such as Drouot, Christie's, Sotheby's,

Morell Wine Auctions, and Acker Merall & Condit organize regular fine wine sales. Auctions have also been migrating from in-person to online over the last decade, with Covid-19 greatly accelerating the process in 2020. For example, the prestigious Hospice de Beaunewine auctions, organized since 2005 by Christie's, allow participants to bid online since 2007.

The very nature of fine wine combined with a two-sided matching market through auctions, however, does make the valuation and estimation of prices a non-trivial endeavor. Fine wines' prices could be more responsive to supply and demand shocks relative to other commodities, since they do not pay any cash flows. Traded on a decentralized and globalized market of multiple trading channels, information asymmetries amongst stakeholders and a fragmentation of market liquidity become even more prominent, which prevents the efficient aggregation of a unique market price or valuation. In addition, unlike most other collectibles, the quantity of each wine available for trading is limited but not necessarily fixed to a single unit. Multiple of a specific wine exist which can all be traded individually. As such, the market for fine wines appears as one of the least illiquid amongst all collectibles.

Given all the layered complexities of selling and purchasing wines through auctions, how goes into the decision processes of participants and how do participants decide and make transactions? Is it the thrill of scoring a rare bottle, the high of winning over other competitive bidders, and the rush of sealing the deal that seems too good to be true?

Philippe Masset and Jean-Philippe Weisskopf collated auction hammer prices of the five First Growths in Medoc throughout the period of 1996-2015 from two auctions houses Hart Davis Hart and The Chicago Wine Company, revealing trading patterns that are perhaps intuitive and sensible in hindsight in the following aspects [Masset and Weisskopf, 2018]:

- Trading Cycles: the trading activity has dramatically increased since 2003 and Number of transactions and median price per vintage and per chateau has reached an initial peak in 2008, when the financial crisis commanded a decline in the number and value of transactions. A rebound in late 2009 then led to wine prices and trading activity hitting an all-time high in 2011, even though turnover has subsequently declined since 2012.

- Seasonality: The market is highly active during three particular periods: around the market release of the last vintage from Bordeaux during the so-called en primeur campaign (March to June); right after summer holidays; and during the Christmas period. Summer months are quiet with very few auctions taking place in July and August.

- Vintage Effects: trading activities concentrated on the very best vintages acclaimed by influential critics like Robert Parker in the case of Bordeaux First Growths. For instance, wines from 2005 generally traded at least once a week, while wines from the less reputed 2004 vintage only traded once or twice a month. Wines from great vintages, such as 1982 or 2005, primary attractions to collectors and investors, were much sought-after and expensive. Lesser vintages, such as 1999 or 2004, on the other hand, mostly attracted wine lovers and amateurs‘ interest and traded at more affordable prices.

These all seem to make a lot of sense. A rational wine buyer or bidder would indeed be willing to shell out more with a rosy economic prospect, during high buying seasons, and for flagship vintages that supposedly yield long-lasting wines. However, are wine buyers largely rational buyers operating in an information-efficient market?

Louis-Michel Liger-Belair, proprietor of the iconic Domaine du Comte

Liger-Belair in Vosne-Romanée, once detailed one time when he was at an auction when a case of Bouchard La Romanée verticals between 2002 and 2005 was on, as well as cases of Domaine du Comte Liger-Belair La Romanée vintages 2002-2005. Because of family ties and sharecropping contracts in early years between Bouchard and Domaine du Comte Liger-Belair, from 2002 until 2005, Louis-Michel in fact made the same wine but half was bottled and labelled as Bouchard La Romanée and the other half Domaine du Comte Liger-Belair. The only difference was the oak treatment and the bottling regime, and perhaps the racking Bouchard did to bring the wine to the cellar, as opposed to no racking in Domaine du Comte Liger-Belair. Louis-Michel himself attested that there wasn't much of a difference during the few vintages, the wines of Bouchard and Domaine du Comte Liger-Belair from the same parcels were very close. Despite the clarification from the auctioneer about such a fact, further confirmed by Louis-Michel in person at the auction, the hammer prices of Domaine du Comte Liger-Belair La Romanée still ended up over three times as much as Bouchard La Romanée.

The irrationality of auction buyers has been well-documented in behavioral economic literature in general. What are the determinants of hammer prices? And what design factors could lead buyers astray? What informational or emotional shortcuts have bidders been taking sub-consciously, more often than not to the detriment of one's own profit? In Section 12.3, let us go through each of these at length, and hopefully avoid such behavioral biases that could cost a fortune (sub-optimally) while bidding next time.

Fine and rare wine auctions are, not unlike fine art or any other collectible auctions, fraught with counterfeits fueled by greediness, lies, and risks. Like art, a great wine is the target of envy, conspiracy, and crime, requiring the most discerning eyes and meticulous minds to safeguard and preserve its authenticity.

Benjamin Wallace's suspenseful book The Billionaire's Vinegar reveals behind the curtains how the high-end wine collecting community operates, those rich and powerful individuals who buy old and rare wines at auction, and their quest for the approachable — a journey full of mystery, competition, ego, wealth, cheating, lying, scandal, toxic masculinity, and wine. It centered around the mysterious individual Hardy Rodenstock, allegedly a perpetrator of elaborate wine frauds that involve a trove of bottles that he believed to have belonged to Thomas Jefferson, the first president and serious wine connoisseur of the United States. It also presented evidences that driven by fortune and fame, the late Michael Broadbent, then director of Christie's wine department, an authority on tasting old wines, and more importantly the auctioneer of Hardy Rodenstock's sketchy bottles, turned a blind eye on the blatant signals of Rodenstock's shady businesses with claims about the provenance and authenticity of these questionable bottles.

In Peter Hellman's In Vino Duplicitas and the gripping documentary Sour Grapes, the masterful trickery of Ruby Kurniawan was put under a microscope. One would never forget when Laurent Ponsot, then proprietor of Domaine Ponsot, unexpectedly showed up in New York and abruptly interrupted an Acker Merrall auction as the lot came under the hammer — a 1945 Domaine Ponsot Clos St Denis — a vineyard from which the domaine only made its first bottling in 1982. This is only one out of thousands of counterfeited bottles of Pétrus, DRC, Lafite, E.Guigal, etc. Despite being imprisoned, released after his term in November of 2020, deported to Malaysia early 2021, Rudy with some of his counterfeited bottles still circulating in the wild, are still constantly talked about and his detrimental impact on fine wine trading felt long after the reveal. The story is perhaps far from over. It's unthinkable, according to Laurent Ponsot, that Rudy alone could have faked the thousands of bottles that flooded the market a decade ago. He is convinced that Rudy had strong and influential accomplices, and promised to disclose them in his upcoming fictional book without naming names.

As was detailed in Section 11.1, AI techniques have been used to combat misinformation, deception, information concealment, and fraud, in various capacities and tailored to different contexts. In Section 12.4, let us focus on fraud and misinformation detection with a review of methods applied to problems readily and potentially addressed in this realm.

12.1 Auction Theory

Among all the trading institutions that determine prices in human society, auctions place somewhere in between negotiations and listed prices, in terms of flexibility, administering cost, and demand sensitivity. On one end of the spectrum, negotiations are costly and time-consuming, but boasts flexibility in determining prices, product qualities, and financing terms, to better tailor to buyers' needs and wants responsively; on the other hand, posted fixed prices are cheap to maintain, but sellers might lose out on opportunities to increase prices when demand spikes or lower prices to avoid lost sales. Auctions appear to enjoy the best of both worlds, with prices somewhat reflecting and responding to demand fluctuations, and yet simpler to administer than negotiations especially when there are many potential buyers and sellers.

How exactly does auction work? In its basic form of transaction, one or more sellers are trying to sell one unit of product to one or more buyers in an auction format. In a forward auction, the potential buyers bid for the product provided by the seller, whereas in a reverse auction, the sellers bid for the contract with which the buyer will honor to purchase the product. Most wine auctions taking place in traditional auctions houses or online auction platforms over fine and rare wines are of the format of forward auction setting, whereas when it comes to business-to-business supply chain transactions, for instance, procurement contacts between wineries and coopers or shippers, reverse auctions are more commonly used especially with repeated transactions over time. Let us focus on the forward auctions for now, where the seller is the bid taker, hoping to sell a case of wine. There are one or more buyers who bid for the lot, each of whom perhaps values the lot at a price known only to himself or herself. In an auction, depending on rules about how bids are submitted, how winners are determined, and what the price should the winner pay for the lot, one of the buyers will win and pay for the lot, or no one wins and the failed auction ends without a buyer.

There are many types of auctions, but the most popular ones fall into perhaps the following four, each of which we will explain further:

- the English auction: the price starts at some reservation level, all the bidders are assumed to be in the auction until he or she decides to exit. The auctioneer gradually raises the price at a constant rate — the so-called English clock — until only one bidder is left in. The winner pays the price at which it ended.
- the English open-bid auction (Figure 70): the English auction implemented as an open-bid auction, in which all the bidders observe the current highest bid, and can submit new bids that must be at least one unit increment higher than the standing bid. The auction ends by a pre-specified ending rule, which may be a hard close such as at 7PM PST on May 1st, 2021, or a soft close, such as after 7PM PST of May 1st, 2021 and when no new bids have been placed for one hour. After the auction has ended, the bidder who submitted the highest bid wins and pays the exact amount of his or her bid.
- the Dutch auction, or the reverse clock auction (Figure 71): the auctioneer begins by calling a high price for the product,

then gradually reduces the price at a constant rate — the so-called Dutch clock — until some bidder claims it for the current price.

- the Sealed-bid First Price auction (Figure 72): all the bidders submit their bids at the same time, and the bidder who submitted the highest bid wins the product, and pays the exact amount of his or her bid.

- the Japanese auction (Figure 73): all the bidders stand as the price increases and sit down when the price exceeds their willingness to pay. The auction stops as soon as there remains only one bidder standing, who wins the auction and pays the last standing price.

- the Sealed-bid Second Price, or Vickrey auction (Figure 74): the same as Sealed-Bid First Price auction, except that the winner pays the amount of the second highest bid, rather than his or her own highest bid.

In an English auction, the product is set at a certain low price. Potential buyers then bid higher and higher prices. The last bidder, who is also the one with the highest bid, wins the product, and pays at the price of his or her own highest bid. This is the one most commonly used in traditional auction houses and online auction platforms, not only in the wine industry but also in almost every other industry where auctions take place. Let us illustrate this process in Figure 70.

In English auctions, eventually the product — for instance, Bartolo Mascarello Barolo 2004, will be sold to the bidder who values it the most, even though he or she will perhaps need to bid at a price slightly higher than the highest bid of other potential buyers. Thus the buyer will not sell it at the highest price possible — the price at which the buyer values the bottle in reality, but rather, slightly higher than what the buyer who values the bottle the second highest.

As a seller in the interest of the highest expected revenue possible, would it be great to sell it at the highest possible price — the price at which the buyer whose values the bottle the most is willing to pay for the bottle? This is exactly what makes optimal auction design challenging. To sell the bottle at the highest price possible, a seller needs to know what the highest price bidders are willing to pay for is. And yet, it is in the bidders' best interest to keep it a secret such that they could buy the lot at a price as low as possible, and definitely not more than how much they value the bottle.

Figure 70: English Auction Mechanism.

As we will dive into later in this Section, the English auction could sometimes drag on for a long while, when the price increments are small and the starting price is much lower than what bidders have valued the lot for. On the other hand, the Dutch auction, originated from how tulip sellers managed to determine the prices of their tulips amongst the tulip financial bubble dating back to the 1600s in the Netherlands, is a type of reverse auction that solves the problem of an auction ending up long-winded. As is illustrated in

Figure 71, in a Dutch auction, the seller would start with a very high price, and keep decreasing it until some bidder claims the lot. For a bidder participating in a Dutch auction, the trade-off he would be facing is that when the price is less or equal to his own willingness to pay, he could wait longer for a lower price while risking it being claimed by another bidder. Just like in a sealed-bid first price auction, the bidder could really use some more information about other bidders in terms of how they value the lot.

Figure 71: Dutch Auction Mechanism.

In the sealed auction illustrated in Figure 72, bidders secretly write down their willingness to pay for the lot being auctioned and submit to the seller, who then awards the lot to the highest bid, just like in the English auction.

In both the Dutch auction and the sealed-bid first price auction, it is in the bidder's best interest to bid the lowest price that would suffice winning the auction, given that it is equal to or below his own willingness to pay for the lot. If every bidder's secret valuation is public information, then this final price would be the same as the second highest valuation among bidders (plus slightly more). This also coincides with the English auction where the product is won by the bidder who values it the most at the price of the second highest bidder's valuation. In reality, however, it is almost never the case that every bidder's valuation is public information. And this is what makes auction design tricky and fun!

Figure 72: Sealed-bid First Price Auction Mechanism.

Another auction format similar to the English, opposite to the Dutch, is the Japanese auction. The seller starts at the low price and slowly increases it. Bidders stand up at the beginning and sit down as soon as they decide to drop out of the auction because the price has risen to the point where they are not willing to pay for it any more. The lot is then sold to the last bidder standing, literally and figuratively. In such an auction, for any bidder, the optimal strategy appears to be keeping standing until the price exceeds their own valuation and willingness to pay for the lot. Let us refer to this notion of behaving and revealing one's true valuation as *incentive-compatible,* in that the Japanese auction incentivizes bidders to bid their true valuation for the product. In most cases, this is ideal from a seller's perspective, because in this way, the seller could sell the product to the bidder who values it the most, and at the highest price equal to the highest valuation of the participating bidders.

Figure 73: Japanese Auction Mechanism.

William Vickrey, then professor of economics at Columbia University, showed that, back in the year of 1961 in his Nobel-winning work, all these basic auction formats — Sealed-bid First Price, the Dutch, the English, and the Japanese — boil down to the lot being auctioned off to the highest bidder at the price of the second highest bidder's valuation, that is a sealed-bid second price auction (Figure 74). They are supposed to yield the exact same expected revenue to the seller. That is, theoretically speaking, if all the bidders value the product independently and are perfectly rational players not influenced by any environmental cues or inherent cognitive biases.

In a sealed-bid second price auction, just like in a sealed-bid first price auction detailed above, all the bidders or potential buyers write down how much they are willing to pay for the lot, and whoever bids the highest wins the lot, exactly the same as the sealed-bid first price auction, except that, the highest bidder only pays the price the second highest bidder submitted. Professor William Vickrey showed that this auction format is *incentive-compatible*, in that bidders have every incentive to write down honestly how much they are really willing to pay for the lot. The result will be the same as in other auctions — the English, the Dutch, the first price, the Japanese, in that the good will go to the highest bidder at the price of the second highest bid.

Figure 74: Sealed-bid Second Price Auction Mechanism.

Giving the product to the person who values it the most seems the right thing to do, but not necessarily what the revenue-seeking seller is looking for. What if we as sellers would like to optimize for the highest possible revenue instead? As tricky a problem as it is, Professor Roger Myerson solved it in the case of auctions of a single item in the year of 1981, the work of which landed him the Nobel prize in 2007. This is what will start us off in the next subsection 12.2. To preview, one of the major breakthroughs in his work is the *revenue equivalence theorem.* Intuitively speaking, it asserts that the seller's expected revenue is fully determined by the allocation rule of the product. In particular, all the auctions we have discussed so far all end up giving the auction item to the person who values it the most. Thus, they all have the same allocation rule. Therefore, thanks to Roger Myerson's *revenue equivalence theorem,* we can assert that they are all *revenue-equivalent.*

12.2 Auction Learning

From the perspective of an auctioneer or seller, designing and implementing an optimal strategy that maximizes expected revenue is an intricate task. How should the auctioneer go about finding out the best auction procedure among all the different kinds of auctions known — the English, the Dutch, first or second price sealed bid auctions, etc.?

In its simplest form, one item — one bottle of wine in our case — is being auctioned, and every potential buyer has his or her own valuation of it, whether it be accurate or not, and the auctioneer, being a diligent market researcher, has some ideas about what potential buyers' valuations are like. For instance, in the year of 2021, if a bottle of Cristal (or DRC) with excellent provenance is being auctioned, it's not far from reality to say, with the help of advanced Internet search engines and the proliferation of price aggregation websites like http://wine-searcher.com, that most interested buyers have a rough estimate estimate of its value already which might manifest in their willingness to pay for the bottle, and so is the seller who might already know very well his or her clientele in terms of preference, purchasing power, taste, etc. Since buyers are always better off pretending their valuation or willingness to pay is lower than what it actually is, the major challenge in designing auctions that maximize revenue is to incentivize buyers to bid on a price at least equal to their real willingness to pay or valuation of the item.

This optimal auction design problem, in its simplest form, has been solved by Roger Myerson's Nobel-winning analysis of optimal auction design. In his work, he reduced the problem to a simple version where only one unit of item is being auctioned off. In addition, each buyer in his setting has his or own private valuation for the product, unknown to other buyers or the auctioneer, at least not the true valuation.

There are at least two reasons why one bidder's value estimates may be unknown to the seller and other bidders. First, the bidder's personal preferences might not be easy to gauge by others, which is more often the case in online auctions. For instance, to what extent would the bidder enjoy Barolo Brunate over Barbaresco Rabaja might not be known to other online bidders or the seller. Let us refer to it as the preference uncertainty. Second, the bidder might have more advanced or even insider knowledge of the intrinsic quality of the wine being auctioned. For instance, the information that Bouchard La Romanée and Domaine du Comte Liger-Belair La Romanée were identical wines from the vintage 2002 to 2005, where the only difference was the oak treatment, bottling, and last-minute racking, might be privy to only the savvy bidders, but not the others. Let us refer to this as the quality uncertainty. The distinction between preference uncertainty and quality uncertainty turn out very important in the optimal auction design.

In an even simpler situation where all the buyers have similar valuations for the item, and none of bidder's valuation for the product could be affected by any insider information about product quality from other potential buyers, assuming everyone would be acting rationally, then the optimal auction becomes a modified Vickrey auction, in which the seller sets a reserve price, and then sells it to the highest bidder at the second highest price. This reserve price depends on how the seller believes the bidders value the product, that is, if he believes the bidders have high valuations, he should set a high reserve price accordingly. Notably this reserve price should not depend on how many potential bidders are in the market, and as we will explore in Section 12.3, in practice sellers always set the price higher if there are more bidders in the room, which is not necessarily optimal for expected revenue maximization.

In the case where all bidders look the same to the seller, Roger Myerson's optimal auction design is simply about adding reserve prices. But in the case where some bidders look more willing to pay than others, Roger Myerson proved that the seller could possibly threaten to sell to other bidders to convince high bidders to bid their true valuations of the item. And this means that the seller should commit himself to not necessarily selling the item to the bidder who values it the most. That is in more general terms, when the bidders' valuations for the product are not similar, then the optimal auction could sometimes sell to a bidder whose value estimate is not the highest among all.

Roger Myerson's optimal auction is not anonymous, in the sense that not all bidders are treated equally. In fact, any careful study of Bayesian theory would tell us that this is quite often the case: optimal decisions discriminate based on beliefs (or, as some people like to call them, prejudices). And one last word about the optimal price: Roger Myerson's revenue-equivalence theorem says that it doesn't really matter. Any auction that allocates the item exactly as Roger Myerson's optimal auction does will win the seller the same amount of revenue, at least in the long term.

Myerson's theory is as beautiful as it is rare. The design of optimal auctions for multiple items is much more difficult, and has defied a thorough theoretical understanding after 40 years of intense research, largely due to severe analytical challenges in going beyond single-item auctions. Even the design of the optimal auction for selling two items to just a single buyer is not fully understood. For instance, a single buyer scenario with i.i.d.[54] values, [Manelli and Vincent, 2006] managed to identify optimal strategies with three items, and was further expanded to six by [Giannakopoulos and Koutsoupias, 2014]. [Yao, 2017] provides the optimal design for any number

[54] I.I.D. refers to independently identically distributed.

of bidders and two items, but only as long as item values can take on one of two possible values. Decades after Myerson's result, we do not have a precise description of optimal auctions with two or more bidders and more than two items.

A promising alternative is to use computers to solve problems of optimal economic design. The framework of *automated mechanism design* ([Conitzer and Sandholm, 2002]) suggests using algorithms for the design of optimal mechanisms. Early approaches required an explicit representation of all possible type profiles, which scales exponentially in the number of auction participants and therefore does not scale. Others have proposed more restricted approaches (for examples, [Guo and Conitzer, 2010], [Narasimhan et al., 2016], etc.) by searching through a parametric family of mechanisms.

In recent years, efficient algorithms have been developed for the design of optimal *Bayesian incentive compatible*[55] (BIC) auctions in multi-bidder, multi-item settings, most of which come from the lab led by Prof. Yang Cai at Yale University (as of August 2021). While there exists a characterization of optimal mechanisms as their proposed concept of *virtual-value maximizers* [Cai et al., 2012, Cai et al., 2013], relatively little is known about the structure of optimal mechanisms so far.

Moreover, these algorithms leverage a reduced-form representation that makes them unsuitable for the design of *dominant-strategy incentive compatible*[56] (DSIC) mechanisms, and similar progress has

[55]A mechanism is incentive-compatible if every participant can achieve the best outcome for themselves by acting according to their true preferences. There exists several degrees of incentive compatibility, out of which Bayesian incentive compatibility is a weaker form, in which all participants reveal their true preferences in that if all others act truthfully then it is in one's best interest to be truthful.

[56]Dominant-strategy incentive compatibility is a stronger form (than Bayesian incentive compatibility) of incentive compatibility where true-telling is a weakly-dominant strategy (in the language of game theory) — one is at least not worse by being truthful regardless of what others do.

not been made for this setting. DSIC is of special interest because of the robustness it provides, relative to BIC. The recent literature has focused instead on understanding when simple mechanisms can approximate the performance of optimal designs.

Thanks to the disruptive developments in machine learning, we believe that there is a powerful opportunity to use its tools for the design of optimal economic mechanisms. The essential idea is to repurpose the training problem from machine learning for the purpose of optimal design. The question of interest in this regard is: can machine learning be used to design optimal economic mechanisms, including optimal DSIC mechanisms, and without the need to leverage characterization results?

In the past few years, promising results surfaced. A group of LSE and Harvard economists [Dütting et al., 2019] explored the use of tools from deep learning for automated design of optimal auctions. They used multi-layer neural networks to encode auction mechanisms, with bidder valuations being the input and allocation and payment decisions being the output. They trained the network using samples from the bidders' values, so as to maximize expected revenue while making sure every bidder's best strategy is to bid for his honest valuation for the product. By re-framing the problem as minimizing the expected post-auction regret over not bidding enough or paying for too much, the deep learning based method that comes up with the optimal auction designs with high probability of achieving high revenue and low regret as long as the auction data on which the method is trained on is of high revenue and low regret. This work inspired a series of incremental improvements from the same research group and other groups such as those at Princeton and New York University. This is definitely a line of research work worth following on the subject.

12.3 Behavioral Auction

From a seller's perspective, how should one design and implement the rules of auctions to maximize one's expected revenue? While William Vickrey showed that all the basic auction formats boil down to the same format, after which Roger Myerson showed that all of them would yield the same expected revenue in theory, in practice, there exists abundant evidence of how different ending rules, seller reservation prices, bidding dynamics, clock speed, bidder characteristics, intrinsic characteristics of the product, etc. affect the expected revenue of the sellers in open-bid auctions.

When comparing the descending price Dutch auction with the Sealed-bid First Price auction, which are in fact strategically equivalent under rather lax assumptions according to Vickrey's Nobel winning theory [Vickrey, 1961], various data and experiments have revealed conflicting patterns. For instance, [Cox et al., 1982, Cox et al., 1983] found the Dutch auction format to score lower revenues than the Sealed-bid First Price for the seller whereas others found the opposite [Lucking-Reiley, 1999], especially in online settings. One potential confounding factor appears to be the speed of the clock [Katok and Kwasnica, 2008], especially when there are a lot of impatient bidders in the market. The two auction formats vary considerably in their dynamic properties, despite being revenue equivalent. Under the Dutch auction, if bidders care about time, they may decide to end the auction earlier; while they would pay a higher price, they may be willing to accept the trade-off of a higher price for time saved. In sealed bid auctions, bidders typically cannot affect the length of the auction with their actions because bids are accepted for some fixed time period — the cost of time in a typical sealed bid auction is sunk. Therefore at fast clock speeds, revenue in the Dutch auction is found to be significantly lower than it is in the sealed-bid auction. When the clock is sufficiently slow, however, revenue in the

Dutch auction is higher than the revenue in the sealed-bid auction.

What are some leverages the auctioneer or seller can pull to steer the auction result more favorably towards the seller? What are the elements of auction design that have been shown to affect expected revenue for sellers?

Reserve price. One classic result on how sellers should set the optimal starting reserve price is that one ought to set a positive reservation price, independent of the number of bidders but dependent on the average market valuation for the product in auction ([Myerson, 1981, Riley and Samuelson, 1981]). However, in practice, it has been found [Davis et al., 2011] that most sellers would set the reserve prices higher if they anticipated more potential bidders, despite the fat chance that perhaps all the bidders value the product at the exact price lower than the reserve price. The underlying drivers of such seller behaviors could be most likely either *regret aversion*, or *probability weighting*, or a combination of them. Sellers who are regret averse might prefer to set a higher reserve price than optimal just to quiet the inner thought of what if — what if I set the price to be higher and raked in better returns? On the other hand, when individuals choose among risky alternatives, the psychological weight attached to an outcome may not correspond to that outcome. In behavioral utility theories such as the Prospect Theory introduced by Nobel laureates Daniel Kahneman and Amos Tversky, the canonical weighting function has an inverse S-shape based on the observation that people attribute excessive weight to events with low probabilities and insufficient weight to events with high probability. Therefore if being prone to probability weighting bias is the reason why sellers would set a higher reservation price than optimal when more bidders are present, he or she might be doing so because they incorrectly assumed the probability of the product left unsold due to the high reserve price to be lower than it was. It turned out to be regret aversion, though, that was identified [Davis et al., 2011] to be the most significant drivers for a larger proportion of buyers in practice.

Ending rules. How a dynamic auction ends also affects how one bids. There are two kinds of endings: a hard close or a soft close contingent on bidder activities. The hard close rule is simple to implement, whereby the auction ends at a pre-determined and pre-specified time that is common knowledge among bidders and sellers. This is widely used in practice in major wine auction platforms. Alternatively, with activity-based rules an auction ends when bidding activities stop. It can be simple to implement too, especially in a clock auction, when the auction ends when only one bidder is left in the game. In open-bid auctions, however, if bidders bid very small amounts little by little, the auction could indeed drag on and on... Therefore, sometimes, a variation is to end the auction when the differences in auction prices falter below a threshold round over round. This is implemented as the online soft close rule: after some pre-specified time, the auction ends when there are no new bids submitted within a pre-specified period of time. For instance, winebid.com has been implementing the hard close rule for a long time until in late March of 2021, a soft close rule called Extended Bidding was put in place to extend the bidding period if any bids were placed within the last three minutes of the pre-specified hard close time, and end the auction if no new bids get placed for 5 minutes. Quite a few auction platforms also implement proxy bidding, a dynamic implementation of a second price auction, which allows bidders to set a maximum price that they would be willing to pay for the product and then allow the computer system to bid for them by the bid increment until someone places a higher bid than their maximum.

It has been found [Roth and Ockenfels, 2002, Ariely et al., 2005] that bidders often exhibit *sniping* behaviors, namely, late bidding, when faced with a hard close rule, rather than a soft close rule. There are several strategic explanations, all of which are well supported by data, as to why bidders snipe. First, last minute bidding is a rational response to naive bidding by bidders who bid as if the auction did not have proxy bidding; second, sniping helps with tacit collusion by avoiding bidding wars when there is a hard close; third, sniping also protects private information of expert bidders who are certain about the true values of the product.

Bid increments. Sometimes in auctions like the ascending English, time is a valuable resource especially when it is conducted online. If the seller allows very small increment, then the auction could drag on, requiring constant attention for a prolonged period of time on the part of bidders. For bidders of rare and fine wines, time is likely a highly appreciated asset, so the choice of bid incremental level becomes a strategic choice. When doing side-by-side comparisons of timed auctions and un-timed auctions keeping all else equal, [Kwasnica and Katok, 2007] have found that in both auctions bidder jumped bids at the beginning of the auction and reduced the bid increment as it draws closer to the end, but the initial and incremental bids were significantly higher — usually meaning more revenue for sellers — when auctions were timed. In general, it has been found that auction formats that allow jump bids could increase sellers' revenues due to bidder impatience.

Rank-based feedback. As is prevalent in practice, sellers could choose not to make public the current winning bid or submitted bids. Instead, only bid ranking information would be released privately to each bidder and each bidder would only be able to know how his or her own bid ranked among competitors. There exists positive evidence [Jap, 2002, Jap, 2007] that this rank-based system ameliorates seller-buyer relationships, and sellers would prefer it due to less information being revealed to competitors whereas buyers might prefer it too as it would lead to less competition from their perspective. "Sealed-bid effect" [Elmaghraby et al., 2012], a rather robust occurrence observed when comparing equivalent sealed-bid auctions with open-bid auctions: sealed-bid prices are lower than open-bid prices because the bidding is more aggressive. Interestingly, when rank-based feedback system is put in place without making bidding information public, the same "sealed-bid effect" kicks in when bidders are of different types, and the average prices end up very close to sealed-bid prices. When bidders are very similar, however, average prices with rank-based feedback generally turn out lower than if sellers provided bidders full information. The most possible explanation is, yet again, bidder impatience, echoing how timed auctions might be more advantageous to sellers when bidders are known to be impatient.

From a buyer's perspective, what are the optimal strategies, as well as potential pitfalls or behavioral biases one might wish to avoid, in order to secure the wine one desires most efficiently in terms of time and cost?

When comparing the ascending price English auction with the Sealed-bid Second Price auction, where the best bidding strategy in both cases is to bid on one's true valuation for the product, rather than trying to game the system by bidding high or low randomly. This is known as *truthful bidding*, theoretically speaking. In practice, bidding behavior in the English clock auction does converge to the truthful bidding strategy, but bidders in Sealed-bid Second Price auctions tend to bid above their true valuations for the product, consistently and persistently in various contexts [Kagel et al., 2009, Kagel and Levin, 2009]. One explanation is that the truthful bidding is highly transparent in a clock auction like the English whereas much less so in the Sealed-bid Second Price when every bidder is supposedly in the dark, and this transparency is highly effective in inducing optimal behaviors due to social learning.

Comparing Sealed-bid First with Second Price auctions, various studies [Maskin and Riley, 2000, Aloysius et al., 2016] have found that in practice, the first price auctions result in lower prices than second price auctions, consistently below the would-be resulting price if every bidder was acting strategically and rationally, whereas the second price auction prices are closer to the prediction, but still lower than if bidders were rational and strategic, under many circumstances.

One consistent and robust finding in various Sealed-bid First and Second Price auctions including their reverse clock formats, of different products, different contexts, and different players is that bidders often bid more aggressively than what they should have if they are perfectly rational and making the optimally economic bidding decisions. There are many possible explanations for such seemingly irrational aggressive bidding behaviors:

1. [Cox et al., 1988, Engelbrecht-Wiggans and Katok, 2009]: bidders might be risk averse and would like to ensure winning rather than risk losing it to opponents or other bidders.

2. [Morgan et al., 2003]: there could be interpersonal social comparison elements at play, for instance, one bidder might overbid after being overtaken by another bidder in the previous round out of spite.

3. [Neugebauer and Selten, 2006]: overbidding might be simply newbie mistakes and as bidders become more experienced at auctions they might learn to bid more optimally over time.

4. [Engelbrecht-Wiggans and Katok, 2007]: for many wine buyers, the regret over not scoring one's favorite bottle which might be hard to come by especially if it is truly rare would overwhelm any sensible decision-making come bidding time.

There exists research studies demonstrating empirical evidences for each of the above explanations though it appears evidence appears to favor the last argument of regret aversion: a bidder might experience winner's regret from winning the auction yet paying too much, or loser's regret if the ending price turns out lower than one's true valuation for the product. And overly aggressive bidding is a consequence of one's anticipated loser's regret overwhelming one's winner's regret.

When it comes to online bidding environments, one key finding across various studies is that even when bidding for products whose value is relatively certain, bidders are influenced by other bidders' behaviors beyond rationality, falling trap to quite a few well-known behavioral biases. One such bias is the *herding* behavior, which refers to the tendency to gravitate toward, and bid for, auction listings with one or more existing bids, ignoring comparable or even more attractive uncontested listings, oftentimes within the same product category, and available at the same time. I myself have definitely been a victim to this bias more often than I would have liked. This is much more common in online settings where bidders are overwhelmed with the sheer amount of available auction listings or wine lots to browse through, and oftentimes take the shortcut by imitating the actions of others, rather than doing due diligence of examining each and every listing on its own merit within one's choice set. And once a bidder submits a bid, another behavioral bias called *escalation of commitment* in the same vein of *sunk cost fallacy* could kick in, and the bidder submits even higher bids to ensure winning the auction. Such herding and commitment escalation behaviors were found to be driven not by how awesome the product in question could be, but how the bidding dynamics played out organically. More interesting findings about the nature of herding behaviors were revealed further by researchers. First, the higher the price of the product increases, the less likely the herding behavior continues. This is because at a higher price point, bidders are more likely to do their own research on what a reasonable price they should be willing to shell out for the product. Second, the more difficult it is for bidders to find out the real value of the product, the more uncertain what the product's value is, the more likely bidders are herding irrationally [Dholakia and Soltysinski, 2001], oftentimes sub-optimally.

Starting prices have also been identified as a critical factor in driving bidding dynamics and final outcomes. Dan Ariely, the behavioral economist perhaps best known for his best-selling books *Predictably Irrational, The Honest Truth about Dishonesty,* etc., together with his colleague Itamar Simonson found that higher starting prices help form anchors to drive final prices up by assimilation [Ariely and Simonson, 2003].

But such a result was refuted a few years later with evidence showing that quite the opposite, lower starting prices could attract more bidders to the auction, causing herding behavior and escalation of commitment that would work in favor of the sellers.

Turns out, as Dan Ariely and his colleague's followed-up field experiments revealed, that the devil is in the details, or in the subtle information cues available to the bidders at the time. They found that higher starting prices had no effects whatsoever on submitted bids when there existed a comparable product with a lower starting price being auctioned at the same time, indicating that bidders perhaps do search and incorporate relevant price information from other auctions in bidding. But if there was no comparable product, a higher starting price would bidders to submit higher bids for the product, despite attracting fewer bidders than lower starting prices. The takeaway message is that, bidders are indeed sensitive to whatever auxiliary information sellers provide, regardless of whether such side information resolves the value uncertainty of the product.

Five years later after the initial experiments, Dan Ariely came up with another observation: for all except the first bidder, it is not the starting price that grabs people's attention, but the current winning price. This means, holding the current price of an auction fixed, more bidders will go after an auction with a lower starting price than a higher one, since lower starting prices encourages more bidder entry from the start, contributing to the notorious herding phenomena. For a bidder, submitting a bid in a crowded auction carries a slimmer chance of winning and a higher expected hammer price, therefore such an irrational herding bias is more likely costlier and more time-consuming to whoever fell victim to it [Simonsohn and Ariely, 2008].

As was briefly touched on in Dan Ariely's experiments about environmental cues, reference prices could be another powerful leverage of sellers to subtly influence bidders' behaviors. Reference prices are standards or benchmarks bidders compare the bid prices against. In wine auctions, oftentimes references prices could be average retail prices listed on wine-searcher.com. Alternatively on many platforms, sellers set an alternative buy-it-now price (BNP) for the same product which is almost certainly higher than the starting price of the ongoing auction, providing bidders with not only potential instant gratification at a higher price, but also a reference price from which bidders anchor their bids and set expectations, somewhat unconsciously. Buy-it-now prices (BNPs) [Leszczyc et al., 2009] are not the only form of reference prices, which could take the form of prices from adjacent auctions [Dholakia and Simonson, 2005], seller-advertised prices [Kamins et al., 2004], unrelated incidental product prices in one's surroundings [Nunes and Boatwright, 2004], starting and reserve prices set by sellers [Kamins et al., 2004], and prices shown on concurrent products [Pilehvar et al., 2017], all of which have been shown to exert powerful influences on bidding behaviors.

When are bidders more susceptible to herding biases? Is it in auctions with only a reserve price, or both a reserve and a starting price, or only a starting price? Researchers [Ku et al., 2006] found that auctions without either a starting or reserve price will more likely lead to a higher final price than auctions with only a starting price, because with the reserve price as a reference price impacting the final price, the absence of a starting price is more likely to attract more bidders, resulting in the herding behavior and escalation of commitment that drive up the final price.
One might argue that not all herding is irrational. If we assume most auction goers are sophisticated wine collectors who sometimes know even better than the seller about the true value of an item, then herding is only rational because the more experts jump onto the bandwagon, the more valuable, or undervalued the product probably is. Fair and square. However, the rather robust phenomenon that bidders who are bidding on items with clear and certain valuations are found to be influenced by incidental prices of unrelated products that so happened to catch their eyes is perhaps indeed irrational by any stretch of imagination [Nunes and Boatwright, 2004]. What's more interesting is that those bidders who succumbed to such effects all stated after the auction had ended that the prices of unrelated prices did not influence their offer prices when in fact they certainly did.

Not all bidders are alike. Researchers [Pilehvar et al., 2017] have also roughly identified two kinds of bidders whose behaviors differ drastically. The first bigger cluster consists of infrequent and less informed buyers, who are less sensitive to environmental information, whereas the much smaller cluster of so-called superbidders are extremely responsive to market conditions in real time and bid more extensively. Despite higher starting bids for auctions participated by novice bidder clusters, the final prices usually end up lower than those participated by superbidders. And that the higher the starting prices, the lower the final prices from auctions where superbidders frequent, the rationale being the effect of fewer bidder entries overwhelmed any positive effect of higher starting prices on final prices.

12.4 Fraud and Misinformation Detection

With the rise of social media, combating misinformation or fraud has become ever more prominent in recent decades. AI could play a major role in preventing the spread of fake news. There has been a lot of work in this exciting domain and even more to be done in the future. Here we detail two major aspects of information manipulation: misinformation and fraud.

As with any precautionary measures, the first step is to accurately identify the source and the diffusion trajectory of the misinformation, especially in popular news articles and social media. **Rumor detection** with machine learning techniques has been widely deployed across social media platforms in recent years, many of which automatically extract discriminative features from social media posts to detect misinformation. Such algorithms are the most impactful when used for early detection of misinformation thus preventing any further diffusion in practice. In general, the models that take into a diverse set of information signals — images, user posting history, texts, emojis, timing, credibility of embedded links, etc., perform the best.

In natural language processing and computer vision, **fake news detection** has been extensively studied in recent years with several large-scale datasets released for benchmarking and comparing algorithms. This line of research goes hand in hand with deep fake research works that focus on generating realistic fake texts or images that could fool humans. When pitted against each other, the fake news generator and the fake news detector could learn from the strengths and weaknesses of each other and improve their performances together.

Another relevant line of research centers on accurately **identifying click-bait headlines** that tricks users into paying attention with propaganda and fanfare. Incongruity or inconsistency between titles and texts, or ambiguous titles or headlines has been incorporated into algorithms and prove rather informative in telling which ones are click-baits.

Social bots that pollute the online social media landscape has also been high on the agenda of many tech companies. Bots are social media accounts that are controlled by algorithms that, once triggered, could post an enormous amount of misinformation within a split second. If fallen in the wrong hands especially in toxic political campaigns, bad bots could be vastly detrimental to the society, therefore **bot detection** has been an active topic in the industrial AI community.

Fraud detection has long been a classic machine learning problem. **Reputation fraud** would distort the potential buyers' opinion on whatever wine being sold in the form of posting online malicious ratings, reviews, and knowledge base entries. In other scenarios, it could also be related to attacks in recommender systems for consumers, and trustworthiness of the evaluation process of the provenance of bottles on sale. As we have detailed in Section 11.1, automatic online review **spam detection** was among the first few attempts within the machine learning community to resolve the problem. A series of research work on reputation fraud detection quickly followed, especially those that are designed to sniff out subtle signals of fraudulent reputation spam between the lines with text mining or natural language processing techniques.

Some other works also leverage the context, and history of user interaction and behaviors to assist the fraud detection algorithms in making judgments. Almost every crowdsourcing website uses one form or another to embed spam detection within the platform now, for instance, Yelp, the popular restaurant review website appears to be combining text analysis and historical user information to identify spam reviews, according to an academic study that reverse engineered how the Yelp spam detector works.

Finally, a third approach is to detect fake reviews based on the interactions among reviewers as well as the review objects — in our contexts it'd be wine — by constructing a network that links review, reviewer, and item being sold together upon which insights could be gleaned based on the evolving structure of the network. For instance, the interaction patterns of malicious spammers were characterized to be very different from genuine potential buyers. Spammers were found to target a wider range of items being on sale. They would naturally co-rate the same items and be tied by such co-rating actions. The ratings given by spammers also tend to largely agree on the co-rated items, since they are instructed to post either positive for promotion or negative ratings for demotion.

Timing could also be a strong signal of fraudulent reviews by spammers, who are often associated with time schedules for how long the spamming activity would or should last. In order to achieve the desired fraud effects, spammers are often required to finish their jobs in time, such that their effects could be aggregated. Therefore this time constraint would necessarily lead to small gaps between the timings of fraud activities. All of these have been leveraged to deploy large-scale online fraud detection algorithms to combat fraud and misinformation. However, in wine-centric websites such automatic and large-scale spam detection practices still appear to be rare so far.

Financial fraud is the attempt to escape the oversight of law or regulations in the pursuit of monetary gains. Business procurement fraud is not uncommon and are being actively combat against by various AI techniques including those in the realms of natural language processing, social network analysis and online learning, as well as real money trading in online games, and cash-out detection in financial services using deep learning methods, some of which have been widely deployed in practice. Fraud in insurance claims is a long standing problem insurance companies have invested interests in detecting and eradicating. As insuring against damage or theft of wine collections rises to prominence with the growth of the fine wine community, identifying and combating insurance claims with AI methods could prove more efficient and accurate than human inspectors, provided that the models are well-trained.

Just like review spams, fraudulent insurance claims were found to exhibit subtle yet distinct linguistic characteristics compared to honest claims, therefore, a series of natural language processing methods have been deployed in practice to understand the texts automatically and pick up subtle cues that sometimes evade even the most experienced human fraud busters. Various methods that identify the topics discussed in the insurance claim, understanding the potential social dynamics between multiple insurance claims, and accounting for temporal evolution of how multiple insurance claims submitted by one account changes, etc. have all been proven helpful in improving the fraud detection accuracy.

SECTION 13

From Vine To Wine

In this chapter, let me walk you through the entire process of wine production from vine to wine with various interactive visualizations, all of which are available, and better viewed online at http://ai-for-wine.com/vine2wine for user interaction. I will sketch out other important aspects of the wine industry where AI applications really shine in subsequent subsections. For the three trees illustrating viticultural, vinicultural, and maturation (and other steps), users can click on nodes to expand further or collapse into top level nodes. Each node represents a vine growing or winemaking practice, which are inter-connected with edges, forming a tree-like structure where the trunks grow into stalks which further grow into stems and leaves, mirroring the hierarchical structure of concepts in viticulture and viniculture. For the four interactive graphs on winemaking for red, white, rose, sparkling, and sweet wines, users are welcome to hover over nodes online to delve into detailed options regarding the practice.

All of these knowledge skeletons are based on several textbooks including *Vines and Vinification* by Sally Eastern, *Viticulture* by Stephen Skelton, and *Science of Wine* by Jamie Goodie, enabled by visualization softwares such as D3 and Dagre.

In the following subsections, I will detail how AI could contribute to many steps of the production and distribution process and make positive changes in terms of improving efficiency and enabling what wasn't possible before. For instance, AI-based tools and softwares have been deployed for the production of agricultural products (grapes being one of them), combating climate change, improving disaster and emergency response for wildfires, snowstorms, earthquakes, severe hailstorms and frosts, etc., improving distribution networks, and so forth, all of which are highly relevant for the supply chain management from vine to wine. In Section 13.1, we detail how AI methods have been and could be assisting viticultural and agricultural activities; in Section 13.2 we illustrate how AI techniques are helping to combat climate change, especially when it comes to weather prediction, disaster response, emergency management, and risk management in general. In Section 13.4, we review ways in which AI have helped with improving distribution and transportation channels and their implications.

This is by no means an exhaustive review of wherever and whatever AI has been applied to address challenges or led to improvements over status quo in the world of wine production and consumption, but I hope it provides a starting point that invites future exploration and even more exciting ideas to be materialized in the near future.

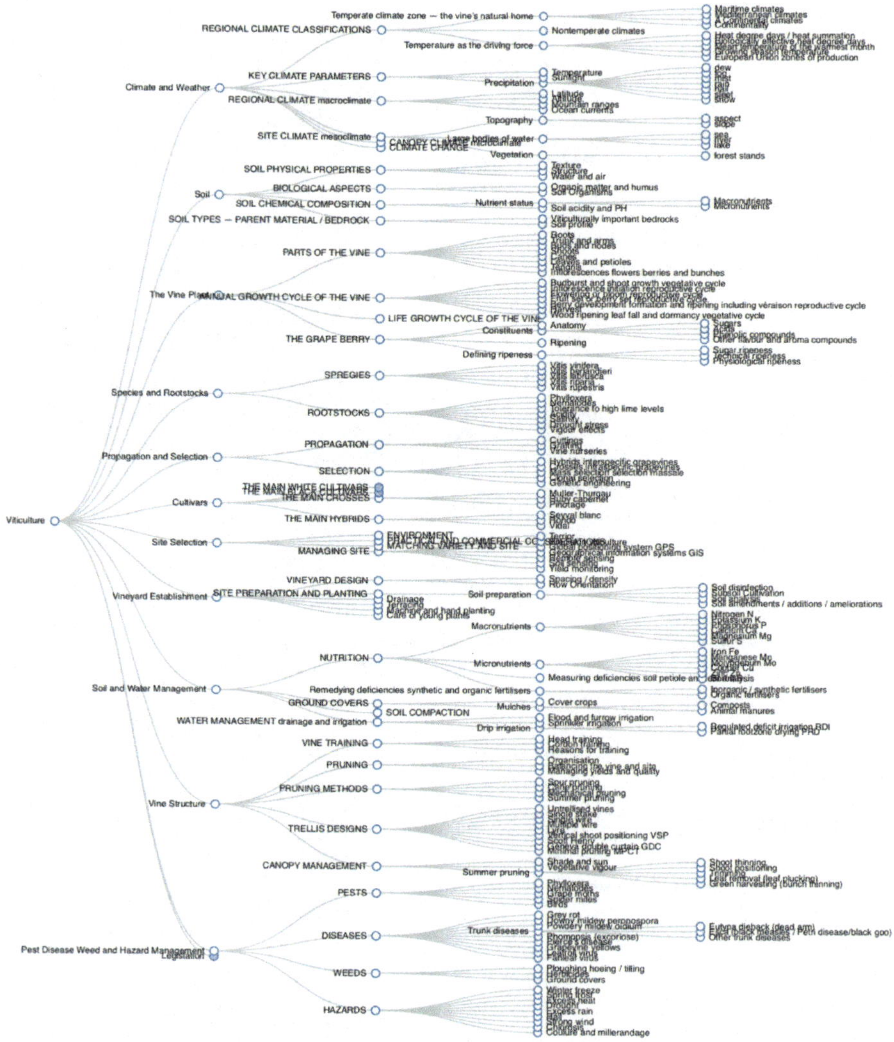

Figure 75: Viticultural Considerations. Due to the densely populated branches, some texts are not clearly rendered. Please refer to http://ai-for-wine.com/vine2wine/viticulture for more interactive details with greater clarity and better representation.

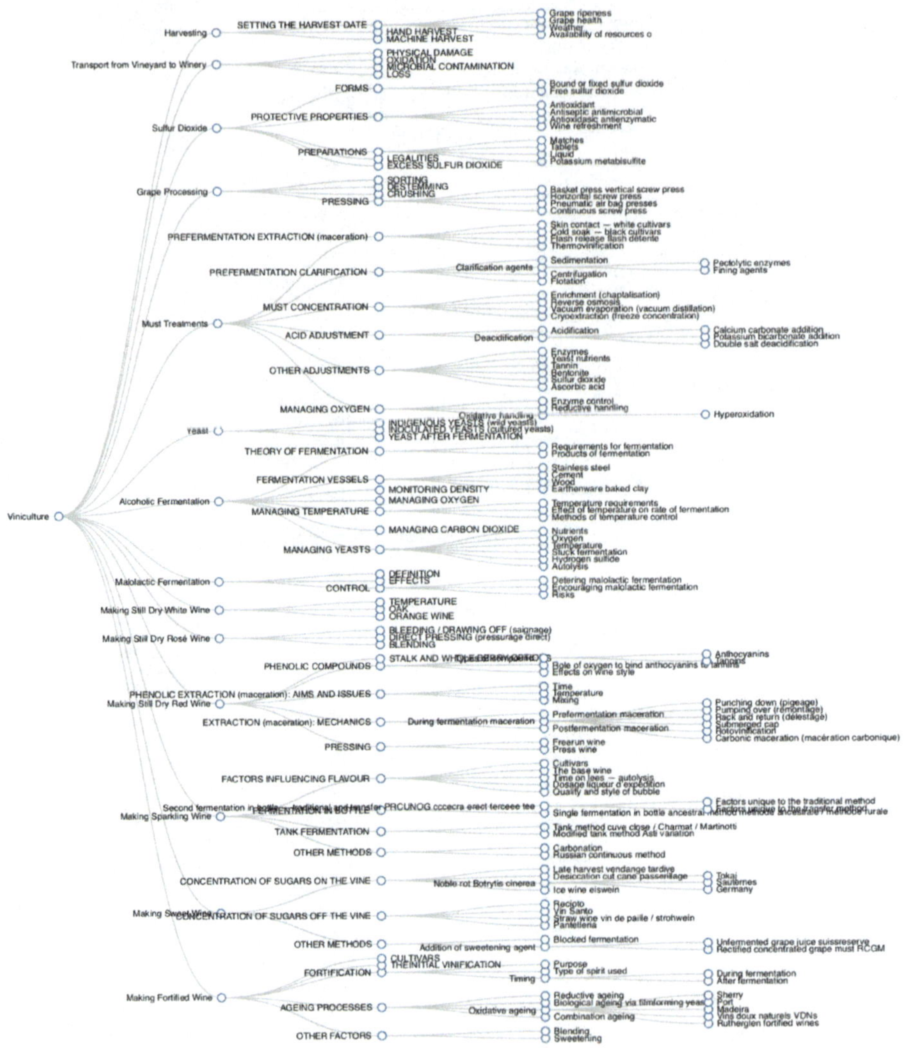

Figure 76: Vinicultural Considerations. Due to the densely populated branches, some texts are not clearly rendered. Please refer to http://ai-for-wine.com/vine2wine/viniculture for more interactive details with greater clarity and better representation.

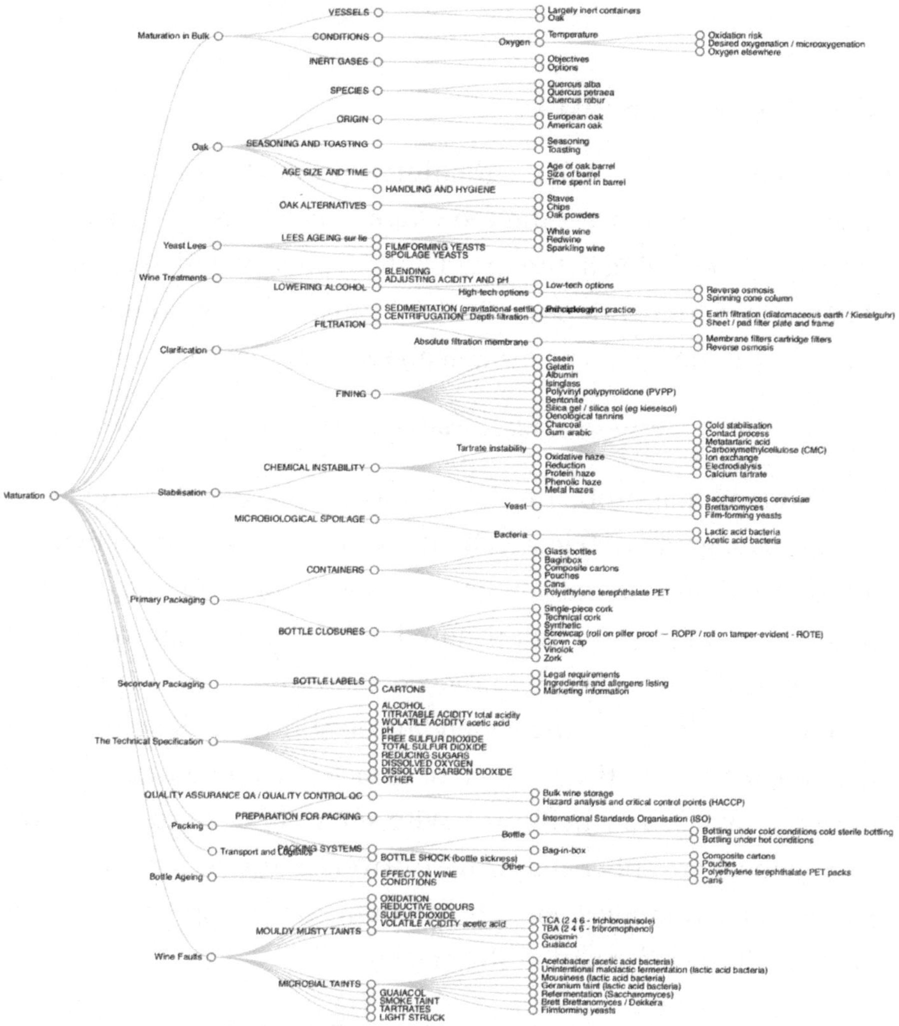

Figure 77: Maturation Considerations. Due to the densely populated branches, some texts are not clearly rendered. Please refer to http://ai-for-wine.com/vine2wine/maturation for more interactive details with greater clarity and better representation.

13.1 AI for Viticulture

Grape vines are essentially agricultural products, and to improve agriculture is to improve the food supply chain that impacts each and every living being in the world both at present and in the future. AI has shown tremendous potential in this realm and there is even more to be done and to be excited about in the years to come.

One fundamental problem AI technologies have direct impact on is crop management, boosted by the progress and commercialization of unmanned aerial vehicles or drones, satellite imagery, and Internet of Things (IoT) that resulted in large-scale high-resolution data. With the help of such immense data sources, AI technologies are better equipped to drastically improve the efficiency of farming, mostly through the practice of "precision agriculture" or more precisely, "precision viticulture". With such, various aspects of crop management are enhanced with AI-driven solutions including crop planning, maintenance, yield prediction, combating vine diseases, and viticultural information sharing.

Crop planning. How could AI help with deciding on what grape variety to grow and when to grow? In a lot of wine producing regions in the new world without centuries of grape growing experience passed down from ancestors, without abundant access to different vine materials at the beginning, the first generation growers and winemakers have often chosen the initial grape varieties to plant by chance, by personal preference, by observation, and by analogy, with trial and error. For this exact purpose, AI researchers have designed and implemented algorithms [Von Lücken and Brunelli,

2008, icr, 2017] to determine the optimal crop level to grow based on soil information such as physical and chemical composition, as soil characteristics are vitally important when determining yield and quality potential. Planting the variety that will best fit the soil characteristics is essential to minimize unnecessary soil treatment, reducing costs and alleviating environmental concerns, and most importantly improving quality potential. The optimization object can be customized and multi-fold: costs of fertilizing and liming, cultivation, expected total return, expected risk, among others. Identification of the optimal sowing and ploughing time has also been explored based on additional information such as weather forecasts. Some wineries have been at the forefront of such experiments deploying automatic mechanical sprayers, drones and robots, in collaboration with researchers at universities and institutions such as Cornell, UC Davis, and University of Montpellier. In 2014, Chateau Coutet was among the first to introduce Vitirover, a drone powered by solar energy and equipped with technology to maneuver in the vineyards at the mercy of vineyard managers' smartphones. It could help growers with instant diagnostics and real-time notification of any ailments in the vines. Vitirover also comes equipped with infrared camera lenses that allow growers the ability to also detect levels of ripeness at the granularity of individual vines.

Irrigation of crops is not a new practice but was known to the Babylonians, the Chinese, the Egyptians, and the early south-American civilization, in the form of simple floor and channel irrigation, which are still in practice today, as the basic needs have not changed since. Vines typically need somewhere between 250mm and 1000mm of water per square metre of land, depending on several factors. First, the evapotranspiration rate of the vineyard, which hinges upon the shading scenario, vegetation cover, soil conditions, wind speed, humidity, and air temperature. Second, the speed at which water leaves the vine, affected by heat and humidity, sunlight intensity, wind speeds, and the stress level which in turn can be induced by undersupply of water. Third, general climate and the amount of natural rainfall certainly count as well. Therefore accurate estimates of crop evapotranspiration rate would greatly enable efficient irrigation management especially in arid, semi-arid, and semi-humid regions, even though such accurate measurements mostly based on daily grass or alfalfa reference ET values and crop coefficients had been limited due to the sparse evapotranspiration network. Researchers at Texas Tech University identified as a practical and accessible alternative an AI-based solution that learns the relationships between non-ET weather station data and the reference ET from ET networks, greatly improving the estimation accuracy of the daily evapotranspiration rate for efficient irrigation management applications. In another study, the authors developed a computational method for estimating monthly mean evapotranspiration rates for arid and semi-arid regions, using monthly mean climatic data of 44 meteorological stations. This method was mirrored in another similar study in which two scenarios and corresponding solutions were presented for the estimation of the daily evapotranspiration from temperature data collected from 6 meteorological stations. Yet another research project developed a machine learning model for accurate estimation of weekly evapotranspiration rate in arid regions based on temperature data from two meteorological weather stations nearby. Symington Family Estates, the time-honored ever-expanding iconic producer in Douro Valley was one of the first few to trial the VineScout robot to measure water availability in the vineyards in real time, among other vine vitals, such as vine vigor, leaf and canopy temperature.

Yield prediction is one of the most significant topics in precision agriculture or viticulture, crucial for yield mapping, yield estimation, matching supply with demand, and crop management to increase fruit quality or productivity. Classical applications include efficient, low-cost, and non-invasive AI-driven solutions for automatic fruit counting on a cluster. The method classifies the fruit into three categories: harvestable, not harvestable, and the maturation percentage of the grape berries, whereas the canonical old-school way is for the winemaker to randomly sample berries from every corner of the vineyards, which is prone to human estimation error and biases. It also automatically estimates fruit weights together with the maturation percentage, providing the growers with the most precise information to assist critical decision-making process regarding the optimal harvest date and sequence. In another line of research, computer vision methods could be incorporated into a machine harvester that automatically shakes and catches fruits during the harvest. The machine segments and detects occluded fruit branches with full foliage even when berries are not visible at first glance. Remote sensing data such as satellite images have been demonstrated by Stanford Management Science and Engineering and Earth Science researchers [You et al., 2017] to be more scalable and accessible alternative sources that enable even more accurate yield prediction based on deep learning models, compared to traditional features such as survey data, weather, and soil properties identified to be useful for such a task. One of the first and the largest deployment in practice was perhaps spearheaded by E. & J. Gallo's collaboration with NASA in a concerted effort to measure canopy size and vine vigor across an enormous span of vineyard plots via satellite imagery updated every 7 – 8 days. With such a computer-vision-based monitoring system, any abnormal changes in the vineyards in terms of environmental conditions, growth patterns, and the likes, could be detected and processed much faster than before, facilitating real-time precision agriculture at the industrial scale.

Detection of vine diseases, pests, and viruses. As with any extensive agricultural or horticultural crop, a wide range of diseases, pests, and viruses could damage vines and leave the production of economically viable crops infeasible, if not treated in time. Common vine diseases include fungal diseases such as Botrytis, downy mildew, powdery mildew, Anthracnose, Armillaria root rot, bacterial blight, black rot, crown gall, Esca, Eutypa dieback, grapevine yellows, phomopsis, and Pierce's disease; viral diseases such as corky bark, fanleaf virus, leafroll, nepoviruses, and rugose wood, whereas common vine pests include beetles, cutworms, erinose mites, fruit flies, grasshoppers, locusts, leafhoppers, leaf-rollers, margarodes, mealy bugs, mites, moths, nematodes, phylloxera, scale insects, thrips, and the aptly-named Western grapeleaf skeletonizer. All of these could require different treatments and manifest in vines and fruits in subtly different ways that confuse the most experienced vine growers. Computer vision methods, specifically Fine-grained Visual Categorization, discussed in greater detail in Section 7.5 with regard to plant diseases, have been used to accurately and automatically identify vine diseases and practical solutions based on images of vine leaves and clusters. Such AI-driven methods are integral to precision viticultural or agricultural management where treatment can be targeted and tailored in time and in situ.

Species recognition. The problem of vine material confusion is widely seen in many parts of the world over the course of wine history. Chilean Carménère has been mistaken for spicy Merlot for centuries as cuttings of Carménère were imported by Chilean growers from Bordeaux during the 19th century, where they were frequently confused with Merlot vines. It wasn't until 1994 when it was first rediscovered as a distinct variety unrelated to Merlot. Sauvignon vert (also known as Sauvignonasse or Friulano) is a white wine grape home to the Friuli region in northeast Italy. It is widely planted in Chile where it was historically mistaken for Sauvignon Blanc. Trebbiano Abruzzese, one of the noble Italian white grapes of high quality potential, have long been confused with other grapes of lower quality such as Trebbiano Toscano or Bombino Bianco. California Zinfandel had long been thought of as a quintessential American grape variety native to Lodi in California until Dr Carole Meredith and her colleagues proved it wrong. Such prevalent vine confusion in history was largely due to lack of information sharing, lack of centralized documentation of the world's wine grapes — in other words, lack of a large-scale database of wine grapes, automatic and accurate scientific methods of species recognition, and the intrinsic difficulty of the task itself since oftentimes the distinction lies in the subtle difference of how leaves grow and look. Luckily, as was detailed in Section 7.5, computer vision methods are especially suited for automatic and accurate identification of plant specifies based on the how the leaves look, enhanced by additional information of plant characteristics. This could greatly clear up or prevent vine material confusions, accelerate scientific development in new grape varieties discovery, assist nurseries from around world in targeted treatment of scions and rootstocks, and ultimately facilitate precision viticulture that improve the quality of the final product.

Weed detection. Keeping weeds under control is one of the most important tasks when taking care of a newly planted vineyard. Weeds pose threats to grapevines by gulping up water and nutrients to the detriment of the vine's needs. In the extreme cases, weeds could crowd out and suffocate the vines, increasing disease pressure especially when moist weed leaves are imposed upon the fragile young vines. Therefore, accurate detection of weeds in the field could prove particularly conducive. Computer vision algorithms coupled with remote sensing data have indeed been developed to accurately detect and localize weeds at low costs without any environmental concerns, which could enable further development of robots or tools to cope with excessive weeds, minimizing or even eliminating the usage of herbicides. Fine-grained visual categorization methods for weed species have also been researched upon to help with pinpointing what the particular weed is and identifying the most effective solution.

Crop quality. How to make the best quality wine possible is the ultimate question every quality winemaker asks. A consensus among the world's best producers appears to be that growing the best quality fruit is the prerequisite. Most producers rely on years if not decades of experience with extensive experimentation, observation, and critical thinking to identify the perfect combination of factors and strategies that lead to the best quality fruit arriving at the winery during harvest. However, humans are notoriously prone to cognitive and behavioral biases, as well as limited working memory and other cognitive capacity, leaving deductions as to what factors lead to the best quality fruit largely anecdotal and by chance. In addition, the distinction between correlation and causation (more thoroughly discussed in Section 10.1) is an important one here: just because something happened and the wine turned out as such doesn't necessarily mean the same thing will definitely lead to the same result the next time around. Machine learning methods therefore have been designed to detect and classify crop quality characteristics to improve upon precision viticulture and ultimately product prices while reducing waste. Another line of research has been devoted to precisely identifying the geographical origin of fruit samples based on applying machine learning methods to chemical components of samples, surfacing the critical chemical components that make distinctive terrior expressions prominent.

Soil management. Soil is a beloved topic among wine professionals, with several books dedicated to it (Alex Maltman's and Alice Feiring's books come to mind), and many more books, magazines, and blogs delving into what that means for wine in the glass. Machine learning models for predicting or identifying soil properties such as estimating soil drying, soil condition, soil temperature, and moisture content have proved especially valuable especially in the era of COVID-19 pandemic when many flying winemakers couldn't get to the vineyards due to worldwide travel bans. Traditionally, soil measurements are time-consuming and expensive in general, and machine learning or AI-based methods provide cheap, accurate, reliable, and scalable alternatives for wide adoption. For instance, one of the seminal works presented an efficient method for estimating soil dryness based on evapotranspiration and precipitation data coupled with site characteristics, thus making remote agricultural decision-making feasible. Another line of study focuses on predicting soil condition [Morellos et al., 2016], more specifically, soil organic carbon, moisture content, and total nitrogen, facilitating the optimization of soil management. Accurate soil temperature estimation [Feng et al., 2019] at different depths and different climatic zones was also researched upon with a machine learning approach applied to daily weather data to assist with better site management. Lastly, a novel method was proposed for estimating soil moisture from data gathered from force sensors on a no-till chisel opener [Johann et al., 2016].

Animal welfare. More and more environmentally conscious producers around the globe, from Macari Vineyard in Long Island to Michel Lafarge in Burgundy, are adopting the idea of vineyard as a living ecosystem. AI-centric models have been developed to track and classify animals' activities in real time such that any abnormal behaviors can be identified and cared for as soon as possible. Such methods take into images of animal movements and audio signals of the sounds they make, and detect in real time actions they take and any deviation from their normal behaviors and sounds captured over time.

Information aggregation. Taking a step back to take a look at the big picture, it is also valuable to aggregate data on where in the world each grape variety is grown and by how many hectares. Without the advancement of computer vision and machine learning techniques, such tasks would be prohibitively time-consuming and labor-intensive to complete at a large scale at high precision. Luckily, with state-of-the-art AI methods applied to satellite imagery, the results could be obtained inexpensively and within a split second. This would enable growers to monitor their crops at low cost via aerial imaging, which relies on computer vision and path-planning algorithms.

Self-driving cars or autonomous vehicles have been receiving tremendous attention as of late, in large part due to the technological boom of Artificial Intelligence. Self-driving cars leverage environmental signals of sight and sound to carry out various AI-centric tasks — localization and mapping, scene understanding, movement planning, and driver state detection — to ensure safe and smooth mobility. Tesla, Zoox, Google (Waymo), Nvidia, Argo AI are among the top contenders in this space. **Self-driving tractors**, on the other hand, take on a slightly different set of responsibilities and are required to work in fairly different environments. A driverless tractor is an autonomous farm vehicle that delivers a high tractive effort (or torque) at slow speeds for the purposes of tillage and other agricultural tasks. Current leading manufacturers are perhaps John Deere, Autonomous Tractor Corporation, Fendt and Case IH.

13.2 AI for Climate and Sustainability

How to adapt vine growing and winemaking practices to climate change is at the forefront of sustainability goals for environmentally conscious vignerons around the globe, so is slowing the progress of climate change or mitigating its effects at the forefront of AI for sustainability goals.

A first step is perhaps to use AI for **monitoring and predicting climate and weather conditions**. There has been a rich body of research on predicting various climate measurements such as temperature and precipitation. Others take advantage of how neighboring regions' climate and weather measurements correlate with those of the focal regions to provide more accurate and combined predictions. When it comes to urban regions, a shortcut for quantifying microclimate characteristics that has proved rather effective by some researchers is to tap into electricity consumption data, which might prove of practical relevance for wine regions around cities such as Ningxia wine producing region in China and Wiener Gemischter Satz DAC around Vienna of Austria.

Air pollution is not only a major threat in a number of world's largest developing economies, but also a not uncommon occurrence in warm or hot Mediterranean regions where wildfires, volcanic eruptions are increasingly frequent with climate change, such as South Australia, California, Mount Vesuvius in Campania, and Mount Etna in Sicily, leading to potential smoke taint left on grapes' skins or even into the pulp, and thus nontrivial crop loss. Existing research works in the AI for Social Good community have used machine learning or deep learning methods to monitor and predict air quality, leveraging community sensing as an alternative to the traditional sensor-based measurement and prediction methods that suffered from the lack of connectivity or coverage. In the community sensing paradigm, any self-interested citizen or non-expert participant could collect environmental data with mobile devices, and contribute to monitoring real-time measurements of air quality, temperature, and humidity, etc. with greater precision and at much lower costs. Researchers [Zenonos et al., 2015] have proposed a coordination and guidance system for such collective sensing efforts by mapping participants to measurements that need to be taken using a deep-learning based search algorithm with very promising results.

Water conservation has been on the mind of many forward-looking vignerons for quite some time. At the current rate of global warming, in 50 years, it will become much warmer and drier and vigerons will have to plant now what's going to be the best then. Temperature might not be as much of a problem as water shortage, therefore water conservation has been and will stay a high priority project for not only environmental scientists but also stakeholders from all walks of life for years to come. AI-driven solutions have contributed to scientific developments of various aspects of water preservation.

In general, there are two main camps of water conservation strategies. First, on the supply side, deploying infrastructures for efficient use of water; and second, on the demand side, reducing water demand by changing consumption habits, perhaps mostly efficiently with behavioral nudging induced by strategic information sharing.

In the first camp, a body of research has been devoted to supporting distributed water resources management through the exploration of trade-offs across different stakeholders' objectives by designing optimization algorithms that efficiently search for and identify the whole *Pareto frontier* that strives for the well-being of everyone involved. This reflects the fact that practical problems are often not fully characterized by a single optimal solution, as they frequently involve multiple competing objectives. It is therefore important to identify the so-called *Pareto frontier*, which captures solution trade-offs.

Another promising line of research, wildly relevant for viticultural site selection and planning, revolves around facilitation, a phenomenon that occurs in water-stressed environments when shade from larger plants protect smaller annuals from harsh and intense sunlight exposure, enabling them to exist on scarce water. This also dovetails with the concept of vineyards as a whole ecosystem as plants can have positive effects on each other in numerous ways, including protection from extreme environmental conditions, which are increasingly common with climate change. AI researchers have developed algorithms that efficiently search for landscape designs that incorporate facilitation to conserve water, by capturing the growth requirements of plant species while encouraging facilitative interactions with other plants on the landscape.

AI planning techniques have also been leveraged to optimize pumping station control in the Netherlands, such that renewable energy is procured at the most cost-efficient manner in real time. Similarly, dynamic programming and mixed integer programming algorithms have been developed and implemented in practice for approximating the *Pareto frontier* in the problem of hydropower dam placement in the Amazon basin, a concerted effort between a dozen earth and computer scientists at Stanford and Cornell University.

In the second camp, studies have shown that providing consumers with usage information of fixtures could help save a considerable amount of water simply through behavioral signaling and social comparison. Water disaggregation has been an emerging research topic along the same vein, which involves taking an aggregated water consumption, for example, the total smart meter readings of a house, and decomposing it into the usages of different water fixtures. Some recent research developments on the topic of water disaggregation proposed efficient and effective reinforcement learning (simply put, machine learning with continuous feedback loops) algorithms to automatically learn the water disaggregation architecture with discriminative and reconstruction dictionaries for every step of the process, thus greatly improving upon the traditional non-AI solution in helping customers with water conservation.

Biodiversity monitoring. Biological diversity enhances the resilience of an ecosystem, and is integral to its survival and recovery after extreme weather conditions or natural disasters. This is in line with the changes we have been seeing in the vineyards over the last few decades, today, and tomorrow, that more future-looking vintners are embracing sustainable, organic, or biodynamic viticulture that encourages biodiversity in the vineyards, leaving the vineyards in a better state to future generations. As we have touched on about AI systems for animal welfare monitoring and tracking in Section 13.1, gathering information about the distribution of animals and plants, as well as real-time information about their conditions or behaviors could pay great dividends in years to come, accelerating scientific innovations and research developments on species preservation and characterization. Various large-scale projects such as Citizen science project, eBird project, the Wildbook project, etc. have tapped into the power of crowdsourcing, combined with computer vision and deep learning techniques to create and maintain the world's most comprehensive records on birds, insects, plants, and other animals both geographically and temporally.

Invasive species management. Invasive species, or species introduced to a new environment to which they are not native, can cause ecological harm and threaten the balance of that environment's natural ecosystem.

Phylloxera, the root-gorging vine louse and the reason why the majority of vines grown in the world are grafted onto rootstocks, is perhaps the best-known tragedy and case in point. It was first introduced into mainland Europe when a wine merchant in a small village next to Avignon in southern France close to Châteauneuf-du-Pape first planted some vines sent by *a friend from America* in 1861. Within five years, many vineyards throughout southern France were under attack by Phylloxera. By 1872, it has reached Douro in Portugal; by 1874, parts of Spain weren't spared, nor was Germany by 1875; by 1879, almost every wine producing region in Italy was suffering; and by 1980 it conquered each and every corner of French wine regions with the last being Champagne furthest away in the up north.

Vintners had learnt it the hard way — injecting Carbon Bisulphide into the soil, burying a live toad under each vine, flooding the vines, etc. — that the cure is to graft European *vitis vinifera* vines onto American rootstock, to come full circle. The solution seemed natural in hindsight. Phylloxera originated from the wild vines in eastern and southern parts of North America — the American vines, with which it managed to live symbiotically through co-evolution with its host on the leaves and roots of the vines, weakening them to some extent but never killing them. Therefore, after centuries of co-existence, American vines' roots have evolved to withstand the damage caused by the insect, a capability European grape vines were not blessed with in the absence of Phylloxera in history. By grafting onto American rootstocks, European vitis vinifera could take on the defense mechanism such that their roots could mend the wounds caused by Phylloxera, sealing them off from further bacterial or fungal invasion, that could cause serious maladies. In addition, saps from American rootstocks have proven effective in repelling Phylloxera as it is particularly unpalatable to it.

It is only in recent years circa 2018 that AI techniques have been proposed to intervene with the spread of invasive species by first simulating the spread trajectories, then deriving and optimizing quarantine along with other intervention strategies. Optimal intervention plans can be tailored to stop invasive species from spreading to particular locations. Others have also proposed to use biological control agents as a both a precaution and treatment, for which a graph vaccination problem is extensively vetted and then solved with AI-driven optimization algorithms.

Species conservation. Every natural ecosystem is delicately balanced by the coexisting species of plants and animals which live in it. The endangerment and extinction of species in the wild, sometimes due to natural disasters, human intervention or activities, disrupts this homeostasis.

As we have mentioned in Section 7, the historic Mastroberardino family in Campania since 1878, had and has been a real champion for the native grape varieties of Campania. When Antonio Mastroberardino, the ninth generation of the family, took over the family business in late 1950s, everything was in shambles after the devastation of World War Two, it was a daunting task to rebuild the viticulture and the winery and restore its former glory at the beginning of 1900s. Taking a leaf out of his grandfather Angelo's and father Michele's books, literally[57], Antonio started once again traveling overseas to open export foreign markets, except that everywhere he went, no one had ever heard of Fiano or Greco after the devastation of World War Two. The decision he took was a lone and usual one, to focus on these obscure native varieties, to identify, preserve, and bring them back to former glory, rather than following suit of planting international grape varieties to cater to immediate demand

[57]The Mastroberardino family are apparently fond of keeping journals of their extensive travel history to pass on for future generations to peruse in awe and nostalgia.

at the time. A small but important part of the family business centers around Pompeii, the ancient city entombed by the explosion from Mount Vesuvius. Producing a wine right inside the archaeological town of Pompeii stemmed from Antonio's dream of bringing back life in Pompeii through the 15 vineyards of theirs, located exactly where vineyards used to be. Each and every vine was planted in the exact same position as over two thousand years ago at a density ancient and modern at the same time at 8,000 plants per hectare in clay, limestone, and volcanic ashes. It was arguably this distinctive volcanic ash that gives the salty edge to the wine of the region. Game theory has been widely used by AI researchers and economists alike to model the adversarial interaction between the conservation agency and the counteracting parties. Game-theoretic models on eco-security interactions have been studied and deployed in practice, making a real difference preserving wild creatures in pristine lands. One of the followup frameworks of green security game addresses wildlife conservation, and its algorithm, aptly termed PAWS, has been deployed in a number of conservation sites. Another body of research on security games has been devoted to protecting forests and coral reefs, among others.

13.3 AI for Crisis Management

Natural disasters such as hails, frosts, wildfires, etc. have wrecked havoc in vineyards around the globe both in recent vintages and remote history, causing traumatic crop loss that could take vignerons years to recover. The hailstorms three years in a row in different parts of Burgundy Cote d'Or around harvest circa 2012, the notorious winter frost in 1956 that wiped out huge areas in Bordeaux and adversely affected almost everywhere in Europe, the spring frost in late March and early April of 2021 that doomed the 2021 vintage of Burgundy still fresh in our memories, and the wildfires that blazed through vineyards causing tremendous losses for many wine estates either directly or indirectly through smoke taint in California and southern Australia in recent years... The heart-wrenching stories are echoed everywhere from northern Italy, to Mendoza in Argentina, from Similkameen Valley in British Columbia, to Shandong province in China.

Disaster detection, prediction, and tracking. To be fully prepared for upcoming natural disasters by putting in place all the necessary precautions is perhaps the first step towards mitigating the disastrous damage these extreme events might inflict. Therefore to be able to accurately predict when and where natural disasters might strike is a first and foremost mission of AI for crisis management. Scientists have come up with machine learning methods to predict the upcoming hail storms in terms of time, location, and size, to forecast how the wildfires could spread, to pinpoint the trajectories of evolving snowstorms. Disaster forecasting has been investigated as a rare event prediction problem in the machine learning and statistics community, and researchers have improved the prediction performance with deep learning. Additional data sources such as social media have also been identified with efficient text mining techniques to surface and track urgent earthquakes in real time.

Disaster response. Timely and efficient routing and adapting disaster response measures such as search and rescue, and evacuation in response to the natural disaster can be life-saving. With effective prediction and forecasting in advance, how to efficiently evacuate a large number of people becomes a network flow problem within the realms of transportation and optimization. Efficient dynamic programming and reinforcement learning algorithms have been proposed and deployed in practice to ensure smooth sailing when dispatching emergency response vehicles.

To come up with accurate algorithms for optimizing traffic flow and routing, real-time information on how an emergency situation evolves and where people and vehicles are moving is indispensable. Twitter has been proved especially useful as a source of real-time sensor data when disasters such as earthquakes strike.

Understanding the severity, the nature, and the urgency of the situation at hand as soon as possible is also a matter of life and death. Computer vision researchers have successfully showcased the effectiveness of using satellite images to detect and segment building damages when flooding happens.

Better understanding and accurate prediction of the dynamics of crowds in a disaster could tremendously help with strategizing optimal crowd control measures to be put in place, leading to more controlled situations where less panic would result and more lives saved.

With the growing popularity of commercial drones in place, information collection in unknown or dangerous environments proves much easier than before, especially with the guidance of human knowledge as to where to navigate. Such human-computer interactive projects have indeed been deployed to help with safer, more flexible, and more granular information gathering during disasters.

13.4 AI for Distribution and Logistics

AI has been leveraged to improve efficiency of transportation systems and methods, reducing the frequency and the severity of traffic congestion, fatal accidents and casualties.

Arrival time prediction. Accurate estimation of travel time of any path is critical for real-time traffic monitoring, optimal route planning, potential ridesharing and vehicle dispatchment optimization. Even though this is a problem that has been studied for many years way before AI and deep learning took off, providing accurate travel time estimation remains challenging, largely due to difficulties in aggregating travel time estimates for individual segments (since the total time is probably not equal to the sum of individual estimates of each segment) and diverse complex factors at work. Deep learning based approaches have been recently proposed and achieved significantly superior accuracy.

Transportation recommendation, the problem of finding the most appropriate transport tools given user preferences, travel constraints such as time or cost, and trip characteristics such as purpose or distance, is at the center of user-centric large-scale system design that aims to satisfy the diverse needs of drivers or passengers and improve the efficiency of transport networks. Recent studies on multimodal (referring to multiple transportation modes) transportation recommender systems have built upon contextualized embeddings (Section 7.4 for improving recommendations in real-time, and such systems have been deployed into large navigation applications to serve hundreds of millions of users, making it more efficient for users to navigate around.

Traffic detection. Accurately detecting the traffic condition in real time is fundamental to traffic management, the reliability of which affects all aspects of traffic prediction and decision-making. Traffic detection started with small-scale vehicle detection from images captured through cameras or satellites based on object detection algorithms at the core of computer vision. A further step up is to estimate real-time traffic conditions — whether congestion or road closure is taking place, and some recent work managed to achieve impressive results even for locations without cameras using videos at nearby intersections. Others have combined social media data or acoustic data indicative of traffic noise to reliably infer traffic conditions at low costs. Yet others have focused on traffic anomaly detection that helps alert on or even prevent accidents. Another work notably attempted to reduce the amount of data needed without compromising prediction accuracy, thus mitigating privacy and security risks in the process.

Traffic forecast. Given detected traffic condition that is supposedly reliable, traffic prediction involves predicting traffic variables with historical data given real-time events that are unfolding. Quite a number of research works have proposed effective solutions through the lens of temporal and spatial networks that simulate the traffic for predictive modeling that leverages both past information and information from a nearby location.

SECTION 14

Wine Investing

Among financially capable individuals, fine wine has been a mainstream investment. According to a survey of Wealth Insights conducted by Barclays in the early 2010s, at least a quarter of high-net-worth individuals around the world own a wine collection, which represents on average 2% of their wealth. Over the last decade, the status of fine wine has considerably shifted as it has become increasingly common to invest in wine. With interest rates as low as 0.5%, it is perhaps only natural that institutional investors, high-net-worth individuals and even retail investors have been on the lookout for new investment channels beyond traditional equity and fixed income. The search for alternative assets has perhaps led to the niche markets of more exotic assets such as commodities, real estates, and collectibles such as fine art and fine wine. It is no wonder that with this niche yet ever-increasing investment demand and the trend towards financialization of the wine market, the development of wine indices has been gaining momentum at an accelerated rate, attracting investors' attention around the globe.

In practice, a variety of wine indices have been developed and proposed over the last two decades, with some gaining industry-wide attention. Let us compare and contrast nine of the well-known wine indices across the industry in Table 25.

Within these, the most internationally recognized and widely adopted family of indexes is provided by Liv-ex — London International Vintners Exchange founded in 1999, which is perhaps considered as the industry benchmark. Several other information and service providers also propose proprietary wine indices.

In France, Idealwine, one of the leading wine trading platforms, publishes its own family of indices WineDex upon which they operate and advise others due to its dominant position on the French auction market.

Wine Spectator is one of the best known wine publications and platforms of information on wine in the world and has been one of the pioneers in wine index construction. The Wine Market Journal also maintains a comprehensive database of auction hammer prices and has therefore the necessary material to compute accurate indices.

WineDecider is one of the few players to track the evolution of retail prices and uses these for their index calculation.

Wine Owners is another player aimed at competing with Liv-ex, with a trading platform and a large set of indices. Cult Wines, yet another leading platform launched in 2007 with the goal of making wine investment more approachable, recently expanded to North America and Canada to cater to the growing fine and rare wine collector community in North Americas. They also rely on their in-house indices that they claim to outperform Liv-ex consistently.

	Liv-ex	Idealwine	Wine Spectator	Wine Market Journal	Wine Deciders	Wine Owners	Cult Wines	Vinfolio (Wine Prices)	Vinovest
Data	Composite Index	Composite Index	Composite Index	Composite Index	Composite Index	Composite Index	Composite Index	Composite Index	Composite Index
Weighted	Yes	No	Yes	No	No	No	Yes	Yes	Yes
Method	Prices from their trading platform	Auction prices in France	Auction prices in US	Global auction prices	Global retail prices	Est. market prices	Est. market prices	Global auction and retail prices	Est. market prices
Frequency	Monthly, daily	Monthly	Quarterly	Quarterly	Quarterly, monthly	Monthly, weekly	Monthly	Monthly	Quarterly
Formula	Not available except explanations	Not available	Not available	Not available	Not available	Not available	Not available	Not available	Not available
List of Wines	Public	Public	Public	Public	Public	Public	Proprietary	Public	Proprietary
Rule of Inclusion	Committee based	Unclear	Unclear	Unclear	Unclear	Committee based	Unclear	Unclear	Committee based
Definition of Weights	Unclear	None	Unclear	None	None	None	Unclear	Unclear	Unclear
Data Availability	Some available	Some available	Some available	Some available	Some available	Some available	Some available	Available	Not available
General Index	Yes	Yes	Yes	Yes	No	Yes	Yes	Yes	Yes
Bordeaux	Yes	Yes	No	Yes	Yes	Yes	Yes	Yes	Yes
Burgundy	Yes	Yes	No	Yes	Yes	Yes	Yes	Yes	Yes
Other Regions	Yes	Limited	No	Yes	Yes	Yes	Yes	Yes	Yes
Tailored Indices	Yes	Limited	No	No	No	No	Yes	No	Yes
Time span	Since 1988	Since 2007	Since 1996	Since 1997	Since 2007	Since 2007	Since 2007	Since 2013	Since 2019

Table 25: Nine Best-known Wine Indices.

Vinfolio, one of the major players in the fine wine scene, houses the website WinePrices.com, which introduced the Wine Prices Fine Wine Indexes, a representative and comprehensive fine wine indexes made publicly available. This set of indices tracks 9 different portfolios of fine wines, with 2 internationally balanced and 7 regional specific indexes. Wines that make up individual indexes are the most actively traded fine wines bought and sold at global auctions. Perhaps one of the new comers is Vinovest in the US, who also introduced their proprietary index Vinovest 100 that tracks 12 different fine wine markets around the world.

As is shown from Table 25, Wine Spectator only computes a general index but the other providers also propose indices covering more specific wine categories, for example, including Bordeaux and finer-grained Bordeaux First Growths.

All indices are computed using the Composite Index approach. This approach is perhaps the simplest and easiest to understand for the general public, which probably accounts for the reason why it is widely adopted in the industry, as opposed to indices introduced in academia that are more complex. With the Composite Index approach, wine indices are calculated as the weighted sum of the last updated prices of a pre-determined set of wines. Despite being simple to implement, this approach operates under the assumption that the previous price of an untraded wine is valid. In many cases, it could lead to using outdated prices and therefore inflate the degree of smoothness of the index, camouflaging the risk therein. Consequently, it is likely to understate the risk associated with wine investment without accounting for the lack of liquidity on the wine market. To put it more concretely, unlike other liquid assets, the investment return of fine wines is highly dependent on the number of potential buyers in the market. By assuming that untraded wine is priced at its last traded price when in fact it might be much lower due to lack of potential buyers when the market is sluggish, such wine indices might paint a rosy picture of high return of investment that's not aligned with reality. In general, indices are updated on a monthly or a quarterly basis, in line with the lack of liquidity on this market. Only Liv-ex computes an index updated daily — the Liv-ex Fine Wine 50 index. Most wine indices suffer from a poor level of transparency as only Liv-ex clearly outlines the index calculation methodology. Liv-ex indices are also the only ones disclosed publicly to be based on weighted average prices and not simple average prices, even though the weights are not disclosed either. Many index providers publish the list of wines included in the indices on their website, but the rules of inclusion and exclusion remain opaque, with even more providers refusing to publicly disclose the composition of their portfolios.

Idealwine, Wine Spectator, Wine Market Journal, make use of auction prices to compute their indices. The key advantage of auction prices is that they reflect actual transactions for which all relevant information is publicly known. Even though due to the very large number of auction houses active in the world and their irregular auction schedules, the process of aggregating market prices tends to be rather complicated. Moreover, auction-specific factors affecting hammer prices should be controlled to avoid biasing the estimation of the index. These factors include differences in reputation among auction houses in different markets, conditions of the bottles being auctioned, and any outliers in auction prices either due to data corruption or measurement errors.

Other platforms such as Wine Decider are more reliant on retail prices, which are more readily available especially with the introduction of Wine Searcher in 2003, that aggregates retail prices of every bottle of wine around the globe. However, retail prices as bases for wine indices are not without limitations. The exact trading volumes of a wine sold through merchants around the world are proprietary and largely not privy to the public. Therefore the same issue of stale prices arise, as a wine could remain in a wine retailer or a restaurant's inventory for months or even years — especially true when COVID-19 hit — before being sold off since the current retail prices do not necessarily correspond to ongoing transactions either. If wine retailers engage in off-line transactions at different prices, or do not update the prices or inventories online frequently enough (as is often the case), then retail prices are even further detached from the true market prices that could evolve swiftly.

In contrast to the above stated auction prices and retail prices, Liv-ex uses the median of the transaction prices that took place on their own trading platform, circumventing the aforementioned drawbacks. However, compared to the large number of auctions and retail transactions taking place everywhere around the world, the number of customers trading on their platform pales in comparison, which in turn could bring greater idiosyncratic sample biases into the process.

Lastly, Wine Owners estimates indices using market prices calculated on the basis of an algorithm which aggregates prices from merchants and transaction prices recorded on their own trading platform, so do Vinfolio's Wine Prices Indices and Vinovest, except that they claim to operate their proprietary algorithms on both auction and retail transaction data around the world.

At the same time, there has been a proliferation of articles published in academia where more sophisticated wine indices are proposed based on statistical methods, mirroring the booming industry indices. Several such academic approaches ensure the reliability and robustness of resulting indices even when the underlying dataset from which the indices are calculated on contains only a limited number of observations. As was touched upon in our discussion on industrial wine indices, it is by no means an easy task to design an index for wine that can be updated timely and regularly, capturing changes in the volatile market in real time. Such is not unique to wine as a tangible asset but also applicable to real estates, arts, and other collectibles, as these markets all suffer from transactional frictions (insurance and storage fees for wines or arts, maintenance fees for real estates, etc.), information asymmetries (sellers know much more than buyers about the product and potentially hide information strategically), limited number of traders and/or assets, among others, making liquidation and asset pricing more challenging than conventional assets such as stocks and bonds.

The reason for more involved methodological development is at least fourfold:

First, fine wine trading takes place in multiple forms, in various highly fragmented markets, and involves stakeholders from all walks of life from everywhere around the globe. Fine wines are traded at the dinner table of a fine dining restaurant in Hong Kong with taxes, markups, and fees, auctioned back and forth at Sotheby's or Christie's in New York with buyer's premiums, shipping or storage fees, purchased off the online catalogue of a retail store in Auckland and shipped across the continent with tariffs and tips. Such a temporally and physically dispersed and fragmented setting makes estimating a single price index that aggregates all the market information in real time particularly challenging.

Second, not unlike other collectibles the value of a bottle of fine and rare wine could be highly subjective and therefore the market price could be highly volatile. A popular singer mentioning it in the lyrics of his or her songs in a widely distributed album release could jack up the sales and the retail price by over 60% overnight.

Third, the limited quantities of fine wines due to production constraints resulting from low yielding ancient vines from small parcels produced in a way that's labor intensive and demands a high level of knowledge, experience, and skills, greatly limit the total volume of sales and liquidity.

Lastly, various transactional frictions such as insurance, storage fees, search costs, shipping fees, duty payment, value added taxes, premiums and markups, as well as wildly prevalent information asymmetries (sellers might withhold critical information about bottle provenance, for instance) and information opacity (information about product quality or transaction costs largely kept in the dark).

Over the past two decades, academic researchers have proposed various methods for calculating wine indices for which various datasets were collected. Some popular methods include *hedonic regression, repeat-sales regression, average adjacent period returns,* and other *hybrid* or *pooled* methods that combine multiple of the aforementioned methods.

Hedonic regression is a classic economic approach for estimating consumers' preferences towards certain products by quantifying its value. This approach dates back to [Waugh, 1928] and has received wider attention in the 1960s and 70s. In wine economics, [Jones and Storchmann, 2001] and [Fogarty, 2006] have used this technique to estimate wine indices. It is based on the idea that the prices are based on the value of the wine which could be seen as a weighted sum of its constituents' values. For example, a bottle of wine might be more expensive if it is made by a reputable or highly sought after producer, if the total quantity is limited, if the grapes are from a highly recognized lieu-dit, if Robert Parker once raved about it, if its vintage gained a lot of hype among notable wine critics, and the list goes on... As you might have already guessed, the main drawback of this method is that without a comprehensive list of all the relevant attributes, the model will very likely be biased and more often than not underestimate the price index.

Repeat-sales regression was first proposed by [Bailey et al., 1963], with various modifications and adaptations over time. More recently,

it has been used by wine economists to calculate wine indices (e.g., [Burton and Jacobsen, 2001, Dimson et al., 2015]). The method computes returns from repeated transactions of the same wine. The main advantage of this approach is to control for all characteristics of a wine, since transactions of the exact same wine are analyzed. Thus, by using repeat sales of a same wine, this approach avoids the heterogeneity issue but loses a substantial number of observations. An index can be constructed based on the repeated sales regression approach without the use of regressions by taking the average of the returns of wines being traded over two adjacent dates to estimate a tendency of the index, which lends itself to the *average adjacent period return* method. It computes index returns between two specific dates as the average return of all wines traded in-between. Some follow up work has improved on this method by removing outliers (i.e., using a winsorized average) or using weighted averages.
To obtain estimations for the *pooled* or *hybrid models* proposed in [Fogarty et al., 2014] one can merge the hedonic regression for wines traded only once with the repeat-sales model. The pooled and hybrid models only differ in the way they are estimated. Hybrid methods, as the name suggests, combines multiple methods such as hedonic regression and repeat-sales regression, with one complementing the other; and pooled methods conceptually similar to the hybrid methods but based on a simpler estimation procedure in a slightly more straightforward way.

Researchers Philippe Masset and Jean-Philippe Weisskoft compared the evolution of various wine indices in both industry and academia over the period of 1996-2015, and some of their findings are worth highlighting here:

1. Various wine indices evolve in a largely similar fashion and share a large proportion of identical wines in portfolio;

2. Wine prices skyrocketed ever since 1990s, even though in more recent decade evolved in a more irregular pattern since 2007, going through the slum of financial crisis and then through the roof after the release of Bordeaux vintage 2010 in 2011;

3. Averaging the longest living wine indices, the annual return to investment in fine wine averaged 6 – 7% over the last two decades;

4. Wine indices are significantly and positively correlated with one another, unsurprisingly. However, Liv-ex appears to be show a higher level of correlation with other indices, whereas Idealwine indices the opposite being slightly more detached from the overall trend;

5. Industrial wine indices exhibits greater volatility than academic indices, which could be due to lower sampling frequency (monthly or quarterly most common), simple composite method of calculation which suffers from stale prices due to illiquidity, delayed information aggregation, and information opacity, among others;

6. Indices traded in currencies other than US Dollars also exhibited greater volatility due to additional risk associated with currency exchange rates;

7. Most monthly wine indices do not seem to correlate with the stock market prices, and sometimes show negative correlations, whereas quarterly indices do show positive correlations. Some academic indices do correlate positively with stock market prices and equities. The use of merchant retail prices that are oftentimes outdated and less responsive to market conditions could be the one of the explanations here, as the indices that heavily rely on auction hammer prices do exhibit more significant positive correlations with the stock market.

Taken together, the risk of a wine investment, especially when it comes to industrial wine indices drawn from merchant prices, seems generally higher than what investors might have expected and has increased drastically in the last decade. As I will detail later in this section, there is a multitude of mixed evidence regarding how return on investment (ROI) and the associated risks of wine investment stack up to traditional investment options.

14.1 Determinants of Fine Wine Prices

Let us take a step back to ask this more fundamental question — what are the determinants of the price differentials of fine wines? There is unsurprisingly a vast body of studies over the last 50 years on this very topic. Unlike any other competitive markets, we could perhaps divide all the determinants into two sides of the market: supply and demand.

From the supply and production side, the place of origin, the associated soil type, vine age, elevation, aspect, exposure, and climate, as well as vintage character, grape variety, the cost of viticulture and vinification as well as the practices themselves, the reputation of the winery and the vineyard, production quantity, the number of bottles or cases produced, and the resulting product in terms of color, concentration, flavor and taste profile, bottle and label, associated critics' review, age, distribution channel, storage conditions or bottle provenance, among others. For each of the these potential factors, there has been at least several academic studies for which the authors collected pricing data, ran economic pricing models against, and provided positive (mostly supposedly causal[58]) evidence for it with certain nuances. For instance, several studies have established the significant impact of the scores and reviews issued by Robert

[58]But many academics would argue that causal inference in the literature is largely flawed, so take your own stock.

Parker on the pricing of Bordeaux wine futures, but none of those by Jancis Robinson.

From the demand side, the question becomes an even more fascinating one — how are fine wines valued among collectors and enthusiasts, and how do fine wines' value evolve over its product life cycle?

Wine enthusiasts and collectors are very much entranced by mature bottles, sometimes over a hundred years old from remote history, gasping about how wine transcends time and space, letting our imaginations run wild. Even though many would argue eloquently that many old wines do not necessarily taste better than young counterparts and it is better to drink a bottle too soon than too late when the wine is way past its peak and deprived of its charm, especially for those who enjoy fruity aromas and floral bouquets, there is still something emotional, ineffable, and almost sacred about opening a bottle that is perhaps the contemporary of our great grandparents, that has braved all the turmoils, and finally found its place right in front of you at this moment of history.

One of the world's priciest bottles of Champagne ever auctioned is the Shipwreck Piper-Heidsieck of vintage 1907, discovered by divers off the coast of Finland in 1997. Left untouched deep under the Baltic sea after a 1916 ship wreck, en route to the Imperial Court of Czar Nicholas II of Russia, caused by a torpedo by a German submarine during World War One, sinking to the bottom of the ocean for over 80 years. On a similar but different occasion, a recent paper published in the Proceedings of the National Academy of Sciences (PNAS) revealed reports on a multiplatform analytical investigation of 170-year-old Champagne bottles found in a shipwreck at the bottom of the Baltic Sea, which provided insights into winemaking practices used at the time, thanks to archaeochemistry as the application of the most recent analytical techniques to ancient samples that provide an unprecedented understanding of human culture throughout history. None of the labels remained, but bottles were later identified as champagnes from the Veuve Clicquot Ponsardin, Heidsieck, and Juglar (known as Jacquesson since 1832) Champagne houses thanks to branded engravings on the surface of the cork that is in contact with the wine. Organic spectroscopy-based non-targeted metabolomics and metallomics give access to the detailed composition of these wines, revealing chemical characteristics in terms of small ion, sugar, and acid contents as well as markers of barrel aging and Maillard reaction products. The distinct aroma composition of these ancient champagne samples, first revealed during tasting sessions, was later confirmed using aroma analysis techniques.

What is **the impact of aging** on wine prices and the performance of wine as a long-term investment, independent of market conditions, vintages, and its gastronomic value? One reason why it is interesting to look at the effects of aging, separate from any vintage premiums, is that even wines that have lost their gastronomic appeal can be valuable as they provide enjoyment and pride to their owners. Estimating the size of such non-pecuniary benefits along with pure financial returns is relevant from a broader asset pricing perspective since non-financial utility may also play a role in the markets for entrepreneurial investments, prestigious hedge funds, socially responsible mutual funds, and art.

In order to answer such questions, financial economists Elroy Dimson, Peter L. Rousseau, and Christophe Spaenjers at London Business School, HEC Paris, and Vanderbilt University, respectively, proposed this theory of pricing a fine wine as an alternative investment. They argue that a wine's value is governed by the following three measurements, in line with how other luxury goods are valued as an asset:

1. the value of immediate consumption — the more drinkable a bottle is at the current time, the more valuable it is for measure of our evaluation, a high quality bottle's drinkability will keep increasing for decades on end whereas a non collectible bottle's drinkability deteriorates from the very beginning;

2. the current value of consumption at its peak, plus any emotional enjoyment from ownership until consumption — that is to say, the more likely the bottle is at its peak, and the older the unopened bottle is, the higher its value;

3. the current value of lifelong storage, in line with other forms of collectibles such as art or jewelry.

By collecting and analyzing auction data provided by Christie's London and retail data by Berry Bros & Rudd for the five First Growth Bordeaux Chateaux classified in the 1855 left bank classification for the period of 1899-2012, the authors showcased the validity and robustness of their proposed framework of wine pricing and surfaced interesting evidence regarding the life-cycle dynamics of fine wines. To begin with, highly rated vintages were found to appreciate strongly for a few decades, but then prices stabilize until the wines become antiques, after which prices start rising again. For supposedly lackluster vintages, however, prices turned out relatively flat over the first few years of the life cycle, but then rose in an almost linear fashion. By considering the difference in financial returns between young and mature wines, a collectible was estimated to deliver a non-financial or emotional return of at least 1% — another piece of evidence for why they call it "emotional asset".

As to long-term financial returns, the authors found that inflation-adjusted wine values did not increase over the first quarter of the 20th century, experienced a boom and bust around the Second World War, and have risen substantially over the last half century. The overall annualized real return was estimated to be 5.3% for the five

First Growths between 1900 and 2012, but after correcting for the insurance and storage costs necessarily lowers the estimated return to 4.1%.

This is some rather strong evidence that equities have been a better investment than wine over the past century, and it is likely that accounting for differences in transaction costs would lower the relative performance of wine investments even further, especially over short horizons. At the same time, returns on wine have exceeded those on government bonds as well as art and stamps, even though art pieces might as well come with even higher emotional return that more than compensate. This well-executed study also indicated a substantial positive correlation between the equity and wine markets.

Lastly, to double down on the not-that-optimistic tone on wine from the point of financial return on investment, the authors further put forth a caveat that these top Bordeaux chateaux are probably on the higher end of market return for wine investment as popular media outlets are highly biased towards them. When tested on Sauternes and vintage Ports, the average returns indeed turned out slightly lower over the same period of time, calling into the question of whether to adopt diversification strategies for wine portfolios.

Media coverage of the wine market has shifted attention to a minority of prestigious areas in which the image, scarcity, and speculation are also the determinants of the price. These wines accounting for only a small share of the total market are more or less referred to as fine wines. There appears to be no precise definition of what a fine wine is. Before mid 2000s, according to Liv-ex Investment reports, “investable fine wines are restricted to the 25 best Bordeaux wines and a minority of wines from other regions.” Researchers analyzed that 95% of Liv-ex turnover was from Bordeaux wines and more than half of it was concentrated on the five first growths of the Medoc. In the most recent decades, however, according to public statements issued by Sotheby's Wine, a diversification has begun. Bordeaux and Burgundy have been going neck to neck, whereas in the past, Burgundy was 20 percent of the total investment wine. The boom of Burgundy wine in the investment market has been widely attributed to the discovery of Burgundy by the rising Asian market, the quality improvement and revolution by new generations (of 1980s) of vignerons who were exposed to scientific viticultural and vinicultural studies at universities and the world wine scene, as well as the minuscule quantities that reinforced the scarcity in light of the sky-rocketed demand. Other authors consider fine wine as a wine allowing an investment with a potential return, as opposed to a non-fine wine. So I guess it is safe to infer that the term fine wine is reserved for exceptional wines from the world's best vineyards, the highest quality grapes and the most acclaimed winemakers. These wines can usually be found in reputable auction houses. Over the past few decades, they have achieved the so-called blue-chip status. The best known are perhaps the five first growths of Bordeaux and a selection of Grand Cru Burgundy, as well as those iconic wines from a selection of other French regions such as Rhone and Champagne, plus some high-profile regions in Australia, California, Italy, Portugal, and Spain.

14.2 Portfolio Management

Ever since the introduction of modern portfolio theory in an 1952 essay by Harry Markowitz, for which he won the Nobel Prize in 1990, on the effects of asset risk, return, correlation and diversification on investment portfolio returns, many scholars and professionals have explored the benefits of diversification strategies for portfolio management, with early works largely focused on potential returns from a single portfolio consisting of different shareholdings. This line of work was soon extended to other types of investment including bonds, currencies, real estates, and commodities. Alternative assets such as art and other collectibles including coins, stamps, cars, cards, etc. have also been extensively vetted for sound financial returns. Here wine is bracketed as a viable financial asset alternative to traditional assets such as stocks and bonds, because of its nature as a hard asset. It was measured by some scholars as less correlated to the equity market because its price adjustment is a slow and gradual process compared to equities, even though whether wine qualifies as an alternative asset with little correlation with equities has remained controversial. Some basic questions we as potential wine investors are interested in include:

- Do wine investment outperforms traditional assets?
- Does the inclusion of wine assets in a portfolio add to the positive diversification effect?
- What are the limits of including wine assets in an investment portfolio?

Let us first simplify the questions by considering building a wine-only investment portfolio first. How will such an investment strategy turn out in the long run, and what is the collective wisdom from past research on how to optimize this portfolio for the highest return possible? Luckily, a multitude of studies have surfaced some rather interesting insights that I will summarize below and in Table 26.

1. The overall returns appear to be consistently positive, across all the fine wine regions, and throughout any decade in the past century;
2. When Bordeaux wines are mixed with other wines in a wine-centric portfolio, the returns appear to degrade to a great extent;

3. Diversification could pay high dividends, provided that sufficiently low correlations among wines in a portfolio are evident, which might include off-the-beaten path strategies;

4. Emerging research on indirect investment with wine funds returns a rather gloomy picture where the capabilities of such managers were questioned and criticized.

Consistent and robust positive ROI on wine portfolios has been widely documented both in academia and industry. The Bordeaux wines included in the Vintage Claret Index averaged strongly at 15.2% annual return for the period 1950-1985, according to one of the first few studies on this topic. The average annual return for Bordeaux Premier Cru classified in the 1855 Classification over the two decades that followed 1988-2000 was reported to be around 8.7%. When zoomed in on the five First Growths from the "en primeur" market (when none had exited), the return turned out to be 4.25% over the period of 1995-1999. Taking a look at the big picture from 1900 to 2012, the annualized return for Bordeaux Premier Crus was around 4.1%, with the most profitable being young wines from highly rated vintages. Outside Bordeaux, there is some positive evidence for including new world fine wines from Australia and California in the portfolio, even though across various studies the estimated annual return on investment in Australian and Californian fine wines ranged between 2.2% and 4.3% depending on the producers, the vintages, and investment time periods.

There is mixed evidence regarding comparing or combining Bordeaux wines and those from other regions in one investment portfolio. Multiple studies have argued for both sides: Bordeaux returns present higher or lower returns than other wines, varying to a great extent in analytical methods and data drawn. For instance, in a series of research papers by James Fogarty, Australian wines have been shown to exhibit comparable, if not even higher return to Bordeaux wines, with more expensive Australian wines generating higher returns than less expensive counterparts but at higher risks. Rhone wines have also been identified for superior investment potential for the period of 1996-2007.

To merit diversification strategies, we need to look for low correlation between prices of different components in a portfolio to hedge against risks. There have been several studies that have identified such mixes: wines from Australia, France, Italy, and Portugal were shown to exhibit sufficiently low correlation between prices for investment potential with diversification in-between. When it comes to wine indices, there appears no sure-fire way for a portfolio to benefit from diversification, as there has been various data points about how an index would provide diversification benefits for a certain period of time but a subset or a superset or for a different period of time wouldn't, even though wine does appear to add to the diversification benefits if it's added to a non-wine portfolio in general.

When it comes to wine funds versus direct investment, there is indeed some evidence from several studies that the returns from wine funds turn out higher. Some argue that it was not an easy task for individual investors to reverse engineer and replicate the performance of a well-managed diverse portfolio, with analyses confirming all the average returns of wine funds exceed direct investment in Bordeaux and Rhone wines. Such high performance on average was achieved not without sacrificing volatility. However more studies criticize the capabilities of wine fund managers in terms of timing and selection, with evidence that many managers do not even know how to properly evaluate the value of wines they manage.

Return (YoY)	Wines Included	Time	Data	Index/Method	Reference
15.2%	Bordeaux	1950-1985	Auction prices	Vintage Claret Index	[Duthy, 1986]
12-13%	Penfold's Grange	1952-1980	Auction prices	Hedonic Regression	[Byron and Ashenfelter, 1995]
18%	Penfold's Grange	1952-1980	Wholesale prices	Hedonic Regression	[Byron and Ashenfelter, 1995]
8.7%	Bordeaux Premier Cru	1988-2000	Auction prices	None	[Bentzen et al., 2002]
18.5%	Bordeaux Premier Cru	1988-1996	Auction prices	None	[Bentzen et al., 2002]
-3.2%	Bordeaux Premier Cru	1996-2000	Auction prices	None	[Bentzen et al., 2002]
9.5-11%	Bordeaux Burgundy Rhone	1976-1992	Auction prices	None	[Weil, 1993]
4.3%	Bordeaux First Growths	1982-1998	Broker prices	Hedonic Regression	[Ali and Nauges, 2003]
9.7%	Australian wine	1965-2000	Auction prices	Hedonic Regression	[Fogarty, 2005] [Fogarty, 2006]
12.8-13.9%	Australian wine	1990-2000	Auction prices	Hedonic Regression	[Fogarty, 2005] [Fogarty, 2006]
2.2-4.3%	Grange St Henri Bin 707 Hill of Grace	1988-2000	Auction prices	Hedonic Regression	[Wood et al., 2006]
4.1%	Bordeaux	1900-2012	Auction prices	Hedonic Regression	[Dimson et al., 2015]
8.2%	Bordeaux Burgundy Rhone	2007-2014	WineDex 100	Composite Index	[Aytaç et al., 2016]
9.3%	Bordeaux	2007-2014	WineDex	Composite Index	[Aytaç et al., 2016]
9.0%	Burgundy	2007-2014	WineDex	Composite Index	[Aytaç et al., 2016]
3.0%	Rhone	2007-2014	WineDex	Composite Index	[Aytaç et al., 2016]
7.3%	Bordeaux First Growths	2007-2014	Liv-ex 50	Composite Index	[Aytaç et al., 2016]
3.9%	Bordeaux Burgundy Rhone Champagne Italy	2007-2014	Liv-ex 100	Composite Index	[Aytaç et al., 2016]
6.0%	Bordeaux Burgundy Rhone Champagne Italy...	2007-2014	Liv-ex 500	Composite Index	[Aytaç et al., 2016]
5.4%	Bordeaux (Top 24)	2007-2014	Liv-ex Investable	Composite Index	[Aytaç et al., 2016]
5.2%	Bordeaux Rhone	1998-2007	Wine funds	Composite Index	[Lucey and Devine, 2015]
3.2%	Bordeaux	1998-2007	Wine funds	Composite Index	[Lucey and Devine, 2015]
5.5%	Rhone	1998-2007	Wine funds	Composite Index	[Lucey and Devine, 2015]

Table 26: A comparison of ROI on wine-centric portfolios.

As we have alluded to earlier while discussing diversification strategies, the inclusion of fine wine in an investment portfolio of conventional assets such as stocks and bonds appears to align with the ethos of diversification. However, it appears we are yet to reach a consensus on that front, and the results are all over the place depending on the time period, how portfolios are compared, and what asset composition is. The seminal paper on this subject pitted French wine returns against a variety of financial assets and came to the conclusion that one should only buy wine for consumption rather than investment. Others that followed either refuted or confirmed with different sets of analyses, such as comparing returns on wine investment with other types of assets within one portfolio, or evaluating the potential of using wine as a hedge for diversification by identifying any correlation in-between.

There appears to be overwhelming evidence of the return of fine wine investment falling short of different types of equities at least in the short run. Bordeaux wines had been compared unfavorably against Dow Jones Industrial Average, equities, or stocks, before the 2000s, and cast in even dimmer lights when insurance costs, storage costs, liquidity concerns, and limited quantities enter the picture, which are mostly irrelevant for other types of assets. On the other hand, there also appears abundant evidence about how wine returns outperform stocks especially when it is longer-termed and after 2000s. For instance, Bordeaux wines during the 2000s were shown to overtake US stock market, and Swiss stocks (but not bonds), and so was a wine index consisting of US, French, and Italian wines. Among studies that pitted wines against bonds, the majority appeared to favor wines, except for a few, such as red Bordeaux and California wines during 1973-1977 which were found underperforming bonds. This result had been challenged by research works that soon followed showcasing superior performance of wines or wine indices over US Treasury bills, art collections, stamps, and bonds.

Different wine investment returns were calculated to vary from 2.4% to 9.5% depending on time periods and wine mixes.

14.2.1 Diversification effects

As we have touched on the controversy revolving around the role of wine as an alternative asset, there are two major camps of scholarly articles in this regard:

First, sentiments towards including wine in a mixed-asset investment portfolio appear positive in general. Government bonds have been documented by researchers to showcase a lower correlation with the wine index than with equities, based on which if we were to optimize our portfolio for the minimum risk, a combination of a fine wine index and government bonds with a smaller weight for equities would be advisable. By applying several industry standard asset pricing models over the period 1996-2003, authors [Kumar, 2005] have found evidence that Bordeaux wines have maintained a low exposure to systematic risk factors. This result was confirmed several times by other researchers [Sanning et al., 2008, Masset and Henderson, 2010] in that Bordeaux wines appear to be solid investment in terms of average returns and volatility because they are relatively uncorrelated with stock markets, with the caveats being the results strongly depend on vintage and critics' ratings. On a similar note, Australian wines were also found to weakly correlate with other types of assets.

Second, evidence [Bouri, 2015, Bouri and Roubaud, 2016] exists that wines could serve as an investment haven to hedge against stock movements during the last decade or so. And to complement the evidence that bonds appear to be less correlated with wines than equities, wine economists have also found that a portfolio that consists of wines and bonds appear to showcase higher returns compared to a portfolio of wines and equities, holding the risk equal. However, there is no free lunch under the sun since fine wine as a safe haven

could be especially weak during market stress or turmoil.
Despite a large number of studies documenting positive evidence for of wine inclusion for the purpose of investment portfolio diversification, it might not be robust enough a causal effect for a surefire positive return over the baseline investment strategy, if investors did not tread carefully with regard to the composition of the wine index or the exact diversification strategy employed. In most recent studies [Faye and Le Fur, 2019], the effect of intrinsic wine characteristics on wine prices were shown to be lacking in robustness or stability with evident cyclical shifts, calling into question again how much could we rely on indices and pricing models for fine wines.

14.2.2 Frontier investments

Most collectors today (at least jokingly) pine over the fact that they didn't seize the moment back in the early 1990s to stock up on the frontiers back then — fine wines from Burgundy and Bordeaux. Which segment within fine wine as a tangible asset to invest in could serve as the new frontier in years to come and how would that compare to the old frontier, and traditional financial assets in terms of investment potential? Wine economists Philippe Masset, Jean-Philippe Weisskopf, and Clementine Fauchery recently made a case for fine Alpine wine from Austria, Germany, Switzerland, Piedmont, and Rhone valley by identifying and examining their performance as frontier investments from 2002 to 2017. They argue their Alpine wines have increased at a pace exceeding inflation, which appears to be driven by a surge in demand at auctions evident from the increased trading frequency and value. So did Alpine wines deliver positive risk-adjusted returns, thus demonstrating diversification potential with low correlations with traditional assets and other better established wine regions. Coincidentally, the growth rate of Piedmont alone has overtaken Burgundy and Bordeaux in the past few quarters according to investment reports by Cult Wines.

Alpine wines in aggregate were shown to display high abnormal returns, moderate levels of risk and low correlations with other assets indicative of high diversification merits. The major challenge of identifying frontier investments lies in predicting the next Bordeaux or Burgundy in terms of performance uptick. There indeed appears strong signals that Northern Italian wines have high potentials with a strong dynamic of high prices, positive returns and good diversification. For Austria, Germany and Switzerland, the evolution appeared more unpredictable with but a few wines showing strong price increases, returns and diversification benefits. When it comes to the old favorites of wines from the Rhone valley, which might have seemed to be of the highest potential as the next frontier but sadly failed to materialize returns comparable to other regions.

14.3 Deep Learning for Portfolio Management

Portfolio management refers to choosing various assets within the investment portfolio for pre-specified period of time to achieve certain investment goals such as maximizing the expected return or minimizing risks. It is at its core a problem of dynamic optimization: what is the best course of action for selecting the set of best performing financial assets given a certain time period? Traditional methods often involve evolutionary algorithms, stochastic modeling, and simulation. Deep learning methods, however, have fueled the new generation of portfolio management systems that takes in historical pricing data, whether it be from stocks, indices, or hedge funds, and predicts future prices, therefore prescribing portfolio optimization strategies thereof and showcasing superior investment performance than traditional methods. Some studies leveraged sentiment analyses extracted from analysts reports through natural language processing methods to predict stock prices, based on which potential portfolio selection could be implemented and evaluated for final strategy recommendation.

Reinforcement learning comes up with autonomous agents that interact with their environments with optimal behaviors learned through trial and error. With deep learning assisting the decision making process especially when it comes to a highly complex high-dimensional decision space, deep reinforcement learning as an AI subfield has gained tremendous momentum in the AI community over the last decade. Due to the dynamic and interactive nature of the portfolio optimization problem, deep reinforcement learning appears to be one of the top choices of how to frame and solve the problem. There are at least three most popular frameworks of solutions to dynamic portfolio optimization problems:

1. Mean Variance: the set of investments that yield the highest potential mean excess return for any given level of risk as the efficient frontier

2. Kelly Criterion: maximize the expected geometric growth rate of a portfolio

3. Risk Parity: assign weights that are inversely proportional to a portfolio component's return volatility to equalize risk from different portfolio components

All of the three criteria collapse into the same criterion under some conditions on return correlation and Sharpe ratio in reality, indicative of potential universal ("model-free") solutions for portfolio optimization. There are two major camps of reinforcement learning methods: value-based, and policy-based.

Value-based reinforcement learning methods learn the optimal state-action value function. Given a current state of the world, and a potential action, the value-based method works out what the corresponding outcome would be. For instance, given the current state of the stock market prices, or index fund returns, as well as a potential trading action one could partake in, what would be the potential rate of return? Such an outcome "value" function is often denoted as the Q function and such a framework is often termed Q-Learning. Deep learning (deep neural networks) has been shown to be particularly effective in learning such complex dynamics, when incorporated into a Q-learning framework, it is aptly dubbed as deep Q-learning or deep Q-networks.

Taking stock in human and animal behavior, as the theory of reinforcement learning is deeply rooted in psychological and neuroscientific perspectives on animal behaviour, of how agents may optimize their control of an environment. In a recently published *Nature* article [Schrittwieser et al., 2020], a dozen researchers at Google DeepMind developed an artificial agent called deep Q-networks by leveraging recent advances in training deep neural networks. It can learn successful policies directly from high-dimensional sensory inputs using end-to-end reinforcement learning. DeepMind researchers tested this agent on the challenging domain of classic Atari 2600 games, and demonstrated that the deep Q-network agent, receiving only the pixels and the game score as inputs, was able to surpass the performance of all previous algorithms and achieve a level comparable to that of a professional human games tester across a set of 49 games, using the same algorithm, network architecture and hyperparameters. This work bridged the divide between high-dimensional sensory inputs and actions, resulting in the first artificial agent that is capable of learning to excel at a diverse array of challenging tasks.

The biggest disadvantage of the valued-based reinforcement learning methods (such as Q-Learning) is curse of dimensionality that arises from large state and action spaces — meaning too many possible actions and immediate results from the actions to be taken into consideration, making it difficult for the agent to efficiently explore large action spaces. Various methods have been proposed to reduce the number of potential actions one could take for agents to investigate thoroughly, the resulting performance tend to vary significantly depending on the type of the outcome value function (Q function) or the type of performance metric, the length of stock price history, and the volatility penalty in the reward. Random noise from how the agent chooses his actions, from how the outcome would turn out, how we measure the outcome, from how we only observe part of the bigger environment we are in, and data collection could all lead to instability of agent's selection of the optimal strategy, thus resulting in volatility of the portfolio performance.

In policy-based methods, the policy itself is directly optimized to represent the optimal portfolio management policy.

A policy-based reinforcement-learning-based portfolio management framework [Cong et al., 2020] was recently proposed as an alternative that improves upon the traditional two-step portfolio-construction paradigm a la Markowitz portfolio theory, to directly optimize investors' objectives. By augmenting deep neural networks such as Transformer (reviewed in Section 7.4) with a novel cross-asset attention mechanism (also reviewed in Section 7.4) to effectively capture the high-dimensional, non-linear, noisy, interacting, and dynamic nature of economic data and market environment. The resulting performance outshines existing traditional approaches even after imposing various economic and trading restrictions, with a particular module tailored for greater transparency and interpretation. Therefore by obtaining the "economic distillations" from model transparency and interpretation, key characteristics and topics that drive investment performance could be revealed.

Another group of researchers at University of Illinois at Urbana Champaign and IBM designed a policy-based deep reinforcement learning framework [Ye et al., 2020] tailored for financial portfolio management where the input data is highly diverse and unstructured — news articles, social media, earnings report, and where the investment environment is highly uncertain — the financial market being volatile and non-stationary. With their proposed reinforcement learning method, asset information is augmented with price movement prediction where the prediction can be based entirely on asset prices or derived from alternative information sources such as news articles, upon which the best portfolio is chosen dynamically in real time. Such methods have been shown to shine in terms of effectiveness compared to standard reinforcement-learning based portfolio management approaches (and other traditional portfolio management approaches) in terms of both accumulated profits and risk-adjusted profits.

Unlike value-based reinforcement learning methods, policy-based methods can be applied directly to large action and outcome spaces, whereas the challenge here lies in approximating the optimal policy with deep learning methods, which has been shown to be largely unstable due to susceptibility to overfitting[59].

According to Ashby's Law of Requisite Variety, if a system is to be stable, the number of states of its control mechanism must be greater than or equal to the number of states in the system being controlled. Experience replay, originally used in the DeepMind's deep Q-network, has the advantage of reducing sequential or temporal correlations in samples, but still couldn't take into account many other possible states. Unlike model-free reinforcement learning introduced above, model-based reinforcement learning methods can simulate transitions using a learned model, leading to increased sample efficiency and stability. For the portfolio optimization problem, model-based

[59]Overfitting is a concept in statistics, which occurs when a statistical model fits exactly against its training data. When this happens, the algorithm cannot generalize with respect to unseen data, defeating its purpose. Generalization of a model to new data is ultimately what allows us to use machine learning algorithms every day to make predictions and classify data.

reinforcement learning methods have also been proposed, where synthetic market data were generated to cope with sample inefficiency and alleviate potential overfitting. More specifically, multidimensional time-series data (i.e., the highest, lowest, and closing prices) were generated to train the models in an imitation learning framework, offering promising results.

All of the above deep learning methods we discussed appear to be based on the assumption that the past asset return is a good predictor of the future asset return, whereas in reality, asset prices behave rather independently of their past performance, thus the past is perhaps not a good indicator of the future at all in the financial markets. The models trained on past financial data would suffer from underspecification — outcome spaces being an underrepresentation of the market environment, with insufficient information for the agent to learn the optimal policy. Therefore, a more efficient and detailed state representation with more informative features such as fundamentals data or market sentiment data that have been shown to exhibit predictive power of future returns, could be fruitful. In addition, domain knowledge certainly still matters in feature engineering and selection, as well as improving the interpretability of deep learning methods.

Interpretability of deep learning models is especially relevant to the portfolio optimization problem, since institutional investors do not want to risk a large amount of capital in a model that cannot be explained by financial or economic theories, nor in a model for which the human portfolio manager cannot be responsible. Deep learning enabled by deep neural networks had been notorious for being a "black box" as their hidden layers exhibit many-to-many complex relationships, even though in the most recent decade, interpretable AI has gone a long way to make things more transparent.

Lastly, there is this well-known credit assignment problem in reinforcement learning where the consequences of the agent's actions only materialize after many steps and transitions of the environment thus it is difficult to pinpoint which actions caused which outcomes, is another potential point of contention in the context of portfolio optimization. Despite always choosing the return maximizing (or whatever the objective is) action, the structure of credit assignment can change over time due to the non-ergodicity of the financial markets in that the price processes converge in distribution, but the limiting distribution is not necessarily uniquely determined, which brings unknown uncertainty, potentially causing the agent to learn in effect a random policy.

14.4 Natural Language Processing for Finance

One of the important components of behavioral finance is emotion or investor sentiment. Given that sentiment extraction or sentiment analysis has been a classic problem in natural language processing for which a wealth of methods have proved to be highly accurate, there has been a growing interest in financial sentiment analysis, in automatic understanding of financial statements, analyst reports, disclosures, conference calls, news articles, social media, etc. There has also been a body of research in finance devoted to forecasting with financial sentiment analysis. Emotions or sentiments extracted from various sources have been used to either complement or replace traditional pricing models with rather promising results. Sometimes sentiments were used as inputs to deep learning models for predicting prices and returns, upon which optimal portfolio selections could be implemented. Besides financial sentiment analysis, natural language processing or more specifically information retrieval has been used to detect different event types from financial news articles to complement stock prices to predict stock movements, co-movements, intraday directional movement, etc. In another line of work, social media news were used to predict index or stock prices and directions with topics identified from the news. In addition, state-of-the-art language models and contextualized word or sentence embeddings (See Section 7.4) have proved highly effective in financial applications too.

Various deep learning methods have been vetted and compared for each and every relevant application in finance: evaluating bank risks, return on assets, information content polarity, besides financial sentiment analysis, based on news, blogs, tweets, emojis, financial statements, etc. There appears no obvious winner in all scenarios, and it requires a non-trivial amount of tweaking with certain domain knowledge to combine or choose between deep learning methods to ensure the optimal performance for the task at hand.

Lastly, the character sequences in financial transactions and the responses from the other side has also been used to detect fraudulent transactions, insurance fraud, market-moving events, and bank stress, sometimes coupled with fundamental data and sentiments and emotions extracted from news articles and social media, with the help of deep learning based methods.

SECTION 15

References

[icr, 2017] (2017). Microsoft and icrisat's intelligent cloud pilot for agriculture in andhra pradesh increase crop yield for farmers.

[Agarwal et al., 2019] Agarwal, A., Zaitsev, I., Wang, X., Li, C., Najork, M., and Joachims, T. (2019). Estimating position bias without intrusive interventions. In *Proceedings of the Twelfth ACM International Conference on Web Search and Data Mining*, pages 474–482.

[Akata et al., 2016] Akata, Z., Malinowski, M., Fritz, M., and Schiele, B. (2016). Multi-cue zero-shot learning with strong supervision.

In *Proceedings of the IEEE Conference on Computer Vision and Pattern Recognition*, pages 59–68.

[Akata et al., 2013] Akata, Z., Perronnin, F., Harchaoui, Z., and Schmid, C. (2013). Label-embedding for attribute-based classification. In *Proceedings of the IEEE conference on computer vision and pattern recognition*, pages 819–826.

[Akata et al., 2015] Akata, Z., Reed, S., Walter, D., Lee, H., and Schiele, B. (2015). Evaluation of output embeddings for fine-grained image classification. In *Proceedings of the IEEE conference on computer vision and pattern recognition*, pages 2927–2936.

[Ali and Nauges, 2003] Ali, H. H. and Nauges, C. (2003). Vente en primeur et investissement: une étude sur les grands crus de bordeaux. *Economie prevision*, (3):93–103.

[Aloysius et al., 2016] Aloysius, J., Deck, C., Hao, L., and French, R. (2016). An experimental investigation of procurement auctions with asymmetric sellers. *Production and Operations Management*, 25(10):1763–1777.

[Anderson et al., 2021] Anderson, C., Teuscher, A., Anderson, E., Larsen, A., Shirley, J., and Farrell, R. (2021). Have fun storming the castle(s)! In *Proceedings of the IEEE/CVF Winter Conference on Applications of Computer Vision (WACV)*, pages 3703–3712.

[Andreas et al., 2017] Andreas, J., Klein, D., and Levine, S. (2017). Modular multitask reinforcement learning with policy sketches. In *International Conference on Machine Learning*, pages 166–175. PMLR.

[Andrychowicz et al., 2016] Andrychowicz, M., Denil, M., Colmenarejo, S. G., Hoffman, M. W., Pfau, D., Schaul, T., Shillingford, B., and de Freitas, N. (2016). Learning to learn by gradient descent by gradient descent. In *Proceedings of the 30th International Conference on Neural Information Processing Systems*, pages 3988–3996.

[Ariely et al., 2005] Ariely, D., Ockenfels, A., and Roth, A. E. (2005). An experimental analysis of ending rules in internet auctions. *RAND Journal of Economics*, pages 890–907.

[Ariely and Simonson, 2003] Ariely, D. and Simonson, I. (2003). Buying, bidding, playing, or competing? value assessment and decision dynamics in online auctions. *Journal of Consumer psychology*, 13(1-2):113–123.

[Arjovsky et al., 2017] Arjovsky, M., Chintala, S., and Bottou, L. (2017). Wasserstein generative adversarial networks. In *International conference on machine learning*, pages 214–223. PMLR.

[Ash et al., 2019] Ash, J. T., Zhang, C., Krishnamurthy, A., Langford, J., and Agarwal, A. (2019). Deep batch active learning by diverse, uncertain gradient lower bounds. *arXiv preprint arXiv:1906.03671*.

[Atzmon and Chechik, 2018] Atzmon, Y. and Chechik, G. (2018). Probabilistic and-or attribute grouping for zero-shot learning. *arXiv preprint arXiv:1806.02664*.

[Atzmon and Chechik, 2019] Atzmon, Y. and Chechik, G. (2019). Adaptive confidence smoothing for generalized zero-shot learning. In *Proceedings of the IEEE/CVF Conference on Computer Vision and Pattern Recognition*, pages 11671–11680.

[Aytaç et al., 2016] Aytaç, B., Mandou, C., et al. (2016). Wine: To drink or invest in? a study of wine as an investment asset in french portfolios. *Research in International Business and Finance*, 36:591–614.

[Bailey et al., 1963] Bailey, M. J., Muth, R. F., and Nourse, H. O. (1963). A regression method for real estate price index construction. *Journal of the American Statistical Association*, 58(304):933–942.

[Bentzen et al., 2002] Bentzen, J., Smith, V., and Leth-Sorensen, S. (2002). *Prices of French Icon Wines and the Business Cycle: Empirical Evidence from Danish Wine Auctions.* Centre for International Economic Studies.

[Berg et al., 2014] Berg, T., Liu, J., Woo Lee, S., Alexander, M. L., Jacobs, D. W., and Belhumeur, P. N. (2014). Birdsnap: Large-scale fine-grained visual categorization of birds. In *Proceedings of the IEEE Conference on Computer Vision and Pattern Recognition*, pages 2011–2018.

[Bianchi et al., 2020a] Bianchi, F., Terragni, S., and Hovy, D. (2020a). Pre-training is a hot topic: Contextualized document embeddings improve topic coherence. *arXiv preprint arXiv:2004.03974.*

[Bianchi et al., 2020b] Bianchi, F., Terragni, S., Hovy, D., Nozza, D., and Fersini, E. (2020b). Cross-lingual contextualized topic models with zero-shot learning. *arXiv preprint arXiv:2004.07737.*

[Bouri, 2015] Bouri, E. I. (2015). Fine wine as an alternative investment during equity market downturns. *The Journal of Alternative Investments*, 17(4):46–57.

[Bouri and Roubaud, 2016] Bouri, E. I. and Roubaud, D. (2016). Fine wines and stocks from the perspective of uk investors: Hedge or safe haven? *Journal of Wine Economics*, 11(2):233–248.

[Brown et al., 2020] Brown, T. B., Mann, B., Ryder, N., Subbiah, M., Kaplan, J., Dhariwal, P., Neelakantan, A., Shyam, P., Sastry, G., Askell, A., et al. (2020). Language models are few-shot learners. *arXiv preprint arXiv:2005.14165.*

[Bruni and Van Natta, 2000] Bruni, F. and Van Natta, D. (2000). The 2000 campaign: The inquity; f.b.i. widens investigation into debate leak. *The New York Times.*

[Burton and Jacobsen, 2001] Burton, B. J. and Jacobsen, J. P. (2001). The rate of return on investment in wine. In *World Scientific Reference on Handbook of the Economics of Wine: Volume 1: Prices, Finance, and Expert Opinion*, pages 247–270. World Scientific.

[Byron and Ashenfelter, 1995] Byron, R. P. and Ashenfelter, O. (1995). Predicting the quality of an unborn grange. *Economic Record*, 71(1):40–53.

[Cai et al., 2012] Cai, Y., Daskalakis, C., and Weinberg, S. M. (2012). Optimal multi-dimensional mechanism design: Reducing revenue to welfare maximization. In *2012 IEEE 53rd Annual Symposium on Foundations of Computer Science*, pages 130–139. IEEE.

[Cai et al., 2013] Cai, Y., Daskalakis, C., and Weinberg, S. M. (2013). Understanding incentives: Mechanism design becomes algorithm design. In *2013 IEEE 54th Annual Symposium on Foundations of Computer Science*, pages 618–627. IEEE.

[Cakir et al., 2019] Cakir, F., He, K., Xia, X., Kulis, B., and Sclaroff, S. (2019). Deep metric learning to rank. In *Proceedings of the IEEE/CVF Conference on Computer Vision and Pattern Recognition*, pages 1861–1870.

[Caliendo and Kopeinig, 2008] Caliendo, M. and Kopeinig, S. (2008). Some practical guidance for the implementation of propensity score matching. *Journal of economic surveys*, 22(1):31–72.

[Chang et al., 2019] Chang, M. B., Levine, S., Gupta, A., and Griffiths, T. L. (2019). Automatically composing representation transformations as a means for generalization. In *7th International Conference on Learning Representations, ICLR 2019*.

[Changpinyo et al., 2016] Changpinyo, S., Chao, W.-L., Gong, B., and Sha, F. (2016). Synthesized classifiers for zero-shot learning. In *Proceedings of the IEEE conference on computer vision and pattern recognition*, pages 5327–5336.

[Changpinyo et al., 2017] Changpinyo, S., Chao, W.-L., and Sha, F. (2017). Predicting visual exemplars of unseen classes for zero-shot learning. In *Proceedings of the IEEE international conference on computer vision*, pages 3476–3485.

[Chao et al., 2016] Chao, W.-L., Changpinyo, S., Gong, B., and Sha, F. (2016). An empirical study and analysis of generalized zero-shot learning for object recognition in the wild. In *European conference on computer vision*, pages 52–68. Springer.

[Chen et al., 2017] Chen, D., Fisch, A., Weston, J., and Bordes, A. (2017). Reading wikipedia to answer open-domain questions. In *Proceedings of the 55th Annual Meeting of the Association for Computational Linguistics (Volume 1: Long Papers)*, pages 1870–1879.

[Chen et al., 2020] Chen, J., Lécué, F., Geng, Y., Pan, J. Z., and Chen, H. (2020). Ontology-guided semantic composition for zero-shot learning. In *Proceedings of the International Conference on Principles of Knowledge Representation and Reasoning*, volume 17, pages 850–854.

[Chen et al., 2012] Chen, S., Moore, J. L., Turnbull, D., and Joachims, T. (2012). Playlist prediction via metric embedding. In *Proceedings of the 18th ACM SIGKDD international conference on Knowledge discovery and data mining*, pages 714–722.

[Chen et al., 2018] Chen, Z., Badrinarayanan, V., Lee, C.-Y., and Rabinovich, A. (2018). Gradnorm: Gradient normalization for adaptive loss balancing in deep multitask networks. In *International Conference on Machine Learning*, pages 794–803. PMLR.

[Cho et al., 2014] Cho, K., Van Merriënboer, B., Bahdanau, D., and Bengio, Y. (2014). On the properties of neural machine translation: Encoder-decoder approaches. *arXiv preprint arXiv:1409.1259.*

[Cong et al., 2020] Cong, L. W., Tang, K., Wang, J., and Zhang, Y. (2020). Alphaportfolio for investment and economically interpretable ai. *SSRN, https://papers. ssrn. com/sol3/papers. cfm.*

[Conitzer and Sandholm, 2002] Conitzer, V. and Sandholm, T. (2002). Complexity of mechanism design. In *Proceedings of the Eighteenth conference on Uncertainty in artificial intelligence*, pages 103–110.

[Cox et al., 1982] Cox, J. C., Roberson, B., and Smith, V. L. (1982). Theory and behavior of single object auctions. *Research in experimental economics*, 2(1):1–43.

[Cox et al., 1983] Cox, J. C., Smith, V. L., and Walker, J. M. (1983). A test that discriminates between two models of the dutch-first auction non-isomorphism. *Journal of Economic Behavior & Organization*, 4(2-3):205–219.

[Cox et al., 1988] Cox, J. C., Smith, V. L., and Walker, J. M. (1988). Theory and individual behavior of first-price auctions. *Journal of Risk and uncertainty*, 1(1):61–99.

[Cubuk et al., 2018] Cubuk, E. D., Zoph, B., Mane, D., Vasudevan, V., and Le, Q. V. (2018). Autoaugment: Learning augmentation policies from data. *arXiv preprint arXiv:1805.09501.*

[Davis et al., 2011] Davis, A. M., Katok, E., and Kwasnica, A. M. (2011). Do auctioneers pick optimal reserve prices? *Management Science*, 57(1):177–192.

[Deng et al., 2009] Deng, J., Dong, W., Socher, R., Li, L.-J., Li, K., and Fei-Fei, L. (2009). Imagenet: A large-scale hierarchical image database. In *2009 IEEE conference on computer vision and pattern recognition*, pages 248–255. Ieee.

[Deng et al., 2019] Deng, J., Guo, J., Xue, N., and Zafeiriou, S. (2019). Arcface: Additive angular margin loss for deep face recognition. In *Proceedings of the IEEE/CVF Conference on Computer Vision and Pattern Recognition*, pages 4690–4699.

[Devlin et al., 2019] Devlin, J., Chang, M.-W., Lee, K., and Toutanova, K. (2019). Bert: Pre-training of deep bidirectional transformers for language understanding. In *Proceedings of the 2019 Conference of the North American Chapter of the Association for Computational Linguistics: Human Language Technologies, Volume 1 (Long and Short Papers)*, pages 4171–4186.

[Dholakia and Simonson, 2005] Dholakia, U. M. and Simonson, I. (2005). The effect of explicit reference points on consumer choice and online bidding behavior. *Marketing Science*, 24(2):206–217.

[Dholakia and Soltysinski, 2001] Dholakia, U. M. and Soltysinski, K. (2001). Coveted or overlooked? the psychology of bidding for comparable listings in digital auctions. *Marketing Letters*, 12(3):225–237.

[Dieng et al., 2020] Dieng, A. B., Ruiz, F. J., and Blei, D. (2020). Topic modeling in embedding spaces. *Transactions of the Association for Computational Linguistics*, 8:439–453.

[Dimson et al., 2015] Dimson, E., Rousseau, P. L., and Spaenjers, C. (2015). The price of wine. *Journal of Financial Economics*, 118(2):431–449.

[Dorie et al., 2019] Dorie, V., Hill, J., Shalit, U., Scott, M., and Cervone, D. (2019). Automated versus do-it-yourself methods for causal inference: Lessons learned from a data analysis competition. *Statistical Science*, 34(1):43–68.

[Dosovitskiy et al., 2020] Dosovitskiy, A., Beyer, L., Kolesnikov, A., Weissenborn, D., Zhai, X., Unterthiner, T., Dehghani, M., Minderer, M., Heigold, G., Gelly, S., et al. (2020). An image is worth 16x16 words: Transformers for image recognition at scale. *arXiv preprint arXiv:2010.11929*.

[Du et al., 2017] Du, X., Shao, J., and Cardie, C. (2017). Learning to ask: Neural question generation for reading comprehension. In *Proceedings of the 55th Annual Meeting of the Association for Computational Linguistics (Volume 1: Long Papers)*, pages 1342–1352.

[Duan et al., 2017] Duan, N., Tang, D., Chen, P., and Zhou, M. (2017). Question generation for question answering. In *Proceedings of the 2017 Conference on Empirical Methods in Natural Language Processing*, pages 866–874.

[Duan et al., 2018] Duan, Y., Zheng, W., Lin, X., Lu, J., and Zhou, J. (2018). Deep adversarial metric learning. In *Proceedings of the IEEE Conference on Computer Vision and Pattern Recognition*, pages 2780–2789.

[Ducoffe and Precioso, 2018] Ducoffe, M. and Precioso, F. (2018). Adversarial active learning for deep networks: a margin based approach. *arXiv preprint arXiv:1802.09841*.

[Duthy, 1986] Duthy, R. (1986). *The Successful Investor: A Guide to Art, Gold, Wine, Antiques and Other Growth Markets.* Collins.

[Dütting et al., 2019] Dütting, P., Feng, Z., Narasimhan, H., Parkes, D., and Ravindranath, S. S. (2019). Optimal auctions through deep learning. In *International Conference on Machine Learning*, pages 1706–1715. PMLR.

[Edunov et al., 2018] Edunov, S., Ott, M., Auli, M., and Grangier, D. (2018). Understanding back-translation at scale. In *Proceedings of the 2018 Conference on Empirical Methods in Natural Language Processing*, pages 489–500.

[Elmaghraby et al., 2012] Elmaghraby, W. J., Katok, E., and Santamaría, N. (2012). A laboratory investigation of rank feedback in procurement auctions. *Manufacturing & Service Operations Management*, 14(1):128–144.

[Engelbrecht-Wiggans and Katok, 2007] Engelbrecht-Wiggans, R. and Katok, E. (2007). Regret in auctions: Theory and evidence. *Economic Theory*, 33(1):81–101.

[Engelbrecht-Wiggans and Katok, 2009] Engelbrecht-Wiggans, R. and Katok, E. (2009). A direct test of risk aversion and regret in first price sealed-bid auctions. *Decision Analysis*, 6(2):75–86.

[Faye and Le Fur, 2019] Faye, B. and Le Fur, E. (2019). On the constancy of hedonic wine price coefficients over time. *Journal of Wine Economics*, 14(2):182–207.

[Feldman and El-Yaniv, 2019] Feldman, Y. and El-Yaniv, R. (2019). Multi-hop paragraph retrieval for open-domain question answering. In *Proceedings of the 57th Annual Meeting of the Association for Computational Linguistics*, pages 2296–2309.

[Feng et al., 2019] Feng, Y., Cui, N., Hao, W., Gao, L., and Gong, D. (2019). Estimation of soil temperature from meteorological data using different machine learning models. *Geoderma*, 338:67–77.

[Finke et al., 1992] Finke, R. A., Ward, T. B., and Smith, S. M. (1992). Creative cognition: Theory, research, and applications.

[Finn et al., 2017] Finn, C., Abbeel, P., and Levine, S. (2017). Model-agnostic meta-learning for fast adaptation of deep networks. In *International Conference on Machine Learning*, pages 1126–1135. PMLR.

[Fogarty, 2005] Fogarty, J. (2005). *Wine investment, pricing and substitutes*. University of Western Australia.

[Fogarty, 2006] Fogarty, J. J. (2006). The return to australian fine wine. *European Review of Agricultural Economics*, 33(4):542–561.

[Fogarty et al., 2014] Fogarty, J. J., Sadler, R., et al. (2014). To save or savor: A review of approaches for measuring wine as an investment. *Journal of Wine Economics*, 9(3):225–248.

[Fornaciari et al., 2013] Fornaciari, T., Celli, F., and Poesio, M. (2013). The effect of personality type on deceptive communication style. In *2013 European Intelligence and Security Informatics Conference*, pages 1–6. IEEE.

[Frome et al., 2013] Frome, A., Corrado, G., Shlens, J., Bengio, S., Dean, J., Ranzato, M., and Mikolov, T. (2013). Devise: A deep visual-semantic embedding model.

[Fu et al., 2015a] Fu, Y., Hospedales, T. M., Xiang, T., and Gong, S. (2015a). Transductive multi-view zero-shot learning. *IEEE transactions on pattern analysis and machine intelligence*, 37(11):2332–2345.

[Fu et al., 2015b] Fu, Z., Xiang, T., Kodirov, E., and Gong, S. (2015b). Zero-shot object recognition by semantic manifold distance. In *Proceedings of the IEEE conference on computer vision and pattern recognition*, pages 2635–2644.

[Gal et al., 2017] Gal, Y., Islam, R., and Ghahramani, Z. (2017). Deep bayesian active learning with image data. In *International Conference on Machine Learning*, pages 1183–1192. PMLR.

[Gao et al., 2020a] Gao, R., Hou, X., Qin, J., Chen, J., Liu, L., Zhu, F., Zhang, Z., and Shao, L. (2020a). Zero-vae-gan: Generating unseen features for generalized and transductive zero-shot learning. *IEEE Transactions on Image Processing*, 29:3665–3680.

[Gao et al., 2018] Gao, R., Hou, X., Qin, J., Liu, L., Zhu, F., and Zhang, Z. (2018). A joint generative model for zero-shot learning. In *Proceedings of the European Conference on Computer Vision (ECCV) Workshops*, pages 0–0.

[Gao et al., 2020b] Gao, Y., Bai, H., Jie, Z., Ma, J., Jia, K., and Liu, W. (2020b). Mtl-nas: Task-agnostic neural architecture search towards general-purpose multi-task learning. In *Proceedings of the IEEE/CVF Conference on Computer Vision and Pattern Recognition*, pages 11543–11552.

[Gao et al., 2019] Gao, Y., Ma, J., Zhao, M., Liu, W., and Yuille, A. L. (2019). Nddr-cnn: Layerwise feature fusing in multi-task cnns by neural discriminative dimensionality reduction. In *Proceedings of the IEEE/CVF Conference on Computer Vision and Pattern Recognition*, pages 3205–3214.

[Ge, 2018] Ge, W. (2018). Deep metric learning with hierarchical triplet loss. In *Proceedings of the European Conference on Computer Vision (ECCV)*, pages 269–285.

[Geng et al., 2021] Geng, Y., Chen, J., Chen, Z., Pan, J. Z., Ye, Z., Yuan, Z., Jia, Y., and Chen, H. (2021). Ontozsl: Ontology-enhanced zero-shot learning. In *Proceedings of the Web Conference 2021*, pages 3325–3336.

[Giannakopoulos and Koutsoupias, 2014] Giannakopoulos, Y. and Koutsoupias, E. (2014). Duality and optimality of auctions for uniform distributions. In *Proceedings of the fifteenth ACM conference on Economics and computation*, pages 259–276.

[Giora, 2003] Giora, R. (2003). *On our mind: Salience, context, and figurative language.* Oxford University Press.

[Goodfellow et al., 2016] Goodfellow, I., Bengio, Y., and Courville, A. (2016). *Deep learning.* MIT press.

[Goodfellow et al., 2014] Goodfellow, I., Pouget-Abadie, J., Mirza, M., Xu, B., Warde-Farley, D., Ozair, S., Courville, A., and Bengio, Y. (2014). Generative adversarial nets. *Advances in neural information processing systems*, 27.

[Gori et al., 2007] Gori, M., Pucci, A., Roma, V., and Siena, I. (2007). Itemrank: A random-walk based scoring algorithm for recommender engines. In *IJCAI*, volume 7, pages 2766–2771.

[Gulrajani et al., 2017] Gulrajani, I., Ahmed, F., Arjovsky, M., Dumoulin, V., and Courville, A. (2017). Improved training of wasserstein gans. *arXiv preprint arXiv:1704.00028.*

[Guo et al., 2020] Guo, D., Kim, Y., and Rush, A. (2020). Sequence-level mixed sample data augmentation. In *Proceedings of the 2020 Conference on Empirical Methods in Natural Language Processing (EMNLP)*, pages 5547–5552, Online. Association for Computational Linguistics.

[Guo and Conitzer, 2010] Guo, M. and Conitzer, V. (2010). Computationally feasible automated mechanism design: General approach and case studies. In *Proceedings of the AAAI Conference on Artificial Intelligence*, volume 24.

[Guo et al., 2018] Guo, M., Haque, A., Huang, D.-A., Yeung, S., and Fei-Fei, L. (2018). Dynamic task prioritization for multitask learning. In *Proceedings of the European Conference on Computer Vision (ECCV)*, pages 270–287.

[Guo et al., 2016] Guo, Y., Ding, G., Jin, X., and Wang, J. (2016). Transductive zero-shot recognition via shared model space learning. In *Proceedings of the AAAI Conference on Artificial Intelligence*, volume 30.

[Guu et al., 2020] Guu, K., Lee, K., Tung, Z., Pasupat, P., and Chang, M. (2020). Retrieval augmented language model pre-training. In *International Conference on Machine Learning*, pages 3929–3938. PMLR.

[Hadsell et al., 2006] Hadsell, R., Chopra, S., and LeCun, Y. (2006). Dimensionality reduction by learning an invariant mapping. In *2006 IEEE Computer Society Conference on Computer Vision and Pattern Recognition (CVPR'06)*, volume 2, pages 1735–1742. IEEE.

[Hamilton et al., 2017] Hamilton, W. L., Ying, R., and Leskovec, J. (2017). Inductive representation learning on large graphs. In *Proceedings of the 31st International Conference on Neural Information Processing Systems*, pages 1025–1035.

[He et al., 2016] He, K., Zhang, X., Ren, S., and Sun, J. (2016). Deep residual learning for image recognition. In *Proceedings of the IEEE conference on computer vision and pattern recognition*, pages 770–778.

[Hein et al., 2019] Hein, M., Andriushchenko, M., and Bitterwolf, J. (2019). Why relu networks yield high-confidence predictions far away from the training data and how to mitigate the problem. In *Proceedings of the IEEE/CVF Conference on Computer Vision and Pattern Recognition*, pages 41–50.

[Herlands et al., 2018] Herlands, W., McFowland III, E., Wilson, A. G., and Neill, D. B. (2018). Automated local regression discontinuity design discovery. In *Proceedings of the 24th ACM SIGKDD International Conference on Knowledge Discovery & Data Mining*, pages 1512–1520.

[Hinton and Roweis, 2002] Hinton, G. and Roweis, S. T. (2002). Stochastic neighbor embedding. In *NIPS*, volume 15, pages 833–840. Citeseer.

[Hinton et al., 2011] Hinton, G. E., Krizhevsky, A., and Wang, S. D. (2011). Transforming auto-encoders. In *International conference on artificial neural networks*, pages 44–51. Springer.

[Hinton et al., 2018] Hinton, G. E., Sabour, S., and Frosst, N. (2018). Matrix capsules with em routing. In *International conference on learning representations*.

[Hinton et al., 2012] Hinton, G. E., Srivastava, N., Krizhevsky, A., Sutskever, I., and Salakhutdinov, R. R. (2012). Improving neural networks by preventing co-adaptation of feature detectors. *arXiv preprint arXiv:1207.0580*.

[Hochreiter and Schmidhuber, 1997] Hochreiter, S. and Schmidhuber, J. (1997). Long short-term memory. *Neural computation*, 9(8):1735–1780.

[Hongsuck Seo et al., 2018] Hongsuck Seo, P., Weyand, T., Sim, J., and Han, B. (2018). Cplanet: Enhancing image geolocalization by combinatorial partitioning of maps. In *Proceedings of the European Conference on Computer Vision (ECCV)*, pages 536–551.

[Hou et al., 2017] Hou, S., Feng, Y., and Wang, Z. (2017). Vegfru: A domain-specific dataset for fine-grained visual categorization. In *Proceedings of the IEEE International Conference on Computer Vision*, pages 541–549.

[Hu et al., 2019] Hu, M., Wei, F., Peng, Y., Huang, Z., Yang, N., and Li, D. (2019). Read+ verify: Machine reading comprehension with unanswerable questions. In *Proceedings of the AAAI Conference on Artificial Intelligence*, volume 33, pages 6529–6537.

[Huang et al., 2017a] Huang, G., Liu, Z., Van Der Maaten, L., and Weinberger, K. Q. (2017a). Densely connected convolutional networks. In *Proceedings of the IEEE conference on computer vision and pattern recognition*, pages 4700–4708.

[Huang et al., 2017b] Huang, X., Li, Y., Poursaeed, O., Hopcroft, J., and Belongie, S. (2017b). Stacked generative adversarial networks. In *Proceedings of the IEEE conference on computer vision and pattern recognition*, pages 5077–5086.

[Huynh and Elhamifar, 2020] Huynh, D. and Elhamifar, E. (2020). Fine-grained generalized zero-shot learning via dense attribute-based attention. In *Proceedings of the IEEE/CVF Conference on Computer Vision and Pattern Recognition*, pages 4483–4493.

[Iacus et al., 2012] Iacus, S. M., King, G., and Porro, G. (2012). Causal inference without balance checking: Coarsened exact matching. *Political analysis*, 20(1):1–24.

[Inoue, 2018] Inoue, H. (2018). Data augmentation by pairing samples for images classification. *arXiv preprint arXiv:1801.02929*.

[Jap, 2002] Jap, S. D. (2002). Online reverse auctions: Issues, themes, and prospects for the future. *Journal of the Academy of Marketing Science*, 30(4):506–525.

[Jap, 2007] Jap, S. D. (2007). The impact of online reverse auction design on buyer–supplier relationships. *Journal of Marketing*, 71(1):146–159.

[Jean et al., 2019] Jean, S., Firat, O., and Johnson, M. (2019). Adaptive scheduling for multi-task learning.

[Jiang et al., 2018] Jiang, H., Wang, R., Shan, S., and Chen, X. (2018). Learning class prototypes via structure alignment for zero-shot recognition. In *Proceedings of the European conference on computer vision (ECCV)*, pages 118–134.

[Joachims et al., 2017] Joachims, T., Swaminathan, A., and Schnabel, T. (2017). Unbiased learning-to-rank with biased feedback. In *Proceedings of the Tenth ACM International Conference on Web Search and Data Mining*, pages 781–789.

[Johann et al., 2016] Johann, A. L., de Araújo, A. G., Delalibera, H. C., and Hirakawa, A. R. (2016). Soil moisture modeling based on stochastic behavior of forces on a no-till chisel opener. *Computers and Electronics in Agriculture*, 121:420–428.

[Johansson et al., 2016] Johansson, F., Shalit, U., and Sontag, D. (2016). Learning representations for counterfactual inference. In *International conference on machine learning*, pages 3020–3029. PMLR.

[Johnson et al., 2019] Johnson, J., Douze, M., and Jégou, H. (2019). Billion-scale similarity search with gpus. *IEEE Transactions on Big Data*.

[Jones and Storchmann, 2001] Jones, G. V. and Storchmann, K.-H. (2001). Wine market prices and investment under uncertainty: an econometric model for bordeaux crus classés. *Agricultural Economics*, 26(2):115–133.

[Kabbur et al., 2013] Kabbur, S., Ning, X., and Karypis, G. (2013). Fism: factored item similarity models for top-n recommender systems. In *Proceedings of the 19th ACM SIGKDD international conference on Knowledge discovery and data mining*, pages 659–667.

[Kagel et al., 2009] Kagel, J. H., Harstad, R. M., and Levin, D. (2009). Information impact and allocation rules in auctions with affiliated private values: A laboratory study. In *Common Value Auctions and the Winner's Curse*, pages 177–209. Princeton University Press.

[Kagel and Levin, 2009] Kagel, J. H. and Levin, D. (2009). Implementing efficient multi-object auction institutions: An experimental study of the performance of boundedly rational agents. *Games and Economic Behavior*, 66(1):221–237.

[Kamins et al., 2004] Kamins, M. A., Dreze, X., and Folkes, V. S. (2004). Effects of seller-supplied prices on buyers' product evaluations: Reference prices in an internet auction context. *Journal of Consumer Research*, 30(4):622–628.

[Kang and McAuley, 2018] Kang, W.-C. and McAuley, J. (2018). Self-attentive sequential recommendation. In *2018 IEEE International Conference on Data Mining (ICDM)*, pages 197–206. IEEE.

[Katok and Kwasnica, 2008] Katok, E. and Kwasnica, A. M. (2008). Time is money: The effect of clock speed on seller's revenue in dutch auctions. *Experimental Economics*, 11(4):344–357.

[Kendall and Gal, 2017] Kendall, A. and Gal, Y. (2017). What uncertainties do we need in bayesian deep learning for computer vision? *Advances in Neural Information Processing Systems*, 30:5574–5584.

[Khattab et al., 2020] Khattab, O., Potts, C., and Zaharia, M. (2020). Relevance-guided supervision for openqa with colbert. *arXiv preprint arXiv:2007.00814*.

[Khattab and Zaharia, 2020] Khattab, O. and Zaharia, M. (2020). Colbert: Efficient and effective passage search via contextualized late interaction over bert. In *Proceedings of the 43rd International ACM SIGIR Conference on Research and Development in Information Retrieval*, pages 39–48.

[Khosla et al., 2011] Khosla, A., Jayadevaprakash, N., Yao, B., and Li, F.-F. (2011). Novel dataset for fine-grained image categorization: Stanford dogs. In *Proc. CVPR Workshop on Fine-Grained Visual Categorization (FGVC)*, volume 2. Citeseer.

[Kilbertus et al., 2020] Kilbertus, N., Kusner, M., and Silva, R. (2020). A class of algorithms for general instrumental variable models. Advances in Neural Information Processing Systems (NeurIPS 2020).

[Kim et al., 2018] Kim, W., Goyal, B., Chawla, K., Lee, J., and Kwon, K. (2018). Attention-based ensemble for deep metric learning. In *Proceedings of the European Conference on Computer Vision (ECCV)*, pages 736–751.

[Kipf and Welling, 2016] Kipf, T. N. and Welling, M. (2016). Semi-supervised classification with graph convolutional networks. *arXiv preprint arXiv:1609.02907*.

[Kirsch et al., 2019] Kirsch, A., Van Amersfoort, J., and Gal, Y. (2019). Batchbald: Efficient and diverse batch acquisition for deep bayesian active learning. *Advances in neural information processing systems*, 32:7026–7037.

[Koch et al., 2015] Koch, G., Zemel, R., and Salakhutdinov, R. (2015). Siamese neural networks for one-shot image recognition. In *ICML deep learning workshop*, volume 2. Lille.

[Koren, 2008] Koren, Y. (2008). Factorization meets the neighborhood: a multifaceted collaborative filtering model. In *Proceedings of the 14th ACM SIGKDD international conference on Knowledge discovery and data mining*, pages 426–434.

[Krause et al., 2013] Krause, J., Stark, M., Deng, J., and Fei-Fei, L. (2013). 3d object representations for fine-grained categorization. In *Proceedings of the IEEE international conference on computer vision workshops*, pages 554–561.

[Krizhevsky et al., 2012] Krizhevsky, A., Sutskever, I., and Hinton, G. E. (2012). Imagenet classification with deep convolutional neural networks. *Advances in neural information processing systems*, 25:1097–1105.

[Ku et al., 2006] Ku, G., Galinsky, A. D., and Murnighan, J. K. (2006). Starting low but ending high: A reversal of the anchoring effect in auctions. *Journal of Personality and social Psychology*, 90(6):975.

[Kumar, 2005] Kumar, M. (2005). *Wine investment for portfolio diversification: How collecting fine wines can yield greater returns than stocks and bonds.* Wine Appreciation Guild.

[Kwasnica and Katok, 2007] Kwasnica, A. M. and Katok, E. (2007). The effect of timing on jump bidding in ascending auctions. *Production and Operations Management*, 16(4):483–494.

[Lampert et al., 2013] Lampert, C. H., Nickisch, H., and Harmeling, S. (2013). Attribute-based classification for zero-shot learning of object categories. *IEEE Computer Architecture Letters*, (01):1–1.

[Lebanoff et al., 2019] Lebanoff, L., Song, K., Dernoncourt, F., Kim, D. S., Kim, S., Chang, W., and Liu, F. (2019). Scoring sentence singletons and pairs for abstractive summarization. In *Proceedings of the 57th Annual Meeting of the Association for Computational Linguistics*, pages 2175–2189.

[LeCun et al., 1998] LeCun, Y., Bottou, L., Bengio, Y., and Haffner, P. (1998). Gradient-based learning applied to document recognition. *Proceedings of the IEEE*, 86(11):2278–2324.

[Lee and Lemieux, 2010] Lee, D. S. and Lemieux, T. (2010). Regression discontinuity designs in economics. *Journal of economic literature*, 48(2):281–355.

[Lee et al., 2018] Lee, H. B., Yang, E., and Hwang, S. J. (2018). Deep asymmetric multi-task feature learning. In *International Conference on Machine Learning*, pages 2956–2964. PMLR.

[Lee et al., 2019] Lee, K., Chang, M.-W., and Toutanova, K. (2019). Latent retrieval for weakly supervised open domain question answering. In *Proceedings of the 57th Annual Meeting of the Association for Computational Linguistics*, pages 6086–6096.

[Lehtiniemi, 2008] Lehtiniemi, A. (2008). Evaluating supermusic: streaming context-aware mobile music service. In *Proceedings of the 2008 international conference on Advances in Computer Entertainment Technology*, pages 314–321.

[Lei Ba et al., 2015] Lei Ba, J., Swersky, K., Fidler, S., et al. (2015). Predicting deep zero-shot convolutional neural networks using textual descriptions. In *Proceedings of the IEEE International Conference on Computer Vision*, pages 4247–4255.

[Leszczyc et al., 2009] Leszczyc, P. T. P., Qiu, C., and He, Y. (2009). Empirical testing of the reference-price effect of buy-now prices in internet auctions. *Journal of Retailing*, 85(2):211–221.

[Levitan et al., 2016] Levitan, S. I., An, G., Ma, M., Levitan, R., Rosenberg, A., and Hirschberg, J. (2016). Combining acoustic-prosodic, lexical, and phonotactic features for automatic deception detection. In *INTERSPEECH*, pages 2006–2010.

[Levitan et al., 2018] Levitan, S. I., Maredia, A., and Hirschberg, J. (2018). Linguistic cues to deception and perceived deception in interview dialogues. In *Proceedings of the 2018 Conference of the North American Chapter of the Association for Computational Linguistics: Human Language Technologies, Volume 1 (Long Papers)*, volume 1, pages 1941–1950.

[Lewis et al., 2020a] Lewis, M., Ghazvininejad, M., Ghosh, G., Aghajanyan, A., Wang, S., and Zettlemoyer, L. (2020a). Pre-training via paraphrasing. *Advances in Neural Information Processing Systems*, 33.

[Lewis et al., 2020b] Lewis, M., Liu, Y., Goyal, N., Ghazvininejad, M., Mohamed, A., Levy, O., Stoyanov, V., and Zettlemoyer, L. (2020b). Bart: Denoising sequence-to-sequence pre-training for natural language generation, translation, and comprehension. In *Proceedings of the 58th Annual Meeting of the Association for Computational Linguistics*, pages 7871–7880.

[Li et al., 2015] Li, Y., Zemel, R., Brockschmidt, M., and Tarlow, D. (2015). Gated graph sequence neural networks.

[Li et al., 2017] Li, Z., Zhou, F., Chen, F., and Li, H. (2017). Meta-sgd: Learning to learn quickly for few-shot learning. *arXiv preprint arXiv:1707.09835*.

[Liang et al., 2016] Liang, D., Charlin, L., and Blei, D. M. (2016). Causal inference for recommendation. In *Causation: Foundation to Application, Workshop at UAI. AUAI*.

[Lin et al., 2013] Lin, M., Chen, Q., and Yan, S. (2013). Network in network. *arXiv preprint arXiv:1312.4400.*

[Lin et al., 2018a] Lin, X., Duan, Y., Dong, Q., Lu, J., and Zhou, J. (2018a). Deep variational metric learning. In *Proceedings of the European Conference on Computer Vision (ECCV)*, pages 689–704.

[Lin et al., 2019] Lin, X., Zhen, H.-L., Li, Z., Zhang, Q.-F., and Kwong, S. (2019). Pareto multi-task learning. *Advances in neural information processing systems*, 32:12060–12070.

[Lin et al., 2018b] Lin, Y., Ji, H., Liu, Z., and Sun, M. (2018b). Denoising distantly supervised open-domain question answering. In *Proceedings of the 56th Annual Meeting of the Association for Computational Linguistics (Volume 1: Long Papers)*, pages 1736–1745.

[Liu et al., 2019a] Liu, S., Johns, E., and Davison, A. J. (2019a). End-to-end multi-task learning with attention. In *Proceedings of the IEEE/CVF Conference on Computer Vision and Pattern Recognition (CVPR).*

[Liu et al., 2019b] Liu, S., Johns, E., and Davison, A. J. (2019b). End-to-end multi-task learning with attention. In *Proceedings of the IEEE/CVF Conference on Computer Vision and Pattern Recognition*, pages 1871–1880.

[Liu et al., 2017] Liu, W., Wen, Y., Yu, Z., Li, M., Raj, B., and Song, L. (2017). Sphereface: Deep hypersphere embedding for face recognition. In *Proceedings of the IEEE conference on computer vision and pattern recognition*, pages 212–220.

[Logan, 2002] Logan, B. (2002). Content-based playlist generation: Exploratory experiments. In *ISMIR*, volume 2, pages 295–296.

[Logan and Salomon, 2001] Logan, B. and Salomon, A. (2001). A music similarity function based on signal analysis. In *ICME*, pages 22–25.

[Lokhande et al., 2020] Lokhande, V. S., Tasneeyapant, S., Venkatesh, A., Ravi, S. N., and Singh, V. (2020). Generating accurate pseudo-labels in semi-supervised learning and avoiding overconfident predictions via hermite polynomial activations. In *Proceedings of the IEEE/CVF Conference on Computer Vision and Pattern Recognition (CVPR)*.

[Long et al., 2017] Long, M., Cao, Z., Wang, J., and Yu, P. S. (2017). Learning multiple tasks with multilinear relationship networks. In *Proceedings of the 31st International Conference on Neural Information Processing Systems*, pages 1593–1602.

[Lopez-Paz and Ranzato, 2017] Lopez-Paz, D. and Ranzato, M. (2017). Gradient episodic memory for continual learning. *Advances in neural information processing systems*, 30:6467–6476.

[Lu et al., 2017a] Lu, J., Hu, J., and Zhou, J. (2017a). Deep metric learning for visual understanding: An overview of recent advances. *IEEE Signal Processing Magazine*, 34(6):76–84.

[Lu et al., 2017b] Lu, Y., Kumar, A., Zhai, S., Cheng, Y., Javidi, T., and Feris, R. (2017b). Fully-adaptive feature sharing in multi-task networks with applications in person attribute classification. In *Proceedings of the IEEE conference on computer vision and pattern recognition*, pages 5334–5343.

[Lucey and Devine, 2015] Lucey, B. M. and Devine, L. (2015). Was wine a premier cru investment? *Research in International Business and Finance*, 34:33–51.

[Lucking-Reiley, 1999] Lucking-Reiley, D. (1999). Using field experiments to test equivalence between auction formats: Magic on the internet. *American Economic Review*, 89(5):1063–1080.

[Maillet et al., 2009] Maillet, F., Eck, D., Desjardins, G., Lamere, P., et al. (2009). Steerable playlist generation by learning song similarity from radio station playlists. In *ISMIR*, pages 345–350. Citeseer.

[Maji et al., 2013] Maji, S., Rahtu, E., Kannala, J., Blaschko, M., and Vedaldi, A. (2013). Fine-grained visual classification of aircraft. *arXiv preprint arXiv:1306.5151*.

[Mallya et al., 2018] Mallya, A., Davis, D., and Lazebnik, S. (2018). Piggyback: Adapting a single network to multiple tasks by learning to mask weights. In *Proceedings of the European Conference on Computer Vision (ECCV)*, pages 67–82.

[Manelli and Vincent, 2006] Manelli, A. M. and Vincent, D. R. (2006). Bundling as an optimal selling mechanism for a multiple-good monopolist. *Journal of Economic Theory*, 127(1):1–35.

[Manski, 2009] Manski, C. F. (2009). *Identification for prediction and decision*. Harvard University Press.

[Maskin and Riley, 2000] Maskin, E. and Riley, J. (2000). Equilibrium in sealed high bid auctions. *The Review of Economic Studies*, 67(3):439–454.

[Masset and Henderson, 2010] Masset, P. and Henderson, C. (2010). Wine as an alternative asset class. *Journal of Wine Economics*, 5(1):87–118.

[Masset and Weisskopf, 2018] Masset, P. and Weisskopf, J.-P. (2018). Wine indices in practice: Nicely labeled but slightly corked. *Economic Modelling*, 68:555–569.

[McFee and Lanckriet, 2011] McFee, B. and Lanckriet, G. R. (2011). The natural language of playlists.

[McInnes et al., 2018] McInnes, L., Healy, J., and Melville, J. (2018). Umap: Uniform manifold approximation and projection for dimension reduction. *arXiv preprint arXiv:1802.03426.*

[Meyerson and Miikkulainen, 2018] Meyerson, E. and Miikkulainen, R. (2018). Beyond shared hierarchies: Deep multitask learning through soft layer ordering. In *International Conference on Learning Representations.*

[Mikolov et al., 2013] Mikolov, T., Chen, K., Corrado, G., and Dean, J. (2013). Efficient estimation of word representations in vector space. *arXiv preprint arXiv:1301.3781.*

[Min et al., 2017] Min, S., Chen, D., Zettlemoyer, L., and Hajishirzi, H. (2017). Knowledge guided text retrieval and reading for open domain question answering.

[Mirza and Osindero, 2014] Mirza, M. and Osindero, S. (2014). Conditional generative adversarial nets. *arXiv preprint arXiv:1411.1784.*

[Misra et al., 2016] Misra, I., Shrivastava, A., Gupta, A., and Hebert, M. (2016). Cross-stitch networks for multi-task learning. In *Proceedings of the IEEE conference on computer vision and pattern recognition*, pages 3994–4003.

[Mobley, 2018] Mobley, E. (2018). Why a cheating scandal is shaking the sommelier world. *San Francisco Chronicle.*

[Morellos et al., 2016] Morellos, A., Pantazi, X.-E., Moshou, D., Alexandridis, T., Whetton, R., Tziotzios, G., Wiebensohn, J., Bill, R., and Mouazen, A. M. (2016). Machine learning based prediction of soil total nitrogen, organic carbon and moisture content by using vis-nir spectroscopy. *Biosystems Engineering*, 152:104–116.

[Morgan et al., 2003] Morgan, J., Steiglitz, K., and Reis, G. (2003). The spite motive and equilibrium behavior in auctions. *Contributions in Economic Analysis & Policy*, 2(1):1–25.

[Morgan and Winship, 2015] Morgan, S. L. and Winship, C. (2015). *Counterfactuals and causal inference.* Cambridge University Press.

[Movshovitz-Attias et al., 2017] Movshovitz-Attias, Y., Toshev, A., Leung, T. K., Ioffe, S., and Singh, S. (2017). No fuss distance metric learning using proxies. In *Proceedings of the IEEE International Conference on Computer Vision*, pages 360–368.

[Muller-Budack et al., 2018] Muller-Budack, E., Pustu-Iren, K., and Ewerth, R. (2018). Geolocation estimation of photos using a hierarchical model and scene classification. In *Proceedings of the European Conference on Computer Vision (ECCV)*, pages 563–579.

[Myerson, 1981] Myerson, R. B. (1981). Optimal auction design. *Mathematics of operations research*, 6(1):58–73.

[Narasimhan et al., 2016] Narasimhan, H., Agarwal, S. B., and Parkes, D. C. (2016). Automated mechanism design without money via machine learning. In *Proceedings of the 25th International Joint Conference on Artificial Intelligence.*

[Neugebauer and Selten, 2006] Neugebauer, T. and Selten, R. (2006). Individual behavior of first-price auctions: The importance of information feedback in computerized experimental markets. *Games and Economic Behavior*, 54(1):183–204.

[Nilsback and Zisserman, 2008] Nilsback, M.-E. and Zisserman, A. (2008). Automated flower classification over a large number of classes. In *2008 Sixth Indian Conference on Computer Vision, Graphics & Image Processing*, pages 722–729. IEEE.

[Nishida et al., 2018] Nishida, K., Saito, I., Otsuka, A., Asano, H., and Tomita, J. (2018). Retrieve-and-read: Multi-task learning of information retrieval and reading comprehension. In *Proceedings of the 27th ACM International Conference on Information and Knowledge Management*, pages 647–656.

[Nunes and Boatwright, 2004] Nunes, J. C. and Boatwright, P. (2004). Incidental prices and their effect on willingness to pay. *Journal of Marketing Research*, 41(4):457–466.

[Oh Song et al., 2016] Oh Song, H., Xiang, Y., Jegelka, S., and Savarese, S. (2016). Deep metric learning via lifted structured feature embedding. In *Proceedings of the IEEE conference on computer vision and pattern recognition*, pages 4004–4012.

[Palatucci et al., 2009] Palatucci, M. M., Pomerleau, D. A., Hinton, G. E., and Mitchell, T. (2009). Zero-shot learning with semantic output codes.

[Pascal et al., 2021] Pascal, L., Michiardi, P., Bost, X., Huet, B., and Zuluaga, M. A. (2021). Maximum roaming multi-task learning. In *Proceedings of the AAAI Conference on Artificial Intelligence*, volume 35, pages 9331–9341.

[Pearl, 2009a] Pearl, J. (2009a). Causal inference in statistics: An overview. *Statistics surveys*, 3:96–146.

[Pearl, 2009b] Pearl, J. (2009b). *Causality*. Cambridge university press.

[Pennington et al., 2014] Pennington, J., Socher, R., and Manning, C. (2014). Glove: Global vectors for word representation. In *Proceedings of the 2014 conference on empirical methods in natural language processing (EMNLP)*, pages 1532–1543.

[Pérez-Rosas et al., 2015a] Pérez-Rosas, V., Abouelenien, M., Mihalcea, R., and Burzo, M. (2015a). Deception detection using real-life trial data. In *Proceedings of the 2015 ACM on International Conference on Multimodal Interaction*, pages 59–66. ACM.

[Pérez-Rosas et al., 2015b] Pérez-Rosas, V., Abouelenien, M., Mihalcea, R., Xiao, Y., Linton, C., and Burzo, M. (2015b). Verbal and nonverbal clues for real-life deception detection. In *Proceedings of the 2015 Conference on Empirical Methods in Natural Language Processing*, pages 2336–2346.

[Peters et al., 2018] Peters, M., Neumann, M., Iyyer, M., Gardner, M., Clark, C., Lee, K., and Zettlemoyer, L. (2018). Deep contextualized word representations. In *Proceedings of the 2018 Conference of the North American Chapter of the Association for Computational Linguistics: Human Language Technologies, Volume 1 (Long Papers)*, pages 2227–2237, New Orleans, Louisiana. Association for Computational Linguistics.

[Pilehvar et al., 2017] Pilehvar, A., Elmaghraby, W. J., and Gopal, A. (2017). Market information and bidder heterogeneity in secondary market online b2b auctions. *Management Science*, 63(5):1493–1518.

[Platt et al., 2001] Platt, J. C., Burges, C. J., Swenson, S., Weare, C., and Zheng, A. (2001). Learning a gaussian process prior for automatically generating music playlists. In *NIPS*, pages 1425–1432.

[Qi et al., 2019] Qi, P., Lin, X., Mehr, L., Wang, Z., and Manning, C. D. (2019). Answering complex open-domain questions through iterative query generation. In *Proceedings of the 2019 Conference on Empirical Methods in Natural Language Processing and the 9th International Joint Conference on Natural Language Processing (EMNLP-IJCNLP)*, pages 2590–2602.

[Qian et al., 2019] Qian, Q., Shang, L., Sun, B., Hu, J., Li, H., and Jin, R. (2019). Softtriple loss: Deep metric learning without triplet sampling. In *Proceedings of the IEEE/CVF International Conference on Computer Vision*, pages 6450–6458.

[Qu et al., 2020] Qu, C., Yang, L., Chen, C., Qiu, M., Croft, W. B., and Iyyer, M. (2020). Open-retrieval conversational question answering. In *Proceedings of the 43rd International ACM SIGIR Conference on Research and Development in Information Retrieval*, pages 539–548.

[Radford et al., 2018] Radford, A., Narasimhan, K., Salimans, T., and Sutskever, I. (2018). Improving language understanding by generative pre-training. *URL https://s3-us-west-2. amazonaws. com/openai-assets/researchcovers/languageunsupervised/language understanding paper. pdf*.

[Radford et al., 2019] Radford, A., Wu, J., Child, R., Luan, D., Amodei, D., and Sutskever, I. (2019). Language models are unsupervised multitask learners. *OpenAI blog*, 1(8):9.

[Raffel et al., 2020] Raffel, C., Shazeer, N., Roberts, A., Lee, K., Narang, S., Matena, M., Zhou, Y., Li, W., and Liu, P. J. (2020). Exploring the limits of transfer learning with a unified text-to-text transformer. *Journal of Machine Learning Research*, 21:1–67.

[Rajpurkar et al., 2018] Rajpurkar, P., Jia, R., and Liang, P. (2018). Know what you don't know: Unanswerable questions for squad. In *Proceedings of the 56th Annual Meeting of the Association for Computational Linguistics (Volume 2: Short Papers)*, pages 784–789.

[Riley and Samuelson, 1981] Riley, J. G. and Samuelson, W. F. (1981). Optimal auctions. *The American Economic Review*, 71(3):381–392.

[Roberts et al., 2020] Roberts, M. E., Stewart, B. M., and Nielsen, R. A. (2020). Adjusting for confounding with text matching. *American Journal of Political Science*, 64(4):887–903.

[Roberts et al., 2014] Roberts, M. E., Stewart, B. M., Tingley, D., Lucas, C., Leder-Luis, J., Gadarian, S. K., Albertson, B., and Rand, D. G. (2014). Structural topic models for open-ended survey responses. *American Journal of Political Science*, 58(4):1064–1082.

[Romera-Paredes and Torr, 2015] Romera-Paredes, B. and Torr, P. (2015). An embarrassingly simple approach to zero-shot learning. In *International conference on machine learning*, pages 2152–2161. PMLR.

[Rosenbaum et al., 2018] Rosenbaum, C., Klinger, T., and Riemer, M. (2018). Routing networks: Adaptive selection of non-linear functions for multi-task learning. In *International Conference on Learning Representations*.

[Roth and Ockenfels, 2002] Roth, A. E. and Ockenfels, A. (2002). Last-minute bidding and the rules for ending second-price auctions: Evidence from ebay and amazon auctions on the internet. *American economic review*, 92(4):1093–1103.

[Roth et al., 2019] Roth, K., Brattoli, B., and Ommer, B. (2019). Mic: Mining interclass characteristics for improved metric learning. In *Proceedings of the IEEE/CVF International Conference on Computer Vision*, pages 8000–8009.

[Rubin, 1974] Rubin, D. B. (1974). Estimating causal effects of treatments in randomized and nonrandomized studies. *Journal of educational Psychology*, 66(5):688.

[Rubin, 2005] Rubin, D. B. (2005). Causal inference using potential outcomes: Design, modeling, decisions. *Journal of the American Statistical Association*, 100(469):322–331.

[Ruder et al., 2017] Ruder, S., Bingel, J., Augenstein, I., and Søgaard, A. (2017). Sluice networks: Learning what to share between loosely related tasks. *arXiv preprint arXiv:1705.08142*, 2.

[Ruder et al., 2019] Ruder, S., Bingel, J., Augenstein, I., and Søgaard, A. (2019). Latent multi-task architecture learning. In *Proceedings of the AAAI Conference on Artificial Intelligence*, volume 33, pages 4822–4829.

[Sabour et al., 2017] Sabour, S., Frosst, N., and Hinton, G. E. (2017). Dynamic routing between capsules. In *NIPS*.

[Sanh et al.,] Sanh, V., Wolf, T., and Ruder, S. A hierarchical multi-task approach for learning embeddings from semantic tasks.

[Sanning et al., 2008] Sanning, L. W., Shaffer, S., and Sharratt, J. M. (2008). Bordeaux wine as a financial investment. *Journal of Wine Economics*, 3(1):51–71.

[Satorras and Estrach, 2018] Satorras, V. G. and Estrach, J. B. (2018). Few-shot learning with graph neural networks. In *International Conference on Learning Representations*.

[Scarselli et al., 2008] Scarselli, F., Gori, M., Tsoi, A. C., Hagenbuchner, M., and Monfardini, G. (2008). The graph neural network model. *IEEE transactions on neural networks*, 20(1):61–80.

[Scheirer et al., 2012] Scheirer, W. J., de Rezende Rocha, A., Sapkota, A., and Boult, T. E. (2012). Toward open set recognition. *IEEE transactions on pattern analysis and machine intelligence*, 35(7):1757–1772.

[Schnabel et al., 2016] Schnabel, T., Swaminathan, A., Singh, A., Chandak, N., and Joachims, T. (2016). Recommendations as treatments: Debiasing learning and evaluation. In *international conference on machine learning*, pages 1670–1679. PMLR.

[Schrittwieser et al., 2020] Schrittwieser, J., Antonoglou, I., Hubert, T., Simonyan, K., Sifre, L., Schmitt, S., Guez, A., Lockhart, E., Hassabis, D., Graepel, T., et al. (2020). Mastering atari, go, chess and shogi by planning with a learned model. *Nature*, 588(7839):604–609.

[Schroff et al., 2015] Schroff, F., Kalenichenko, D., and Philbin, J. (2015). Facenet: A unified embedding for face recognition and clustering. In *Proceedings of the IEEE conference on computer vision and pattern recognition*, pages 815–823.

[See et al., 2017] See, A., Liu, P. J., and Manning, C. D. (2017). Get to the point: Summarization with pointer-generator networks. In *Proceedings of the annual conference of Association of Conputational Linguistics*.

[Sener and Koltun, 2018] Sener, O. and Koltun, V. (2018). Multi-task learning as multi-objective optimization. In *Proceedings of the 32nd International Conference on Neural Information Processing Systems*, pages 525–536.

[Sennrich et al., 2016] Sennrich, R., Haddow, B., and Birch, A. (2016). Improving neural machine translation models with monolingual data. In *54th Annual Meeting of the Association for Computational Linguistics*, pages 86–96. Association for Computational Linguistics (ACL).

[Seo et al., 2019] Seo, M., Lee, J., Kwiatkowski, T., Parikh, A., Farhadi, A., and Hajishirzi, H. (2019). Real-time open-domain question answering with dense-sparse phrase index. In *Proceedings of the*

57th Annual Meeting of the Association for Computational Linguistics, pages 4430–4441.

[Shyam et al., 2017] Shyam, P., Gupta, S., and Dukkipati, A. (2017). Attentive recurrent comparators. In *International conference on machine learning*, pages 3173–3181. PMLR.

[Simonsohn and Ariely, 2008] Simonsohn, U. and Ariely, D. (2008). When rational sellers face nonrational buyers: evidence from herding on ebay. *Management science*, 54(9):1624–1637.

[Simonyan and Zisserman, 2014] Simonyan, K. and Zisserman, A. (2014). Very deep convolutional networks for large-scale image recognition. *arXiv preprint arXiv:1409.1556*.

[Snell et al., 2017] Snell, J., Swersky, K., and Zemel, R. (2017). Prototypical networks for few-shot learning. In *Proceedings of the 31st International Conference on Neural Information Processing Systems*, pages 4080–4090.

[Socher et al., 2013] Socher, R., Ganjoo, M., Sridhar, H., Bastani, O., Manning, C. D., and Ng, A. Y. (2013). Zero-shot learning through cross-modal transfer. *arXiv preprint arXiv:1301.3666*.

[Sohn, 2016] Sohn, K. (2016). Improved deep metric learning with multi-class n-pair loss objective. In *Advances in neural information processing systems*, pages 1857–1865.

[Song et al., 2018] Song, J., Shen, C., Yang, Y., Liu, Y., and Song, M. (2018). Transductive unbiased embedding for zero-shot learning. In *Proceedings of the IEEE Conference on Computer Vision and Pattern Recognition*, pages 1024–1033.

[Stuart, 2010] Stuart, E. A. (2010). Matching methods for causal inference: A review and a look forward. *Statistical science: a review journal of the Institute of Mathematical Statistics*, 25(1):1.

[Sullivan, 1896] Sullivan, L. H. (1896). *The tall office building artistically considered.*

[Sun et al., 2019a] Sun, F., Liu, J., Wu, J., Pei, C., Lin, X., Ou, W., and Jiang, P. (2019a). Bert4rec: Sequential recommendation with bidirectional encoder representations from transformer. In *Proceedings of the 28th ACM international conference on information and knowledge management*, pages 1441–1450.

[Sun et al., 2019b] Sun, X., Panda, R., Feris, R., and Saenko, K. (2019b). Adashare: Learning what to share for efficient deep multi-task learning. *arXiv preprint arXiv:1911.12423.*

[Sung et al., 2018] Sung, F., Yang, Y., Zhang, L., Xiang, T., Torr, P. H., and Hospedales, T. M. (2018). Learning to compare: Relation network for few-shot learning. In *Proceedings of the IEEE conference on computer vision and pattern recognition*, pages 1199–1208.

[Szegedy et al., 2015] Szegedy, C., Liu, W., Jia, Y., Sermanet, P., Reed, S., Anguelov, D., Erhan, D., Vanhoucke, V., and Rabinovich, A. (2015). Going deeper with convolutions. In *Proceedings of the IEEE conference on computer vision and pattern recognition*, pages 1–9.

[Tan et al., 2018] Tan, C., Wei, F., Yang, N., Du, B., Lv, W., and Zhou, M. (2018). S-net: From answer extraction to answer synthesis for machine reading comprehension. In *Proceedings of the AAAI Conference on Artificial Intelligence*, volume 32.

[Tan and Le, 2019] Tan, M. and Le, Q. V. (2019). Efficientnet: Rethinking model scaling for convolutional neural networks. *arXiv preprint arXiv:1905.11946.*

[Taramigkou et al., 2013] Taramigkou, M., Bothos, E., Christidis, K., Apostolou, D., and Mentzas, G. (2013). Escape the bubble:

Guided exploration of music preferences for serendipity and novelty. In *Proceedings of the 7th ACM conference on Recommender systems*, pages 335–338.

[Thapa et al., 2020] Thapa, R., Zhang, K., Snavely, N., Belongie, S., and Khan, A. (2020). The plant pathology challenge 2020 data set to classify foliar disease of apples. *Applications in Plant Sciences*, 8(9):e11390.

[Tokozume et al., 2018] Tokozume, Y., Ushiku, Y., and Harada, T. (2018). Between-class learning for image classification. In *Proceedings of the IEEE Conference on Computer Vision and Pattern Recognition*, pages 5486–5494.

[Tran et al., 2013] Tran, N. K., Zerr, S., Bischoff, K., Niederée, C., and Krestel, R. (2013). Topic cropping: Leveraging latent topics for the analysis of small corpora. In *International Conference on Theory and Practice of Digital Libraries*, pages 297–308. Springer.

[Tran et al., 2019a] Tran, T., Do, T.-T., Reid, I., and Carneiro, G. (2019a). Bayesian generative active deep learning. In Chaudhuri, K. and Salakhutdinov, R., editors, *Proceedings of the 36th International Conference on Machine Learning*, volume 97 of *Proceedings of Machine Learning Research*, pages 6295–6304. PMLR.

[Tran et al., 2019b] Tran, T., Do, T.-T., Reid, I., and Carneiro, G. (2019b). Bayesian generative active deep learning. In *International Conference on Machine Learning*, pages 6295–6304. PMLR.

[Uzzi et al., 2013] Uzzi, B., Mukherjee, S., Stringer, M., and Jones, B. (2013). Atypical combinations and scientific impact. *Science*, 342(6157):468–472.

[Van der Laan and Rose, 2011] Van der Laan, M. J. and Rose, S. (2011). *Targeted learning: causal inference for observational and experimental data.* Springer Science & Business Media.

[Van Horn et al., 2021] Van Horn, G., Cole, E., Beery, S., Wilber, K., Belongie, S., and Mac Aodha, O. (2021). Benchmarking representation learning for natural world image collections. In *Proceedings of the IEEE/CVF Conference on Computer Vision and Pattern Recognition (CVPR)*, pages 12884–12893.

[Vandenhende et al., 2019] Vandenhende, S., Georgoulis, S., De Brabandere, B., and Van Gool, L. (2019). Branched multi-task networks: Deciding what layers to share. *Proceedings BMVC 2020*.

[Vandenhende et al., 2020] Vandenhende, S., Georgoulis, S., and Van Gool, L. (2020). Mti-net: Multi-scale task interaction networks for multi-task learning. In *European Conference on Computer Vision*, pages 527–543. Springer.

[Vaswani et al., 2017] Vaswani, A., Shazeer, N., Parmar, N., Uszkoreit, J., Jones, L., Gomez, A. N., Kaiser, L., and Polosukhin, I. (2017). Attention is all you need. *arXiv preprint arXiv:1706.03762*.

[Veitch et al., 2019] Veitch, V., Sridhar, D., and Blei, D. M. (2019). Using text embeddings for causal inference.

[Veličković et al., 2017] Veličković, P., Cucurull, G., Casanova, A., Romero, A., Lio, P., and Bengio, Y. (2017). Graph attention networks. *arXiv preprint arXiv:1710.10903*.

[Vickrey, 1961] Vickrey, W. (1961). Counterspeculation, auctions, and competitive sealed tenders. *The Journal of finance*, 16(1):8–37.

[Vinyals et al., 2016] Vinyals, O., Blundell, C., Lillicrap, T., Kavukcuoglu, K., and Wierstra, D. (2016). Matching networks for one shot learning. *arXiv preprint arXiv:1606.04080*.

[Vinyals et al., 2015] Vinyals, O., Fortunato, M., and Jaitly, N. (2015). Pointer networks. *Advances in Neural Information Processing Systems,* 28:2692–2700.

[Vo et al., 2017] Vo, N., Jacobs, N., and Hays, J. (2017). Revisiting im2gps in the deep learning era. In *Proceedings of the IEEE International Conference on Computer Vision (ICCV).*

[Von Lücken and Brunelli, 2008] Von Lücken, C. and Brunelli, R. (2008). Crops selection for optimal soil planning using multiobjective evolutionary algorithms. In *AAAI,* pages 1751–1756.

[Vuorio et al., 2019] Vuorio, R., Sun, S.-H., Hu, H., and Lim, J. J. (2019). Multimodal model-agnostic meta-learning via task-aware modulation. *Advances in Neural Information Processing Systems,* 32:1–12.

[Wah et al., 2011] Wah, C., Branson, S., Welinder, P., Perona, P., and Belongie, S. (2011). The caltech-ucsd birds-200-2011 dataset.

[Wang et al., 2020a] Wang, A., Cho, K., and Lewis, M. (2020a). Asking and answering questions to evaluate the factual consistency of summaries. In *Proceedings of the 58th Annual Meeting of the Association for Computational Linguistics,* pages 5008–5020.

[Wang et al., 2018a] Wang, H., Wang, Y., Zhou, Z., Ji, X., Gong, D., Zhou, J., Li, Z., and Liu, W. (2018a). Cosface: Large margin cosine loss for deep face recognition. In *Proceedings of the IEEE conference on computer vision and pattern recognition,* pages 5265–5274.

[Wang et al., 2017] Wang, J., Zhou, F., Wen, S., Liu, X., and Lin, Y. (2017). Deep metric learning with angular loss. In *Proceedings of the IEEE International Conference on Computer Vision,* pages 2593–2601.

[Wang et al., 2018b] Wang, S., Yu, M., Guo, X., Wang, Z., Klinger, T., Zhang, W., Chang, S., Tesauro, G., Zhou, B., and Jiang, J. (2018b). R 3: Reinforced ranker-reader for open-domain question answering. In *Proceedings of the AAAI Conference on Artificial Intelligence*, volume 32.

[Wang et al., 2019] Wang, X., Han, X., Huang, W., Dong, D., and Scott, M. R. (2019). Multi-similarity loss with general pair weighting for deep metric learning. In *Proceedings of the IEEE/CVF Conference on Computer Vision and Pattern Recognition*, pages 5022–5030.

[Wang et al., 2014] Wang, X., Wang, Y., Hsu, D., and Wang, Y. (2014). Exploration in interactive personalized music recommendation: a reinforcement learning approach. *ACM Transactions on Multimedia Computing, Communications, and Applications (TOMM)*, 11(1):1–22.

[Wang et al., 2020b] Wang, Y., Zhang, H., Zhang, Z., Long, Y., and Shao, L. (2020b). Learning discriminative domain-invariant prototypes for generalized zero shot learning. *Knowledge-Based Systems*, 196:105796.

[Ward, 1995] Ward, T. B. (1995). What's old about new ideas. *The creative cognition approach*, pages 157–178.

[Waugh, 1928] Waugh, F. V. (1928). Quality factors influencing vegetable prices. *Journal of farm economics*, 10(2):185–196.

[Wei et al., 2019] Wei, X.-S., Cui, Q., Yang, L., Wang, P., and Liu, L. (2019). Rpc: A large-scale retail product checkout dataset. *arXiv e-prints*, pages arXiv–1901.

[Weil, 1993] Weil, R. (1993). Do not invest in wine, at least in the us unless you plan to drink it, and maybe not even then. In *2nd*

International Conference of the Vineyard Data Quantification Society, Verona, February.

[Weinberger and Saul, 2009] Weinberger, K. Q. and Saul, L. K. (2009). Distance metric learning for large margin nearest neighbor classification. *Journal of machine learning research*, 10(2).

[Wemple, 2016] Wemple, E. (2016). With question-leaking, cnn has a scandal on its hands. *The Washington Post*.

[Weyand et al., 2016] Weyand, T., Kostrikov, I., and Philbin, J. (2016). Planet-photo geolocation with convolutional neural networks. In *European Conference on Computer Vision*, pages 37–55. Springer.

[Wong and Gesmundo, 2017] Wong, C. and Gesmundo, A. (2017). Transfer learning to learn with multitask neural model search. *arXiv preprint arXiv:1710.10776*.

[Wood et al., 2006] Wood, D., Anderson, K., et al. (2006). What determines the future value of an icon wine? new evidence from australia. *Journal of Wine Economics*, 1(2):141–161.

[Woodward and Finn, 2017] Woodward, M. and Finn, C. (2017). Active one-shot learning. *arXiv preprint arXiv:1702.06559*.

[Wu et al., 2017] Wu, C.-Y., Manmatha, R., Smola, A. J., and Krahenbuhl, P. (2017). Sampling matters in deep embedding learning. In *Proceedings of the IEEE International Conference on Computer Vision*, pages 2840–2848.

[Wu et al., 2020] Wu, L., Li, S., Hsieh, C.-J., and Sharpnack, J. (2020). Sse-pt: Sequential recommendation via personalized transformer. In *Fourteenth ACM Conference on Recommender Systems*, pages 328–337.

[Xian et al., 2016] Xian, Y., Akata, Z., Sharma, G., Nguyen, Q., Hein, M., and Schiele, B. (2016). Latent embeddings for zero-shot classification. In *Proceedings of the IEEE conference on computer vision and pattern recognition*, pages 69–77.

[Xian et al., 2018] Xian, Y., Lorenz, T., Schiele, B., and Akata, Z. (2018). Feature generating networks for zero-shot learning. In *Proceedings of the IEEE conference on computer vision and pattern recognition*, pages 5542–5551.

[Xing et al., 2014] Xing, Z., Wang, X., and Wang, Y. (2014). Enhancing collaborative filtering music recommendation by balancing exploration and exploitation. In *Ismir*, pages 445–450.

[Xu et al., 2018] Xu, D., Ouyang, W., Wang, X., and Sebe, N. (2018). Pad-net: Multi-tasks guided prediction-and-distillation network for simultaneous depth estimation and scene parsing. In *Proceedings of the IEEE Conference on Computer Vision and Pattern Recognition*, pages 675–684.

[Yang et al., 2020] Yang, R., Xu, H., WU, Y., and Wang, X. (2020). Multi-task reinforcement learning with soft modularization. *Advances in Neural Information Processing Systems*, 33:4767–4777.

[Yang and Hospedales, 2017] Yang, Y. and Hospedales, T. (2017). Trace norm regularised deep multi-task learning. In *5th International Conference on Learning Representations*.

[Yao, 2017] Yao, A. C.-C. (2017). Dominant-strategy versus bayesian multi-item auctions: Maximum revenue determination and comparison. In *Proceedings of the 2017 ACM Conference on Economics and Computation*, pages 3–20.

[Ye et al., 2020] Ye, Y., Pei, H., Wang, B., Chen, P.-Y., Zhu, Y., Xiao, J., and Li, B. (2020). Reinforcement-learning based portfolio management with augmented asset movement prediction states. In

Proceedings of the AAAI Conference on Artificial Intelligence, volume 34, pages 1112–1119.

[Yoo and Kweon, 2019] Yoo, D. and Kweon, I. S. (2019). Learning loss for active learning. In *Proceedings of the IEEE/CVF Conference on Computer Vision and Pattern Recognition*, pages 93–102.

[You et al., 2017] You, J., Li, X., Low, M., Lobell, D., and Ermon, S. (2017). Deep gaussian process for crop yield prediction based on remote sensing data. In *Thirty-First AAAI conference on artificial intelligence*.

[Yu and Tao, 2019] Yu, B. and Tao, D. (2019). Deep metric learning with tuplet margin loss. In *Proceedings of the IEEE/CVF International Conference on Computer Vision*, pages 6490–6499.

[Yu et al., 2020a] Yu, T., Kumar, S., Gupta, A., Levine, S., Hausman, K., and Finn, C. (2020a). Gradient surgery for multi-task learning. *Advances in Neural Information Processing Systems*, 33.

[Yu et al., 2020b] Yu, Z., Zang, H., and Wan, X. (2020b). Routing enforced generative model for recipe generation. In *Proceedings of the 2020 Conference on Empirical Methods in Natural Language Processing (EMNLP)*, pages 3797–3806.

[Yuan et al., 2020] Yuan, M., Lin, H.-T., and Boyd-Graber, J. (2020). Cold-start active learning through self-supervised language modeling. In *Proceedings of the 2020 Conference on Empirical Methods in Natural Language Processing (EMNLP)*, pages 7935–7948.

[Yuan et al., 2019] Yuan, T., Deng, W., Tang, J., Tang, Y., and Chen, B. (2019). Signal-to-noise ratio: A robust distance metric for deep metric learning. In *Proceedings of the IEEE/CVF Conference on Computer Vision and Pattern Recognition*, pages 4815–4824.

[Yuan et al., 2017] Yuan, Y., Yang, K., and Zhang, C. (2017). Hard-aware deeply cascaded embedding. In *Proceedings of the IEEE international conference on computer vision*, pages 814–823.

[Zenonos et al., 2015] Zenonos, A., Stein, S., and Jennings, N. R. (2015). Coordinating measurements for air pollution monitoring in participatory sensing settings.

[Zhai and Wu, 2018] Zhai, A. and Wu, H.-Y. (2018). Classification is a strong baseline for deep metric learning. *arXiv preprint arXiv:1811.12649*.

[Zhang et al., 2018a] Zhang, H., Cisse, M., Dauphin, Y. N., and Lopez-Paz, D. (2018a). mixup: Beyond empirical risk minimization. In *International Conference on Learning Representations*.

[Zhang et al., 2017] Zhang, L., Xiang, T., and Gong, S. (2017). Learning a deep embedding model for zero-shot learning. In *Proceedings of the IEEE conference on computer vision and pattern recognition*, pages 2021–2030.

[Zhang et al., 2018b] Zhang, Z., Cui, Z., Xu, C., Jie, Z., Li, X., and Yang, J. (2018b). Joint task-recursive learning for semantic segmentation and depth estimation. In *Proceedings of the European Conference on Computer Vision (ECCV)*, pages 235–251.

[Zhang et al., 2019] Zhang, Z., Cui, Z., Xu, C., Yan, Y., Sebe, N., and Yang, J. (2019). Pattern-affinitive propagation across depth, surface normal and semantic segmentation. In *Proceedings of the IEEE/CVF Conference on Computer Vision and Pattern Recognition (CVPR)*.

[Zhang and Saligrama, 2015] Zhang, Z. and Saligrama, V. (2015). Zero-shot learning via semantic similarity embedding. In *Proceedings of the IEEE international conference on computer vision*, pages 4166–4174.

[Zhang and Saligrama, 2016] Zhang, Z. and Saligrama, V. (2016). Zero-shot learning via joint latent similarity embedding. In *proceedings of the IEEE Conference on Computer Vision and Pattern Recognition*, pages 6034–6042.

[Zhao et al., 2020] Zhao, T., Lu, X., and Lee, K. (2020). Sparta: Efficient open-domain question answering via sparse transformer matching retrieval. *arXiv preprint arXiv:2009.13013*.

[Zheleva et al., 2010] Zheleva, E., Guiver, J., Mendes Rodrigues, E., and Milić-Frayling, N. (2010). Statistical models of music-listening sessions in social media. In *Proceedings of the 19th international conference on World wide web*, pages 1019–1028.

[Zheng et al., 2019] Zheng, W., Chen, Z., Lu, J., and Zhou, J. (2019). Hardness-aware deep metric learning. In *Proceedings of the IEEE/CVF Conference on Computer Vision and Pattern Recognition*, pages 72–81.

[Zhong et al., 2020] Zhong, Z., Zheng, L., Kang, G., Li, S., and Yang, Y. (2020). Random erasing data augmentation. In *Proceedings of the AAAI Conference on Artificial Intelligence*, volume 34, pages 13001–13008.

[Zhou et al., 2017] Zhou, Q., Yang, N., Wei, F., Tan, C., Bao, H., and Zhou, M. (2017). Neural question generation from text: A preliminary study. In *National CCF Conference on Natural Language Processing and Chinese Computing*, pages 662–671. Springer.

[Zhu et al., 2019] Zhu, H., Dong, L., Wei, F., Wang, W., Qin, B., and Liu, T. (2019). Learning to ask unanswerable questions for machine reading comprehension. In *Proceedings of the 57th Annual Meeting of the Association for Computational Linguistics*, pages 4238–4248.

[Zhu et al., 2017] Zhu, J.-Y., Park, T., Isola, P., and Efros, A. A. (2017). Unpaired image-to-image translation using cycle-consistent adversarial networks. In *Proceedings of the IEEE international conference on computer vision*, pages 2223–2232.

Made in United States
Orlando, FL
04 November 2026

90200623R00267